Hitler Youth

HITLER YOUTH

Michael H. Kater

HARVARD UNIVERSITY PRESS

Cambridge, Massachusetts

London, England

First Harvard University Press paperback edition, 2006

Library of Congress Cataloging-in-Publication Data

Kater, Michael H., 1937–
Hitler Youth / Michael H. Kater
p. cm.
Includes bibliographical references and index.
ISBN 0-674-01496-0 (cloth : alk. paper)
ISBN 0-674-01991-1 (pbk.)
1. Hitler-Jugend. 2. National socialism and youth.
3. Germany—History—1933–1945.   I. Title.

DD253.5.K28'2004
943.086'0835—dc22   2004047359

Designed by Gwen Nefsky Frankfeldt

For my daughter Anja

Contents

Hitler Youth

"Make Way, You Old Ones!"

In 1992 a former Hitler Youth or Hitler-Junge, now a respected historian, sat down to reflect upon his childhood and early adolescence in Nazi Germany. Hermann Graml, who was born in 1928, concluded that there were many aspects of his life as a member of the Hitler Youth (HJ) that had appealed to him. Most important was that he, along with his friends, was "wooed and flattered beyond limits" by the powerful political system of the Third Reich, and thus he was proud to be a part of the largest ever youth organization that it had created. He was attracted by the spiritual and national hymns they sang and by the cult-like activities that initiated young people into the movement, such as swearing an oath of fealty to Adolf Hitler, the supreme leader. In the struggle for ultimate authority over the children that sometimes took place among the church, schools, parents, and Hitler Youth, Graml and his friends enjoyed being the center of attention and the object of adult desires. However, they tended to side with the Hitler Youth more often than not because it seemed to be "more modern" and forward-looking than any of the other institutions. Indeed, they found that the Nazi regime appeared to be more supportive of youth in terms of granting autonomy from parents and allowing liberal relations with girls of their age. Unlike family, church, and school, the HJ was not weighed down by tradition and taboos and seemed to offer an exciting opportunity for young people to be respected and responsible.

When Graml's time came to be drafted as a young soldier, he and his friends accepted the incipient war as a given because of the paramilitary training he had received in the HJ. He, and other youth, had been preparing for war's eventuality for years and were not frightened by the prospect of active combat at the front. On the contrary, Graml remembers being motivated by a "lust for adventure, daring, and risk," a love of flirting with danger. Not everything in the Hitler Youth appealed to him, however, and some of the training went against the grain of his experience. Lessons in "biological racism" and ideas of a "Germanic world empire" seemed abstract and far-fetched to a young boy. National Socialist visions of enlarged living space could not stir his interest, nor could the concept of a German "master race." Despite his training, he remembered contravening Nazi dogma by making friends with Soviet prisoners of war forced to work in local factories, and when serving as a flak cannoneer he continued such friendships with Soviet mercenaries fighting alongside him and members of his platoon. Thus, in retrospect, he saw himself as having resisted total submission to the HJ despite his positive reaction to its spirit and activities.[1]

Margarete Hannsmann, a German actress and novelist born in 1921, recently composed a memoir entitled "The Sun is Rising: A Child Becomes Nazi." In the book she tells about slowly emancipating herself from her parents, especially her authoritarian father, with the help of the Hitler Youth, and how, as a girl in her mid-teens, she felt like a responsible adult when helping a farmer in the fields during a special HJ agricultural program. She describes being flattered by the attentions of an older, handsome Hitler Youth leader and her sense of liberation in a subsequent affair with him, her first. The highlight of her years in the Hitler Youth was her appointment to an intermediate leadership post and the assumption of responsibility toward other, younger girls. But she reports being deeply disillusioned by the Hitler Youth leader's callous, coldly controlling treatment of her when the affair ended, and she was incensed when comrades wrongly accused her of having stolen money from a communal locker room. Growing up in the HJ had its humiliations as well as its pleasures.[2]

Bittersweet experiences of joy and suffering may have characterized the life of younger, ordinary Hitler Youths such as Graml and Hannsmann, at least according to their post-1945 recollections. However, the extant memoirs of more highly elevated HJ leaders, apart from all the post-1945 self-criticism they contain, are suffused with a scarcely veiled sense of pride in their former power, and are graphic in their description of the type and extent of this power. They demonstrate that the very authoritarian nature of the Nazi regime, coupled with its merciless ideology of the survival of the fittest as it was eugenically implemented, constituted a major point of attraction for adolescents who were searching for certitudes in a swiftly changing and newly structured world, however harshly regimented. According to a well-defined Nazi leadership creed, this authority made them strong vis-à-vis a multitude of younger, weaker juveniles who were their charges, and it gave them an incomparable sense of superiority over average German citizens of any age, even when they were Nazis, and nearly absolute power over those who were not.[3]

These observations raise a number of questions about the complicity of members of the Hitler Youth, both the young ones and the older ones, in the consolidation and, by extension, the breakdown of the Third Reich. These questions must be asked, even if they cannot all be answered. For example, can children of ages ten to eighteen (the usual range for membership in the HJ), who usually are not culpable in a court of law, be held responsible for having participated in the activities of a dictatorship's youth organization, even when those activities were criminal? Or were they culpable at a somewhat more advanced stage of their life, when they were either drafted or volunteered to wage war against innocent neighboring states? Many youth were inducted into the HJ as children and had little choice in the matter. Either they were placed in the movement by their parents or teachers, who thought this offered the best opportunity for mobility in the state before HJ membership was made compulsory, or it was difficult to escape the pressure of peers for uniformity and solidarity. Furthermore, one can understand young people's attraction to spiffy uniforms and to the paraphernalia of premilitary drill, such as air guns. Similarly, it is not hard to understand the appeal and satisfaction of belonging to a large, dominant, and protective community and participating in their communal singing, marching, and camping. Above all, there was the omniscient and omnipotent father, Adolf Hitler, who provided immense guarantees of safety at a time shaken by continued economic depression and recurrent fears of war. As much as authority overawes children and instills fear in them if they are disobedient, it also provides security as long as the children agree to conform to prescribed standards of behavior that do not strike them as too odious. It was one of the great propaganda achievements of the Nazi rulers that they were able to offer a political and ideological world view that granted status, certainty, and power to young people, so much so that teenagers of both genders could accept and abide by the prescribed behaviors with hardly any qualms. Through the elaborate propaganda process and its propagation of racial theory and the superiority of the *Volk,* Hitler was able to shape private and public behavior as well as reinforce public support of the Nazi regime and the people's intimate ties to him, their Führer. Young people, with their ideals and energies, would have been especially vulnerable to such values in their own search for identity and meaning.[4]

The issue of complicity changes as one focuses on Hitler's youths in their transition from juveniles to young adults. It is necessary to determine at which stage a youth would have had the option either to accept or to reject an opportunity for advancement to higher leadership responsibilities. Members' compliance with such advancement from the lower HJ ranks was voluntary and necessitated a fair amount of ideological conviction in the Nazi cause, something that a youth from age sixteen to eighteen could evince as persuasively and sometimes even as eloquently as a diehard Nazi in his early thirties. It is fair to say that seventeen-year-old HJ leaders with a few hundred charges under their command, in contrast to the ten-year-old underlings, made themselves culpable, to the extent that they knowingly imparted Nazi values to these underlings, inciting them to racial hatred and war-

fare against Poles, Russians, and Jews. As they got older, precondi-
tioned, brainwashed children would swap air guns for machine guns
and willingly be drafted to use them against Hitler's foes.

The issue becomes even more difficult as young people made the
transition from mature Hitler Youth membership to tours of duty in
the armed forces or associated branches such as the Reich Labor
Service. Even if such duty was the consequence of general conscription, the subsequent behavior of a former Hitler Youth in war could
depend on how seriously he had taken the paramilitary routines he had
practiced throughout his youth, and the catechism of beliefs he had
been taught. These would influence his comportment in war: whether
he would kill his adversary or make him a prisoner of war; whether he
would shoot when ordered to kill civilians. The certainty which the
Nazi regime had provided to a Hitler Youth in peacetime through a
tightly structured totalitarian dictatorship would be continued in the
armed forces, albeit slightly changed: instead of a chain of command
dominated by National Socialist ideology, it would now be one determined by the Wehrmacht's tried-and-true rules of war. As it turned
out, Nazi rules and Wehrmacht rules often coincided after 1938 to create conditions under which a German soldier, as a former Hitler Youth
member or leader, would find it difficult to be guided by a humane
conscience. The pattern of order and authority that a Wehrmacht soldier was able to cling to during war was his strength to a great extent
but, ultimately, his weakness as well. It canceled out all gray areas and
made choices simple by reference to what the Führer thought best—
but that only lasted as long as the Führer did.

The seemingly coherent world view offered by the Third Reich was
a far cry from the atmosphere of a disintegrating democratic republic
in the waning years of the Weimar state and society. The pluralistic
public arena was filled with competing ideologies and plans. Few
among the young had confidence in the government to provide jobs,
security, or national stature. The suicide rate among university students, beset with uncertainty and poor morale, was three times as high
as in the general population—a phenomenon not seen before or after

in modern German history.[5] As Peter Loewenberg has shown, the youth cohort born between approximately 1903 and 1915 was afflicted with various economic, social, physical, and psychological problems. This group of young men and women were between the ages of eighteen and thirty in 1933, when they constituted nearly one-third of the German population.[6] Brought up as children during World War I, they and their mothers were abandoned as the fathers fought in the trenches. Malnutrition, inadequate shelter, and deficient heating resulted in hunger, illnesses, and deaths well into the post-1918 Allied blockade period. The children's pain was prolonged when the fathers returned from the war as losers who had been thrashed. Many were nominal fathers who did not understand their children anymore and were often regarded by them as rivals for the affection of their mothers.[7] Others never returned: two million men had been killed in the war, leaving war widows alone with their children.[8] The disastrous results of the postwar runaway inflation, which lasted until 1924, left many children feeling frightened, dreading real or potential impoverishment—a feeling exacerbated by the high unemployment and wage loss during the Great Depression starting in late 1929. This deflationary recession was still in full swing when Hitler assumed power.[9] As this generation of young people became apprentices, journeymen, young merchants, or university students, and hence prospective full-fledged members of the nation's workforce (or, as females, future wives of putative breadwinners), their sense of economic uncertainty led to profound doubts about their social station. Those from the middle to the lower strata accustomed to moving up in society experienced barriers in their path; those from the middle to the upper strata despaired over unsuccessful attempts to stave off downward social mobility. Many if not most of the youth cohort for the period of the 1920s and very early 1930s felt cheated out of whatever chances they had thought were theirs and increasingly looked to radical alternatives. The time was ripe for a new source of promise and support for young people, a source that gave them hope for themselves and their state in the future.[10]

These multiple difficulties were complicated by extraordinary tensions between this young generation and their elders. Indeed, intergenerational conflict was a dominating theme in Germany from the beginning of the twentieth century up to Hitler's attainment of power.[11] This conflict found expression not only in day-to-day socioeconomic and political relations but also in the arts and literature; it became a subject for many plays and novels and was starkly evident in graphic art and even music.[12] It was a determining factor in the German youth movement, in which youth sought refuge to escape from some of their difficulties, including problems with their elders. Some young people were members of the *Antifaschistische Junge Garde* (*Antifa*), the youth wing of the Communist *Rotfrontkämpferbund,* and at the close of the Weimar Republic battled Nazi storm troopers in the streets of the large cities. Others, on the other end of the ideological scale, belonged to the *Jungnationaler Bund,* a group patronized by the piously Lutheran and national-conservative establishment.[13]

The German youth movement had been founded in 1901 in Steglitz, then a thoroughly middle-class suburb of Berlin in a semirural setting, by Protestant male adolescents who were reacting against the materialism and bourgeois complacency that characterized the new German Empire's rapid industrialization in the late nineteenth century. Calling themselves *Wandervögel,* or hiking birds, they became suspicious of and bored with what the British historian Walter Laqueur, a former member of a Silesian youth group of the 1920s, has labeled a "world of growing plenty and rapid technical advance." Laqueur writes that the incipient youth movement was "an unpolitical form of opposition to a civilization that had little to offer the young generation, a protest against its lack of vitality, warmth, emotion and ideals." These young people, boys as well as girls, stressed individualism; inspired by cultural pessimists like Lagarde, Schopenhauer, and Nietzsche, they wanted to lead their own lives beyond urban confines, away from homes, parents, and teachers. They roamed the countryside, following their own rules of simplicity and honesty, dressed in makeshift garb, singing rediscovered folksongs, eating simple food by the campfire, and espousing a sexually clean life. They were in search of a romantic absolute, what since the nineteenth century had been called the "Blue Flower." They became enthralled by mysticism, whose sources they found in Cossacks of the Russian steppes or Buddhist priests in Far Eastern temples. Most of this was alien to their parents' experience and barely understood by them. Thus the theme of intergenerational conflict was already built into the very first chapter of German youth-movement history. Although the youths' activities were apolitical, they occurred within the wider framework of pre-liberal, romantic, and in some respect resurrected medieval social and political values. In conscious opposition to the ideals of the Enlightenment, they eschewed rationality in favor of emotion.[14]

With its professed contempt for society, politics, and the state, the early German youth movement did not hesitate to wholeheartedly embrace the Empire's entry into World War I. War was viewed as highly idealized combat, and struggle in battle as natural and organic. The concept of the nation, too, had never been forsaken. As an idea unrealized, it had played a role in medieval times, as it did in the early-nineteenth-century Romantic movement and then again in the post-1848 restorative era. World War I was therefore welcomed as the catalyst in a huge cleansing process that would purge European nations, especially the new modern German nation-state, of their materialism and would resurrect archaic values. (A similarly idealistic goal was upheld by young French and English fighters for their countries, though in different ways, as their letters and diaries illustrate.)[15] In a battle near the Belgian village of Langemarck on November 10, 1914, thousands of voluntarily enlisted *Wandervögel* threw themselves against the British and were mowed down. They were regarded by their surviving peers as symbols of a tremendous sacrifice for the nation as well as for their own cohort and the youth of future German generations.[16] Henceforth, celebrations eulogizing Langemarck became a characteristic part of the developing youth movement.[17]

After November 1918, when it was realized that not even half of the 12,000 *Wandervögel* who had rushed into battle had returned,[18] the center of gravity of the German youth movement shifted. While it had always been elitist and anti-modernist, it now became increasingly martial, hierarchical, attached to discipline, uniforms, and drill, racist, and suspicious of girls in its midst—all of which was a departure from the days of the Empire. As such, the youth movement was alienated from the new republican system of Weimar, whose essence was equality as expressed in parliamentary democracy and whose representatives had signed the humiliating Treaty of Versailles (1919). In fact, the movement became downright hostile. The successors to the *Wandervögel* were the ascetic *Bünde* (leagues—because of their mystical connotations, most of these terms defy translation), who wanted nothing to do with Weimar party politics.[19] They always maintained that they were above political parties, but in fact they were ideologically right of center. Soon, however, dedicated political youth wings of the Weimar parties also came into being, as well as Protestant and Catholic youth leagues. Inasmuch as they all overlapped with the core *Bünde*, they shared the defining characteristic of the postwar German youth movement, namely its anti-democratic stance and concomitant rejection of all that Weimar stood for, in particular its modernism. A tiny minority of republican-inspired youth leagues arose that supported the new political order, but they were only a drop in the bucket.[20] On the overtly political side, there were offshoots of the parties such as the *Bismarckbund* (aligned with the German National People's Party—DNVP) and the *Antifa,* which had evolved from an earlier Communist youth league. On the extreme right, there was a youth league called the Hitler Youth, after the Führer of the Nazi Party.[21]

Because of countless disagreements on means and objectives among the multiplicity of youth leagues, serious structural weaknesses developed, resulting in flux. As typified by the Communist youth groups, change was becoming the only constant in the youth movement, giving it a notorious volatility at a time when the Weimar regime itself was becoming increasingly unstable. From 1918 to 1933 the history of the youth movement was one of an "uninterrupted chain of unions, splits and reunions."[22] Adding to this instability was the fact that the intergenerational conflict that had once defined the archetypal youth movement of 1901 itself became a problem for the youth leagues. By the end of the 1920s, members who refused to leave when reaching adulthood often took charge of new generations of members and increasingly were resented by them.[23]

In the years from 1929 to 1933, a faltering political regime, pressing economic hardship with little hope for the future, non-sympathetic parents, and self-serving and static youth groups left many young men and women with few places to turn to. This was the opportunity that some leaders of the National Socialist movement under Hitler had been waiting for. One of their war cries in those years, which could not help but impress Germany's alienated youth, was "Make Way, You Old Ones!"[24] Many Nazi leaders drove home the point that the government of the Weimar Republic was leaving young people in the lurch, providing no agencies to care for them and leaving their problems in the hands of the disparate youth leagues. They skillfully exacerbated the existing generational tensions to their own ends.[25] Aware of the joblessness that stigmatized the young, ancillary organizations of the Nazi Party sought to help in job creation and tried to broker gainful work. The HJ was one of these organizations, appealing, in particular, to the lower strata of society, for which the elitist *Bünde* had not been created.[26]

While Hitler appeared to many young people as the father or older brother they had never had or had already lost, the Nazi movement, with all its factions, was coming across to many as a party made for youth. Its visible formations in the street seemed to be young—the SA, the SS, and the National Socialist Student League, which from bastions in the universities had acted as a vanguard of Nazism in Germany's educated middle class since the mid-1920s.[27] Above all, the members of the Nazi Party themselves were visibly young, with a mean age of approximately thirty-one for all new joiners in the period from 1925 to 1932. This compared favorably to any other Weimar party except for the KPD.[28] Moreover, during national elections toward the end of the Republic, the support of youthful voters for the NSDAP tended to be stronger, at least within the urban electorate, than that of older voters, because it was in the towns that economic problems were greatest.[29]

If disenchanted young men and women at the end of the Weimar Republic put stock in the growing Nazi movement with a view to their own future, the Nazi leaders in turn regarded youth as companions on their immediate road to success and as indispensable in the realization of their planned millennium. Although a uniform Nazi policy on youth did not exist from 1919 to 1933, the words and deeds of individual Nazi officials at certain points in time reflect an exalted view of youth. At first Hitler had been oblivious to the problems of youth, since adolescents were too young to vote or attain Party membership. Thus he could not understand why anyone among his followers would want to found, during the mid-1920s, a Nazi Students' League.[30] But once he had been persuaded by his supporters of the importance of young people, and when he realized that adolescents over sixteen were useful in big-city street fights, he acquiesced and made overtures to the youth. No doubt influenced by more astute tacticians such as Joseph Goebbels and Gregor Strasser, Hitler acknowledged by 1930 that young people were needed as recruits and guarantors of the longevity of the movement. And so he said to Munich students in the summer of that year, when their social and economic situation was becoming acute, that they should "acquire rich knowledge, in order to assume leadership positions in a coming Reich."[31] Albert Speer's later statement that Hitler was always particularly interested in youthful enrollments for the survival of his regime is true only for the post-1930 era; this was an interest forever in need of shoring up by Hitler's advisers.[32] The Führer's ambivalence toward youth helps explain why his circle of associates aged without younger reinforcements until the end of the Third Reich, and why the Nazi Party itself suffered from senescence.[33] This ambivalence and the central problem of structural ossification to which it led are connected to fundamental weaknesses in the organization of the Hitler Youth and the training it sought to provide for its members.

Apart from Hitler, there were astute Nazi lieutenants who realized early on the importance of leadership issues and how these related to the timely enlistment of youth, but their pronouncements and decisions never possessed the authority of those made by the Führer himself. In the period after World War I, when it was known that the birth rate in Germany was declining,[34] Goebbels, whose intelligent insights into policy matters were second to none in Hitler's entourage, stated precisely: "True leaders are born. Leadership cadres, however, may be trained. To engage in politics one must be called, yet to function administratively it suffices to be instructed, drilled, trained, and bred."[35] Two years after that 1930 dictum, Strasser, the chief of the Party's bureaucracy, decreed that it would be incumbent on the young generation, together with the front soldiers, to be "the sole bearers of future politics."[36]

By 1933, the young generation whom Strasser addressed consisted of those born after 1915. The common denominator of the members of this young cohort was their incorporation in the Hitler Youth between the start of Hitler's reign and its termination, that is, between 1933 and 1944, the year when the last batch of youths was initiated. By this criterion, the "Nazi Regime Youth Cohort" was not a "generation" in the classic sense, but in the sense of a group that shared a major experience within a relatively short time span.[37] Hitler Youths usually were between the ages of ten and eighteen, and thus the oldest members of the "Nazi Regime Youth Cohort" were born in 1916, and the youngest in 1934. They all "grew into the Nazi state," as the German parliamentarian Erhard Eppler, a former HJ boy, has described it in his memoirs. It is to their collective experience that we now turn.[38]

Serving in the Hitler Youth

In 1938, a story by Hitler Youth Hans Wolf, entitled "Comradeship," was published as part of a public-school primer. This is how it began: "It was a hot day and we had far to march. The sun was burning down on the heath, which was bereft of trees. The sand was glistening, I was tired. My feet were hurting in those new walking shoes, every step was hurting and all I could think about was rest, water, and shade. I clenched my teeth to keep walking. I was the youngest, and this was my first outing. In front of me strode Rudolf, the leader. He was tall and strong. His backpack was heavy and pressed down on his shoulders. Rudolf carried the bread for us six boys, the cooking pot, and a pile of books, from which he would read us wonderfully thrilling stories, at night in the hostel. My backpack only contained a shirt, a couple of sneakers, washing utensils, and some cooking gear, apart from a tarpaulin for rainy days and straw beds. And yet I thought I could not lug this backpack any longer. My comrades all were somewhat older and had camping experience. They hardly felt the heat and hardship of the march. Every now and then they would sigh and drink lukewarm coffee from their canteens. More and more, I remained behind, even though I tried to make up for my slack by running. Suddenly Rudolf turned around. He stopped and watched me crawling up to him from a distance, while our comrades continued in the direction of a few trees on the horizon. 'Tired?' Rudolf asked me, kindly.

Ashamed, I had to say yes. Slowly, we walked side by side. I was limp-
ing. But I did not want to let on to Rudolf. When we got to a juniper
bush, the leader sat down and said: 'For a little rest!' Relieved, I threw
myself down. I did not want to talk, for I was shy. Rudolf gave me
something to drink. I thanked him and leaned back comfortably, glad
to be able to stretch my aching feet, and before I knew it I was sleeping
... When we resumed our march, my feet hurt much less and my
backpack did not press down on me so. I was very glad about that."[1]

Hans Wolf's story encapsulates the essence of the communal Hitler
Youth experience. In exemplary fashion, it illustrates why the Hitler
Youth was so attractive and worked so well for millions of boys and
girls, certainly in the early years of the Nazi regime. Because it demonstrated key Nazi values, this story was thought fit to be distributed as
primary reading material to school children in their early teens. The
very title conjures up the important sense of belonging, as one small
individual, to a larger community, the organic *Volksgemeinschaft*. The
shared experience of marching, as the youngest of a group, in a difficult
environment reminds the young pupils of how small and weak they are
by themselves and how important it is to be supported by a group of
stronger friends. The leader of these friends is Rudolf, the strongest of
them all, who not only looks after the physical needs of his charges—
he carries the bread for them—but also acts as their spiritual mentor,
through stories he reads to them. In the larger Hitler Youth, too, the
strong members would support their weaker pals, and knowledgeable
leaders would be at hand for physical as well as mental direction. If
physical activity—much like the march in the scorching heat of the
treeless heath—however unbearable, would steel the boys' muscles and
sinews, readings and discussions in the evenings would train their
minds in Germanic lore and Nazi ideology, part of which was the
Führer cult. As a Führer in the heath, Rudolf himself is a shining
example. Sacrifice and fealty are important to him, especially in adversity, yet in the end he will save his troop, as he saves little Hans from
fatigue and total breakdown.

In 1938, as that story was being read in German classrooms, the

Third Reich was not far removed from a time of much longer marches, in territories of even more heat and fewer trees than in the story's scenario, yet undertaken for the ultimate Nazi goal of winning new living space in foreign lands. To condition German youth to serve such a goal was the principal purpose of the Hitler Youth, just as it was the purpose of Hans's story to remind all boys and girls of eligible age how important it was for them to join.

To be sure, like many institutions of the Third Reich, the Hitler Youth did not originate as a result of systematic planning and was not always an expression of monolithic cohesiveness as might have been expected in a totalitarian dictatorship such as Adolf Hitler's. Indeed, this dictatorship itself was less streamlined and much more heterogeneous than the Führer and his lieutenants would have preferred.[2] To that extent, then, Hans Wolf's depiction of comradeship, harmony, and sacrifice under the authority of a strong and omniscient leader might have overstated the actual efficiency and inner workings of the *Volksgemeinschaft* and its political agencies, if not the Hitler Youth itself. However, there is no denying that most Hitler Youths in the fold loved its program of activities and did feel looked after, knowing that they would graduate to become bearers of the new Reich. From their subjective point of view, the sentiments of belonging, of sharing, of being willing to follow orders from tough but caring leaders, were very real. It is against this backdrop of a broad and general consensus among youth in Nazi Germany that exceptions and inconsistencies must be judged.

In Search of Monopoly and Uniformity

The Hitler Youth emerged from the highly polarized pattern of youth leagues in the Weimar Republic. It had been a group of young people tied to the National Socialist German Workers' Party (NSDAP, or Nazi Party). Its origins go back to early 1925 when Adolf Hitler, just out of Landsberg prison after the abortive Beer Hall Putsch of November 1923, was rebuilding his Nazi Party. The youth group was initiated by

Kurt Gruber, a law student and admirer of Hitler from Plauen in Saxony, home to many blue-collar workers. Thus the beginnings of the Nazi youth affiliate were in the proletarian realm, and at least until Hitler's takeover in January 1933, the groups emphasized their working-class mystique. However, the proletarian image became more and more threadbare over time, as more middle-class youths joined. The groups were first called Hitler-Jugend (or HJ as a short form) in July 1926, when they were placed under the command of Hitler's SA; Hitler himself did not take a great interest in them at that time because he focused only on adults old enough to vote for his Party.[3]

Until 1930, in comparison with the *Bündische Jugend,* the HJ remained insignificant. Politically, the *Bündische* were right-wing (including anti-Semitic) enough to attract the majority of German youths who detested the Weimar Republic. The difference was that they were not fixated upon a single leader, as was the HJ, and their social composition was much more middle- to upper-class. There were about 50,000 *Bündische* when the Nazis became the second-largest national party after the Reichstag elections of September 14, 1930. By this time the HJ membership had increased to 18,000, and their social base was broadening from working-class members to middle-class youths from secondary schools, or Gymnasien, concerned about career mobility in industry, state administration, and the academic professions. It was at this time that the HJ instituted a female section, the Bund Deutscher Mädel (League of German Girls or BDM), to be part of the larger HJ organization. In addition, a Jungvolk was created for teenagers from ten to fourteen (later these would be known as Pimpfe). By the end of 1930, the age range for the HJ of both genders was from ten to eighteen.[4]

In October 1931, Baldur von Schirach was appointed by Hitler as chief of all the youth activities for the NSDAP. Schirach had led the Nazi University Student League since 1928, as well as the Nazi Pupils' League. He would soon give up both, to devote himself entirely to the Hitler-Jugend. (The Student League lived on, whereas the Pupils merged with the HJ.) In 1931 the HJ already had close to 35,000 members, which still comprised about 69 percent young workers, 12 percent pupils, and 10 percent white-collar shop clerks. It was assumed that during this time of the Great Depression, about half of the parents of these adolescents were unemployed.[5]

Baldur von Schirach, a handsome man although always on the flabby side, was three-quarters American and one-quarter German. His great-grandfather, Karl Benedikt von Schirach, once a German judge, had emigrated to the United States in 1855, where his son Karl Friedrich fought in the Civil War, on the Union side as a Major. Having lost a leg in the Battle of Bull Run, Karl Friedrich von Schirach was an honor guard at President Lincoln's funeral in 1865. Major von Schirach, Baldur's grandfather, married Elizabeth Baily Norris from a patrician Philadelphia family, but his son Karl Norris von Schirach, Baldur's father, was born back in Berlin, and eventually he too wed an American, Emma Tillou, from another good Phildelphia family. Karl Norris von Schirach was an American citizen until he joined the Prussian Army, from which he retired as a Colonel to become Generalintendant of the Weimar court theater in 1908. From this position he was ousted—unjustly, he claimed—by the revolutionary currents after World War I. Until that time, between the hallowed aura of Goethe and Schiller on the one side and the visionary modernism of the Bauhaus on the other, the Grand Duchy of Weimar was marked by mostly mediocre artistic achievements, including those in the theater directed by Karl Norris von Schirach.[6]

Into this moderately well-off family with high but frustrated cultural ambitions, Baldur von Schirach was born in 1907, in Berlin. Since his family had strong monarchist and nationalistic leanings and hated the revolution and its republican aftermath, Baldur was predisposed to the radical right even as a child. Adolf Hitler passed through Weimar one day in March of 1925, and Hans Severus Ziegler, a local right-wing culture broker close to the Schirach family, introduced Baldur and a friend to him. "Hitler pressed our hands for a long time, looking us deeply in the eyes . . . Running home, I composed one of my many bad poems: 'You stand a thousand strong behind me / And you are me, and I am you / I have not lived a single thought / Which did not quiver in your hearts.'" Hitler visited the Schirach home in the fall of that year, whereupon Baldur's American mother exclaimed: "At last a German patriot!"[7]

By the spring of 1927 Schirach had moved to Munich University to take up the study of German and English literature as well as art history; already fluently bilingual, he fancied himself a budding poet and wanted to lead the stimulating life of an artist and intellectual. As he became involved in the machinations of the Nazi Student League, he participated in its ongoing boycott of Jewish students. Again he met Hitler, who made him leader of the League in July 1928. At the same time the Führer reminded him: "Schirach, you are studying with me!"[8]

After Hitler appointed him the Party's youth chief in October 1931, Schirach nominally became a subordinate of Ernst Röhm, who now, for the second time, was the leader of the SA, or storm troopers. In 1932, Hitler elevated Schirach to the same Party status that Röhm himself enjoyed, and the HJ was set free. To emphasize his new position as a leader much closer to Hitler, Schirach organized his first youth mass rally on October 1 and 2, 1932, at Potsdam, near Berlin. There were marches, speeches, drills, and fanfares, and, naturally, both Schirach and Hitler addressed the crowd. The occasion appears to have attracted an impressive 70,000 boys and girls from all over Germany, all of whom had paid for the journey themselves.[9] December 1932 capped a period of turmoil for socially insecure people in large cities, with the radical left fighting the radical right in the streets. On the Nazi end, the SA and Hitler Youth were the main participants. In Kiel, one day in 1932, when the Party and its affiliates had been forbidden to wear Nazi uniforms by the Papen Cabinet, a clutch of HJ butcher apprentices walked down the street in their white butcher aprons, with everyone afraid that they were hiding huge butcher knives underneath.[10] By the end of the Republic, the HJ had lost twenty-two comrades in these fights, the most glorified of whom was Herbert Norkus, son of an SA man from the lower-class Moabit district of Berlin, who was hounded down by Communist youths and stabbed to death in late January of 1932.[11]

As soon as Hitler became Chancellor of the German Reich on January 30, 1933, Schirach tried to consolidate all of Germany's youth. His aim was to take over as many as possible of the diffuse youth leagues, large and small, that existed by then and turn them into Hitler Youths. On June 17, Hitler appointed Schirach Youth Leader of the German Reich. Schirach would remain in this position until August 1940, when he would be promoted to regional chief or Gauleiter of Vienna; Artur Axmann, the twenty-seven-year-old head of the Berlin social services office of the HJ, would replace him as Reich Youth Leader. Axmann's loyalty could not be doubted; born in Westphalian Hagen, he had become active in a Berlin HJ cell in 1928. But Schirach always maintained his grip on German youth: in October of 1940 Hitler appointed him Reich HJ Inspector and Plenipotentiary for Youth Education of the NSDAP, charging him with the responsibility for KLV, a program for children to be moved to the safety of the countryside, under the guidance of the HJ.[12]

By any standards, the growth figures of the Hitler-Jugend are impressive: over 100,000 by the time of Hitler's assumption of power, over 2 million at the end of 1933, and 5.4 million by December 1936. At that time Schirach, who had just been granted additional powers by the Führer, claimed to have the allegiance of 60 percent of all young people from ages ten to eighteen. While this was truly remarkable, demonstrating the attraction of the authoritarian Nazi system for young Germans, it still did not constitute the 100 percent that Schirach craved.[13]

In early 1933, the Hitler Youth showed much promise for development but was still based on a relatively small, voluntary membership. Because it prided itself on the voluntarist principle, the HJ depended during the first years of the Third Reich on the voluntary flow of new members. In order to fill the comparatively small membership rolls more quickly, Baldur von Schirach tried soon after January 1933 to manipulate the wholesale takeover of the entrenched youth leagues.

This was not too difficult, since many of their leaders sympathized with the HJ and could be lured with promises of instant leadership positions, as had been done before 1933. What these groups had in common with the Hitler Youth was a generic hatred of the Weimar republican system, its parliament and democracy; they preferred authoritarian leadership structures. What had to be overcome was individual allegiances to many single chiefs, in exchange for a unitary commitment to one national leader and his deputy.[14] Those of the republican youth groups that had derived from Weimar political parties such as the *Jungnationaler Bund* became amalgamated first because the presidential Emergency Ordinance for the Protection of People and State of February 28 paved the way for the banning of all political parties and their ancillary organizations. As the former West German Chancellor Helmut Schmidt, who was fifteen in 1933, recalls, this provoked non-organized teenagers like himself to join the HJ, so as not to be left out in the cold.[15] Schmidt speaks for many who were then under considerable peer pressure to join. Stigmatized groups, like the Communist youth league, KJVD (*Kommunistischer Jugendverband Deutschlands*), were simply dissolved and their leaders sent to a concentration camp; residual Marxist splinter groups who attempted resistance were all but snuffed out by 1935.[16]

The bourgeois and politicized youth groups who were known under the overarching label of *Bündische Jugend,* including such groups as the *Wandervögel* and *Deutsche Freischar,* whose members were given to hiking in the countryside to get away from their elders and tended to be suspicious of the Republic, had all officially been neutralized by 1936. This Nazi victory had been achieved by totalitarian methods: the terror and wounds of street fights, generally initiated by Hitler Youths despite Schirach's official ban on such confrontations.[17] But doubtless, Schirach had issued his order only perfunctorily, and it was gleefully ignored by his followers. In southwest German Baden in the summer of 1934, for example, where the *Deutscher Pfadfinderbund* (German Boy Scouts) had so far gone unmolested, forty Hitler Youths attacked two of their members without apparent cause, sending one to the hospital.[18] In another instance the charismatic Eberhard Koebel, whom his followers in the *Deutsche Jungenschaft* knew as "Tusk," after flirting with Communism had made overtures to the HJ in the autumn of 1933. However, in January 1934 the Gestapo arrested Koebel, who then slit his wrists and was sent to the hospital, where he jumped out of a window and suffered a concussion. After his release a few days later, he fled to England via Sweden.[19] Other bourgeois youth leaders were murdered outright. A typical incident occurred in June 1934, when in Plauen the former leader of the *Deutsche Freischar*, Karl Lämmermann, was killed by a frenzied HJ mob. Lämmermann had already come over to the HJ as leader in 1928; after January 1933 he continued to indoc- trinate his charges in the spirit of individual freedom which had typi- fied most of the pro-republican youth leagues, and thus he reached a violent end at Nazi hands.[20] By 1935, the Hitler Youth leadership cal- culated that youth groups with a total membership of almost 3.5 mil- lion remained outside its influence.[21] On February 8, 1936, the Gestapo forbade all those bourgeois youth leagues to exist or meet, using again the emergency decree of February 28, 1933.[22] This order had to be repeated several times because problems persisted with some *bündisch* youth formations, especially with the markedly Catholic ones among them.

The Hitler Youth faced less of a challenge in trying to incorporate the Protestant leagues. Many Protestant youths and their leadership had already declared their sympathy with the HJ before 1933, as had their parents, disproportionately, with Hitler and his Nazi move- ment.[23] To the extent that Protestant youth leagues wished to preserve their independence after January 1933, it was on account of claims for their institutional freedom rather than religious beliefs. To the racist Nazi "German Christians" in the Protestant Church, who thought that the Jewish Jesus really was a blond "Aryan," Hitler appeared as hav- ing been directly sent by God in order to save Germany. But even their rivals in the church, the Confessional Christians led by Pastor Martin Niemöller, believed in ceding to Caesar what they thought was Caesar's. And so easily enough, Schirach and the Protestant Youth leadership arrived at an agreement in December 1933 that merged Protestant youth groups seamlessly with the Hitler Youth.[24] A positive feature for the church leaders, or so they thought, was that Bible study could be continued in groups beyond the ranks of the HJ. But within a few months those who did so were regarded with open suspicion by local HJ leaders and harassed to the point of suppression or absorption.[25]

Catholics had been more skeptical toward the Nazis from the beginning, not least because since the Wilhelmian Empire they had had their own Catholic Center Party. The situation for Catholic youth groups, with over a million members, seemed ambiguous, but then in July 1933 the Concordat between Berlin and the Vatican was concluded, guaranteeing the Catholic Church in Germany sovereignty over all religious matters, but proscribing any sort of political activity and closing down the Center Party itself.[26] Organized Catholic youths now thought they could coexist with the Hitler Youth, but Schirach would have none of this. He accused them of being political even when they were not. There were many fracases especially in heavily Catholic regions between HJ and Catholic groups, involving notably the largest, the *Katholischer Jungmännerverband,* and the athletic organization *Deutsche Jugendkraft.*[27] Symptomatic of Nazi brute force was an incident in the Bavarian countryside near Berchtesgaden, where in May 1934 Hitler Youths accosted young Catholic churchgoers and ripped their *Jugendkraft* club signs from their clothes.[28] The shutting down of the Catholic youth leagues occurred in stages between 1935 and 1939; even youth groups with harmless names, such as "Franciscan Youth" or "Catholic Young Men's Association," could not convince the HJ leadership of an absence of political intentions.[29]

Thus the growth of the Hitler Youth from January 1933 to the beginning of World War II was in large part contingent on the forced incorporations of previously organized leagues and less on voluntary memberships, as Schirach and his minions had claimed.[30] Indeed, of three statutory provisions concerning the HJ before September 1939, only the last one called for compulsory membership of boys and girls aged ten to eighteen. The first of these provisions was Schirach's formal appointment by Hitler as Reich Youth Leader of Germany on June 17, 1933, which gave his office of youth supervision high priority without elevating it to the status of a Reich ministry.[31] Schirach could issue patriotic appeals and use psychological ploys such as invoking peer pressure, which would serve as a powerful incentive for non-organized German youths to join, but he could not force them outright. The second provision, the Hitler Youth Law of December 1, 1936, stated that "the entire German youth within the territory of the Reich is coordinated in the Hitler Youth." This was wishful thinking in the guise of a decree, but it had not actually been accomplished, even though it created a strong illusion in Germany that Schirach was right, thus adding more power to peer pressure.[32] The third provision, on March 25, 1939, specified that "all adolescents from age 10 to 18 are obligated to put in service in the Hitler Youth."[33] With war in the offing, Hitler now thought it prudent to fashion the HJ more strictly as a training cadre for the Wehrmacht, and this could not be accomplished without coercion. These three consecutive administrative measures are reflected in the Hitler Youth's growth statistics. According to the HJ's own figures, at the end of 1933 there were 2.3 million young people, or 30.5 percent of the total age cohort, in its ranks. This figure had climbed to 64 percent at the end of 1937, and by early 1939, undoubtedly because of the March decree, membership briefly reached a respectable 98.1 percent.[34] To all intents and purposes, Schirach with his carrot-and-stick policy—a typical governing ploy in the formative years of the Third Reich—had been resoundingly successful.

German locales were affected unevenly by these developments. Of 137 elementary schools in the region of Vechta in northern Germany, 80 had co-opted all students in the last four grades by July 1934, meaning those from ten to fourteen years old; the rest claimed a success rate of at least 80 percent.[35] By contrast, schools somewhat further south in the area of Lippe at about the same time could barely win half of the students for the Hitler Youth.[36] In June 1935 in a trade-school class in Hamburg only seven of twenty students were in the HJ, and thus the Party representatives were handing out questionnaires asking: "Why are you not a member?"[37] Students of trade schools throughout southwest German Baden in October of that year managed an HJ membership of less than 80 percent, whereas Gymnasien were higher than 90 percent, and elementary schools just under 90 percent.[38] Eight Gymnasien in the vicinity of north German Brunswick (always a Nazi stronghold) in February 1936 boasted HJ membership figures from 94 to 99 percent, but in Catholic Bavaria, in elementary and trade schools, merely 44 percent followed Schirach's call.[39] In all of Württemberg, to the northwest of Bavaria, less than a year before the compulsory order of March 1939, 89.7 percent of students in all schools had joined, with those in Gymnasien at the highest rate, those in trade-oriented schools the lowest, and elementary pupils somewhere in between.[40]

Although these figures are respectable, they also show that not all schools attracted HJ recruits equally and that religious and regional factors had something to do with a teenager's willingness to join. As individual case histories bear out, the membership rate in a Gymnasium tended to be high because, contrary to its pre-1933 lower-class motto, the HJ leadership now wooed older and socially well-placed students who could lead youths two or three years younger than themselves. This incentive was absent in elementary schools, from which students graduated at age fourteen with apprenticeships or jobs in mind that allowed little room for HJ interests. And that situation was even more pronounced in designated trade schools, some of whose students were already engaged in a job.[41]

Wherever it existed, the porousness of the HJ membership structure until March 1939 still allowed some flux. Obviously, when young Germans chose not to join, they were challenging the societal or labor-market sanctions that such an attitude would evoke. One of these Germans was the budding Nobel Prize novelist Heinrich Böll in Cologne, sixteen years old in 1933: "I just *could not* go to the HJ and I did not go, and that was that."[42] Local HJ pressure to join was often overcome with the help of parents, more precisely the mother, and in

Catholic regions the local priest could strengthen any anti-HJ resolve.[43] In the summer of 1936 country girls in the Bavarian village of Weildorf refused to attend BDM evenings, citing lack of parental permission, church obligations, and fatigue after a hard day's work in the fields.[44] Once they were members, some boys and girls played hooky because they were bored, did not like the songs, found exercising and marching too strenuous, or did not get along with the (scarcely older) group leaders.[45] One Nazi publication hints at something more sinister: in the story of Hitler Girl Ursel and her friends, a BDM newcomer, Marga, refuses to fit in. She does not abide by the BDM cleanliness code and is interested only in silly pranks. She sticks her tongue out when told to behave, all to no avail, until the leader, Ursel, strips Marga of her uniform and insignia. Marga turns on her heel, slams the door shut, storms out, and is never seen again.[46] The willingness of well-conditioned Hitler Youth teens to brand outsiders as enemies of the Nazi community, even in those early years, was effective then and foretold of things to come.

Because members could leave at will if they were disgruntled, social and political sanctions were brought to bear. At least in theory, Gymnasium students absent from the HJ were not permitted to pass the Abitur, the mandatory entrance examination for university. Working youths were to be denied apprenticeships in trades or factories, and could not become hereditary farmers (*Erbhofbauern*). The political consequence of non-participation was to be barred from the Nazi Party or any of its affiliates forever. This was supposed to amount to "political ostracism and a ban from all public life."[47] But already in 1936, with a dearth of workers for the incipient war economy, these stipulations were rendered meaningless, and for those who hated the HJ enough to avoid it, public office in a Nazi state would have been loathsome in any case.

Even after the Youth Ordinance of March 1939 the constancy of HJ attendance was still not what it should have been, as too many teenagers came and went or did not enroll at all.[48] The HJ leadership got some help in November 1939 when it was decreed that it could use the state bureaucracy to enforce its rulings. This meant notifications to local and regional government agencies, such as county heads (Landräte) and, subsequently, the police.[49] Henceforth the HJ aimed to solve the truancy problem at two levels. If, for example, boys or girls had missed three meetings, the local gendarme could put them behind bars for an entire Sunday (so they would not miss school), on a diet of water and bread. Once parents were held responsible, Nazi Kreisleiter or district chiefs could threaten them with the withholding of social benefits until their children became faithful members.[50]

In the following months many HJ outposts tried this route, but with mixed results.[51] Indeed, government agencies such as the judiciary doubted the efficacy of currently available sanctions, not least because of the red tape involved.[52] Everyday practice bore this out. In Biberbach near Ulm on a Sunday in April 1941, several HJ members chose to go to church rather than attend a specially scheduled morning drill. They were supported in this not only by their parents but also by virtually the entire village population, of which it was said that "it holds the position that the boys belong in church, as there is enough time during the afternoon for drills."[53] Only in rare cases did young repeat offenders appear to have been actually arrested, tried, and punished.[54] And so throughout the Reich, not much improvement was seen. In some places, such as the Bavarian district of Landsberg, by the middle of 1942 "there had not been any Hitler Youth activity for 2–3 years."[55]

Although at the national level, these incidents appear not to have had great importance, they still irked the Hitler Youth leadership. Thus the HJ leaders decided to solicit Heinrich Himmler's aid in his capacity as Chief of SS and Police, including the Gestapo, in order to enforce total service in the HJ. Through the Youth Service Compulsion Decree of November 24, 1942, Himmler laid down much tougher laws that did not require bureaucratic channels to implement. The police were empowered to move quickly against a culprit's parents, who could be fined or imprisoned. Alternatively, the youths themselves could be held accountable. They, too, could receive a fine, be incarcerated on the express order of the Hitler Youth, or be taken into special custody by the criminal police or, worse, the Gestapo, as asocial aliens and unreconstructible criminals.[56] Subsequently, this regulation served as the basis for much more rigorous attempts to stamp out absenteeism, especially when combined with the ultimate social punishment meted out by the HJ, expulsion.[57] However, all this could not change the fact that Hitler Youth attendance even at the height of the war was not perfect.[58]

Young Germans who mustered the courage to resist HJ incorporation often did so not just out of boredom or dislike of annoying routines and drills. Many were individualistic enough to reject, on their own behalf, the stereotypical mold into which the Hitler Youth leadership wished to press all of its members, thereby allowing for no deviations from the norm, no idiosyncrasies whatsoever. The HJ's idealized self-image was stiflingly uniform and militantly exclusive at the same time—in keeping with the vision of a future Nazi elite, in which many ruthless political führers were needed for every governmental echelon.[59] This uniformity was manifested not just by the required clothing—black shorts or trousers and khaki shirts for the boys, and dark-blue skirts with white blouses for the girls—but also by the military short cut (with hair the length of matches) for the boys, and long braids or rolls for girls.[60] Within specifically German frameworks, the ideologically racist Hitler Youth defined itself for practical purposes through folk songs, life in the outdoors, and physical exercise—said to be the opposite of international decadent Jewry, American-style films and jazz, and modern international art forms.[61]

Thus, even during times of (officially) universal HJ membership, when most members, like Hermann Graml and Margarete Hannsmann, loved the daily cult and sports routines, there were always some reflective adolescents of both sexes who were different. They protested against the stifling rigor by refusing the state's youth conscription. In this they were mostly acting alone and only sometimes with the backing of parents or friends. One boy in northern German Rendsburg, supported by his father, risked total confrontation with his leaders

simply by growing his hair long.[62] Another, Max von der Grün, later a
writer, resented the demanding HJ because his father was incarcerated.
Peter Wapnewski, later a professor of German literature, as a youth was
hypnotized by American jazz and swing and thus forged a doctor's letter to stay away.[63] A Frankfurt boy who skipped the Hitler Youth meetings in favor of the movies altered his HJ identity card in order to view
the adult-only films.[64] A particularly sensitive girl in Hamburg risked
expulsion from the BDM because she found its views to be drivel, after
she had seen paintings by Emil Nolde, George Grosz, and members of
the Bauhaus school which were displayed as deterrents at the 1937
Exhibition of Degenerate Art.[65] Karma Rauhut, too, was a Hollywood
film and jazz aficionado, who exchanged her meetings with BDM pals
for ones with Eleanor Powell and Clark Gable. Like Wapnewski, Rosemarie Heise, socialized by Social Democratic parents, forged a medical
certificate in order to stay home and listen clandestinely to the BBC.[66]
The noted Hitler biographer Joachim C. Fest, who even at seventeen
was a critic of the Führer and his Nazi regime, had never bothered to
join the HJ. After he carved a small caricature of Hitler on his wooden
desk in 1941, he faced expulsion from school as well as political
recriminations from the Hitler Youth. Without hesitation, his sympathetic father took Joachim out of the Berlin Leibnitz-Gymnasium and
quietly moved the family to Freiburg.[67]

   Although these exceptions were quite rare, they still contradicted,
from the hopeful beginnings in 1933 to the catastrophic finale in 1945,
the image of a uniform monopoly by the Hitler Youth that its leaders
consistently projected. And few as they might have been, they constituted the basis for several of the HJ's growing problems. Yet there is no
denying that the Hitler Youth, beginning with Schirach's watch and
continuing under Axmann, managed to gather by far the greater part of
German youth between the ages of ten and eighteen into its fold.

Authoritarianism, Militarism, Imperialism

Although this was always denied by Hitler Youth leaders after 1945,[68]
the hallmark of HJ socialization was militarization, with a view to a

war of territorial expansion and, as its predetermined goal, the neutralization of Europe's Jews. To be sure, matters of military import had already played a role in the late Weimar republican youth movement, but, because of post–World War I disarmament, they were never as central or as significant. This situation had already begun to change with the rhetoric of Nazi leaders after January 1933, and it did change in April of 1935, after the introduction of universal conscription on March 16. Armed Forces Minister Werner von Blomberg announced: "Service in the Wehrmacht is the last and highest step in the general educational process of any young German, from the home to the school, to the HJ and Labor Service."[69] At the same time, the youngest HJ boys of ages ten to fourteen were officially quoted as saying: "What are we now? Pimpfe. What do we want to be? Soldiers!" In 1937 Lieutenant Colonel Erwin Rommel, destined to be famous as Hitler's Desert Fox in the North African campaign, was appointed by the German Army High Command as the first liaison officer to the Hitler Youth leadership.[70] During World War II, the connection between premilitary training in the HJ and actual combat in the field was of course made much more explicit, as one became a precondition for the other.[71]

Even before the beginning of the global conflict in September 1939, the most ingenuous Hitler Youths found this trend quite normal: they had been told in school and at home—to say nothing of the HJ itself—that Germany was preparing for an "unavoidable war."[72] The most common Hitler Youth activities involving premilitary training were camp and hiking exercises, practiced in a far more rigorous way than the Weimar youths or the Boy Scouts in England had done. Local HJ groups enthusiastically played "war games" against each other, during which boys could be roughed up badly in order to steel themselves for greater adventures.[73] Local camp events often took place in tents, with mandatory overnight stays; the game plan included many military features, such as roll calls during flag ceremonies, military trumpet fanfares, and rifle practice, all controlled by a strictly hierarchical command rule.[74] Much importance was given to the study of maps and the spotting of imaginary or designated enemies (usually an opposing HJ posse, perhaps from an adjacent city district). In the guise of games and play, constant vigilance and discipline were practiced.[75] This applied as well to the regional and national hikes, which would take the Hitler Youth on strenuous marches to historically important sites, preferably near the borders of countries to be conquered later, such as Schleswig (Denmark) and East Prussia (Poland).[76] Once the war had begun, these routines were well in place and were continued with the express purpose of immediately transferring eighteen-year-old youths into the armed forces.[77]

A large part of this premilitary training consisted of sports, in keeping with Hitler's own tenets in *Mein Kampf,* where he had singled out boxing as his favorite.[78] Indeed, boxing was one of the preferred sports in the Hitler Youth.[79] Programmatically and in accordance with the biopolitical principles underlying the Nazis' *völkisch* community, it was held that sport was not a matter of individual relaxation, but a "necessity for keeping the *Volk* healthy"—hence to be entrusted exclusively to the national monopolist youth organization.[80] From 1933 until well into the war, the Hitler Youth leadership organized large-scale regional and national competitions among its members, after having attained a state monopoly in the organization, administration, and conduct of all types of sport.[81] Again, the connection with war was obvious: through sport the body was trained for combat, and certain sportsmen were needed for special tasks, such as skiers in the spring of 1940 after Germany had invaded Norway under General Eduard Dietl.[82]

Whether they were aware of the military implications or not, most Hitler Youth members liked the sports, since there was plenty of variety. There were calisthenics, swimming, fencing, ball games, and the nationally beloved soccer, which was said to further a mutual feeling of community.[83] The writer Siegfried Lenz reports that he was fond of spear throwing, preferring it even to handball and the high jump.[84]

But not all Hitler Youths were so happy with the sports and drill because much of it overextended them physically. Although this was not unusual in premilitary groups of any day or age, the Nazis perfected sports and drill techniques so as to humiliate their young

charges to the point were they lost their self-respect, becoming deper-
sonalized and totally malleable. "We had to run for hours," writes one,
"crawl through filth, and hop up and down." "Did we feel degraded,
drilled, demeaned, or caught?" writes another, in retrospect claiming
not to have known that he was being readied "for a war."[85] The HJ,
explicitly honoring the Social Darwinist principle of the superiority of
the fittest, encouraged individual and group sadism, physical and mental torture, and peer-group hazing, more than any republican youth
league would have done. There were forced tests of courage such as
making youths jump from five-meter boards into water, often when
they could not swim, making them climb up the side of ravines without proper support, and forcing them to perform endless knee-bends.
In one camp, a non-swimmer drowned in the deep end of a swimming
pool.[86]

Learning how to shoot was a key element in premilitary training and
a regular part of the agenda early on for all boys, from ages ten to eighteen. Those up to fourteen years practiced with air guns, while the
older boys were taught how to use small-caliber rifles. The instruction
was theoretical as well as practical.[87] On the whole, these exercises were
understandably very popular with the HJ membership, who for some
years could not foresee but only guess to what uses their skills would be
put one day.[88] But their enthusiasm did not diminish after the war
began and the need for gun training became wholly transparent. If
anything, more frequent and elaborate shooting matches such as those
prescribed by an ordinance of October 15, 1939, sharpened the boys'
appetite for real-life combat, since they had already been sufficiently
conditioned in a martially attuned society.[89] Frequently, the increased
familiarity with and casual handling of guns led to accidents, as in February 1941 in Munich, when a sixteen-year-old Gymnasium student
shot his friend to death with a handgun during play-acting. The
revolver was a Browning, which at the time was routinely handed out
to Hitler Youths by their superiors.[90]

Although gun sports were prevalent throughout the Hitler Youth,
they may have mattered less in some branches and more in others,

depending on their specialization. Apart from the general HJ, there
were some specialized units that were regarded as more elite than
others, such as those with gliders, then turning into the Fliers' HJ. In
these units, experience in the air was paramount, often after courses in
model-plane construction, and playing with handguns or rifles took
second place.[91] It is obvious that these eager young pilots were coveted
by Göring's Luftwaffe when the war was on, just as the ground forces
would claim experienced members from special details for motorcycles
and even automobiles (Motor HJ). In the Motor HJ, some of the
vehicles were owned by senior HJ members or their well-to-do fathers;
others could train on the HJ's own vehicles, which again incited much
enthusiasm in the boys.[92] In the North, the Marine HJ was sought-
after, since many youths in Hamburg, Bremen, or Kiel were already
familiar with sailboats and kayaks.[93] After 1938 these young men easily
found their way into the Navy, which most of them joined just as willingly as others did the Luftwaffe. Like the motor branches, members of
the Equestrian HJ and the Communications HJ, which trained with
the telephone and Morse code, would also merge with conventional
ground troops.[94]

   There also was a music division in the Hitler Youth. The boys
and girls who flocked to it were artistically inclined and, because of
their sensitivity, less interested in physical activities and therefore
more subject to harassment by their peers than was the norm.[95] The
music cadres usually were attached to radio stations (HJ-Rundfunk-
Spielscharen), where HJ choirs or small orchestral ensembles performed alongside other offerings, frequently political ones, broadcast
live from the studios. These HJ musical groups also performed at public recitals, and whenever the Hitler Youth leadership needed them for
inspiration at its own political and disciplinary exercises, such as
regional camp meetings or occasions when the HJ had to reinforce
Nazi Party rallies.[96] At drill time the repetitious use of a song helped in
the numbing of young minds, as part of the Nazi educational canon.[97]
Such music could be turned exclusively to serving ideological ends,
aided by a plethora of ideologically charged texts. Fully aware of this,

the HJ leadership maintained music academies and chairs at universities to help in the forming of politicized musical Nazi servants. Some respectable German composers, including Heinrich Spitta and Wolfgang Fortner, contributed their talents to this effort, and Carl Orff wanted to put together at least one songbook for HJ mass consumption in 1933.[98] Indeed, most of the songs that the Hitler Youths were encouraged to chant, in the manner of soldiers on the march, were clearly martial in character, related to Fatherland, duty, honor, blood and soil, and above all fighting and death.[99] A prime example of this is "Our Flag Is Showing Us the Way," with lyrics by the would-be poet Schirach himself, used for HJ propaganda as early as 1933 in the Ufa film *Hitlerjunge Quex,* which glorified the 1932 Nazi martyrdom of Herbert Norkus. The song conjures up a battleground, speaks of defying danger, of a glowing Germany, of possible doom, of Hitler the Führer ("We are marching for Hitler through night and dread / With the banner of youth for freedom and bread"), and reassures the enraptured singers that "we are the soldiers of the future."[100]

As one might expect, even in peacetime the Hitler Youth boys and girls spent a good many hours per week in HJ-owned houses, after school or work and regularly on weekends. Here indoctrination took place and plans were made for extracurricular outdoor activities, such as bivouacs, sports, and drill. In the early years of the Third Reich, existing Weimar youth movement hostels were confiscated and new HJ clubhouses were built from scratch or by renovating rudimentary structures such as stables and tool sheds. During this construction and the meetings following it, the beloved HJ hymns were intoned.[101] These clubhouses (HJ-Heime) became much more important in the winter time, when the teenagers could not be sent away to rural areas to do some practical work for the nation. For the regime, the most valuable of these tasks, especially during summer school vacations, turned out to be the work of aiding the peasants on the farms. Such field activity helped serve the purpose of keeping the youths physically fit, while at the same time honoring the Nazi dogma of "Blood and Soil," which tried to put a stop to the current exodus from the land to the cities. Not least, such work was good for the overall economy and was, once again, an important preparatory step toward premilitary recruitment and, eventually, the deployment of young people in battle, the occupied territories, and for war emergencies at home.[102]

From the beginning of organized agricultural service, around 1934, the Nazis targeted eastern territories in particular, first German ones adjoining the Polish border such as Pomerania and Silesia, with a view to occupying them in a sweep of conquest behind the German Wehrmacht.[103] Thus helping on the farms and in the fields, whether this involved harvesting, cutting wood, or milking cows, was complementary to the barely disguised imperialistic hikes by Hitler Youths to the coveted borders.[104] When the time came, these youths would know those territories and how to exploit them. HJ-Landdienst, or agricultural service, was always characterized by an imperialist quality. Its ideology was based on that of the racist *Artamanen,* a pre-1933 youth league on the extreme right of would-be eastern settlers, to which leading National Socialists had once belonged, among them Heinrich Himmler, Reich Peasant Leader Richard Walther Darré, and the future commandant of Auschwitz, Rudolf Hoess. It is telling that the *Artamanen* were among the few Weimar republican youth groups to blend easily with Schirach's budding Nazi youth movement, when it absorbed them in 1933.[105]

It was during the war that the agricultural youth service revealed its true predatory character. Teenagers were sent to the newly conquered western areas of Poland where many Germans lived in the countryside, most of them adhering to a standard of nutrition and hygiene typical of their Polish neighbors, which the Germans in the Reich despised. The mission of German youth was to re-educate those ethnic Germans, or *Volksdeutsche,* and lead them back to the proper ways of the life and livelihood of their forefathers. Eventually, such Nazi hubris even extended to Germans living in the western borderlands such as Eupen and Malmédy, which had been reconquered from Belgium, and Alsace-Lorraine, reconquered from France. In the Southeast adjacent to annexed Austria, Lower Styria, too, once part of Yugoslavia, was targeted.[106]

In 1940 this HJ service was still voluntary, and tens of thousands of teenagers moved to the borderlands. Not only did they willingly toil on the farms, in the forests, and in the fields, but they also gave German lessons to ethnic Germans who had lost or adulterated their language.[107] Nazi-specific culture, such as that derived from traditional German music or folk dance, and ideological issues also became part of the broader catechism.[108] Many of the Germans from Poland were to be resettled in the Reich, and this number was greatly increased after 1941, when approximately 350,000 emigrants from rural areas of the Soviet Union, mostly the so-called Volga Germans, had to be cared for as well, in large resettlement camps.[109] By 1942 this colonization work had become mandatory for members of the Hitler Youth, and they were typically deployed during the summer or fall for a period of six weeks, when entire classes were taken out of school and sent on the job.[110] During such sojourns German youths were also commanded to guard the youth of conquered nations in special camps, in particular Polish youth, and in this way were taught the techniques of subjugation, which not all of the Reich's teenagers were immediately comfortable with.[111] Now more than ever the Hitler Youth leaders—as did Himmler's SS—worked with the concept of *Wehrbauerntum,* or fortified farmsteads, as border bastions in an incrementally conquered East, where young German families would be settled, plow in one hand and gun in the other. The goal, originally projected by the *Artamanen* in the 1920s, was to subjugate the indigenous populations and use them as slaves on the land that had been taken from them, with the Germans as sole beneficiaries and absolute masters.[112]

On the home front during the war, the Hitler Youth went from door to door collecting valuable raw materials, such as rags, paper, and scraps of metal for recycling, an activity that was essential for the war economy. HJ members also had to participate in the search for mushrooms and for herbs, used for tea and medicinal purposes, as well as helping out in town and country in various auxiliary positions, such as tram conductor, ersatz-coffee dispenser at train stations, or letter carrier.[113]

But the ultimate trial for the Hitler Youth came during direct contact with the effects of the war itself, on the home front as the tide turned against the Germans. HJ members had to assist soldiers who were home on furlough or sick leave, many exhausted or disabled, some of them maimed beyond recognition. The boys and girls helped in the building of fortifications in the streets or close to the fronts and were on call for emergencies and war-triggered catastrophes such as flooding.[114] Teenagers functioned as air raid wardens and helped to fight fires, often at lethal risk to themselves. One former Hitler Youth, sixteen years old in 1940, remembers what he saw: "People under shock, with burns and singed hair, old women who had gone insane, mothers with an injured toddler in a blanket, momentarily blinded people, men weeping quietly. Pictures which carried me into many nightmares."[115] The worst such experience occurred after half of Hamburg had been leveled by British phosphor bombs, in July and August of 1943. The Nazi regime praised those youngsters as heroes—twelve, thirteen, or fourteen years old—who had saved civilians from burning ruins, even as some were themselves consumed by flames. One of those who made it through the inferno, which killed 42,000, writes that "we didn't have any sun at all for three or four days; it was completely dark out. We only saw a blood-red ball in the distance, which didn't penetrate the dark cloud that hovered over Hamburg for days: smoke, cinders, and ashes. The dead were piled in the entrances of houses. And when you went by you just saw a heap of feet, some barefoot, some with burned soles. The corpses were beyond identification. We would dig entire families out of their basements, sometimes two, three weeks later; they'd fit into a bathtub. Even the adults were very small. They were completely mummified, burned, and melted together by the heat."[116]

One might think that youth cohorts thus conditioned by a totalitarian regime were, like Sparta's young, toughened by removal from their primary environments of nurture and formal education, whether parental homes or schools. This was undoubtedly the ideal of the Nazi state in recruiting suitable leaders and followers, to keep the millennial Reich on track. However, Nazi socialization of the young in the long run was difficult because in Germany it had to contend with traditionally strong mainstays of society, namely parents and teachers and in some cases employers, with whom Hitler Youths might be apprenticing. Although the employers became less of a problem because the primacy of a war economy was recognized early and shops might make fewer demands on a youth's available time, ties to home and school posed difficulties which the HJ leadership took pains to overcome. In this struggle, the HJ leaders knew they could count on Hitler himself, who in the 1920s had declared in *Mein Kampf* (a book that few Germans bothered to read or take seriously) that developing a fit body was paramount, and anything else, including "the development of intellectual acumen," took second place.[117] In December 1938, after the Sudeten crisis, Hitler made clear his concept of the total politicization of youth when he announced publicly: "After these youths have entered our organizations at age ten and there experienced, for the first time, some fresh air . . . we shall under no circumstances return them into the hands of our old champions of class and social standing, but instead place them immediately in the Party or the Labor Front, the SA or SS . . . And then the Wehrmacht will take them over for further treatment . . . And thus they will never be free again, for the rest of their lives."[118]

To be sure, in the beginning the Hitler Youth leadership, with its revolutionary self-image, paid lip service to the institutions of old, but only to trick them into submission and subsequently to defeat them. Pronouncing on a three-pillar theory of home, school, and HJ, Baldur von Schirach early on attempted to assure parents that their traditional role as nurturers would not be interfered with, and educators that they would remain role models in the classrooms. But even then he left no doubt that the HJ's task of indoctrinating the young with the Nazi weltanschauung and developing their physical and martial prowess

took precedence over any traditional grooming.[119] Still, to pacify especially the teachers, Schirach in conjunction with the Reich Education
Ministry allowed for a Staatsjugendtag or State Youth Day in June
1934. This meant that much of the weekly HJ service encroaching on
school time would be concentrated outside of school on Saturdays,
during which those teenagers of ages ten to fourteen not yet organized
in the HJ were allowed to remain in regular school attendance. Wednes-
day evenings were to belong to the HJ.[120] To placate parents, Sundays
were to be reserved for them, and Schirach made a special point
in 1937 that Christmas, now as ever, was "the festival of the German
family."[121] Even in 1940, after the HJ had achieved unassailable state
monopoly status, the three-pillar theory was still upheld, with the family being singled out as the avatar of pre-school socialization.[122] By this
time, however, the HJ leadership had not only made service in its ranks
a national obligation, but was also able to use the exigencies of war as a
rationale to step up its battle against parents and teachers alike.

   In *Fear*, a play from 1944, Bertolt Brecht depicts the situation of a
couple fearing they will be denounced by their son, Klaus-Heinrich, as
he steps out of their flat for a short period to buy himself some candy.
Even after his return home, they have no way of knowing whether or
not he has turned them in to the Gestapo. They are certain that Klaus-
Heinrich has overheard anti-regime remarks, and they know that he is
a member of the Hitler Youth.[123] This fictionalized scenario was a very
real one for many parents of Hitler Youths who could not hold their
tongues, certainly in the period before the beginning of the war when
the official status of the HJ often seemed arbitrary and parents still
assumed their traditional educational prerogative. Indeed, there are
documented cases where children turned in their parents to the police,
for whatever reason—such as a certain Herr Hess, once a Communist,
who had called the Führer "a blood-crazed maniac." Reported by his
son, a mid-level HJ leader, he was arrested on the very night of the
remark and sent to Dachau, where he died at age forty of a sudden
"heart failure."[124] There are other instances where brazen HJ leaders,
callow youths of sixteen or seventeen in uniform, confronted the

fathers of sons in their cadres and threatened them en masse.[125] Girls did the same to mothers.[126] Much more numerous, however, were those cases in which, as Brecht describes, parents *thought* some anti-regime remark had been made or where the HJ child *knew* of their former political affiliation, such as Communism, Social Democracy, or membership in a religious sect like the anti-Nazi Jehovah's Witnesses.[127] Nor were political or ideological factors the only reason for a denunciation. Normal intergenerational conflict may have somehow been resolved in the democracy before 1933. But in Hitler's totalitarian *Volksgemeinschaft*, which often pitted son against father or daughter against mother as a matter of tactics, such conflict was being politicized, to be exploited subsequently by Schirach's HJ in order to keep the adults in check.[128] Thus perhaps unwittingly, children often became pawns in a fundamental confrontation between the regime and its less than pliant subjects.

Without a doubt, regime leaders knew and took advantage of the fact that for many youngsters the parental atmosphere was too narrow, or that they could not abide a family's religious practices, now frowned upon in the Hitler Youth.[129] Melita Maschmann, later an influential BDM leader, once met a young sympathizer who disliked his father, a professor of psychology, because he was a devotee of Freud.[130] Aesthetic reasons, such as a distaste for the plebeian Nazi uniforms, motivated many parents to try to keep their children from joining the HJ when this was still not compulsory, and this provoked resentment in their children.[131] National Socialism as celebrated in the Hitler Youth symbolized something new. The "revolution" that Schirach liked to invoke was seen as genuine by adolescents who often thought their old-fashioned parents were behind the times. Many young people wanted novelty and change and perceived the HJ as offering it.

Still, there is no denying that tension between the HJ and parents constituted only one side of the coin, for on the other was the huge reservoir of sympathy that a plurality of parents harbored for the Nazi cause. HJ leaders could always count on Nazi parents, some of whom had been Old Fighters in Hitler's Time of Struggle in the 1920s, to win over the lukewarm or resistant ones. These parents frequently went to great lengths, for example organizing "Parent Friends of the HJ," a lobby that was formed in early 1936 in Hanover.[132]

The situation was more complicated in the case of schools and teachers: whereas the HJ was an institution of Party and State, educational institutions nominally were its equal because they came under the time-hallowed State Ministry of Education. By contrast, the family was traditionally in the private, not public, sphere. Hence Schirach had a freer hand whenever the Ministry elected to cooperate with him on behalf of its teachers, but he got exercised whenever the Ministry or teachers attempted to restrain him. Fortunately for him, Schirach was a much more dynamic, and certainly much younger, Nazi official than the former secondary-school teacher Bernhard Rust, the Minister of Education, whose love of the bottle was the stuff of Nazi gossip.

In his struggle with the schools Schirach was indirectly able to claim victory after the proclamation of the Law for the Reconstitution of the Civil Service on April 7, 1933, whereby unreliable teachers, such as Social Democrats and Communists (to say nothing of the Jews), were summarily dismissed. What followed were screening routines of the remaining teaching staff by the police, which, as irreversible actions, could only work in the future interest of the HJ leadership.[133] Thus when the Staatsjugendtag was introduced in May 1934, it looked like a concession by Schirach to the teachers, but its concept and practice were still so much to the disadvantage of the schools that it was abandoned in December 1936—significantly, at just the time when Schirach claimed to have united all of Germany's youth under his leadership. One telling sign that the Staatsjugendtag had been a shabby compromise for teachers was that although on Saturdays it had kept non-HJ pupils under fourteen in the classrooms, about a quarter of youths over fourteen had been missing class on Saturdays because, as HJ leaders, they had to supervise the younger HJ pupils in the field.[134] By May of 1938 Schirach felt strong enough to launch a massive public attack on the school system, claiming that it was hopelessly out of date, counter-revolutionary, and statically tied to the civil-service tenure of its teachers. Schirach echoed Hitler's sentiment in *Mein Kampf* when he asked: "Why is it that almost all the men our nation takes pride in have advanced themselves not because of their school education, but in spite of it?"[135]

With some good will, Schirach could have found common ground with the teachers, for the majority were neither Nazis nor anti-Nazis but German national conservatives, who despite the defeat of 1918 had adapted themselves in the Weimar Republic and did not find it too difficult to acquiesce in the post-1933 order. In 1980 Alfred Andersch drew a portrait of this type: a Gymnasium teacher with a pot belly, always smartly dressed in suit and tie, smug, a believer in law and order who would vacillate between dispensing favors and picking on students for the sake of maintaining absolute power, and, inevitably, proud of his World War I record. This particular teacher, under whom Andersch studied Greek and history at the Wittelsbacher Gymnasium in Munich in 1928, was the principal of that well-regarded school. His name was Secret Counselor Gebhard Himmler, at that time sixty-three years old and the well-respected father of Heinrich.[136]

The authoritarian and militaristic persona of teachers like the older Himmler eventually blended easily with the ideal of totalitarian educators which the Third Reich espoused, even before the pressure of the second war. Indeed, constant classroom references to personal war experience between 1914 and 1918 bolstered the self-esteem of teachers and—this Schirach could appreciate—kept most of the students spellbound. The teachers were able to accommodate Goethe, Beethoven, Nietzsche, and Schopenhauer, as they lauded the demise of modernism which they had experienced during the Republic. As called for, the moribund monarchic idea of the Hohenzollerns was easily supplanted by the notion of a National Socialist Reich, and for the teachers, too, Fatherland turned into *Volksgemeinschaft*. The concentration in Nazi-style history classes on figures of the Germanic past, such as Arminius the Cheruscan, Luther, Frederick the Great, and Bismarck, was little different from that in the schools in the decades after German Unification in 1871.[137]

Even within this conservative yet adaptable set, there were those who embraced Hitler and Nazism fully only in the aftermath of the threatening Law of April 1933.[138] This law was much more on the minds of that minority of anti-Nazi teachers who were forced to hide their opposition to the regime under various guises. They had to walk a tightrope between internal rejection of the Hitlerites and postures of approval. Many had been lucky not to have been caught by the law, for once found out and denounced—by malevolent colleagues or fanatical HJ pupils—they could not only be dismissed but also arrested and incarcerated, especially if they had already once been demoted.[139]

The courage of those teachers often bordered on the miraculous, and their ruses in cheating Nazi superiors were nothing short of ingenious. One teacher called Krättge, "a young man with thick glasses, a high forehead, and unkempt hair," taught German literature in Berlin. He was hated by many and beloved by few. He emphasized themes of peace where everyone spoke of struggle, exposing the cruelty in a poem about a soldier lying mortally wounded at the front for two days without anyone tending to him. The torture ballad "Feet in the Fire," from the Huguenot Wars in France, was subtly twisted to point at the Nazis' victims.[140] Heinrich Böll reports that Herr Schmitz, his German teacher in Cologne, used *Mein Kampf* as a mandatory text, by way of a bad example, to teach his pupils concision.[141] There is a touching story of a teacher who clandestinely approached Max von der Grün as a young boy, whose father, a Jehovah's Witness, was then languishing in Flossenbürg concentration camp and whose hatred of the Nazis was ferocious. The teacher removed newspaper wrappings, produced the Jewish author Stefan Zweig's *Decisive Moments in History*, and implored his student not to show it to anybody. "For me, this was the hour of destiny in my life," writes von der Grün. "I began to read with awareness. I began to develop an interest in history, and the history I read was very different from what we were taught at school." In short, says von der Grün, he began to read "the history of the vanquished rather than that of the victors."[142]

Predictably, the Nazi concept of the superior Aryan race constituted the framework for subjects such as biology, history, and geography, and some teachers adapted neutral subjects like those in the hard sciences or mathematics to ideology by dwelling on military examples, as could be done with ballistics. In music, Beethoven and Wagner were stressed and Jewish composers like Mendelssohn ignored.[143] Invariably, such teachers humiliated pupils who were wholly or partially Jewish for as long as they were allowed to be in the classrooms.[144] The comportment of these teachers conformed closely to Nazi etiquette: some of them arrived in mustard-colored Party uniforms, barked in a tone of military command, offered the Hitler salute, or boasted of honorary positions in the regime.[145]

Not least because of the growing cooperation of many of those teachers, Schirach was slowly but steadily winning his campaign against the schools. Until the outbreak of the war, more and more teachers complied with his demands that they act as recruiting agents for his youth groups, and more and more of the younger ones donned HJ uniforms, thus symbolizing the increasing subservience of formal education to Nazi indoctrination.[146] Building on earlier efforts, Schirach by February 1938 had succeeded in creating the category of "liaison teachers" (*Vertrauenslehrer*), educators as mere stooges of the Hitler Youth.[147] Pupils themselves eagerly arrived in their classrooms dressed in HJ outfits; as Manfred Rommel, son of the general and a future lord mayor of Stuttgart, described it, "we tended to be against the school and in our HJ uniforms felt like grown-ups and strong in a group."[148]

By 1937 it had become obvious that the mounting politicization of the teachers combined with the growing neglect of school matters in favor of HJ service by many students was leading to a dilution of conventional pedagogical standards; students were learning less. Schirach seized the moment in early 1938 by once again ridiculing teaching as a profession and insisting on the superiority of ideological and character training, HJ-style, over the acquisition of formal knowledge. In a gesture of defeat, Minister Rust then shortened secondary education by a year, with the dire consequence that even fewer young men and women were willing to enter the teaching profession than before. This was on the eve of the war, when the teachers' collective strength was already being sapped by countless individual conscriptions.[149]

The war years served merely to demonstrate further the capitulation of the conventional school system to the HJ, against the background of continuing powerlessness in parental homes. Teachers, no less than parents, in the spring of 1940 and again in the fall of 1942, complained about the broken relationship between schools and families on the one side, and the Hitler Youth on the other, despite the necessities of a global war that was ideologically sanctioned.[150] The HJ leadership remained unmoved; it had further disparaged the family with impunity, and it knew that millions of its charges had been weaned from the schools and were now putting in service in the armed forces or in the Party echelons.[151] Denunciations of dissident teachers on the indictment of defeatism had become easier and more frequent; moreover, large numbers of the younger and more fanatical teachers who were at the fronts returned to the classrooms on furlough, in order to incite an already militarized student body further.[152] The school curriculum itself had become less substantive, shortened and progressively corrupted by ideology or applied war-related arts.[153] Isolated protests by school principals against the widespread alienation of students from the classrooms, because of services required for Party and State, remained unheard, as exemplified by a particularly urgent letter from a secondary-school official in Goslar, in September 1942.[154] As one schoolboy, Hitler Youth, and soldier, not without cynicism, later recorded in his memoirs: "Learning was postponed to the period after the Final Victory."[155]

Early in the war the Hitler Youth was provided with an additional opportunity to strengthen its powers over both parents and teachers. By September 27, 1940, Hitler had decided to create a program called Kinderlandverschickung (KLV), or "Save the Children in the Country," with the HJ in charge. Its purpose was to protect children old enough to be separated from their parents, from about age four to the early teens, from the bombs increasingly falling on German towns and cities, by removing them to out-of-the-way, non-urban places. Children could be sent away for six months at a time, and once installed in specially prepared HJ living quarters, they were subject to rigorous disciplinary controls beyond the purview of their parents. While children up to age ten were sent to live with Nazi families by state social workers, those between ten and fourteen were in HJ-controlled locations. Usually themselves members of the HJ, these children came to be supervised by somewhat older Hitler Youths. Thus, the parental home appears to have been totally eclipsed.[156]

This expansion of HJ jurisdiction over the nation's young posed new problems for parents and teachers alike. The main question for the parents was whether they should allow their children to leave at all. But while that decision was indeed their own, most of them had little choice because the Nazis' argument that children should be protected from bombs was a sensible one; moreover, since pupils were removed from schools by grades as class units, peer pressure made it virtually impossible for a single child to stay behind.[157]

The boys and girls were carried by special trains to rural locations all over Germany, but also—and here the imperialism of the Nazi regime was the underlying factor—to villages in Axis countries such as Romania, Hungary, Bulgaria, and Slovakia, and more significantly, to conquered areas, such as Luxembourg, the Protectorate of Bohemia and Moravia, Denmark, and western Poland. Depending on their luck, the children and their warders might be quartered in the shabbiest of surroundings, such as run-down hospitals or school buildings in poverty-stricken parts of Bohemia, or in luxury hotels and even beach resorts and castles, as in Tirol and Luxembourg. The camps in Poland were almost always wretched, while the ones in South Germany tended to be in swank little pensions in alpine resorts with names like Garmisch-Partenkirchen and Berchtesgaden. If the statistics are reliable, 200,000 special trains transported approximately five million German children to as many as 12,000 camps by early 1945, at which time the actions were officially called off.[158]

More often than not, the fear among parents was great, for however much they trusted this program in their heads, they were suspicious of it in their hearts—unless they were the sturdiest of Nazis. The HJ knew this and therefore discouraged visits by parents to their camp sites wherever they could, even though they were not always successful.[159] Children found it difficult to communicate with their mother or father because their letters home were censored; sometimes they were even ordered by their HJ supervisors to write that they were doing well, homesickness and illnesses notwithstanding.[160] However, the regulations were still on the parents' side; so if they really wanted to have their children back home, there was nothing that could be done to stop them.[161] Usually it was sufficient for children to convince the HJ or their parents that they were quite ill, so that they could be brought home.[162]

Not only was it clear that the HJ was winning more victories over parents through the KLV program, but the HJ also found ways to further aggravate the teachers. The regime had fiendishly made use of its scheme of multiple responsibilities by which no agency knew who was ultimately in charge of public administration, and representatives of the Party, symbolizing the Nazi revolution, usually prevailed over the State's civil servants. In the case of KLV, the teachers who were transplanted from the classrooms to the HJ camps were supposedly responsible for a continuation of the pedagogical process and were even told to exercise supervision, whereas in fact the much younger Hitler Youth leaders who controlled the logistics of the camps were the true bosses. Even though the regime saw to it that most of the teachers sent out were trusted members of the National Socialist Teachers' League (NSLB), this arrangement turned into a true humiliation of the educators and a triumph for Baldur von Schirach and his successor, Artur Axmann.[163]

To settle the control issue, altercations between teachers and HJ camp leaders were common; these ended with an academic victory for the former and an actual one for the latter.[164] The HJ leaders enjoyed the added advantage of easy recourse to local Party powers, such as regional Hitler Youth chiefs or, as in the Protectorate, a regent such as the egregious Karl Hermann Frank.[165] To a greater extent than earlier in the Reich, normal school routines were reduced and sacrificed to HJ exercise and drill, often led by thoroughly corrupt young chieftains, with the result that the evacuated pupils were reading even fewer school texts than before.[166] The ultimate affront to the teaching profession occurred after a low point of the war in early 1943, when many more of the younger teachers were conscripted for the trenches, while the remaining older ones came under the command of ever younger Hitler Youths, because the older HJ members were at the fronts.[167]

At the KLV sites, in total disregard of the encumbered teaching personnel, the HJ extended its proven drill regimen from the home bases, again with calculated attention paid to premilitary training. Children were bullied, especially if they were found to be bed wetting—a frequent occurrence in the camps and indicative of the sense of loss they generally must have felt.[168] "Often they were simply beaten up," recounts one-time inmate Ralf Dahrendorf, today a British subject and member of the House of Lords.[169] In some places, ten- or twelve-year-olds who were starting to masturbate had their hands covered with thick gloves and then tied to the bed frames. But in other sites there were masturbation contests, and the entire practice became part of the entrenched hazing regimen.[170] Regular HJ announcements at roll calls about the air-raid death of close relatives, designed to toughen the charges' character, often broke the spirits of the stunned youths.[171] Unsanitary conditions and inferior nutrition frequently caused diseases that could not be cured because of lack of medications and medical staff, although the HJ did not hesitate to use medical students.[172]

The darkest aspect of this entire exercise, in keeping with the racist-imperialistic aims of the Nazis, was that they purposely planted their youth in surroundings known to be hostile to them. This afforded the HJ ample opportunity to point out the difference between HJ children as heirs of the master race on the one side, and those slaves who had already been vanquished, on the other. This was not without danger to the youngsters, who in Occupied Poland and the Protectorate in particular were always regarded with unmitigated hostility in the streets, to the point where it was dangerous for them to be alone or in small groups without the protection of firearms held at the ready by accompanying senior Hitler Youths.[173] Children were being taught to hate in the field, as it were; they would have to use this skill later at the extended fronts, to defend their status as members of the German ruling caste.

Problems of Training, Discipline, and Leadership

To liberate itself completely from the conventional school system, the Hitler Youth attempted to create educational institutions of its own. These were the Adolf-Hitler-Schulen (AHS), which Baldur von Schirach, behind Reich Minister Rust's back, in early 1937 conceived in an alliance with Robert Ley, the leader of the German Labor Front (DAF) and a fellow Party dignitary. Not surprisingly, Rust was furious when he found out. Hitler, however, was on the side of Schirach and the schools that would bear his name.

The first of these schools was opened on April 20, 1937, the Führer's forty-eighth birthday, in Pomeranian Crössinsee, at one of Ley's own training establishments. The projection was for about fifty such schools, at least one for each Nazi Gau or region, with a projected enrollment of 15,000 altogether. By 1941, however, there were only ten schools, and at the end of 1943, a mere 2,027 pupils attended. One reason was lack of money, for the Party's purse was notoriously tight as the war progressed. Upon graduation, after six years of schooling (subsequent to their initial six in a primary school), AHS students were supposed to enter one of Ley's own "order castles" for further Party training. Thereafter, a special Nazi university, the Hohe Schule, under chief Party ideologue Alfred Rosenberg, was to take over as a political-elite finishing school.[174]

As a new type of secondary school, the Adolf-Hitler-Schulen were Nazi Party–specific, and therein lay their early promise for Party leaders like Schirach and Ley. Beginning with the process of recruitment, the schools' entire structure rejected previous educational ideals:

they were anti-traditional, anti-knowledge, anti-Gymnasium, and anti-parent. The schools' charter was supposed to be inspired by a revolutionary dynamic, which would motivate its pupils always to put Nazi dogma first. The selection of AHS pupils was to be made by HJ leaders in conjunction with regional representatives of the Party, a certain contingent of them being assigned annually to each Gau. Although the sons of proven Nazi parents were to be preferred, the parents themselves could not apply for their children's admission and later were forbidden to take their offspring out of an AHS school. Selection criteria focused on Hitler Youth boys at least twelve years old, racially attractive, fit for sports and drill—hence with already outstanding pro-Nazi dispositions and what was called "character," a quality deemed superior to intellect and based on Nazi notions of honor, bravery, and devotion to the Führer. The ultimate career objectives for AHS students, as far as the regime was concerned, were jobs in the Party hierarchy, such as HJ leader or Gau administrator, and, as a second choice, jobs as conventional civil servants.[175]

Because of the lack of synchronization of curricula with ordinary secondary schools, the pattern of continuing education beyond primary school, and the very restricted role of parents during initial selection, the prescribed quotas for these new institutions were never attained. It was not at all surprising, Albert Speer pointed out in his postwar memoirs, that "the top functionaries did not send their children to those schools themselves."[176] When toward the end of the war the Party officials saw the error of their ways, they decided to allow intelligence more weight than "character," and to create, upon graduation, the formal learning prerequisites for entry to the Reich's universities. But it was already far too late; the damage had been done.[177]

The inferior quality of instruction was a result of the collective profile of the teachers handpicked by the HJ leadership. Whereas the older teachers tended to be staunch Party cronies, the younger ones, still in their twenties, were HJ liaison teachers, for whom Nazi politics and ideology ranked above scholarship. Shunning the time-honored school books, they worked with study aids manufactured by the social engineers of the Hitler Youth.[178] A specially dedicated Educators' Academy in Sonthofen was on the drawing board as early as 1938, in order to mold the AHS instructors of the future, but by 1943 these plans still had not been realized.[179] One and all, those teachers were "good comrades," concedes former AHS student Harald Grundmann, "they strove admirably, but they did not know enough."[180]

This lack of teaching qualifications was reflected in the curriculum. Although Schirach himself maintained in 1938 that in his new schools the substance would remain the same and only the teaching methods would change, the reality was different.[181] To a large degree, AHS instruction consisted of an intensification of the physical and mental exercises favored during regular HJ service. Among conventional school subjects, those which emphasized the German past and racial superiority were stressed, as in history, geography, and biology; foreign languages were to be studied for the sole purpose of communicating orders to future subject peoples.[182] Still, on any given school day, only an hour and a half was to be dedicated to such academic pursuits, while five hours were given over to sports.[183] Subsumed under sports were the old drill and physical tests and trials, again with the ultimate goal of warfare. "Love of war and the readiness to embrace a hero's death" was the didactic motto.[184] Since Nazi character was deemed superior to intellect, ideological indoctrination was at the top of the list. AHS students were taken to concentration camps to get to know the internal enemy. A professor of medicine explained to them the "euthanasia" program, the killing of the handicapped and infirm. And there were "combative discussions" revolving around questions of Nazi weltanschauung, politics, and novel Nazi doctrines, such as why the Aryan race was thought to be superior to any others.[185] During his school years he was always challenged physically, Grundmann remembers, but "never intellectually."[186]

The Hitler Youth had hoped that extensive school enrollment would further the Nazis' overall aim of a social revolution which would give opportunity to all classes, an ideal the HJ had held high before 1933 and still paid lip service to. Hitler himself said in 1942 that the

Adolf Hitler Schools should enable "even the poorest boy to rise to any position for which he is potentially suited."[187] Therefore almost no fees were charged to the students, either for class instruction or for room and board.[188] Nonetheless, even though the children of the lower classes turned out to be somewhat more heavily represented in AHS schools than in traditional ones, their number was insufficient to change the middle-class character of the entire student body in the Reich.[189] Proclaiming social equality had done nothing to heighten the schools' prestige.

Yet another reason for the schools' lack of success as training grounds for a future Party elite lay in the unsuccessful promise of follow-up institutions. Ley's Ordensburgen or "Order Castles"—Crössinsee and one more each in West and South Germany—which AHS graduates were to enter around age eighteen, were conceived neither as traditional universities, which some of these young men would ordinarily have preferred for an academic career, nor as military academies such as those offered by the Wehrmacht. Their didactic concepts were shrouded in racist mysticism, and with only a small number of students and an insufficient staff, they never reached even a rudimentary stage of functionality.[190] Nor was the final plateau in this hierarchy, Rosenberg's Party university Hohe Schule, ever realized—it remained a chimera for the time after the Final Victory.[191]

Yet another Party high school, the partially subsidized NS-Deutsche Oberschule in Feldafing on Lake Starnberg, was not considered as competition for the AHS by HJ leaders. This school, housed in no less than forty villas, was more for sybarites than ascetics (often the offspring of self-important Party leaders); students played golf there or went sailing after a minimum of formal lessons. No one ever received a grade, and no one ever failed a course. The school, for pupils from twelve to eighteen, had been founded as a recruitment instrument by SA chief Ernst Röhm in 1933, and was maintained, after his execution in July 1934, by Deputy Führer Rudolf Hess. It posed hardly any competition to the HJ because it was comparatively small, and its instruction staff was no more qualified than Schirach's or Ley's.[192]

But if this multiplicity of Nazi training institutes was not yet a threat to the HJ's own pedagogical ambitions and its goal of monopolistic control, the threat from the SS-run former military cadet academies was real. For these Nationalpolitische Erziehungsanstalten (NPEA) did everything the Adolf-Hitler-Schulen were attempting to do; only they did it much better and with tangible results. Three NPEA had been established under Schirach's old rival, Minister Rust, in April 1933. By 1940, there were twenty-one.[193] Himmler's SS, in connivance with Rust, assumed control over them in 1936, when SS General August Heissmeyer became their chief inspector. His teaching staff were not only academically schooled in the traditional manner, but also, for the most part, genuine SS members.[194] Generally, more boys from the upper-middle and upper classes—with merely nominal ties to the HJ—attended the NPEA.[195] The complete submersion of their egos through inhuman drill and calculated psychological torture eventually led these graduates, who had flocked in large numbers to the SS by September 1939, to commit killings as "political soldiers" without the slightest qualms.[196] And yet their academic achievements were quite respectable, hardly below the average in the Reich's Gymnasien.[197]

One striking indication that the Hitler Youth's own schools fared badly in their attempt to replace the conventional education system is that problems of discipline arose with the first of these institutions and escalated after the start of World War II. Even beyond the schools, lack of discipline permeated the entire HJ. The Hitler Youths were "a chaotic bunch," writes Heinz W. Kämmer, who joined in 1933 in Thuringian Erfurt.[198] As early as 1933, Hitler told Schirach that Reich President Paul von Hindenburg was cross with him because "the young people did not show the necessary respect to old officers, teachers, and ministers of the church."[199] Later in the Third Reich, HJ miscreants in their early teens were known for committing petty theft, obstructing railroad tracks, and accosting civilians in the streets.[200] As for the older ones, traffic violations such as racing with staff cars became a serious problem, sometimes resulting in the injury of innocent bystanders. HJ leaders were habitually driving their cars with such speed that often "they cannot be brought to a necessary stop," according to an official complaint.[201] Homosexuality and sadism became rampant among HJ members.[202] In one notorious case in the summer of 1938, a mid-level teenage leader inflicted long-lasting torture on his charges by tying their wrists and ankles during an outing and then beating them with his steel-studded belt.[203]

The public, no less than other Party agencies, blamed the older HJ supervisory personnel, who did not appear capable of assuming the responsibilities of leadership that Schirach had envisioned. Indeed, arrogant HJ members went out of their way to seek altercations with representatives of the SA, the police, the Party and, after the spring of 1935, even the Wehrmacht.[204] Thus the problems continued to mount.

Even though soldiering inspired greater discipline among the Hitler Youth rank and file, especially after 1938, these difficulties did not go away. During the war years boys and girls continued to engage in crimes like theft, impersonation, or gross acts of vandalism. As a result, clashes between the police and other agencies of the regime and the HJ multiplied.[205] "Our HJ is being hoodlumized," charged one Swabian Party leader in January 1943, two weeks before the catastrophe of Stalingrad.[206] Nazi character training notwithstanding, homosexuality could not be curbed, and more women were being sexually molested than had been the case in peacetime.[207]

The root causes of this situation were the Hitler Youth's leadership structure and the principles by which it was governed. Schirach had taken an adage from the Weimar youth movement culture, which had prided itself on independence from an older generation, real or imagined: "Youth must be led by youth."[208] Of course, Schirach himself was barely twenty-six when Hitler appointed him Reich Youth Leader in June 1933, and his policy was to have boys (or girls) of any given age lead those who were perhaps only a couple of years younger. This conformed to his anti-intellectual view that shaping a person's character through experience was superior to a formal schooling of the mind.[209] However, in accordance with the National Socialist leadership principle—and often in contrast with Weimar youth movement practice—these leaders and sub-leaders were appointed from

above and never held responsible for their actions toward their subordinates.[210] As alluring as this may have seemed to German teenagers
at the time, it opened the floodgates to incompetence, abuse, and
corruption.[211]

Schirach and, after August 1940, his twenty-seven-year-old successor Artur Axmann tried to establish checks and balances on abuses by
setting up their own leadership courses, seminars, and academies for an
ever-growing number of ever-younger HJ leaders. The first of such
schools opened, even before Schirach's formal appointment, in April
1933 in Weyarn, south of Munich, under the direction of a police lieutenant. Not surprisingly, more attention was paid here to matters of
discipline, as a "soldier's posture" was said to be paramount.[212] Soon
there was a Reich Leadership School in Potsdam as the HJ's principal
training institution, and later several smaller ones all across the Reich,
offering individual weeks of command training as well as ideological
instruction, for example in race science and German history. By January 1935 Schirach boasted that some fifty thousand youth leaders of
both genders and all ranks had been trained.[213] This number grew to
78,000 in 1936, but since at that time there were 496,000 leaders
of one sort or another (part of a total membership of approximately
five million), it meant that only 16 percent of them were actually
trained.[214]

And even by HJ standards, there were doubts concerning the value
of the instruction offered. In a speech of January 1935, Schirach himself had alluded to the difficulty of securing adequate staff.[215] Two
years later, one of his regional commanders criticized the deplorable
quality of HJ training thus far and the subsequent reliance on inferior
trainers. One could not adequately educate one's own trainers, he
grumbled during a Berlin staff meeting, because educators in the HJ
were too badly paid for anyone to choose that occupation.[216] A few
months after that, in Tübingen, senior instructor Oskar Riegraf wrote
that he had recently completed teaching fifty-six courses only as a favor
to Stuttgart's Gauleiter Wilhelm Murr, and that now he was "finished
with the HJ."[217]

Especially during the war, when staff was at a premium, the instructional standard for tens of thousands of presumptive Hitler Youth leaders of both genders appears to have sunk quite low. One young trainee in March 1943, who actually liked physical drill under duress (similar to the way some twenty-first-century youngsters like extreme sports), told of indoctrination sessions that featured themes from *Mein Kampf,* the history of the Nazi movement, and the subsequent rise of the Third Reich since 1933. In the afternoons, he wrote, they discussed Göring, Himmler, and Goebbels.[218] One of his more mature comrades, an Austrian, was sent to the training camp in Thuringian Eichsfeld, after he had already fought at the front. "I was supposed to be reacquainted with Nazi weltanschauung and brought up to date. But to my surprise I did not quite get it. I soon noticed what the difference was: the candor of the soldier was missing." This combat-experienced warrior deplored the bureaucratization of home-based HJ functionaries who had forgotten how to be leaders. "They had settled into many spots and made themselves indispensable . . . They allowed no one to speak who had something else, something better to say." Moreover, "They felt they had a monopoly on heroism."[219]

Early on, the HJ heads had thought that help was on its way in the form of a so-called Academy of Youth Leadership in Brunswick. Schirach declared in October 1935 that he had reached an agreement regarding real estate with the town of Brunswick. In 1936 it was announced that the institution would be commencing its work by the end of the following year.[220] But it took until April of 1939 for the newly constructed Academy to open, with an allegedly demanding course of studies. Even then, the first semester had to begin at a sports site in Berlin; the move to Brunswick did not take place until August, when the building was finally completed. Requirements for the Academy included graduation from Gymnasium, strict pre-selection, four months of apprenticeship in a HJ region, and eight weeks at the leadership school in Potsdam, to be followed by twelve months of residency at the Academy. Thereafter candidates had to work for three weeks in some war-related industry and undergo six months of training abroad.

Successful graduates were to be officially designated as "Youth Leaders of the German Reich," but had to sign on for full-time service for at least twelve years with the Hitler Youth. In those positions, they would enjoy the status of one of Schirach's virtual generals.[221]

As it turned out, the Academy could not live up to its promises. Even though its quarters were sumptuous, it was quickly hampered by the war's manpower needs and its makeshift courses lasted barely five months instead of the required twelve. The Academy's "thorough training" was deceptive at best, for it could not even come close to the level of what today would be called a community college.[222] The "famous scholars and university teachers" whom Axmann invented for his 1995 memoirs in reality were third-rate guest lecturers—Nazified faculty from outlying universities. The students attending that first summer semester stayed only a few weeks, after which they rode off to the front lines. Those who arrived after September 1939 were mostly mid-level youth leaders who had been wounded in the war and had combat experience under their belts. There was little the Academy could now teach them.[223]

How ill-suited the academy was for the the average HJ member is illustrated by two postwar reports. One veteran wrote that life in Brunswick was the equivalent of "a comfortable vacation"—cynically noted by those who had already fought at the fronts. Drill consisted of relaxed marches through the picturesque town of Brunswick. Nothing from the lectures by the visiting university teachers made any impression at all: "nothing really stuck, the metaphysically argued ideology remained incomprehensible to us." And when Schirach himself deigned to address these students, "one after the other fell asleep."[224] Another former student spoke of the visit of a high HJ leader who had received the Knight's Cross in the war—in other words, a nationally admired paragon for all future leaders. But he chose to display only arrogance during his inspection. The student, an apprentice with the Stollwerk chocolate company in Cologne, "intellectually could not follow the arcane training program" at Brunswick although, in 1942, he was already among the highest ranks of the HJ. In his memoirs of 1994 he admitted to dozing off during what were advertised as intellectually challenging lectures.[225] Summing up his overall impression up to 1945, this onetime regional HJ chief wrote that as "the leaders became younger, their training became shorter."[226]

Chronically inadequate leadership recruitment and training inevitably contributed to systemic faults in the HJ leadership structure, as a result of the lack of capable chiefs. Whether in the Palatinate, Brunswick, or Bavaria, the HJ had to accept as leaders just about anybody who showed interest, with predictably distastrous results.[227] This was true especially in the countryside, where boys and girls tended to pass up the HJ for work on the farms, during weekends and after school.[228] Meanwhile, Schirach tried to mollify his critics by claiming that youth leaders were not born "ready-made" and that, after all, leaders still had to be found for this, "the largest youth movement in the world."[229]

The beginning of World War II exacerbated these difficulties because now the older set of leaders, aged seventeen and up, were incrementally conscripted. On October 1, 1939, of the very top full-time chiefs in Schirach's administration, 273 had been called to fight, out of a total of 424; by January 1, 1940, 25 percent of all leaders were at the fronts. Not yet two years later, this rate had swelled to 60 percent.[230] The war intensified what had already been a problem in peacetime: as older leaders vanished, they had to be replaced by ever younger ones who lacked expertise for any HJ governance.[231] By 1944, boys in their mid-teens were commanding comrades of equal age, and during the last two years of the war, many youths could not believe that suddenly they had been promoted to what in the Wehrmacht was the equivalent of Major or higher.[232] Lina Heydrich, the widow of the SD chief, was beside herself when in July 1944 she had to inform Himmler that because sixteen-year-olds were guiding the HJ, her little son Heider was being unduly neglected. Himmler granted her wish that henceforth Heider be relieved from all HJ duty.[233]

Constant personnel changes in individual locales made the teenagers nervous, as well as their parents, teachers and, not least, the Party brass.[234] In some places, HJ posts disappeared altogether because there was no staff.[235] The Party Chancellery, under Martin Bormann, intervened as early as March 1940 in an effort to shift local youth chief authority to its own representatives, but since this amounted to an ill-disguised attempt by Bormann to make the HJ subservient to him, Schirach did not even deign to respond. In November 1942 the Reich Interior Ministry once again insisted on this change, also with no result. Right up to early 1945, the Party tried to exert an influence on the personnel department of the HJ leadership, from regional leaders to the highest levels. But until the end, Schirach and Axmann remained impervious to external intervention and retained sole control.[236]

To insiders, as well as many on the outside, the HJ appeared corrupt and diseased to the core. As early as 1934, lower-down leaders were embezzling money through bullying and double book-keeping.[237] Local HJ officials often appeared vain and arrogant.[238] "You probably know," wrote the high-placed Riegraf to a former comrade in November 1938 from Nürtingen, "what kind of an outfit the HJ currently is. Things are going on which no decent person can possibly tolerate any longer."[239] Others observed "HJ leaders who were smoking, lewd BDM maidens, and drunken youth chiefs," and, inevitably, Hitler Youth personnel of both genders having sex in their offices.[240] By 1943 Axmann was socializing with Goebbels, who was well known for his habit of procuring film starlets for intimate parties at his various Berlin hideaways. Axmann helped Goebbels chauffeur these young women and himself held some parties on the side, to which he invited those starlets and pretty BDM maidens.[241] Instead of causing the reins to be tightened, Schirach, too, appeared to be acting irresponsibly. In early 1945, for instance, as Gauleiter charged with the defense of Vienna against the Red Army, he donned a red-and-gray "sort of general's uniform" in the mode of Göring and invited his lieutenants, a group of higher HJ leaders, for a dinner of chicken with rice and polite conversation. They had been expecting stern direction in their fight against the Russians. Earlier, after putting in some weeks of nominal service at the western front in 1940, Schirach appeared with a huge bandage around his head which, he pretended, stemmed from action at the front. In reality, he had only had a car accident.[242]

Hess and Bormann had tried to interfere with Schirach's erratic recruitment and training policies because, understandably, they had an interest in a regular, orderly replenishment of Nazi Party personnel. As early as the spring of 1934, Schirach had agreed to the wishes of Party executives that more senior HJ leaders should serve as adjutants to local and regional Party bosses, down to the level of Ortsgruppenleiter, or local chapter leader.[243] How popular this arrangement was with the HJ rank and file is shown by the fact that it was never put into place. Nonetheless, Hess and Bormann persisted with their demands, so that subsequent ordinances were drawn up. But especially after the beginning of the war, when the Party and its affiliates needed fresh leaders because military conscription had taken the older ones away, the HJ leadership countered that they too lacked leaders for the very same reason and thus they could not comply with the Party's request.[244] In any event, Hitler and Goebbels continued to depend on the reserves they believed the HJ could furnish. Goebbels remarked in August 1941 that recruits in his propaganda sector were "very thinly planted" and that he was looking forward to an agreement with the HJ administration for a deployment of "a large contingent of seasoned HJ leaders."[245] This was half a year before he had occasion to bemoan the fact that "the first generation" of old Nazi Party fighters was beginning to die out.[246] In May 1942 Hitler complained to his inner circle that for leadership functions, he had to remain dependent "on the same old people."[247] A year later, after tens of thousands of German men in their prime had died on the battleground in Stalingrad and large numbers of youth leaders were on the verge of taking their places on the eastern front, Bormann quoted Hitler as saying that the Nazi Party could "rejuvenate itself only from the ranks of youth and the ranks of soldiers."[248]

As before, the youths themselves regarded the Party's plans far more skeptically. In the period from 1941 to 1944, the number of HJ volunteers for Party office was minimal, so that by the fall of 1943 the Party had to concede that its echelons had been staffed by HJ leaders only "to a certain degree."[249] And in early 1945, when the war was all but over, a revealing conversation took place between Melita Maschmann, a high BDM leader, and her colleagues. One of them had said that now they had proof that Party Chancellery chief Bormann was leading Germany into the abyss, by systematically misinforming Hitler. Wishing to pursue the point, Maschmann asked her comrade why he and his companions did not cause Bormann to disappear. "For what other reason are you lugging around your large handguns? I only know one answer to this question: you are too cowardly to sacrifice yourselves for such an act, as important as you think it might be." Maschmann was assured that after the Final Victory, youth together with the front soldiers would ally themselves with Hitler in order to send the old Party bosses to the devil.[250]

Such sentiment was indicative not only of the naïveté of many in the upper youth echelons, but also of the common belief of most Germans during the entire reign of the Third Reich that however much the Nazi bureaucracy was wanting, Hitler himself could do no wrong.[251] Some Hitler Youths were even willing to exempt from their criticism that branch of the Nazi movement known to be closest to the Führer, namely the SS. To the extent that the Hitler Youths regarded themselves as the young elite of the movement, they knew that by current standards the SS represented its mature elite. The SS, too, knew of this real or imagined affinity, and early on attempted to exploit it.

This became apparent on June 27, 1934, when Hitler made his wish known to reinforce his SS elite unit "Leibstandarte Adolf Hitler" with seventeen-year-old Hitler Youths, who had to be at least five feet ten inches tall (the SS norm then was five feet seven inches). The date is significant, for at that time Hitler knew he would quell what he said was a budding revolt within the disobedient SA under Röhm. Hitler also knew that in 1931–32 Schirach had resented being formally under Röhm's command, with the HJ an affiliate of the SA. When the purge actually occurred on June 30, it was the Leibstandarte that was the executioner.[252] Hitler Youths may indeed have been proud to be recruited by such a unit (albeit too late to participate in the purge), but in

December of that year Schirach's headquarters had to caution the SS to stop wooing and admitting to its ranks mere youths of seventeen. He feared they would be lost prematurely to the HJ's own designs.[253]

Himmler pushed the issue of HJ recruitment further when in May of 1936 he addressed Schirach's youths on the Brocken mountain in the Harz range, not far from Brunswick where the SS had just opened its leadership school. In his speech, he explained the essence and the task of the typical SS leader and then invited the HJ up to Brunswick—the town where Schirach was planning, at that very time, to erect a leadership academy of his own.[254] Exchanges of this kind between the SS and the HJ were intensified through 1937 until August 1938, when increased conscription into the Wehrmacht posed a real threat to SS recruitment and Himmler started using the HJ-Streifendienst (SRD) as a convenient feeder mechanism for his units. From its founding in July 1934, the Streifendienst was to consist of male Hitler Youths between sixteen and eighteen, who in close cooperation with the Gestapo and other SS branches were charged with the policing of, first, wayward members of the entire uniformed HJ and, second (and especially important for the war), any suspicious members of the Reich's youth as a whole. For the SS, the deployment of the Streifendienst, which would have comprised the most enthusiastic Hitler Youths, possessed two major advantages: it conditioned already convinced young Nazis as potential policemen and hence readied them for serious enforcement duties inside and beyond the Reich later, such as subjugating conquered peoples and killing civilians; it also attracted an elite-conscious youth group eager to step far over conventional boundaries at the very site of their HJ commands. Because of close personal and organizational liaisons, transfer protocols were set up, bringing into line, for putative converts, the HJ ranks with SS ranks.[255]

By the end of 1938 Himmler was, in addition to the SRD, recruiting from the agricultural service of the HJ (Landdienst), whose imperialist ideology was akin to that of the 1920s *Artamanen,* in whose ranks Himmler himself had served. At this point—the Sudetenland was being occupied—Himmler and Schirach jointly made mention not only of the general black-shirted SS, but also the SS-Verfügungstruppen (which after the beginning of the war were to turn into the Waffen-SS), and the SS Death Head's Squads that already guarded concentration camps.[256]

Two years later Himmler showed himself pleased with the performance of the Streifendienst as a youthful vanguard of the SS; there were 50,000 members, and he was aiming for 80,000.[257] Regional reports asserted that HJ candidates who had applied had to be turned away for lack of qualifications. Individual testimonials from HJ boys who made it into the SRD mention the advantages of superior boxing and jujitsu instruction, to say nothing of pride in "the duties of the police." They suggest that for the HJ boys, these adventurous sojourns were vastly attractive—exercises which they knew could lead to politically more important tasks.[258] But if indeed SRD service was as popular with the boys as the sources suggest, this could not have been so without prior training in Nazi racist ideology.

Such training meant acquaintance, from an early age, with the dogma of German racial superiority and, conversely, the inferiority of other peoples, especially Slavs, Sinti and Roma (colloquially known as Gypsies), and Jews. That such indoctrination went on more or less systematically in HJ ranks from age ten and up has characteristically been denied by post-1945 apologists of the Nazi youth culture.[259] Of particular significance in this connection is the assertion that there was no HJ participation in the signally anti-Jewish pogrom of Kristallnacht in November 1938.[260] The truth is that participation did occur, even though HJ boys and girls were not generally dispatched to these actions in any organized fashion. While a few took an active part, the great majority became involved by way of being forced to watch and digest the experience and learn the required racial lessons from it. However, in Alzey in Rhenish Hesse the SA, who had been commissioned for these schemes by the regional Party leaders, co-opted the local HJ group and led them to the apartment of a Jewish family, where, with the frightened victims looking on, the boys proceeded to demolish all the furniture with an ax.[261] In Munich the HJ drove around in ostentatious staff cars to the residences of Jews who were known to be rich, taking money from some and intimidating others into deserting their villas.[262]

More important to the HJ leadership was exposing its charges directly to the mêlées of Kristallnacht, which were to serve as an example of how to treat the Jews—a first or second step in an ever-escalating sequence leading up to the Holocaust. Many boys and girls, already ideologically formed, found the spectacles as fascinating as they found them justified.[263] Some Hitler Youths struggled with it all, attempting an argument or seeking an explanation from their leaders, particularly after soul-searching discussions with parents.[264] Others were disturbed, choosing nevertheless to close their eyes and then to accept what they thought to be unavoidable after all.[265]

For the HJ command, the Jews appeared at the center of a carefully constructed profile of aliens that was to be conveyed to the foot soldiers through daily propaganda and well-scheduled training sessions. These were intended to dispel doubts that teenagers might still harbor, especially in the early years of the regime, about how to identify a Jew, or why Jews were different, or why indeed they were considered evil.[266] After all, significant questions revolved around the physical appearance of a role model like Goebbels: he was dark-haired, "very small and narrow," and walked with a limp because of a clubfoot. Did this correspond with the antipodal Aryan stereotype conjured up during ideological schooling?[267]

This schooling had both a theoretical and a practical side. The theory of the Jew as subhuman was taught by older HJ leaders during routine camp and chapter meetings, with the help of special training materials (*Schulungshefte*) or Julius Streicher's semi-pornographic rag *Der Stürmer*. The latter depicted ugly Jews with curly hair and fleshy noses in the shape of a 6, always on the lookout for blond German maidens to seduce.[268] At one of those gatherings during the war, a local Berlin HJ chief, Stammführer Karl-Heinz Wirzberger, warned that "world Jewry had decided to fight the Germanic race."[269] Boys and girls were assembled to listen to special addresses such as the one by Reich Economics Minister Walther Funk in May 1938, who explained to them why German Jews had to be expropriated. After taking from them their businesses and their wealth, Funk declared, one could grant them a kind of inferior leaseholder status, "so long as we do not have the capability to move them completely out of Germany."[270] HJ teenagers sang anti-Semitic songs with texts that sanctioned "Jewish blood dripping from the knife," and in 1943 they were dispatched en masse to watch Veit Harlan's film *Jud Süss* (Jew Sweet), by all accounts the most anti-Semitic feature film ever made in Nazi Germany.[271] One HJ boy who during the war was living in Nazi-occupied Lódz (then called Litzmannstadt) was taken for a car ride by a German policeman who told him, when passing the large Jewish getto, that "we should fire into this vermin on a daily basis." Thinking back to this incident in 1998, the writer remembers he agreed because it was the right thing to do.[272]

Hitler Youths were told to seek out practical experience in dealing with Jews. In Vienna during the Anschluss, uniformed boys were commandeered to supervise the chicanery inflicted upon bearded orthodox Jews in their characteristic caftans, as they were shoved into synagogues or ordered to clean the pavement with toothbrushes or, in some cases, their bare hands.[273] (Later it would be Schirach who, as Gauleiter of Vienna, would stand out from among his colleagues by impressing upon Hitler the necessity of cleansing the city of its Jews—60,000 of them that might easily be sent to, say, Occupied Poland.)[274] In 1941 a contingent of Hitler Youth was taken to Theresienstadt concentration camp in the Protectorate, to view the Jewish enemy first-hand. They were confronted with one of them who, they were told, had to stand upright for twenty-four hours on end. "And if he faints?" asked an incredulous visitor. "Then he gets a bucket of water over his pelt," replied the swaggering HJ leader, with a laugh. "And then you will see how quickly he will get on his feet!" And he continued: "Of course these are no ordinary criminals, they are depraved creatures, detritus, you understand?" An SS guard hastened to add: "The Jews are our most repulsive cases. One has to approach them like a disease, like an epidemic."[275]

Victor Klemperer, a Jewish retired professor of French literature with a gentile wife who was precariously tolerated in a so-called privileged marriage, has recounted the regimen of indignities that Dresden Hitler Youths subjected him and his coreligionists to during the height of the war when ever younger HJ chiefs were called up for special home front duty. During a roundup of Jews for transport to concentration camps, Hitler Youths would officiate. Others were told, on marches, to turn their heads and "eye the Jew, so you will know what the Jews are all about." In 1944 Hitler Youths appeared, in lieu of Gestapo or SS, to organize "privileged Jews" such as Klemperer for Sunday cleanup in enemy-bombed houses.[276]

Undoubtedly, some of the anti-Semitic currents the youths were exposed to originated in their homes and schools, to the extent that Jew-hating parents and teachers were vocal there. It is clear that the hatred of Jews was an integral and critical factor in the rise and coming to power of Nazism and that such sentiment pervaded people's homes after January 1933. Inevitably, those in the younger generation were steeped in this attitude and were socialized as little anti-Semites—who were not so little any more when they were called to fight in the war at age seventeen or less in 1944.[277]

The situation in the schools was similar, if one considers that it did not necessarily take a teacher of finely distilled Nazi convictions to spout anti-Semitic slogans. There were far too many German nationalists on the staff of schools, some of them front soldiers from World War I and ex-*Freikorps,* for whom the hatred of Jews, who allegedly had sold Germany down the river in 1918, was an article of faith.[278] Add to this the fact that some of the younger teachers were coming to the Hitler Youth as liaison personnel, that some read *Der Stürmer* on a regular basis and drew caricatures of Jewish noses on the blackboard, rejoiced in telling anti-Semitic jokes, and enthusiastically used anti-Jewish teaching aids in their profession, and one has a lethal combination.[279] Even a mathematics instruction book read as follows: "In Germany the people of foreign race are the Jews. In 1933 the German Reich had 66,060,000 inhabitants. Of those, 499,682 were practicing Jews. How much is that in percent?"[280]

The children of many of these practicing Jews still went to school with their gentile fellows during the period 1933–1936, until, one by one, they were forced out. The Nuremberg race laws of September 15, 1935, legally defined Jews as persons having at least three Jewish grandparents; thereafter *Mischlinge* of the first degree (those with two Jewish grandparents) and of the second degree (those with one) were still allowed in German schools, but always at their own risk. This risk was evident when they became victims of vicious teachers or their applauding Aryan flocks. The situation was worse, of course, for the full Jews, as long as they were in the classrooms. Not everybody was as fortunate as the historian Peter Gay, born in 1923, whose name in Berlin was Peter Fröhlich when he attended the Goethe-Gymnasium in the early years of the regime. "Our teachers were on the whole free of bigotry and did not set out to make their Jewish pupils' lives harder than those of our gentile classmates," he writes.[281] Most tell a different story. The class in another Berlin school shortly before the war was told by its teacher that "all Jews are bad," and, as he pointed to the dark, curly-haired Esau, who had done nothing wrong, "even Esau and the other two Jewish students in this class."[282] Ineluctably, school children were overwhelmed by the pervasive anti-Semitism in their classrooms, where it would take merely one of several potentially anti-Semitic teachers to push the whole class toward hatred against Jews. As one former student remembers a Jewish classmate: "I did not want to have anything to do with him. Of course I ignored him, but then I did not hurt him either. Somehow he had fleas, I did not like him. Not because he was personally unpleasant, I did not relate to him in any way, it's just that he was a Jew, and therefore I could not stand him."[283]

It is not surprising that such sophistry, in this case driving perhaps one of the duller German pupils, could also propel the marginalization of mere *Mischlinge,* be they of the first or second degree, for only the Nazi law books were at pains to make such specious distinctions. There are many examples of how these partly Jewish pupils were degraded by fellow students and teachers alike. One "Aryan"-looking girl, whose gentile father enjoyed that rarefied German status of having fought in the front lines of the Great War but who had a Jewish mother, was ostracized by the entire class as soon as her pedigree became known. Former friends would touch her and then cry: "Ouch, I have come into contact with Steinbrecher, and now I smell of garlic."[284] She was then taken to a Jewish school where pupils had to sit at some distance from the windows lest they be hurt by rocks hurled by German passersby. The Tübingen neurologist Jürgen Peiffer, born in 1922, recalls that in Stuttgart in the early 1940s the two *Mischlinge* in his class had to wear white shirts during school ceremonies, when everybody else wore their uniforms. And of course after October 1941 they had to wear the Yellow Star. A "half-Jew" named Hanns-Peter Herz reports: "We had a tough, hard-core Nazi as a physical education and swimming teacher. The first day we had to put on our bathing trunks and stand alongside the pool. When we were all lined up, he said: 'Herz, step forward. And you stay there. We won't go into the pool with a half-Jew.' From then on I spent swimming class, two hours every week, standing at the edge of the pool in my trunks. I didn't learn to swim until 1963."[285]

One former Nazi remembers that while in the Hitler Youth he had always heard that the Jews were Germany's destroyers and that the Führer had described them as a race that was parasitical and reponsible for Germany's defeat in 1918.[286] In this statement the first archetypal cliché about Germany and the Jews was matched exactly by the second regarding Hitler's infallibility as the ultimate bearer of truth. From 1933 to 1945, belief in the Führer was the bedrock of any Nazi education as carried out by diehard Nazi parents, teachers, and HJ leaders alike. It was the anchor of Nazi conviction, and it sank into even the most doubting of these young acolytes.

Führer worship was at the center of all HJ and school activities, and in the average German dwelling there hung at least one portrait of Hitler.[287] The schools made Hitler's personal and political biography part of history or German lessons; the *Schulungshefte* of the HJ did the same. The two holiest of Nazi holidays, Hitler's birthday on April 20 and November 9—the approximate time of Germany's World War I defeat, of Hitler's Munich Beer Hall Putsch of 1923, and, not coincidentally, of Kristallnacht in 1938—were punctiliously observed; the April date was the time of official Hitler Youth initiation. (For the SS, including its promotions, both dates were used.)[288] Young people of both genders were ecstatic whenever they had the opportunity to see and hear Hitler in person, as happened more often during the beginning of his regime. And if they were not so fortunate, they collected small Hitler pictures made by cigarette manufacturers like Reemtsma for trading and putting in albums on the model of American sports heroes.[289]

The most satisfying way for the youths to experience the Führer vicariously was during broadcasts of his many speeches or, even better, to be able to witness his speech and gestures during mass meetings such as those held at the Olympic Games in the summer of 1936.[290] One of the most effective of these, because it happened early and was brilliantly orchestrated by Speer and Leni Riefenstahl, was during the Nuremberg Reich Party rally in September 1934. In her classic masterpiece *Triumph of the Will,* Riefenstahl recorded this event both graphically and sympathetically: on September 8, 60,000 Hitler Youths marched into the stadium to salute the Führer. The cries of "Heil" resounded for seemingly endless minutes. Fanfares rang out. A Hitler Youth band played "We Boys." Then Schirach spoke, introducing the Führer. "Twelve months ago," Hitler shouted, "the struggle for power granted us success. And since then our movement, whose young vanguard you are and whose standard bearers you will be, has repossessed one position after the other in this state and thus returned to the German people . . . We know, nothing in the life of the world's peoples is for free. Everything has to be fought for and conquered . . . You have to learn to be tough, to accept sacrifices without ever succumbing . . . Within yourselves, Germany will live on, and when we are long gone, you will be clutching the flag in your fists which once we pulled up from nowhere!" As he finished, a storm of applause filled the stadium, and then the 60,000 boys belted out their signature song, "Our Flag Is Showing Us the Way."[291] "It was the most fascinating thing I could imagine," remembers Bertram Otto, who was ten years old at the time and saw Riefenstahl's film repeatedly at the theater. "He was illuminated and revered: the Führer, *my* Führer."[292]

All of this demagoguery was well engineered, and for a higher purpose. The Third Reich needed its young generation to continue what it now was molding as tradition, to ensure a fresh reservoir of leaders for the most ambitious—and of obedient followers for the more complacent. Above all, it needed young Germans to fight, sooner rather than later, against foes who had long been excoriated by propaganda. Continued allegiance to Hitler, of the kind Schirach had shown since 1925, was key in this effort. The Reich Youth Leader expressed it succinctly when he said, in 1939: "We are marching to the Führer—and if he wants us to, we shall also march for him!"[293]

German Girls for Matrimony and Motherhood

In the 1920s and early 1930s, Irma Grese was growing up in the village of Wrechen in Mecklenburg, not far from Berlin. She was in her early teens when she joined the Hitler Youth as the daughter of a farm laborer. The blond girl, who had lost her mother early, was beautiful if not delicate. She was "a frightened young girl," as she later admitted, predestined to be bullied by her classmates. She wanted to excel, but her schoolwork left something to be desired. However, service in Hitler's youth squads, of which her father disapproved, pleased her. Soon she was a fanatical member of the HJ organization for females, the BDM. First a nursing assistant, then a dairy helper, Irma was merely eighteen in 1942, when she was somehow persuaded to enter the SS Female Helpers' training base at the nearby women's concentration camp of Ravensbrück. In that camp, these helpers, or SS-Helferinnen, were subjected to tough routines. Nazi-style discipline was to be learned by watching and practicing cruelty on inmates and engaging in promiscuous sex with male SS guards. Such discipline was designed to rob the girls of any vestiges of conventional morality.

Her SS training completed, Irma was transferred to Auschwitz in March of 1943. Here she became notorious as the Beautiful Beast. "She was one of the most beautiful women I have ever seen," recalls former inmate Gisella Perl. "Her body was perfect in every line, her face clear and angelic and her blue eyes the gayest, the most innocent eyes one can imagine." Conscious of her stunning looks to the point where she became obsessed with the idea of becoming a film star after the war, Grese, in a tight-fitting uniform, her golden hair carefully coiffured, and always carrying a whip, was feared because of her sadism toward women inmates. A prosecutor later accused her of beating "women until they fell to the ground" and then kicking them "as hard as you could with your heavy boots." Grese acquired the reputation of a nymphomaniac who would coerce male or female prisoners into sex as well as taking Nazi lovers, among them camp physician Josef Mengele and commandant Josef Kramer. In Auschwitz, she was the youngest female guard and also the most cruel, in charge of 30,000 women inmates. Because of a liaison with an SS guard who was transferred to Bergen-Belsen camp in the spring of 1945, around the time that Anne Frank was succumbing to typhus there, Grese moved to that camp as well. Here British soldiers encountered her when they liberated the gruesome site. Along with other SS-Helferinnen, Grese became a defendant in the Bergen-Belsen Trial conducted by the British Military Government in Lüneburg. Her case was highly publicized in the German press, and Hitler's former subjects could not believe that such a lovely young woman would be capable of evil. Grese was convicted of war crimes and hanged at Hamelin prison on December 13, 1945. Together with two other condemned SS women, she had stayed up the night before, laughing and singing non-stop the well-known Nazi hymns. Her face showed no remorse when she told the hangman: "Quick, get it over," as he was placing the noose around her neck. At the hour of her death, Irma Grese was twenty-two years old.[1]

Grese's career was hardly typical of those pursued by other girls who had also been trained in the BDM. Yet her story raises the important question not only of what girls did after graduation from the Hitler Youth, but also how active they were in the shaping of the Nazi Reich. To date, there have been two main theories regarding the latter point. One holds that women were just as responsible as men for the rise of Hitler before 1933 and for what happened in the Third Reich thereafter. Even though women could not fight at the fronts and usually did not murder Jews, they supported their men in these actions, either directly, by sharing their Nazi beliefs and giving the men active moral support, or indirectly, by remaining silent yet giving tacit approval to anything political or military their men might be up to.[2] The second view is that by Nazi ideological definition, women were a subordinate group ruled by the exponents of male supremacy, and they were forced by biology and circumstances into roles they did not want to play and even into the status of victims, which was especially obvious as the war neared its terrible finish.[3]

It would seem that young girls in Nazi Germany between the ages of ten and eighteen who were forced by parents, teachers, or peer pressure to join the BDM were more passive participants than malefactors. Just as in the case of boys, however, as young girls became older they were charged with more responsibility, got used to it, and liked it, so that with increasing age they also became more culpable. This is true despite the fact that girls and women in Nazi society never attained positions of supreme responsibility, for even the Reich Women's Leader, Gertrud Scholtz-Klink, had as her superior a man.[4] Girls did not possess the same degree of herd instinct that characterized the males, which motivated them to join groups, gang up on others, and eventually made them complicit in crimes such as assault and murder. Girls had constituted only one-third of the total membership in the Weimar youth movement,[5] which suggests a greater tendency to maintain their individuality rather than submerging it in a mass group. Many young women, as former members of nationalist Weimar youth groups such as the *Jungnationaler Bund,* were too old to join the BDM after 1933, but neither did they join the Nazi Women's League of Scholtz-Klink. Their only political commitment might have consisted of hanging a Hitler portrait in their living rooms and having husbands who eventually joined the Nazi Party.[6]

Girls could attain their share of power, and could exhibit a measure of cruelty. However, it was never quite as extensive as that exhibited by the boys or young men.[7] Two factors should be kept in mind when considering the fate of girls and young women in Hitler's youth organizations. First, girls were integrated into the larger Nazi youth movement in a manner similar to the way boys were treated, with little planning from above to account for gender difference. Nominally, Hitler boys and Hitler girls were coequals, in terms of the leadership structure, the basic psychological and ideological schooling, and many of the daily tasks to be performed. It never occurred to the Nazi authorities that perceived mental and physical attributes of females, based on their lower rank in the Nazi hierarchy of the human species, made a political mass organization unsuitable for them. Consequently, Hitler boys and Hitler girls, pressed into one organizational mold, often behaved dysfunctionally. Second, as the entire purpose of the Hitler Youth changed after September 1939, girls not used to martial regimens were much more severely shaken than the boys. The conversion from folk dancing and hikes to outright political tasks and military postures was more radical and traumatic for girls, as more of them suddenly were needed for the war effort. Consequently, in the phase of actual warfare, especially toward the end, however much boys were exploited as children required to be soldiers, young girls suffered even more in an environment that was, by definition, anathema to the German notion of girlhood and female virtue to which they had been conditioned.

The Bund Deutscher Mädel in Peacetime

The Bund Deutscher Mädel (BDM) or League of German Girls originated in the late years of the Weimar Republic, as a part of Nazi organizations for women. The development of these organizations occurred within a specific value system consistent with Nazi ideology and practice. In a patriarchal movement based on the biological-eugenic tenets of Adolf Hitler, women had three important interrelated functions: to serve as helpmates to the men, to bear them children and rear them according to Nazi values, and to be faithful homemakers.

These functions were reflected in the earliest Nazi pronouncements, which were aimed at a conservative group of followers who championed what they regarded as a naturally determined sexual division of labor.[8] In Hitler's mind, the biologically defined *völkisch* state was ruled by laws of male supremacy and was in need of women "who could again give birth to men." Educating women would be tantamount to grooming future mothers.[9] Hitler's Gauleiter for Bayreuth, Hans Schemm, enlarged on this theme when he declared that to be a mother of Germans meant being a devoted woman, a conjugal mate to a German man.[10]

Such emphasis on women's secondary role vis-à-vis that of men translated into relative passivity for women and a constant state of subordination. Early Nazi women themselves posited the superiority of men, especially as embodied in Hitler. Women tended to shy away from the male-dominated Nazi Party; only about 5 percent of females had joined by early 1933.[11] When in the Nazi movement's Time of Struggle Nazi women began to organize themselves locally in order to serve the menfolk better, they did so on their own accord without any substantial help or sanction by the Nazi men, and in a haphazard fashion. A national Nazi Womens' League (NS-Frauenschaft or NSF) did not come into being until 1931 and was regarded with suspicion by husbands as well as fathers, brothers, and boyfriends.[12] As much as women might busy themselves in the service of Hitler's movement, the popular consensus was that politics was a man's game and they had better stay out of it. Thus conditioned, they acquiesced when Deputy Führer Rudolf Hess told comrades at the Nuremberg Party rally of 1938: "Talk to your wives only about such matters which are expressly designated for public discussion."[13]

In the late years of the Weimar Republic, Nazi women supported the members of a political party that was often small, dispersed, and illegal. At that time the Nazi Party, being on the right-radical fringe, was held in contempt by a plurality of Germans, especially the truly dedicated citizens of the Weimar Republic. In such adversity, women's service to their men's cause often assumed victim if not martyr status.

Not the least of such female ministrations consisted in presenting themselves at public meetings, to achieve a respectable Nazi body count and to cheer on male speakers through their sheer physical presence. In March 1925, many women attended a Nazi convention in Nuremberg, at which Hitler and the city's Gauleiter, Julius Streicher, spoke. The Party had barely been reborn with Hitler's release from Landsberg prison. Streicher later praised the fact that "so many women" were in the movement.[14] In August of 1927, Streicher's Nuremberg was host to the third annual Nazi Party rally, which drew up to 20,000 visitors from all over the country. A local police report commented that "among the participants many were youthful and female persons. Several women and girls were wearing Hitler dress and even joined the SA march through the town, although they were prevented from parading before Hitler."[15] Among these women at Nazi meetings, the younger ones often were fanatical, and even more so the closer they found themselves to the Führer. As Baldur von Schirach's father-in-law Heinrich Hoffmann, Hitler's personal photographer, recounted, young girls frequently interrupted the leader enthusiastically with "frantic applause." The wealthy and sophisticated Ernst ("Putzi") Hanfstaengl, a Hitler acolyte and Harvard-educated art publisher in Munich, whose sister Erna had hidden Hitler in her villa after the 1923 putsch, wrote after a Nazi rally: "Only a few yards away there was a young woman, her eyes fastened on the speaker. Transfigured as though in some devotional ecstasy, she had ceased to be herself, and was completely under the spell of Hitler's despotic faith in Germany's future greatness."[16] Susceptible to the leader's charisma, some young girls found an idol to be adored.

Apart from flocking to meetings for the sake of full attendance and a sense of communal belonging, women performed the kind of household and nurturing work for their men that was expected in a Nazi home. The early Nazi movement considered young women's Party obligations as preliminary practice for the properly run Nazi family, once Hitler had come to power. Local organizations of women as caregiver groups to the Nazi Party and its affiliates are documented for the period before the Munich Beer Hall Putsch in November 1923, such as the one in Saxony which included Henriette Mutschmann, mother of the future Saxon Gauleiter Martin Mutschmann.[17] When Hitler was in prison in 1924, many women undertook pilgrimages to Landsberg to visit and console him, and some sent care packages. To one women's group Hitler wrote, in November of that year, that the package had arrived undamaged "and provided much joy to all of us, on the anniversary of the uprising."[18] (Hitler continued to collect bric-a-brac from admiring women during the republican period, which later he exhibited in his *Berghof* above Berchtesgaden, as he could not part with it for emotional reasons.)[19] Times were difficult for a largely lower-middle-class and proletarian Nazi following, even in the so-called Golden Twenties of the Weimar Republic, and women had to help their men, whose jobs were often at risk as they tried to revive the frequently illegal NSDAP. Women darned socks and mended trousers, collected money from door to door, and helped to distribute flyers. In February of 1927, for instance, Joseph Goebbels, then the propaganda chief of the Party, received some money from groups of women to help men recently wounded in street fights. Goebbels wrote back with "many cordial thanks for the sacrifice."[20]

A new phase of Nazi women's work began in 1929, at the beginning of the Great Depression, when conditions for Nazi fighter families worsened while Nazi membership numbers were rising. This was the time when the SA, Hitler's brown-shirted storm troopers, held sway in the proletarian sectors of large towns, where they were battling the Communists.[21] Women's groups organized soup kitchens for the SA and shelters for wounded comrades, often harboring men who were wanted by the republican police.[22] Earlier work such as providing clothes and collecting money continued unabated.[23] Since 1928 Party comrade Frau Thieme in Halle, for example, had been known for her large Open House with a swastika flag on the roof. It served as a generous SA kitchen for those in need, despite having its windows broken every day and being under constant police surveillance.[24]

One factor motivating Nazi women was a virulent hatred of Jews. It was not a hatred derived from abstract anti-Semitic theory, although undoubtedly Nazi ideology fanned fires that had been set long before. Rather, it was a feeling based on the women's everyday experience, in their encounters with the Jewish store owners and professionals on whom they depended for goods and services. Nazi women focused on the well-worn, gender-specific stereotypes of Jewish physicians, especially gynecologists, as documented around Heidelberg in 1927, or Jews as perpetrators of cosmopolitan, "un-German" fashion in 1930 Königsberg, or Jews as the owners of chain stores in 1932 Berlin, where women were accustomed to shop daily.[25] Nazi men augmented these racist dispositions with eugenic arguments to the effect that pure German women, as future mothers of heroic males, must not allow themselves to be defiled through sexual congress with Jews.[26] The caricature of the male Jew as sexual predator, no less than the derogatory economic and religious images, corresponded to the same kind of anti-Semitism on which Nazi women would thrive after Hitler's assumption of power. And it was this racism of the adult females that was passed on to their daughters who eventually made their way into the BDM.

The earliest gatherings of Nazi girls came about as offshoots of local women's associations. They originated haphazardly, locally and regionally, and were different from one another; some, the Party chronicle alleges, began as early as 1923. The affinity with the women's groups was clear. From the beginning, the girls' chores were "to help, where they were needed . . . to stitch flags and brown shirts, cook meals, lend medical first aid and post guard at some political demonstrations and pass along warnings," underlining a similarly servile role vis-à-vis the men.[27] In 1931 the Hitler Youth leadership claimed central control of the disparate girls' groups with a view to merging them with its own fledgling girls' league, in existence since 1930 and now called Bund Deutscher Mädel. In July 1932, Schirach succeeded in neutralizing the cloying interference of the NS-Frauenschaft, the Party's organization for adult women, which thereafter would become a permanent, if ultimately unsuccessful, rival for supervision of young girls.[28] Nazi concern with teenage females was evident in the choice of a "uniform." Initially, drab and frumpy uniforms had little appeal for fashion-conscious teenagers even of the Nazi persuasion. However, in 1932, Hitler himself seems to have had a hand in commissioning professional designers to come up with a costume which would appeal to the girls and which eligible young men would find attractive. This was another signal by Nazi leaders that the female's biological goal in life was to attract the male for future procreation.[29]

The theme of subordination to men's needs and desires characterized the subsequent history of the BDM. The BDM never acquired an independent leader directly responsible to Hitler, as was the case with Schirach as leader of the boys. Instead, after an interregnum lasting until June 1934 when no particular woman was consistently in charge, a so-called BDM-Reichsreferentin (Reich Deputy) was appointed, reporting directly to Schirach. She was Trude Mohr, formerly of the German youth movement, who had lately been head of the BDM's division in the East. Thirty-two years old, from a middle-class family, she was suitably undereducated; never having completed Gymnasium, she had worked in the lower echelons of the national postal service. Her motto for the BDM was in keeping with the tradition of the past and aptly pointed the way for the future: "Don't talk, don't debate, live a National Socialist life in discipline, composure, and comradeship!"[30]

After her marriage, which disqualified her from this position, Mohr was succeeded in November 1937 by Jutta Rüdiger, a twenty-seven-year-old woman with a doctorate in psychology, who had belonged to the pre-regime Nazi Student League. Rüdiger would serve under Schirach and later Axmann in that role until the end of the Third Reich.[31] It is unclear why a woman with a Ph.D. was chosen at that time—Rüdiger was far better educated than both Mohr and Schirach himself. Apparently a northern regional leader, Lisa Husfeld, had been the first choice, but this young woman had declined, pointing to Rüdiger as one who "can do this better than I can."[32] There are two possible explanations. Perhaps the HJ leadership, displeased with the fact that Mohr married and left the BDM, reasoned that highly educated women would scare away potential husbands, and thus Rüdiger was perceived as having a fairly good chance of remaining dedicated only to her girls. As it turned out, she did stay single. Another possible reason for the choice of Rüdiger is that Schirach, a man with some university education, may have realized that psychological understanding of girls would be helpful in a difficult-to-supervise mass organization like the BDM. Even in the macho Nazi Reich, there were paths that no marching boots could tread. However anti-academic the Nazis were, they exploited the applied arts and sciences for their own purpose. In this case, they believed that the use of "organic" (as opposed to "Jewish" Freudian) psychiatry and psychology to get inside the minds of German girls would make it easier to rule them.[33]

The BDM, with its members from ages ten to eighteen, grew somewhat more slowly than its male HJ counterpart. After March 1939, the Third Reich made membership in the HJ obligatory for both girls and boys. Earlier there had been a gap in the post-fourteen-year cohort in the BDM, probably because more girls would join the work force after primary school at age fourteen than boys. There was also less job-site pressure on girls to join the BDM, at least until the policy of compulsory HJ membership by the summer of 1939.[34]

The BDM was built on a command structure analogous to that of the male HJ. The female leaders in the more responsible positions would be schooled in special training centers, especially as those with the highest authority became full-time salaried staff.[35] However, there were significant differences in the schooling and treatment of these young women which set them apart and actually demeaned them in relation to boys and young men. Apart from the leadership structure as such, most other factors were identical, and leadership shortage problems plagued both the female and the male HJ.[36]

What set the girls' BDM division apart from the boys' division in the wider Hitler Youth? To answer this question one can explore further the rudimentary service routines of these girls, which had been pre-charted by Nazi women as early as 1923. In keeping with an officially projected feminine image, the BDM's approach to young recruitable girls was softer and gentler than that employed for boys, although this was primarily true during the period of voluntary membership until 1939. It was especially so with the youngest and most impressionable age cohort from ten to fourteen, a group called Young Girls, or Jungmädel, the female equivalent of the Pimpfe. The BDM's approach was designed to emphasize the ideal of physical passivity (vis-à-vis boys and men) and lack of activism, which were commensurate with the hoped-for future eugenic role of girls as Nazi childbearers.

Accordingly, the memoirs of former BDM inductees reflect the published propaganda of the organization itself, with an emphasis on pleasure, friendship, the warmth and charisma of somewhat older leaders, communal fun, and play rather than physical exertion in drills, athletics, and competition. Many young recruits of those days typically recall the joys of joining the BDM and being welcomed by sympathetic leaders and groups of like-minded friends.[37] Since Schirach openly condoned "the games of young girls" (1934), including much of the outright romanticism of the late-Weimar youth movement, these activities, such as watching a full moon and then spending the night in a barn, were self-consciously continued, whereas in the case of the boys, they had been discouraged.[38] Military aspects of BDM service could easily be disguised as innocent contests and games; anything that might look like a military exercise or that presaged war was played down.[39]

Much as with the boys, the girls were given the very positive experiences of going on hikes in the country, roasting sausages over campfires, communal singing, enacting fairy tales and theatrical plays, and performing puppet shows, folk dances, and recorder trios. "The weekends were crammed full with outings, campings, and marches when we carried heavy packs on our backs. It was all fun in a way and we certainly got plenty of exercise . . . These young BDM leaders taught us songs and tried desperately to maintain a certain amount of discipline without ever really succeeding."[40] In winter, handicrafts and needlework shops in the BDM clubhouse were very popular.[41] Whatever political message the HJ leadership wanted to convey to the girls, it was imparted subliminally. In the early years of the regime, and certainly for the younger groups, political indoctrination was practiced lightly and hardly noticed by the (admittedly innocent) target group. Play and games, however, were decoys for sterner things to come.[42]

One clever bait for the girls was the aesthetic appeal of fashion. The early attention paid by leading Nazis to the BDM's attire bore fruit. It is true that the standard costume—dark blue skirt, white blouse (both reminiscent of the youth movement), and black kerchief with a knotted tie of leather strips—made girls look alike. Judged singly, however, the garments were generally thought to be attractive, especially the spiffy tie. A mustard-yellow vest (*Kletterweste*) was not so popular with most, but a few found it especially fashionable.[43] Fashion here catered to a remarkable blend of impulses, and the Nazis knew how to exploit that. On one hand, there was a sort of lemming effect, where peer group pressure motivated girls to belong by imitating. "I thought this was really chic and I just had to have this too," said one former member in explaining her feelings at the time.[44] On the other hand, girls wishing to express their individual personalities through the style in which they dressed still felt they had leeway to do so, for instance by making slight modifications or by ignoring (or emphasizing) the somewhat controversial yellow vest, wearing different knee socks, or paying attention to the hairdo—mostly braids for the youngest girls, but they could be of different lengths, and hairstyles could change with increasing age.[45] Indeed, as the girls got older and developed a sense of adult fashion, the uniforms too were invariably altered, as they were for the leaders: universally admired insignia were added, such as the green leadership cord, or fashionable overcoats were worn. There were other opportunities to dress up in different clothes, for instance the white dresses with colorful aprons and ribbons that were worn for the public performances of folk dance—a very satisfying experience for the girls involved.[46] To the boys, attire mattered much less; their vanity would be satisfied in other ways.

The various sports offerings for the girls were also attractive, particularly since they were treated more as group play than individual competitions. Usually, rhythmical gymnastics took the place of athletic strain. This kind of exercise emphasized harmony and the sense of resting within one's own physical body as well as the collective body of the group. Thus the girls practiced organic *Volksgemeinschaft*. At the same time, the flow of gymnastic movements was closely related to the feminine anatomy and the future role of women as childbearers. Where boys had to be forceful, girls had to show grace. And while there were opportunities for female competitive sports such as swimming for points or Nazi honor badges,[47] the overall emphasis was not on individual performance but on collective movement, not unlike women's aerobics of a later era, but less driving and challenging even than those.[48] Games with softballs were popular, and during the 1936 Berlin Olympics more than a thousand BDM girls gyrated simultaneously, in a synchronized show of unity—a symbol of totalitarian strength that was later successfully imitated by other dictatorships such as the People's Republic of China.[49] Such scenes were brilliantly captured in the films of Leni Riefenstahl.[50]

Communal, synchronized sport was a technique to ensure what, according to Schirach, was the duty of young women, "to correspond with the beauty ideal of male adolescents and grown-ups."[51] Officially, this ideal was of a woman who did not use lipstick or makeup, did not arrange or dye her hair—all the denigrated attributes of slick Weimar-republican city girls or French seductresses.[52] The perfect German woman did not wear pants, nor did she smoke.[53] For women in German society generally, and older girls in the BDM in particular, the Nazis projected the paragon of a Nazi female as a woman who tied her hair in a bun and dressed tastefully yet simply. In the BDM, the white and blue uniform was considered feminine enough without even a touch of elegance or sensual suggestiveness, and except for a ring and a watch, no jewelry was allowed. High-heeled shoes and silk stockings were off limits.[54] As BDM members became older and obtained leadership positions, however, especially during the war, those rules were relaxed, although too stark a transgression could still raise eyebrows in public.[55]

The regime dictate of a well-groomed and well-dressed young woman was designed to attract a German man for breeding and child-rearing. Hence the ideal of a healthy mother was always proclaimed, and so were her typical chores as a homemaker. Hitler himself made certain that training in the BDM did not stray too far from the domestic path when he reiterated at the 1936 Nuremberg Party rally that "motherhood was woman's supreme function, and that a woman could make no greater contribution to the nation than the birth of several children."[56] Toward that end, special BDM physicians constantly watched over the health of their young charges, in particular with a view to preventing physical overexertion (for instance, after sports), and monitoring prenatal potential.[57]

Many of the things that BDM girls did while hiking or congregating in the clubhouse amounted to practical exercises in preparation for wifehood and motherhood. Certain activities were thought to appeal to the girls because of their gender-specific nature: the door-to-door selling of trinkets for welfare purposes, or the household collections of toys and clothes for the needy.[58] Girls were valued as servants of the muses when the BDM performed in choirs, played in amateur orchestras, or told stories for the little ones during "Children's Hour" on the radio.[59] As early as 1934 *Mädel im Dienst,* an official manual for the Jungmädel cohort between ages ten and fourteen, listed their goals as the "warmth of the homey hearth fire," needlework, proper cooking practices, and how to outfit and furnish a home.[60] Considerable space was apportioned to family celebrations, such as Mother's Day, which had been celebrated in the Weimar Republic but which the Nazis elevated to a state holiday and used as an instrument of propaganda for women.[61] Ultimately, of course, there was much talk and writing about giving birth and bringing up children, the high duty of every German woman.[62]

It was also thought in the BDM that two excellent ways for young women to prepare to be future housewives and mothers were learning to help out as maids in households and working in the country as farm hands, or in the farmer's house. These were both accomplished in various programs under the labels of Pflichtjahr, or Duty Year, or the Landdienst or Landjahr, these latter two simply denoting service in the country.

The farm programs lasted anywhere from a few months in the summer to two solid years, and until early 1938, they were voluntary. They arose from a combination of ideological motives, grounded in the racist *Artamanen* doctrine of the 1920s, which aimed at rooting more young Germans in the soil and further developing the infrastructure of the rural East. This formula would provide the basis for recolonization of the non-German East once the war against the Third Reich's eastern neighbors commenced. Beginning in early 1934 the BDM took care of employment for fourteen-year-old girls just released from school, who were looking for jobs in industry. On the one hand, the Nazis discouraged the gainful employment of women, as there was still unemployment in the cities because of the lingering Depression.[63] On the other hand, farm jobs were not popular, and this labor shortage had to be filled for the sake of the economy. Here, the BDM's program satisfied ideological as well as economic objectives. In 1934, 7,000 German girls started farm work; by 1937, 43,000 had been sent out—mostly to farmsteads in the East, in Silesia, Pomerania, or East Prussia. The girls lived and worked with the farmers and in the evenings mingled socially with the youths of the village. Nazi social engineers such as demographic planners looked upon this as creatively molding the *Volksgemeinschaft*.[64]

Between 1936 and 1939, this farm program was expanded. Retraining and schooling facilities were established to help as many city girls become farm girls as possible. Rural farm labor was seen as developing feminine qualities and readying a girl for marriage and motherhood all the more effectively. With the girls kept away from urban ills and corruption, it was hoped that young women would be more likely to choose an occupation consonant with the Nazi agenda for females: nurse, social worker, teacher, or—in the rarest cases and at a higher plane—pediatrician.[65] The girls' farm service became compulsory after January 5, 1938, when Schirach, now in complete control of the BDM, decreed it as such.[66] But because membership was still voluntary and the need for farm workers great, Hitler's Economic Plenipotentiary, Hermann Göring, weighed in a few weeks later with a decree that established the Pflichtjahr within his Four-Year Plan for all teenage girls, whether in the BDM or not.[67] This Pflichtjahr was for a full year, so that before a young woman could accept a permanent position in the work force, she had to complete her service either on a farm or in city homes as a maid—another unpopular job category. Thus by 1940, there were 157,728 German girls starting Pflichtjahr work in agriculture, and another 178,244 in domestic service.[68] In addition to the agricultural training centers, already existing *Haushaltsschulen,* or household schools for domestic service, were built up and new ones founded.[69] Girls' memoirs of those years in either work branch tell varying stories of happiness and woe; what was evident in all the girls' experiences, however, whether they realized it then or not, was a ruthless exploitation of unpaid menial labor, in the country as much as the city households.[70]

Conveniently, these two interrelated programs, the farm service and the household aid, would be followed and amplified by the Reich Labor Service for young women, the Reichsarbeitsdienst (RAD). It observed the same triple goals of ideological indoctrination, discipline, and national economic improvement as did the BDM. Even though the RAD had been around for some years as a voluntary institution, its real mission and force would only emerge in wartime.

The Challenges of World War II

As the Pflichtjahr continued to be mandatory for younger BDM members during the war, the Reich Labor Service came to the fore for older girls, as part of the general Labor Service. That service had already been established in the Weimar Republic on a voluntary basis. It was made compulsory for young men in 1935, as a prerequisite for the newly

introduced general conscription, whereas it became a duty for the girls only with the beginning of hostilities in 1939. Female volunteer work camps had existed since 1935. They were expanded to receive all girls from ages seventeen to twenty-five who were single, not yet employed, or not in some formal training or educational institution.[71] In 1938, there had been about 25,000 "Reich Labor Maidens," as they were officially called. By April 1940 more than twice that number were concentrated in over two thousand camps all around Germany, and shortly thereafter in annexed and occupied territories such as the Protectorate, Alsace, and Denmark.[72]

The original term of service was six months, and the work was very similar to (and often merged with) that delineated by the Pflichtjahr—in households or farmers' homes and in the fields. Things were much less carefree in the RAD, however. The girls in these camps were ruled by a different regimen from the one they had experienced in the regular BDM. Paramilitary drill replaced communal gymnastics, and an atmosphere of compulsory service supplanted the genial, voluntary spirit. The changed atmosphere manifested itself in a change of attire: unflattering navy or olive-green work dresses and a plain hat replaced the stylish BDM costumes; roll calls demanding quick changes in uniform, interrupted only by tasteless meals and noxious sports and drill, became the daily routine. The girls' labors took up thirteen hours of the day, and they were free only every second Sunday.[73] Such extended BDM service resembled the much tougher HJ obligation for the boys from the age of ten on. However, young men of around seventeen were drafted into a separate two-year RAD service which immediately took them closer to the fronts—something that these early RAD Maidens never experienced.[74]

But the situation changed after June 1941, when Reich Munitions Minister Fritz Todt convinced Hitler that he needed more man- and womanpower toiling in war-related industries, specifically the processing of mass ammunition. As far as the women were concerned, they were supposed to take the place of industrial workers who had recently been conscripted by the Wehrmacht. By October 1, 1941, to aid

the newly opened campaign against the Soviet Union, those RAD
Maidens who were just due to be released were ordered to serve an
additional six months, for a total of twelve, in what was called Kriegshilfsdienst, or Auxiliary War Service. From then on, every RAD cohort, upon its release, had to do secondary duty in the war industry.
For this work, each of the girls was paid 45 marks a month (in contrast
to unpaid regular RAD service), which was still a pittance in relation to
what they were commissioned to do. Although farm labor or house-
work was to be continued in some of these cases—for instance, working in a bakery in Alsace or herding cattle in Posen (Poznan)—work in
the Reich's munitions factories became the norm. This could mean
sorting and crating ammunition like grenades, gluing together rubber
gas masks for horses, or sewing up Army uniforms. Many young
women were trained as radio and telephone operators, telegraphers,
and stenographers.[75] Toward the end of the war, when the situation for
the government was becoming desperate, hundreds of young women
were earmarked for the construction of anti-tank obstacles and anti-
aircraft artillery aid, and some were actually deployed.[76] This meant
that large numbers of women were, at one time or another between
October 1941 and May 1945, moved to the proximity of the fronts,
though still behind the lines. Yet especially in early 1945, facing the
advancing Russians, this became a frightening experience for many. A
smaller proportion of these girls still labored in households or in fields,
as well as in hospitals, particularly military ones. While most found
themselves far from home, a few were fortunate enough to be placed in
venues close to their parents' residences.[77] Because of the large number
of personnel involved, the lack of adequate supervision and organization, and the fact that the Maidens had neither sufficient experience
nor on-the-job training, the efficiency rate of the overall work in both
the regular RAD and its Kriegshilfsdienst ancillary turned out to be
dismally low.[78]

For the younger girls in the BDM, those who had not yet reached the
RAD stage, the tone changed also, as did their tasks, after September
1939. One of these tasks was taking charge of ethnic German peasants

in conquered Poland, in a caregiving role. The program was named Osteinsatz, or Eastern Service; its work could also be shared by the older girls in the RAD.[79] The BDM had already had a similar experience in peacetime with Polish-Germans in the traditional eastern provinces. Either as part of their obligatory Pflichtjahr or on a volunteer basis, girls usually aged sixteen and older would assist Polish-Germans and German resettlers from eastern Europe in the arts of keeping a house, using the mother language properly, and bringing up their children in accordance with Nazi hygienic standards.

Their work took place mostly in the so-called Wartheland (the Nazis preferred the term "Warthegau"), which was Polish territory around Posen, and in the southern tip of Upper Silesia, which had been German until the outcome of World War I had forced its cession to Poland. After Poland was conquered by Hitler in 1939, it was divided into the Wartheland (now again considered a German province) and Poland proper, which was militarily occupied and governed as the Generalgouvernement under Hitler's old Munich lawyer, Hans Frank. The situation was very confused ethnically and culturally in the Wartheland: there were ethnic Poles with German names speaking mostly German, and Germans with Polish names speaking mostly Polish. Many other combinations between these two extremes were possible, and the problem for Heinrich Himmler, as Hitler's newly minted Reich Commissar for Ethnic Resettlement, was to distinguish and separate the ethnic populations from each other and settle them accordingly. The grand scheme was to drive the Poles out of Wartheland and into Occupied Poland, leaving the ethnic Germans behind on much larger homesteads. As the war in the East progressed, other ethnic Germans from the Baltics, Bukovina, Volynia, and Bessarabia, eventually even from the Soviet Volga Basin, were supposed to join them. In this scheme of things, the crucial task for the regime demographers was to establish beyond a doubt who was truly German and who was Polish.[80]

Once the distinctions had been made, however haphazardly, by the specialists of the SS, Schirach, Axmann, and Rüdiger's girls were supposed to help settle the ethnic Germans. The population transfer of

Poles and Germans was massive and complicated. It has been estimated that approximately one million Poles were removed from Wartheland to the Generalgouvernement, to make room for 350,000 ethnic Germans from outside Poland, including up to 200,000 juveniles. This does not include the tens of thousands of ethnic Germans who were already in Poland. To facilitate Nazi resocialization, 19,000 of the Reich's BDM girls and their youthful leaders were called in and billeted in 160 special camps, for an average stay of four to six weeks at a time. The girls were ordered to work in teams of up to fifteen, each team being responsible for four or five Polish villages, often in collaboration with the SS who had just finished driving out the Poles.[81]

The girls usually found their chores distasteful throughout because, according to their inculcated dogmatism, the Poles were dirty people and kept a filthy house. One report talks about having to hack away at layers of caked dirt in a former Polish dwelling, to make room for cleaner ethnic Germans.[82] What surprised and shocked these girls even more, however, was that the Germans they then had to help resettle were hardly cleaner than the Poles, and few of them knew how to speak their mother tongue. "Romantic illusions" were being destroyed after confrontation with reality, wrote one intermediate BDM chief; it was clear that "good Germans" could not easily be made out of "half Poles" within a short time.[83] Although most ethnic Germans were very friendly with their "liberators" and dreamed of a Golden Age under Nazi rule after the Final Victory, for the time being they continued speaking Polish with the remaining Poles in the village "and viewed them as their total equal." They often slept in a bed with them, ate from a common bowl, and shared the same fleas, lice, and scabies. Frequently illiterate, these ethnic Germans had an extremely high infant mortality rate, incest was rampant, and some could not be weaned from their wood alcohol. Above all, they could not understand why German girls like the BDM zealots would want to work so hard on their behalf.[84]

Such impressions of ethnic Germans caused them to be ranked a notch or two beneath the racial benchmark of the BDM themselves.

One former BDM leader recalls that she was forced to tell Polish-reared German colleagues in the Warthegau that they were to be replaced by young women from the Reich, because in the end they were not seen as fit to lead.[85] This leader's action was in accord with official ideology: in the Nazi racial hierarchy, Germans ranked at the very top, followed by the ethnic cousins of dubious quality, then the alien Poles, and finally, insofar as one could be aware of them there, the Jews.[86]

The prejudices against Poles were reinforced by tales of Polish suppression and even murder of ethnic Germans, which were bruited about by the surviving relatives of the slain from before World War II.[87] The BDM had been instructed at home by their leaders and were reminded again and again that Poles were a people "worthy of disgust, genuine sub-humans, who deserved to be ruled by a master race. Any shyness or even politeness on the part of Nazi representatives would be tantamount to a betrayal of the ethnic Germans."[88] Back home, one girl had been lectured by a family friend that finding a place to live in Poland was not a problem at all. "You can look at all the apartments of rich Poles and can then select the ones you want. All you have to say is: Get out, you pigs!"[89] Finally placed in a Polish village in the Osteinsatz, the same girl was asked by an ethnic German woman to venture out into the field and beat up the small Polish boy who failed to mind the cows: "With Polacks you cannot be squeamish; you have to hit them, or they will not obey." The frightened girl actually did go out to confront and then to hit the undernourished little lad, symbolically, with a stick. She felt terrible about it and could not help noticing his eyes, "wild with rage and hatred," the memory of which then pursued her day and night.[90]

Another girl, in Cracow, saw the bloodied corpses of two German policemen who had been assassinated by the Polish Underground. The next day at the same site, she discovered forty Poles lying side by side on the grass, shot in retaliation by the Germans. An SS soldier was keeping watch. Poles, this girl took note, had to keep their distance from the Germans in all public places. Fully recognizing their subjugated status, the Poles viewed their conquerors with hate.[91] BDM girls were recipients of this hatred, as when a girl, Carola, on the way to contact future German settlers in Volynia, entered a train compartment in her BDM uniform. She saw that all civilians were immediately forced to vacate her compartment, only to threaten her, through the window of the adjacent one, with clenched fists.[92]

After stressful weeks of work in Poland, important new duties awaited the BDM girls back in the Reich as part of their regular service. Although they were still expected to prepare to be model wives and mothers, the war's exigencies temporarily put the national economy and war-related matters first. This meant fewer drills and sports, and almost no hiking, camps, or cookouts in the peacetime mode. By 1941, bombing raids were already making these activities impossible.[93] What was required instead was the equivalent of man-hours, tangible work for the benefit of civilians and soldiers. There was a plethora of chores on an almost daily basis, with the effect that school or occupational instruction suffered markedly. Many of those chores were gender-specific or at least gender-neutral, as HJ boys of similar ages were drawn to warrior-like tasks in the war effort, some in paramilitary postings and increasing numbers close to or at the fronts.[94]

Apart from the continuation of household or farm labor service within the Pflichtjahr or, for the older girls, the RAD, other girls were increasingly involved in the collection of medicinal herbs—some for ersatz tea—in the countryside. In the entire Reich in the period 1939–1940, over a million BDM members spent 6.5 million work hours on the collection of various herbs and tea. In Mecklenburg in the Northeast, the BDM's collection of herbs more than doubled from 1939 to 1941, but then fell off again somewhat in 1942 because of increasing air raids.[95] In the countryside, additional jobs were done within the KLV program, where somewhat older BDM teens with some intermediate leadership rank were called upon to supervise younger children in the HJ evacuation camps. Thus Hildegard Morgenthal, from a workers' family in Berlin, at the age of sixteen became the HJ camp director in Steinseifersdorf, Lower Silesia, in March of

1941. There she was to function alongside four female teachers and three junior BDM leaders, to manage 130 girls from ages ten to thirteen. She and other camp directors of comparable age and rank were joined by representatives of the BDM health corps, who had been trained by and were deployed in conjunction with the German Red Cross.[96] More mundane services had to be rendered in towns and cities, where BDM girls replaced tram conductors, postal employees, and sales personnel in corner stores—presumably filling in for all the conscripted males or the older girls now staffing the RAD. Already in the first year of the war, more than eleven thousand girls were performing clerical work in police stations and fifteen hundred of them were with emergency fire departments.[97] Some girls were minding municipal day-care centers, while others designed toys for toddlers.[98]

As the war progressed, it became more important to aid those immediately affected. In the civilian sector, BDM members were regularly found at train stations, where they assisted mothers with children or handed out sandwiches and hot drinks to hungry passengers; this work became ever more significant as the conflict wound down and fugitives, mostly from the East, were crisscrossing the Reich in search of an elusive safety.[99] Collection of herbs tended to be replaced by collection of those items needed quickly by the air-raid-stricken: emergency utensils for personal hygiene such as combs, toothpaste, towels, and brushes.[100]

Of paramount importance was assistance to the afflicted themselves, immediately after air-raid hits. A program described as Katastropheneinsatz, Action in Catastrophe, employed teenagers for grueling tasks which were far removed from the dreams of eleven-year-old Hitler Girls in 1934. The larger and more strategic the German city, the greater were its chances of being attacked. Hence in Bremen, a major northern port, scores of BDM girls were toiling in kitchens trying to feed 1,500 suddenly homeless people three times a day—and the girls themselves were always on the run from the next bomb attack.[101] How such an event could shape up is told by thirteen-year-old Ilse Koehn. In the capital she was preparing sandwiches with comrades, who were cooking soup, in 1942. Then the sirens sounded. "The lights go out, tumult and screams. 'Take cover, everyone take cover! Into the cellar!' Flashlights shine on these masses of people, pushing and screaming and screeching." And then: "All the noise is drowned out in the rush of the falling bombs. The walls tremble, and the horrified screams almost tear apart my ear drums . . . Fearful eyes glance at the ceiling. Will it hold?"[102] It was always worse when the raids were over and the dead had to be hauled up from below. A year later in Berlin, a BDM girl was helping survivors surface from the ruins when she herself was hit and, "in order to save herself, cut off her own leg, which had been caught in the rubble."[103]

Many of the girls' first-aid tasks were shifting from the field to the hospitals, for civilians and soldiers alike. Already in the first year of the war more than 60,000 BDM girls were lending a hand in sickrooms.[104] In early 1945 in Ulm, northwest of Munich, when the personnel shortage was most acute, one schoolgirl was supervising four patients in a local hospice. These were not strictly medical tasks, but nonetheless, such nursing took the place of school work, regular BDM duty, and any free time she would otherwise have had—until the next Katastropheneinsatz occurred, and then she had to be in the shelters to help those hurt by air raids.[105]

Increasingly, such patients turned out to be soldiers. More immediately and symbolically, the girls were finding themselves back in the service of German men, for whom they had been said to be destined. Many of those soldiers had already received care packages and morale-supporting letters at the fronts from the BDM girls, or group entertainment like folk singing during furlough. In the former cases, the names of the front soldiers had been pulled out of a hat by the girls' leaders, who then urged their charges to write comforting letters to the soldiers.[106] But with the wounded in the hospitals, it was disturbingly different. Certainly, the girls would bring flowers and gifts to the wounded men and would serenade them to cheer them up.[107] But increasingly, they would attend to the soldiers' wounds, and often the sight of these maimed young men was too much for them to bear. In one bed a BDM veteran found a "barely living wreckage, in it lies what is left of a very young man, his face suffused with a translucent pallor and his head attached to what appears to be a rectangular package under the sheets—the first quadruple amputee we have seen."[108] Maria Eisenecker, another nurse's helper, wrote that she just could not get over the fact that "young men without legs, with bullet wounds were lying there, who could neither live nor die."[109]

Such was the service of girls on behalf of the Reich and the young men who served it in the Army. However, there was also service to the SS. Some three thousand young girls, coming straight out of the BDM, allowed themselves to be recruited as assistants to the SS, and several became concentration camp guards. This meant complete subservience to the dictates of brute force and male domination associated with Himmler's Black Shirts. Many of these young women were caught up in the brutal practices around them and became cruel themselves, thus moving far away from the feminine ideal of nurturance which the BDM leadership had preached to them earlier. Girls like Irma Grese succumbed completely to the abandonment of all humanity and indulged in grossly criminal behavior without a backward glance. Others could do so only with major doses of cigarettes and cognac. One of the female SS assistants was a stenographer behind the lines at the eastern front. She took minutes during the SS interrogations of suspected saboteurs and was part of a process during which some victims went mad during torture and were "screaming like wild animals." For a few like Grese, such sadism became addictive. Evidence shows that a few others who could tolerate it no longer eventually were allowed to make arrangements to return home.[110]

Eugenics and Race

In a more developed stage, the Bund Deutscher Mädel strove to cultivate an elite group to serve as a test object in the Nazis' wider racial-eugenic planning. Much of this occurred in close cooperation with the SS, which, of course, ultimately groomed the male elite, the incarnation of male supremacy in the Third Reich. The program, announced by Baldur von Schirach on January 19, 1938, ran under the trademark "Glaube und Schönheit," or Faith and Beauty.[111] This was an emblematic designation inspired by aesthetic ideals promoted by Albert Speer, the architect, and Leni Riefenstahl, the filmmaker. Not coincidentally, Speer and Riefenstahl, who were themselves unusually attractive, collaborated on cultural projects such as the filming of Party rallies and the Olympics, with heightened concentration on beautiful young bodies in synchronized motion.[112]

With the SS in the background, "Glaube und Schönheit" was a model blueprint for eugenically perfect propagation of Germans in the National Socialist interest and therefore of the highest significance to Nazi social engineers. At first glance the program seemed to be out of line with other Nazi phenomena. Its first leader was a veritable Countess, Clementine zu Castell (formerly the Nuremberg regional BDM chief). She remained at her post until she got married to another Count in 1939 and resigned. However, her title had already served its purpose of attracting aspiring young women.[113] "Glaube und Schönheit" recruited young women from seventeen to twenty-one and older, some of whom could still have been regular members of the BDM while others, the older ones, might have been in the process of being claimed by different (mass-oriented) Nazi Party affiliates. The program made a point of appealing to especially beautiful and Nordic-looking young women who were already physically mature. These women had to be unmarried and could be gainfully employed; their course of duty would be for four years, and normally they would meet once a week. Membership was entirely voluntary, even in wartime, as if there were no dictatorship and women were free to make their own decisions.

As with the early BDM, fashion—this time glamorous apparel for women with film-starlet figures—was a major enticement. The young women were encouraged to peruse fashion magazines in an attempt to create well-fitting attire for themselves; during the summer they were clad in tight teeshirt-like tops and well-cut, pleated, very short skirts, all in suggestively innocent white. Photographs show leggy blond beauties with medium-length hair, not tied in the usual Nazi-type bun, presumably without makeup and casually playing with hoops. By any standards, they were sexually alluring.[114]

These girls were to congregate for workshops where they could engage in all the leisure and sports activities open to the pre-war BDM during a typical month, such as swimming, needlework and shop work, or running and softball. They had to register for courses that were optional; group gymnastics, however, was mandatory at least once.[115] There were modeling shows at which the girls put themselves on display like professionals, either publicly or for a more select Nazi male audience. Moreover, three very elite sports were offered that the ordinary BDM girls never had access to: tennis, horse riding, and fencing.[116] Another activity was home design, but of a more sophisticated and elaborate kind than in the common BDM program. These young women were to help create a Nazi-specific home-decoration and furniture aesthetic, the capstone for an elite Nazi family.[117]

In the official literature the description of these goals was embellished with phrases betraying the true eugenic nature of this venture in the Nazis' demographic blueprint. "We know that especially the beautiful girls will embrace these activities enthusiastically," wrote Schirach's top lieutenant, Günter Kaufmann, in 1938.[118] And "the themes of these workshops demonstrate that all issues which concern girls and women in our *völkisch* life are covered here." In straight biological terms it was explained why a girl would ideally have to be around twenty years old in order to join this program. "It is only when they are about twenty-one that German girls outgrow their girlhood and, as women and mothers, move into the great German *Volksgemeinschaft*. Therefore, we want to use this time of adolescence, as the developmental stage of our Nordic race between childhood and womanhood, to learn as many pedagogical lessons as is possible for us in our *völkisch* existence." The most revealing statement regarding the ultimate mission of this program was made in 1943, when it was written that "the ideal of the lovely, beautiful, and proud girl" was equal to the ideal of the "courageous, chivalrous boy."[119]

And herein lay the key to the whole enterprise. It was Himmler, that inspiring mentor to Schirach and Axmann in the business of human recruitment, who had very distinct notions about Nordifying the German people and already was on record for coveting superior Hitler Youths for his SS. In addition, he was interested in outstanding young women as future mates for his prized warriors, as was common knowledge throughout the BDM.[120] As he explained to his masseur Felix Kersten early in 1941, when the "Glaube und Schönheit" program was fully implemented, Himmler wished to see blond, blue-eyed girls molded according to German racial and eugenic criteria. By the time they were no older than twenty-eight, they would be ready to assume the title of *Hohe Frau*, or High Woman. (Himmler also thought that ordinary Party leaders should divorce their wives for the sake of marriage with a *Hohe Frau*.)[121]

Himmler, a former chicken farmer and south German *Artamanen* chief, was ruled by very strong beliefs regarding the application of breeding theories to humans—by way of positive selection for the "Aryans" and negative selection for their natural enemies, the Slavs, Gypsies, and Jews. Positive selection, as he was attempting to prove within his SS and as was routinely discussed in the higher BDM echelons, meant that biologically superior males should be allowed to sire as many children as possible, consensually with a eugenically appropriate partner, out of wedlock.[122] These children would then be brought up in special SS homes, the Lebensborne or Founts of Life, which were being erected all over Germany (although never quite the breeding institutes that popular belief imagined, where strapping SS inseminated eager blondes).[123] To that effect, Himmler issued a "Procreation Order" to his men in November 1939, and he barred SS officers from promotion if they did not marry and, if married, did not beget offspring, ideally sons.[124] In the SS view of cohabitation, libido or eros per se was not allowed to matter, only as a vehicle to national biological fulfillment; hence the sex act was merely a technicality, a clinical necessity. This was stated unmistakably by J. Mayerhofer in the summer of 1943, in an article entitled "Love and Marriage" in Himmler's internal publication *SS-Leitheft*.[125] It was for this reason that Himmler, who obviously underestimated his men's basic sex drive, had to issue an SS ordinance in June 1942, prohibiting the seduction of innocent girls for the sake of mere carnal pleasure.[126]

Hohe Frauen were supposed to be beautiful and expert in everything the "Glaube und Schönheit" curriculum taught its candidates. The young women were expected to be of above-average intelligence and to have mastered gymnastics and superior modern skills such as driving a car, using a handgun, riding a horse, and, especially, fencing, which Himmler considered an "intellectual exercise." In this he was no doubt encouraged by his top aide, Reinhard Heydrich, himself a champion fencer. Eugenically, these young women were expected to be fit to bear children, at least three in their lifetime, in accordance with the assumed feminine ideal of the Germanic tribes of two thousand years ago, who, Himmler said, were "racially outstanding."[127] This corresponded with the genetic assumption underlying the "Glaube and Schönheit" program, which emphasized that all Germanic women, like the current students, espoused the Aryan "union of body and soul."[128] Thus it followed that for practical purposes both Himmler's SS and the BDM grooming program would pay close attention to a girl's more immediate Aryan ancestry, traceable, in church records, through two or three centuries.[129]

With eligible young SS leaders in view as breeding partners, "Glaube und Schönheit" placed a remarkable emphasis on the virtues of race, particularly the uniqueness of the German race in contrast with that of "foreign peoples," especially in the East.[130] It helps explain Himmler's *Wehrbauern* scheme in which elite women were viewed as the ideal biological mates for SS leaders who, for "hundreds of kilometers," would farm and stand guard in a conquered European East with no more Jews and with Slavs as slaves.[131] It was suggested that some SS leaders should even have two women, and perhaps some high Party brass too. Himmler's friend Martin Bormann was already practicing such a policy officially, with a wife and many children in Berlin, and his mistress Manja Behrens, a beautiful actress, constantly at his side.[132] Himmler heartily aided and abetted such attitudes, if more discreetly. In addition to his dour wife Marga (with whom he had his daughter Gudrun), he too had a mistress—his attractive secretary, Hedwig Potthast. With her he sired a boy, Helge, and a girl, Nanette Dorothea.[133] Indeed, if things went according to Bormann and Himmler, bigamy was to become universal in the *Volksgemeinschaft* after the war.[134] These ideas were further rationalized by the bloodletting at the fronts, which meant that the Third Reich, for a generation at least, would be left with a surplus of women over men, and hence the biological survival of the *Volk* would be imperiled.[135]

The racial bias of "Glaube und Schönheit," especially as it was implicitly endorsed by Himmler's SS, was reflected in instruction on "circumstances conditioned by race" and "Questions of *völkisch* Life."[136] This racial ideology was mirrored on a much more massive scale in the general BDM. It was anchored in four particular conditions: early Nazi women's hostility against Jews, especially physicians, viewed as dangerous predators; the ongoing racial indoctrination in the BDM, starting with the younger cohorts and accelerating with the older girls; the BDM's imperative to its members, as future child-bearing mates to German males, to keep themselves racially pure; and the first-hand experience of mature female teenagers with Poles and, by extension, Jews, in Poland after September 1939. These experiences and their implicit racial indoctrination constituted the single significant exception to an otherwise largely non-political socialization for girls in the Bund Deutscher Mädel after 1933. It was their racial identity which was central to the Nazi agenda.

In the Third Reich, enduring images of racial aliens as biological foes, with Jews in the first rank, followed by Gypsies and Slavs, underlay much instruction. Such views were routinely imparted through teach-in sessions in the BDM clubhouses, for instance under the label "Race and Volk." Here, the basic principles of what Nazi scholars understood by "race science" were carefully taught.[137] The governing anti-Semitic canon spawned malicious commonplaces about the necessity for a "racial rebirth" of the German people, on the model of a racially pure German *Volksgemeinschaft.*[138] German girls were to be the guardians of "German blood, German culture, German way of life and customs, physical and spiritual health and correctness."[139] One former BDM girl remembers that she and her comrades were lectured about being the better people in this world, and aesthetically the more perfect. "And the Jews were the opposite—this is how they interpreted it to us."[140] At the height of the war, an intermediate BDM leader repeated Hitler's mantra to her charges: "By destroying the Jews, I am doing the work of the Lord."[141]

Lectures, films, and history books taught these girls about a political and biological danger posed by Jews in recent history, particularly as far as women were concerned. BDM instructors and manuals spoke of the "Oriental" origins of the Jews, how they deviously made their way into German lands and in 1812 even received civil rights.[142] That was a result of a "false" doctrine, said *Mädel im Dienst,* namely "that all men are equal."[143] Jews were said to be responsible for the shameful outcome of World War I, the predominance of a gutter culture in the subsequent Weimar Republic, and questionable practices during that period, such as fraudulent cattle-vending in the countryside and cheating through chain stores in the cities.[144] All told, there was "racial degeneration" during the Republic resulting from the presence and dominance of Jews. Since his time in Palestine, the Jew was said to have absorbed Negro blood and to have a particular affinity to those French colonial Negroes who terrorized the German population under the French occupation of the Rhineland in the early 1920s, notably through their compulsive rape of women. And then, the story went, Jews already settled in Germany facilitated the entry of hordes of eastern Jews, who were easily recognized by "a stocky, short figure, the short head with the flat back cranium, somewhat protruding eyes, the Jewish nose in the shape of a 6, and the chin set back."[145] The Nazi stereotypes of Jews abounded and were conspicuously directed at the core of German womanhood. Such propaganda fell on fertile soil. As one eighteen-year-old noted in her diary in early 1940: "We just had political training, for an hour and a half. The origins of the Great War,

the mood in Germany, and the consequences of Jewry. I like this training very much and I am glad to be able to keep my knowledge up to
date."[146]

In 1940, Veit Harlan's feature film *Jud Süss,* with his wife, the
Swedish blond actress Kristina Söderbaum, playing the innocent German girl Dorothea who is raped by the Württemberg court Jew Süss in
the eighteenth century, was shown to large numbers of girls.[147] It was
designed to serve as a timely warning to them about the sexual devasta-
tion Jews had wrought in the past, and also as a reminder of the
Nuremberg Race Laws of September 1935, which had prohibited such
alleged crimes and which were constantly under discussion.[148] The
eugenic purity of German virgins vis-à-vis the predatory designs of
Jewish infiltrators was a primary theme in the instruction of girls. It
was elaborated upon with graphic clarity by Julius Streicher's semi-
pornographic rag *Der Stürmer,* in the most coarse and virulent terms.
In one story, in 1935, Streicher depicts a slender young girl reclining
on a doctor's couch, with the bald and fat physician, his 6-shaped nose
prominently displayed, leering at her with a salacious grin. Underneath
the prominent caricature, the story reads: "Inge is sitting in the waiting
room of the Jew doctor. She has to wait for a long time. She leafs
through the journals on the table. But she is much too restless to read
even a few sentences. She constantly has to think about the warnings of
her BDM section leader: 'No Germans can go to a Jew doctor! And
especially not German girls! Many a girl who sought treatment from a
Jew doctor found only decrepitude and shame.'" The story about Inge
continues, as she waits and then hears a girl crying in the physician's
office and a man laughing viciously. She again thinks of what her
BDM superior had told her. "And then the door opens. The Jew
appears. A scream escapes from Inge's mouth. Terrified, she drops the
journal. Mortified, she jumps up. Her eyes stare into the face of the
Jewish doctor. And that face is the face of the Devil. In the middle of
that Devil's face there sits a huge hooked nose. Behind the glasses glis-
ten the eyes of a criminal. The bulging lips are contorted in an insolent
smirk. A smirk that says: 'Finally I've got you, little German girl!' And

then the Jew approaches her. His fleshy fingers grope her."[149] Such stories terrified young girls and their mothers and bred revulsion toward
Jews.

Anti-Semitism attained even more currency when framed by theories about German superiority and the contemptible inferiority of
others. The concept of the strong, virile Germans as the master race
provided a particularly protective feeling for a German teenage girl. "I
always was under the impression," said one girl born in 1929, "that we
alone were the great rulers of the world and nothing could ever go
wrong for us. And all the others were, well, something like lower subjects."[150] Most Germans traditionally despised the "others" in their
midst, such as Gypsies who, unlike Jews, were not known to ravish
German girls—rather, the lore was about promiscuous Gypsy women
seducing German men.[151] The point about French colonial blacks was
driven home repeatedly, for France, though defeated by 1940, was still
the arch-enemy, and "from France we are threatened by the Black Danger, the bastardization through Negroes and Negro mongrels."[152] And
in southern Austria, now called Ostmark, visiting BDM girls working
on the land were made aware of local disdain for *Windische,* or half-
assimilated Slovenians, "whom one must now get rid of."[153] These ethnic groups threatened the purity of the *Volk,* and young girls who were
potential vehicles of such infection needed to be taught to loathe the
"alien."

Next to the Jews, of course, came the Slavs in Eastern Europe and,
farther afield, even the Mongols, regarding all of whom the Party as
late as spring 1944 exclaimed in terror that they "multiplied like rab-
bits," hence the need for a German "victory of the cradles."[154] Even in
1934, *Mädel im Dienst* taught that the Poles and other eastern peoples
were extremely fertile, and therefore it was possible to figure out by
what year Poland would be overpopulated.[155] It was in 1938, a year
before Hitler's premeditated attack on Poland, that the BMD's primary
song book, *Wir Mädel singen,* published songs with insidious verses to
be chanted communally, such as "Let's ride against the eastern land"
and "Into the east wind throw your banners / For the east wind makes

them wide / Over yonder we shall start building / Which will defy the rules of time."[156]

Thus it was maintained that, with the eugenic tasks to be solved for the preservation of the *Volksgemeinschaft,* the German girl was "the racial conscience of the nation." Every German girl, whose prototype was firmly planted in the BDM, had to be a "guardian for the purity of the blood and the people, in order to bring up heroes from among the sons of the *Volk.*"[157] This defined the mutual relationship between German girls and German boys, as future biological partners who in the HJ and BDM were being conditioned for their reproductive missions. Their roles were stereotyped in line with Nazi ideology, which, it is true, took cues from German conservative thinking, but with the biological functions vastly exaggerated. A Hitler Youth boy had to be chivalrous and protective toward a Hitler Youth girl; the girl would not be his "to play with," but his "comrade." Such ethics sprang from the Nazi theory of the reciprocation of the sexes in that both were considered equal, albeit with different pursuits, duties, and goals. The differentiation derived from the naturally assumed biological variance, as in the cliché of the boy being strong and protective and the girl meek and dependent; yet each, in his or her own way, was conceived of as a fighter.[158] As the historian Jill Stephenson has observed: "The 'difference' lay in both their contrasting natures and their complementary functions. In essence, this confirmed the traditional division of labor, with men dominating the public sphere and women controlling the private sphere."[159] What this amounted to in everyday life, and what made it uniquely Nazi, was that "women, like men, were to serve their 'ethnic community' [*Volksgemeinschaft*] in the manner decreed by their political masters, for goals over which only these masters had jurisdiction."[160] None other than Hitler himself underwrote this view, when at the 1934 Party rally he conjured up the curative tasks of the women of the Time of Struggle and then went on to say, at the top of his voice: "The emotional capacity of women has, since time immemorial, corresponded to the intellect of man . . . and this then is the miraculous effect of Providence, that no conflict between the two genders is possible, as long as each part observes whatever is its specific requirement by nature."[161]

Thus the rhetoric about the equality between the sexes translated in practice into an unqualified subordination of the female to the male, as could be seen within the Hitler-Jugend and Bund Deutscher Mädel, as well as in all other Party affiliates and Nazi society at large. There are telling examples of true inequality for the girls. Political training did not exist in any form, with girls generally shying away from discussing the politics of the day because they knew they would be laughed at or censored by their HJ peers.[162] Cadre schooling of any kind, in comparison to that for the males, was deficient, so that there were no Adolf Hitler elite schools and only two Nationalpolitische Erziehungsanstalten for the girls (compared with ninety-three NPEAs for the boys). And not only was the BDM formally a branch of the male-dominated HJ as a matter of course, but the Brunswick leadership academy, which opened in spring 1939, was accessible to girls only for a very brief period because of the lack of males to fill its spaces.[163] Even a higher BDM leader could never issue an order to the lowest HJ boy.[164] On many occasions, despite the chivalrous reputation that theoretically preceded them, HJ male leaders were gratuitously condescending or downright offensive to their female comrades.[165] Girls were reminded, especially before and during the war, that they were not made of the stuff that could fight in the trenches or that they could not share in the "tough, masculine romanticism" and camaraderie which allowed boys to sing the old fighting songs of storm troopers.[166] Several of the more ambitious BDM members suffered from this attitude. "I thought it was an unkind fate that had caused me to be born a female," remembers Gudrun Pausewang, "for I could not offer my life to the Fatherland."[167]

Some women thought they had broken through to that hallowed goal when in the course of the war the personnel shortage manifested itself, especially at leadership levels. All of Nazi society was afflicted with manpower shortages, so that women physicians, for instance, who earlier had not been allowed to practice, were called into service to stand in for colleagues at the fronts. But there were disadvantages: the women were always in dependent postings, they were ill-paid, and they were on notice to return to civilian life as soon as the men came back to reclaim their rightful, prestigious positions.[168] However, just as the male HJ had to be led by ever younger boys, ever younger girls moved up to take the place of older BDM female leaders who were called up to assume some of the functions of male leaders now in the Wehrmacht or SS.[169] Thus, service on the farms by girls increased by a ratio of 2 to 1 vis-à-vis boys in 1940, and 6 to 1 by 1944.[170] But it could not have helped their egos: many a full-time BDM leader, around age twenty or so, was unable to easily master the new and ambitious tasks thrust upon her.[171] Trained for the home more than the field, these young women often found the adjustment difficult and dangerous.

The uppermost figure in the male-supremacist hierarchy was of course Hitler. Despite the myth that the Nazi Party attained power because in pre-1933 elections the women's vote had tipped the scale, there is little doubt that women of all ages were captivated by Hitler's persona, and at mass rallies often reacted to his presence with complete hysteria. It cannot be overemphasized that this hysterical adulation continued well into the Third Reich.[172] Hitler exuded a sexual magnetism for German females which today can only be compared with the mass appeal of an international rock star. Hitler understood his intense appeal to women and used it strategically. His rationale for remaining a bachelor (until the day before his suicide) was that of a seasoned demagogue: if he were married, he would be seen as having been spoken for and would lose the support of many German girls and women. He wanted to be indelibly imprinted in their hearts as an eligible bachelor and potential spouse. Not unlike a nun's marriage to Christ, the female Aryan would always be joined to her Führer.

In the BDM, Hitler may have been a kind of father figure for many of the younger girls, although in Freudian terms even this image has serious sexual overtones.[173] As the girls became older, that sense of sexuality escalated, and the BDM leadership itself reinforced this disposition. Hitler's persona as a virtually omnipotent male was held up in training sessions at all levels, where one talked about "the life of our

Führer," and joined in the "Song of the New Era" which proclaimed: "Across the streets the columns march / A Führer strides ahead / He opens the path to freedom / Huge shouts from everywhere / Hitler leads the way!"[174]

Girls loved their Führer as a father and a god.[175] And they were erotically enraptured when they were fortunate enough to see him in person. "I have seen our great Führer," wrote Lore Walb in her diary in October 1933, "twice! On the way to the Niederwald Monument and back. So solemn, yet so strong and great he stood there, with his raised right arm in his car! At that moment, tears welled up in my eyes."[176] Doris K. also saw him twice, first in 1934, during Thanksgiving on the Bückeberg mountain near Hameln. "I still remember the eyes this man had. Eyes, in which you could almost drown. Dark-blue eyes, some say they were black, but I saw them as blue. And this man gave me his hand, and thereafter I did not wash my hand for three days." Four years later Doris saw him again in Stuttgart; this time she was fourteen. "Everybody screamed like crazy. Mass suggestiveness! The scream became a roar . . . Especially the women were fascinated. Their emotions were strongly touched and so were, without a doubt, unfulfilled sexual wishes and desires."[177] Helga Giessel was fourteen as well when she fell totally in love with Hitler. She was old enough to wish strongly to travel to Berlin to give a child to the Führer, although she had not quite figured out how, technically, this was to be done.[178]

"Giving a child to the Führer" was a favorite, ritualized rationale for sexually active teenage girls before, as much as during, the war, and this alone gave the lie to Baldur von Schirach's affirmation that a "sexual problem of youth" did not exist in the Hitler Youth.[179] Indeed, against the intentions of the regime, Nazi racial-eugenic policy provided an alibi of sorts for its young protagonists, causing its originally clinical-biological function to be extremely sexualized. The chief consequence of this was a constant release of libidinal energies among HJ adolescents of both genders who would have been constrained under more traditional sexual mores. Once fully recognized, unabashed sexual promiscuity among youth turned out to be a slap in the Nazis' face, but, seemingly paradoxically, it played to the prurience of men like Bormann and Streicher and quietly amused outright philanderers like Goebbels.

It is characteristic of male-supremacist Nazi society that in most contemporary accounts it was the girls, rather than the boys, who were singled out as sexually abnormal or seduction-driven culprits. However, it is likely that boys and girls were equally responsible, acting on their own accord (for they both welcomed the new revolutionary freedom of being out of reach of traditional homes). But because girls had previously lacked the opportunity for this sexual freedom, being well guarded by their parents, the change was viewed primarily as an emancipation for girls and young women, who thus posed a threat to males.[180] For it is generally true in any authoritarian polity that by "all those who see military discipline, self-sacrifice, austerity, and worship of the Leader as the highest social ideals, the power of female sexuality will be seen as a dire threat."[181] And misogynist Nazi males steadfastly subscribed to the traditional German view that where there was sexual seduction, women were doing the seducing, and if anyone was to be blamed, it had to be them.[182]

Rumors about sexual indecency filtered through to various Party headquarters, including the HJ's own, as early as 1934. From Saxon Bärenstein it was reported in March that a BDM leader and her HJ counterpart were found alone in a HJ home and then were spied upon to see what they were up to. Unambiguous reputations preceded BDM girls, so that in neighboring Frohnau, HJ boys invited recent BDM recruits over in order to accost them sexually. As a result, the Frohnau BDM chapter never materialized.[183] Matters progressed in a similar vein elsewhere. In Mannheim in the following year, twenty-five BDM girls were confirmed in a Protestant church; fifteen and sixteen years old, every one was pregnant. In Saxon Heidenau, parents complained about "the sexual depravity in the Hitler Youth and in the League of German Girls." During this time in nearby Chemnitz a BDM girl, after giving birth to a baby and being asked who its father was, answered that it could have been any one of thirteen boys.[184] In 1936

young girls serving in the Landdienst often camped out near a corresponding boys' camp, and then became pregnant by the dozens.[185]
During the Reich Party rally of that year, nine hundred BDM girls
returned home from Nuremberg carrying a child; in only half of the
cases was the father known.[186] As a result, to curb the worst excesses,
camping out was prohibited for the BDM in 1937.[187] As far as the girls
were concerned, the escalation of sexual libertinage during the war was
mainly a result of two factors: the general sexual frustration of girls and
women left without men on the home front and on the farmsteads,
and the steady escalation and indoctrination to induce what the German historian Adelheid von Saldern has defined as the "pronatalist
racial welfare state," as exemplified in the "Glaube und Schönheit"
program, among others.[188]

Mature German women left behind by their men after September 1939 at first accepted their fate of loneliness and sexual depriva-
tion with equanimity and then increasingly turned to lovers, such as
prisoners-of-war or, less frequently, other German soldiers returning
from the fronts on furlough. Their affairs with POWs or, more commonly in the countryside, with conscripted foreigners working as farm
hands, became widespread. Among these men, Poles were the most
ubiquitous and also the most dangerous to be caught with (the men
were always hanged after the act); Frenchmen were sought after for
what was considered a refined sexual technique, and Italians were only
slightly less popular.[189] A German woman, married or not, who was
convicted of an affair with a foreigner usually was imprisoned, often
in a concentration camp such as Ravensbrück, while in villages, according to medieval custom, many had their heads publicly shaved.[190]
Extramarital affairs with soldiers, mostly in cities, were looked upon
less harshly and often depended, for a solution, on the attitude of the
duped husband (if he returned from the war alive). Nonetheless, mar-
riages were breaking down at a record rate.[191] It reflects the male-
chauvinist character of the Nazi Reich that German men caught
sleeping with Polish servant girls received incomparably milder treat-

ment: males could receive a reprimand, while the Polish girls landed in concentration camps.[192]

Many of these sexually experienced women—sometimes sisters or even mothers—were models for BDM girls. It is not hard to imagine how sexual desire and experience would be rife among girls' groups in wartime Germany. By 1940, BDM members in the Ermland area preferred affairs with conscripted Polish laborers and prisoners of war; in the Upper Danube region, work-drafted Czechs, Poles, and Bulgarians were the chosen paramours. In the Thuringian countryside near Halle a sixteen-year-old girl, together with her girlfriend, had herself locked into a Polish POW camp. "She did nude dancing and had sexual intercourse with several men."[193] By early 1942, after the Wehrmacht had attacked Russia and the first Soviet prisoners were brought into the Reich, they were preferred for sex around Berlin, second only to the Poles; all Slavs were thought to be exotic.[194] Two sixteen-year-old girls in a small town near Munich entertained French POWs, who were employed in shops next to their own; the trysting place was a wooden shack near the prisoners' camp.[195] For much of 1942, another Bavarian eighteen-year-old had sex regularly with a French POW who was helping out on a farm; this girl had been sexually active since she was fourteen and well into the BDM.[196] There was mounting evidence for such incidents until 1944, when a subordinate of Bormann's exclaimed, probably in mock surprise, that "even BDM girls had carried on with aliens."[197]

Often these girls had earlier been sexual partners of German soldiers, or had been in multiple relationships, and knew how to play foreigners against Germans for best advantage. In 1943 one seventeen-year-old, working off her mandatory year in a household, was told by a Wehrmacht soldier wooing her that German men were just as good in bed as Frenchmen. But she stunned him with the reply that her Frenchman knew exactly where to touch her all over and that she had come to expect "full satisfaction."[198] If foreign men were exotic and ravishing especially to simpler country girls, philandering German soldiers appealed to the more sophisticated, patriotic maidens, particularly in the large cities, and the dashing officers among them were often seen as nothing less than gods. Hitler Youths attending Gymnasium at the time recall that especially in more well-to-do circles, comely girls dreamed of handsome officers in uniform and more often than not became their prizes, leaving their jealous comrades with short pants in the dust.[199] Many of these casual sexual encounters were the result of those comfort letters that BDM girls had been exhorted to write to the men at the fronts; the girls then became "comfort women" as the men visited on furlough in hotels.[200] Soldiers as well as anyone in Germany knew about the changing reputation of the Bund Deutscher Mädel, whose acronym, BDM, popularly came to stand for *Bund Deutscher Matratzen* (League of German Mattresses) or *Bubi Drück Mich* (Come on Boy, Press Me Hard).

If BDM teenagers did not meet their soldier lovers through prior correspondence, they encountered them daily among civilians on the home front. In early 1940, after she had seen an older man platonically a few times before he became a candidate for officer training, one girl confided to her diary: "When he bid me goodbye by kissing my hand, he said—and I am sure he was sincere—that he enjoyed having met me and that he was hoping to see me again. Momentarily, that is my greatest wish as well. Being so much in love perhaps may be terrible, but I don't care that he is married (that is: I am actually sorry that he is). Still, this does not render him 'taboo' for me. He could have kissed me, I was longing for that."[201] Deprived of many of the more usual pleasures and satisfactions of peacetime life, young girls were susceptible to the attentions and desires of lonely men.

More daring girls went to the local train station to be picked up by a soldier for a one-night stand. This widespread phenomenon all across Germany became a social problem of the highest order as the war dragged on and fewer men were available to sexually satisfy a growing contingent of women left alone at home. BDM girls knew they had an advantage over older and, particularly, married women, because they were young and unattached, and in their uniform they could move about quite freely under the guise of official duties. Soldiers got to know this situation well and ruthlessly took advantage of it, to the point where authorities were charging them with gross irresponsibility, indecency, and rape. Wehrmacht personnel quartered in youth hostels across the country for longer terms, apart from the regular barracks, exacerbated the situation. Girls as young as twelve hung around these residences and threw themselves at the soldiers, using lines such as: "Don't worry, you can go with me, I am already sixteen." In some places such as the town of Dachau, park benches and adjoining lawns were notoriously occupied by soldiers and their teenage consorts, and every spot was littered with condoms. As a result of such promiscuity, illegal pregnancies increased further, and so did cases of venereal disease.[202] Because the BDM, as well as somewhat older RAD girls, often accepted small gifts and even money from men, authorities were inclined to speak of "covert prostitution."[203] Indeed, reports from Berlin as early as 1941 indicated that the red-light districts were disappearing, as professional whores were being pushed out of their jobs by BDM amateurs.[204] All this constituted a particularly unseemly aspect of the Nazi militarization of German society, the ideals of which had been preached at length to the boys in the HJ.

As the more perceptive girls would have been able to tell, sexual exploitation pervaded the HJ itself. A report from the summer of 1940 tells about a HJ-Bannführer, high up in the hierarchy, whose Streifendienst was raiding a small hotel: "There are two beds in the room, each containing a couple. Naked . . . In the other rooms the situation is very similar. Everywhere the SRD has surprised young couples. In one room there are even twelve straw mattresses."[205] RAD maidens kept in work camps were especially susceptible to sexual temptations by HJ boys stationed in surrounding, similar establishments.[206] However, all BDM girls were easy prey for boys in the HJ, with the females frequently taking the initiative.[207]

During the second half of the war, young women appear to have suffered the highest incidence of venereal disease in the entire civilian population.[208] At that time, the proverbially loose morals of the BDM in the Third Reich made all of its members into obvious targets, even for Party officials, who thought the girls were theirs for the taking.[209] Rather than emancipation vis-à-vis males, which can either precede or follow sexual freedom, this exploitation symbolized the subjugation of young females to the twisted value system of the male-supremacist Nazi rulers. There were only a very few girls who were strong enough to resist what they experienced in the Hitler Youth in a serious way, and one of them known to have done so paid for her courage with her life. She was a former BDM leader from Ulm, and her name was Sophie Scholl.

Dissidents and Rebels

Dissidence in Hitler's Germany was the exception. Despite an occasional lack of structural cohesiveness, an extremely well organized Hitler Youth mobilized the great majority of Hitler's young subjects toward Nazi ends. It is against the background of this all-encompassing youth recruitment that rebellious actions, mostly on the part of courageous individuals and groups, appear so dramatic.

The story of the German resistance to Hitler has often been told, beginning with a classic account by Hans Rothfels, printed by H. Regnery, a right-wing American publisher, in 1948. Rothfels was a converted Jew who had to emigrate to England and then the United States from Germany in August 1939, two weeks before the war broke out. Until his return to Tübingen in 1951, he taught at Brown and the University of Chicago. Significantly, he had included for treatment in his original volume only groups and individuals he deemed to be worthy traitors of the Third Reich, ideally conservatives and those associated with the attempt on Hitler's life on July 20, 1944. The Bielefeld historian Hans-Ulrich Wehler, who as a German youth was almost killed by Allied bombers during the final months of the war, observed that in Rothfels's view "the resistance was dominated by members of the old upper stratum—the officer corps, senior civil servants, and the clergy." Rothfels himself, who had lost a leg during patriotic service in World War I, was politically a reactionary. Before his forced emigration he had condemned the Peace of Versailles, and, as a conservative, had been a staunch enemy of the Weimar Republic. He had advocated *völkisch* expansion in the East and had in fact hoped that he could stay in Nazi Germany after some kind of accommodation to the new regime. Thus in his 1948 book, which served as self-justification and legitimation for the German ultra-conservative establishment, marginal groups that resisted Hitler were not mentioned. These would have included high-minded but unorganized individuals, adherents to religious sects such as the Jehovah's Witnesses, members of the political left, and a large number of young people. It is significant that Hans and Sophie Scholl of the White Rose resistance group in Munich made their appearance only on one page of his book, even though they quickly attained the status of icons in the historiography of resistance to the Third Reich, in the judgment of more progressive authors.[1]

Rothfels's original argument in 1948 was that the Third Reich had been such an evil monolith that resistance was well-nigh impossible, and where it did occur, it was tantamount to the highest form of heroism. Such an undifferentiated view put no stock in the possibility that more modest figures might have attempted resistance, that their resistance might sometimes have been on a smaller scale than political or military opposition, and that the everyday dysfunctionality of Hitler's regime invited attitudes and acts along a broad spectrum from disagreement to implacable defiance. This is not to deny the difficulties inherent in non-Nazi-aligned behavior. As the Canadian historian Robert Gellately has persuasively shown, even though the police apparatus of the Third Reich may have been deficient or too small, there were plenty of ordinary Nazis ready to turn in their neighbors on a daily basis and for the slightest of infractions—to the point where a Gestapo was hardly necessary.[2] That ever-present danger is underscored by a recent recollection of George Wittenstein, once a close friend of Hans Scholl and himself a member of the White Rose in Munich, who writes: "I witnessed an illustrative incident in a movie theater: During the newsreel—which always showed Hitler—the Gestapo suddenly arrived and arrested a man two rows ahead of me.

He likely had made a derogatory remark about Hitler, which was over-heard by someone who instantly reported him . . . There simply was no way of communicating safely."[3]

And yet there were youth in the Third Reich who decided to break ranks. Some were members of the Hitler Youth, but others never even bothered to join and instead opted for nonconformity or sabotage of one kind or another. Some were members of the White Rose, and some were paracriminal juveniles. Did the latter act in opposition to the regime because they had a criminal disposition, or were they crimi-nalized by a regime that chose to define deviant behavior in such a way as to entrap them? That the Nazis simply labeled them deviant is sug-gested by the savagery with which the leadership struck at them in the final years of the war. However, this savagery could equally have been a manifestation of furious despair, after the regime's leaders realized that their claim to the total control of youth was harder to achieve than they had at first imagined. The youth who were to be the next genera-tion's Nazi elite were not a monolithic cadre committed to the Führer. There were some who dissented.

The Varieties of Dissidence

Individual withdrawal from the Hitler Youth in peace or war consti-tuted an important form of dissidence in the Third Reich, although it hardly ever endangered the institution's monopoly. However, loosely organized groups of dissenters caused the HJ to worry that the spirit of opposition could be spread far and wide. On the one hand, the HJ had reason to fear organizations that were remnants of the republican past, which it thought it had neutralized, but which were reappearing again. On the other, there were signs of new group formations that tended to move beyond the HJ's control. Adherents to such dissenting groups might still be formally incorporated in the Hitler Youth, but they tended to miss meetings often. Others had already been expelled, and some had never joined.

The first category of officially suppressed youth consisted of those who belonged to groups that had for the most part surrendered their existence to the state monopoly early on, but who continued to maintain illegal offshoots. Nostalgic for the individual liberties they had enjoyed before Hitler came to power, they bore names invoking the Weimar period and usually harkened back to the traditions and practices of the *Bündische Jugend,* or Eberhard Koebel's Communist-inspired *Deutsche Jungenschaft,* or Catholic youth leagues, or a romanticized and fuzzy combination of some or all of these. The main thing was that to varying degrees they had been and continued to be anti-Nazi. In June 1935 an athletic association, calling itself *Turnverein Burg-Lesum,* was detected by the police near Bremen. During the Whitsunday weekend they had gone camping dressed in garb typical of the *Bündische Jugend,* such as blue shirts, white stockings, blue pants, and blue jackets. Clashes with the HJ were feared, and so the police and Hitler Youth collaborated in disbanding this group.[4]

Similar groups, including some with female members, were maintained all over Germany; some persisted even into the war years. In Leipzig and Berlin a *Jungenschaft* chapter coalesced around Horst Vanja and lasted until 1942. They, too, planned hiking weekends; they wore characteristic hiking dress and took along mandolins to accompany songs by Bertolt Brecht and Russian Cossack melodies, and books to read by censored authors such as Ricarda Huch and the early Weimar youth movement mentor, Stefan George. Politically, the spectrum of youth groups ranged from Communism to liberal democracy to the Catholic Center of Heinrich Brüning, one of the Republic's last chancellors. Another clique that had originated around Frankfurt, the *Orden der Pachanten,* had no less than fifty members. Its tradition was that of the *Nerother Bund,* which had long been forbidden by the Nazis.[5] This group and another Frankfurt group named *Bündischer Selbstschutz* hiked to secret camp sites as far away as Berlin, Bremen, and Nuremberg in defiance of Nazi rules. They were kept alive by apprentices, many from the graphics trade, who supported and joined their activities. The Don Cossack male choir, which gave concerts across Europe to some of these youths, symbolized freedom of expression and spirit against the totalitarianism of the Third Reich and the Soviet Union. Yet another group that stood outside the HJ was the *Schwarze Schar* in Berlin, which managed to hold a camp meeting on the Baltic island of Rügen in 1938 and whose male members kept in contact with one another even while serving in the Wehrmacht.[6] In spring 1939 the Gestapo spotted similar groups around Munich, which they could not name but were able to identify by their strange outfits, often with "laughable headdress"; without a moment's hesitation, the policemen earmarked these groups "as a danger for the state youth."[7] Even in Vienna in 1940 and thereafter, several hundred *bündische* youths rapturously attended Don Cossack choir concerts before they were interrogated and imprisoned by the secret police.[8]

On the Roman Catholic side, the oppositional *Graue Orden* (Gray Order) was founded in 1934, at a time when Catholic youth organizations were already heavily under fire. The group seems to have had at least 150 members in 1936, mostly from West and Southwest Germany. In 1934 they hiked to Lapland, and in 1936 to Montenegro. Although they behaved like the *bündisch* youth, and carried similar paraphernalia such as the peaked *Kote* tent which had been proscribed by the HJ, they were much more interested in spiritual content. They read texts by the Catholic theologian Romano Guardini and the Jewish philosopher Martin Buber. In January 1938, eighteen of their members were arrested by the Gestapo, but during their subsequent trial for subversion they were freed because of a general amnesty in celebration of the Anschluss with Austria.[9]

Considerably more risky was the behavior in Bruchsal in the Baden region of a Catholic Gymnasium student group named *Christopher,* which in May 1941 was being led by Wilhelm Eckert. On the twelfth of that month the Gestapo caught him red-handed in his parents' house with a copying machine, used for the manufacture of a pro-Catholic, anti-Nazi group letter intended for soldiers at the front. This was after Baldur von Schirach's compulsory Youth Ordinance of March 1939, and so the members of Eckert's group, who had avoided the HJ, were expelled from Gymnasium and their parents punished.

Franz Schmitt, a mentoring priest to the group, was apprehended and later executed in the aftermath of the anti-Hitler July 1944 putsch. Eckert himself received a comparatively mild sentence of eight months in prison. Upon his release he was to be conscripted for work in Occupied Ukraine, but he preferred to join the Wehrmacht, and there he died as a soldier during a battle in Sicily in July 1943.[10]

Walter Klingenbeck, a Munich mechanic's apprentice, age sixteen in May 1940, fared worse. Over the radio he had heard about the massive destruction of Rotterdam at the hands of German troops invading Holland. By 1941, he had gathered around him a number of equally outraged young Catholics, formerly from Catholic youth groups like his own, *St. Ludwig*. At first they listened to enemy radio stations, which could have cost them their lives even then, but later they printed and duplicated flyers with slogans such as "Down with Hitler," and they painted the British victory symbol "V" on Munich residences. In 1941 and 1942, they assembled three radio transmitters and did a trial broadcasting of anti-Nazi propaganda. The police got to Klingenbeck and two of his friends in early 1942. The friends were sent to the penitentiary, but Klingenbeck was beheaded in Munich's Stadelheim prison in August of 1943.[11]

Given the irreconcilable differences between Nazis and Catholics on core issues of dogma and ideology, it is not surprising to find the remnants of Catholic youth groups so persistent even after official proscription. The Protestant youth tended to be much more tame and accommodating. But even among the Protestant youths there were some who dared to stray from the official path. In February 1939 in Rothenburg ob der Tauber, Protestant HJ and BDM members organized themselves, with the help of their church, in an illegal group, which local Nazi officials urged be disbanded.[12] And in November 1940 Augsburg's HJ leadership criticized get-togethers of Protestant youths in church-owned buildings in nearby Lechhausen for more than two hours every Saturday, a prime time during which the HJ itself would schedule major events.[13]

The last of the former youth leagues who attempted independence or considered resistance to the Third Reich were the Marxist ones. In addition to illegal hiking trips, they discussed Karl Marx, Communism, the Soviet Union, and possibly active resistance in secret meetings.[14] A *Schwarze Schar,* or Black Band, originated illegally in Berlin in January 1934. Its leader was Heinz Steurich, "Jonny" to his friends. Steurich offered a roof for other "red leagues" to congregate under: *Rote Pfadfinder, Rote Jungpioniere, Turnverein Mariendorf.* Until many of their members were caught in 1937, these leagues organized hikes and, during the Olympic Games in summer 1936, attempted to make contact with foreign youth representatives. The *Schwarze Schar* even conducted rifle training at a shooting range, although it does not seem to have been overtly conspiratorial. Nevertheless, one leader, Rudolf Wernicke, or "Ajax," committed suicide during the Gestapo raids of 1937. Some members of this group survived in a loose network until May of 1945.[15] A similar group of fifteen young Marxists, previously tied to the *Sozialistische Arbeiterjugend,* was broken up in Bremen in November of 1938 and their members, two of them girls, were put behind bars.

Some dissenting youths in the German Reich had not been organized earlier, but had found each other and then collaborated in the interest of a common goal, which was hatred of the Nazi system and its large, odious youth cohorts. One such group existed in Vienna, led by the Gymnasium student Josef Landgraf. He was only fourteen when the Anschluss occurred in March 1938, and even though we do not know how he had been socialized as a child in the Austrofascist system of Engelbert Dollfuss and Kurt von Schuschnigg, it is certain that it did not take him long to develop a dislike of the new regime. At first a member of the Hitler Youth, he soon avoided its meetings and drills altogether. Unusually mature for his age, he gathered around him other students, three of whom were put on trial alongside Landgraf for treason in late summer 1942.

Landgraf and his friends had been listening to the BBC even before the war and had collected newspaper clippings about Churchill, Roosevelt, and Anthony Eden because they saw them as guarantors of world peace. By autumn 1941 they were authoring anti-Nazi texts and distributing them in flyers. Hitler, "The Bloody," and his paladins were depicted as rapacious world conquerors, bent on subjugating other nations, including of course Austria. Adverse military news from enemy broadcasts and anti-Hitler jokes completed Landgraf's leaflets. In one of these, directed toward Austrian farmers, he wrote: "Do you want to deliver your crops to market so that Göring and his cronies can become even fatter?" Another said: "Copy this flyer and help us enlighten the others! Turn only to good and reliable friends! You must convince the undecided by handing them the flyer in such a way that they cannot recognize it was you!" The sheets were sent to others by mail or were distributed in the streets or near buildings. A fellow student and a suspicious teacher, who later testified against him, betrayed Landgraf and his friends to the Gestapo. He was apprehended on September 20, 1941.[16] Landgraf was condemned to death but later was pardoned.

These activities demonstrated a great deal of courage and idealism, especially for so young a fighter. Helmuth Hübener, a Hamburg youth from a Mormon family, was similarly motivated. Only seventeen years old, he was a clerk in the civil service when he was executed after a trial by the infamous People's Court on October 27, 1942. Even though he was a Mormon, it is not certain how much his religion had to do with his anti-Nazi attitude, because Mormons in Germany were law-and-order people who were generally pro-Hitler.[17] Hübener, too, got together with three friends, listened to enemy broadcasts, and distributed what he had heard through leaflets. Among these was one with a message to the HJ: "German Boys! Do you know the country without freedom, the land of terror and tyranny? Well, you know what it is all right, it's just that you do not wish to say it. They have already oppressed you to the point where you don't dare any more, for fear of punishment. Yes, you are right, it is Germany, Hitler-Germany."[18]

In a similar manner the Berlin publisher Wolf Jobst Siedler, at age seventeen, got together with Ernst Jünger, the son of the famous novelist of the same name, whose trench novels from the Great War were then studied in Nazi elite schools.[19] Jünger and Siedler had long been friends in a Gymnasium class in Berlin, where Siedler's father, critical of Hitler, moved in industrialist circles. Ernst Jünger Sr. was posted to the Wehrmacht in Occupied Paris; a self-professed non-Nazi of dubious fascist distinction, he still adhered to elitist ideas of a handpicked Spartan caste.[20] His son and Wolf Jobst in November 1943 were part of a group of auxiliary cannoneers (Flakhelfer), all Berlin classmates, at an airport on the North Sea island of Spiekeroog. "The two of us founded a group to oppose the Hitler Youth at our boarding school," Siedler recalls. "We also discussed what would happen if the war was lost." Young Ernst, who according to Siedler shared his father's dislike of vulgar mob rule, wrote, for others to read: "This war will never be ended unless an assassination attempt on Hitler succeeds. As long as Hitler is alive, there will never be an armistice." And: "When Hitler is hanged, I will personally walk barefoot from Berlin to Potsdam to help pull on the rope." Siedler and Jünger listened to enemy radio stations and then disseminated what they heard. The group was exposed by a spy in their midst, and Siedler and Jünger had to stand trial in January 1944. A military court sentenced them to a term in prison, but eventually both ended up as soldiers at the Italian front. Here Ernst was deliberately put at risk by his superiors, and he was killed by a bullet to his head, near Carrara, early in January 1945. Siedler suffered a kinder fate: an explosion that injured his left hand resulted in a lengthy stay in the hospital, which undoubtedly saved his life.[21]

Jünger and Siedler had derived much of their resentment against the Third Reich and its youth movement through first-hand experience with Hitler's military machine. This was also the case with the male members of the Munich-based White Rose resistance group; at the same time its female members had to accept at face value alarming stories about the Wehrmacht and SS which they heard from their brothers and boyfriends. Of these young women, Sophie Scholl was by far the most important. But as a teenager, Sophie too had been in the Hitler Youth. "Sophie at that time was very enthusiastic, very fanatically in favor of National Socialism." So reports Eva Amann, who at the age of twelve was in the BDM of Ulm when Sophie, the sister of Hans, Inge, Werner, and Elisabeth Scholl, was a leader of the Jungmädel, the BDM cadre under Jutta Rüdiger consisting of girls aged ten to fourteen. Back then, in 1936, Sophie was fifteen. Although in most respects she was an enthusiastic BDM girl like the others, in some ways she was different from the other girl leaders; she wore her hair short and took the socialism in Nazism seriously by distributing the food rations during BDM hikes painstakingly evenly. "Sophie always liked to sing ballads, very heroic ballads. They dealt with Siegfried, who carried the gold from the heath." She accompanied herself on the guitar, and the atmosphere was romantic, with a campfire. "Yes, Sophie was very romantic and idealistic and also fanatic." She loved exercising her girls while marching: "Left, two, three . . . that was really dashing."[22]

The graphic artist Otl Aicher, then a classmate of Sophie's younger brother Werner, remembers Sophie from their shared adolescence in Ulm. "She leaned her head back a bit, blinked against the disappearing sun and walked with her hip a tad forward, her feet somewhat apart." In contrast to her sister Inge, tall and four years her senior, Sophie was diffident and indulged an almost extreme physical and mental rigorousness. "She had a straight intellect and could catch up quickly," says Aicher. Sophie was certain the invasion of the Western Allies was imminent when she talked with Aicher at the end of 1942; Aicher was a soldier home on furlough, and they both anticipated a catastrophe at Stalingrad.[23] By that time Sophie was receiving letters from her boyfriend, twenty-five-year-old Wehrmacht Captain Fritz Hartnagel, who informed her of the desperate situation around the doomed city before he was flown out. He wrote about "thousands of fugitives, women and small children and old men without shelter or food," and that he had assisted one old man, scarcely able to walk, as well as a young woman.[24] Already in April 1940 Sophie, nineteen years old and in her last year at the Ulm Gymnasium, had written: "Sometimes I shudder because of the war, and all hope for a better future is leaving me. I just do not wish to think about it, but soon there will be nothing more than politics, and as long as that is so confounded and so evil, it would be cowardly to turn one's back on it." Sophie was at that time still a leader in the BDM.[25]

Sophie's brother Hans, born in 1918, was tall and handsome in a manner more immediately striking than his pretty, inner-directed sister. Aicher admired him deeply, although some of Hans's friends, while not denying his charisma, thought him "self-serving, filled with a sense of his own importance" and manipulative of people.[26] "He thought when he talked," remembers Aicher. "His was a rhetorical existence, dialogue as well as dialectics. Insights came to him as to a constantly turning spotlight on a beacon." He was "always radiating, always receptive. This technique invariably placed him in the center, even when he did not wish it." Like Inge, whom some remember as a much tougher BDM superior than Sophie, Hans was seen as a born leader, with an aura of natural authority for his friends.[27]

Like Sophie and Inge, Hans had been a junior chief in the Ulm HJ. When he joined the Hitler Youth in 1933, he did so, at the time, in protest against his father's thoroughly democratic convictions. Hans was then calling his father, Robert Scholl, a former Swabian small-town mayor and civic administrator, a "reactionary." Soon Hans became "an enthusiastic standard bearer." He carried the flag, representing 4,000 Ulm Hitler Youths, at the nearby Nuremberg Party rally in September 1935—the one at which the noxious Race Laws were promulgated. Significantly, this marked Hans's departure from Nazi ideals. He began to resent the pronounced militarism, the overt racism, the victimization of the weak. When a higher HJ leader was bullying a younger lad who could not hold the banner straight, Hans boiled over and hit the older boy in the face. In 1937 Hans joined one of the forbidden resurgent *bündische* groups, the *d.j.1.11* with secret ties to the exiled Eberhard Koebel.[28] At the end of the year he was arrested, in the wake of the police ordinances prohibiting such gatherings. Even Inge and Hans's younger brother Werner came under suspicion and spent weeks as a guest of the Gestapo, while Sophie was screened and quickly released. As a fresh volunteer for the Wehrmacht, Hans too won his freedom before long. In April 1939 he began to study medicine in

Munich, and in 1940 he was in a medical student company as an orderly with the advancing troops in France. By that time his opposition to the regime had clearly crystallized.[29]

The four other members of what was to become the active core of the White Rose resistance group were Willi Graf (b. 1918), Alexander Schmorell (b. 1917), Christoph Probst (b. 1919), and Jürgen (later George) Wittenstein (b. 1919), all of them friends and colleagues of Hans Scholl as university students of medicine. Wittenstein's rich industrialist mother had already smuggled a Jewish woman into Switzerland, from her country estate on Lake Constance.[30] Originally from Saarbrücken, Graf had been in the Catholic youth movement of the Republic and after 1933 was one of those German boys who steadfastly refused to join the Hitler Youth. Instead, in 1936 he became a member of the Gray Order, until it was extinguished in 1938. Graf was then studying medicine in Bonn, but he remained equally interested in history, philosophy, and theology. From June 1941 to April 1942 he served at the Russian front. After witnessing German war crimes at first hand, he wrote: "The war, especially here in the East, leads me to see things which are so terrible as I could never have thought possible." He was posted to Munich in spring 1942 to enable a completion of his medical course of studies.[31]

Schmorell had a German physician father, who was born in Russia and returned to Germany after the October Revolution, and a Russian mother who was the daughter of an Orthodox priest. After his mother died, his father began practicing medicine in Munich. Alexander learned fluent Russian from his nanny, Nanja, and was raised in the Russian Orthodox faith. When the group of *bündisch* youth he belonged to was conflated with the HJ, Schmorell withdrew immediately. He was something of a roamer, wandering around by himself and seeking new and strange friendships, often communing over jugs of wine with vagrants. Much like Hans Scholl, Schmorell was what the Hitler Youth coveted as "leadership material": he was a first-rate swimmer and fencer who also played the piano and sketched and turned into an expert sculptor. Wittenstein today calls him "a multifaceted and multigifted artist at heart."[32] But such an individualist had problems subordinating himself to the Wehrmacht, which he tried to leave once drafted, in 1938. While still in training he met up with the medical student Jürgen Wittenstein, one of the few White Rose survivors and today a distinguished thoracic surgeon in southern California. Schmorell himself began his medical studies in 1939, and in the fall of 1940 was a medical student at the University of Munich.

Christoph Probst's father was a passionate private scholar of Sanskrit with ample money and time, who lived in Zell near Berchtesgaden. Eventually Christoph was sent to a Gymnasium in Munich, where he met Schmorell. He too remained aloof from the HJ but, like Scholl and Graf, showed no interest in any of the illegal or secret groups. Probst tried to overcome his revulsion against the Reich's labor and military service by immersing himself in art, literature, and music. He began his medical studies in Munich out of a general love of humankind, and specifically out of hostility to the euthanasia program of the Nazis, to which, as many Germans were becoming aware, the mentally and physically infirm were increasingly falling victim after 1939. He was the only one of the five main principals in the White Rose who, at the time of their arrest in February 1943, was married and had children.[33]

In the fall of 1941 Otl Aicher informed Hans Scholl of the written protests by Clemens Graf Galen, the Catholic Bishop of Münster, against Hitler's euthanasia campaign. Letters and flyers with such contents had been dropped into people's mailboxes in Ulm, which was in the vicinity of the killing centers at Grafeneck and Kaufbeuren. They originated with three Gymnasium students, one of whom, Hans Hirzel, knew the Scholls. This was the first time that Hans Scholl commented on the expediency of owning a print duplication machine.[34] By early 1942, in Munich, the medical students were already active, preparing their resistance flyers. Hans reluctantly initiated his sister Sophie into his circle only after her urging, when she joined him in

Munich in May to take up the study of biology and philosophy. Between June and July, the first four of a total of six *Weisse Rose* flyers were sent out to the students in the university.[35]

Soon afterward, the medical student company with Hans Scholl and his friends was ordered to leave for the eastern front, to work as auxiliary physicians right behind the lines. Passing through Poland, they were appalled by the treatment of the population and what they saw of the abuse of the Jews. Utterly shocked, Wittenstein photographed the victims of the Warsaw Ghetto. These German medical students were impressed by Russia because of the simplicity of the peasants, the nostalgia of their folk songs (just as the Cossacks had impressed the Weimar youth movement), and the expansive landscape in which they sensed the Russian soul. Dostoyevsky became their quintessential author, as he had been for earlier generations of pro-Russian Germans. Schmorell, who with his knowledge of the language and of the mentality of the people was able to arrange meetings with the peasants, further advanced this idealization of Russia. This romance with Russia was in stark contrast to the human tragedies of pain and death which the medical students had to cope with in the field hospitals. At the end of August, Scholl wrote that he could hear the moaning of his wounded patients day and night, and neither music, nor Dostoyevsky, could help him get over it. Small, simple acts of kindness, whenever possible, helped to ease the young men's own pain from day to day. When Scholl met an old, suffering Jew in a work detail, he handed him his entire tobacco rations, and Schmorell risked court-martial after he chided a Wehrmacht soldier who had beaten a Soviet prisoner to a pulp. Wittenstein took pictures of "some of the horrors: shot-down Russian planes, willfully desecrated churches and icons." And he saw "trucks crowded with people disappear into a forest, heard rifle shots, and saw the trucks return empty." In a train on their way back home, the group of medical students sang anti-Nazi songs, unmolested. Their mood was one of invincibility and soaring hope as they returned to Munich in November 1942.[36]

By that time, there existed a loose circle of more mature friends who were supporting the Scholl group spiritually and psychologically. Probably the most important of these was Professor Carl Muth, a left-leaning Catholic writer and scholar whose journal *Hochland* had been prohibited by the Nazis in 1941. Although Hans Scholl himself was Protestant, Graf and Probst and a few others in the outer circle were Catholics. During the summer of 1942, Scholl catalogued Muth's extensive library and had many heart-to-heart conversations with the older man. In spring 1942 Scholl met the architect Manfred Eicke-meyer, who confided in him what he had seen in Occupied Poland, where he had supervised construction work. Eickemeyer told Scholl of "shootings by the SS of Poles and Russians," and, since he had gotten around quite a bit, of "how the Germans had carried on there." Another influential mentor was the philosopher Theodor Haecker, who had written about human nature and had been silenced by the authorities in 1935. Haecker conveyed to Scholl that the current suffering of the Jews was due to Germans in their capacity as Christians and represented true evil—perhaps not a strikingly original hypothesis, but one which impressed Hans deeply.[37]

And then there was Kurt Huber. Born in 1893, he taught psychology at the university, but his formal training was in musicology and he was also very interested in philosophy. His specialty was Bavarian musical folklore. This had probably made him fall in line with the Nazis easily after their assumption of power. In 1935–36 Huber wanted to help found a "German School of Folk Music and Dance" in Munich, to counter "the champions of Marxist tendencies and Jewish products." He was interested in music to be played by laymen and folk dance "in the spirit of National Socialist weltanschauung." Toward that end, he wished to enlist the aid of the Hitler Youth.[38] At that time Huber believed in musicianship that was "rooted in the soil," to retain the "purity of German folk art," in the song of the fathers, "whose *völkisch* race was congenitally tied to our own."[39] Huber had moved to Berlin in 1938 to assume the direction of the newly created folk song archive, but had to return to Munich when he clashed with Nazi authorities over his professional future. As late as 1940 he had joined the Nazi Party, probably to increase his chances for a full chair at the university, where he was teaching as a poorly paid adjunct professor. His ingrained Catholicism, his treatment at the hands of the authorities, and possibly a growing concern over what he cumulatively witnessed in the dictatorship slowly turned him into an enemy of the Third Reich. He certainly was opposed to the regime when he met the Scholls for the first time in July 1942, although it is still unclear exactly how altruistic his motives were then.[40] An indication of his state of mind during this phase can be gathered from a lecture that Wittenstein heard him give on Spinoza. The seventeenth-century philosopher Benedict Spinoza was a Jew, and it was forbidden to teach his ideas. "But Professor Huber managed his lecture so brilliantly that it became evident that this 'despised, decadent Jew' was one of Germany's most important philosophers."[41]

In December of that year there was another important meeting between Huber and the White Rose group. The emblem of the White Rose was now on the flyers that were circulating. It had been taken from writings by the nineteenth-century romantic Clemens Brentano, who had composed songs of liberty against Napoleon, and it symbolized freedom of thought and expression. In January 1943, the most active month for the White Rose, Huber was an integral member of the group. More leaflets were prepared; they were sent off in the hundreds by mail and distributed in people's mailboxes in the towns surrounding Munich, some as far away as Frankfurt and Vienna. Several thousand leaflets were placed in Munich itself. On the fourteenth of the month, Munich's Gauleiter, Paul Giesler, asserted in a speech at the university that women were useless as students and thus "had better give a child to the Führer"; they could easily produce academic credentials in the form of one son a year. Those girls not attractive enough to find a boyfriend might be taken care of by his own adjutants. The crude import of his speech first provoked a riot among those students who had heard him in the lecture hall and then caused a larger disturbance among the entire student body. The Gestapo arrested a few students but let them go after several days.[42]

Then came news of the German defeat at Stalingrad on February 2, 1943. Against the background of the recent altercation with Giesler and the demonstration of student dissent, White Rose members felt certain that their own victory was not far away, and they became fool-hardy. For several nights they engaged in dangerous actions, painting slogans such as "Freedom," "Down with Hitler," and "Hitler mass murderer" as well as crossed-out swastikas on university walls and free spaces in the streets surrounding the massive main building.[43] One incensed observer reported that they had used red paint to print those slogans on the sidewalks of the major thoroughfare, Ludwigstrasse.[44] Wittenstein wrote similar graffiti in the restrooms of the university.[45] The group then mass-manufactured a sixth flyer, which Huber actually conceived and wrote for them, in which he cleverly capitalized on the disaster of Stalingrad. On February 18, nearly two thousand copies of this flyer were distributed by Hans and Sophie Scholl in broad daylight throughout the university building on Ludwigstrasse and were thrown over the balcony of the inner, glass-covered light well. They were observed by a caretaker, who immediately took them to the university rector, Professor Walther Wüst, a Colonel in the SS and an intimate of Himmler's. Wüst held the two in his office until the Gestapo came to take them away.[46] Hans and Sophie Scholl together with Christoph Probst were tried before the People's Court on February 22. Graf, Schmorell, and Huber followed a few months later. (Schmorell had tried to flee to Switzerland, but had been hindered by deep snow. A former girlfriend, Gisela Schertling, allegedly betrayed him after recognizing him in a Munich air raid shelter.)[47] The sentence for all was death by guillotine.[48] When Hans put his head on the block, he shouted: "Long live freedom!" Sophie said to her parents, who had come to say good-bye from Ulm: "This will make waves."[49] But as courageous as her remarks were at the time, they were not prescient.

The leaflets distributed by the White Rose in 1942 and early 1943 are characterized by a mixture of high idealism and crass naïveté. But the contents of these flyers and the consequences of their fearless distribution made these young Germans, most of whom had barely

graduated from the Hitler Youth, into the few true heroes of the
unevenly organized resistance movement against the Nazi regime,
from beginning to end.[50] What stands out most clearly from the White
Rose group's proclamations is the clear characterization and condemnation of tyranny, abhorred by civilized societies since the Enlightenment. "Nothing is less worthy of a cultured nation," began the first
flyer, "than to allow it to be 'governed' without protest by a clique of
rulers who are dependent on irresponsible and dark drives." In the second flyer it is astutely observed that, from the beginning, the Nazi
movement was predicated on a need to defraud the citizens; always rot-
ten to the bone, it was built on lies. This assertion was at odds with the
widespread German belief, until about January 1945, that with all its
faults, the Nazi movement was always salvageable because it had the
virtuous Hitler at its center.[51] Hans Scholl and his friends showed a
healthy democratic sense when they urged, in the fifth flyer, that in the
future, a viable Germany could only be based on a federal system as an
integral part of a rejuvenated Europe.

Also notable in the White Rose leaflets is the frequent allusion to
German classical and romantic ideals and icons—in particular Goethe,
Schiller, and Novalis, but also the universally adopted Aristotle and
Lao-tzu. Such references are characteristically couched in the jargon of
the German *Bildungsbürgertum,* the humanistically educated intellectual elite, of which these young men and women would have been
future members. In that spirit, the second flyer began: "It is impossible
to take on National Socialism intellectually, because it is itself anti-
intellectual." In their last leaflet the group's members identified themselves shrewdly, using the National Socialists' own terminology, as
"workers of the brain," and condemned the Hitler Youth, the SA, and
the SS as primitives who for years had tried to anesthetize "the most
formative educational years of our lives."

Alongside the western-humanist commitment, a strong religious
conviction shines through these pages. "Christian and Occidental culture" is a phrase that appears early in the first leaflet and is echoed
throughout. The idea of a cleansing through suffering, the concept of

"guilt" or "shared guilt," and that of "punishment" are key Christian notions. The Nazi state is identified as "the dictatorship of evil" and Hitler is likened to Satan, the fallen angel, and his mouth to "the stinking pharynx of hell." A reference to "the fight against the demon, against the messenger of the anti-Christ" reflects the deep Catholic beliefs of approximately half of the White Rose core group.

What renders the six leaflets ultimately persuasive are the succinct references to past and current crimes of the regime, those things that for all Germans were unspeakable, if they were known at all. The White Rose states that "since the conquest of Poland three hundred thousand Jews in that country have been murdered in the most bestial manner." There is reference to the wholesale liquidation of the Polish intelligentsia and to the gruesomely onerous advance of the Wehrmacht on the eastern front, requiring the death of many German soldiers. This is in contrast to the "hero's death" of a husband, brother, or fiancé usually celebrated in the daily press, and for most Germans long a bitter cliché. In this regard, the leaflet of February 1943 is the most strongly worded, as it makes cutting allusions not only to the recent insult of the female university students by the prurient Giesler, but also, and more significantly, to the catastrophe at Stalingrad: "Thoroughly shaken, our people is witnessing the destruction of the men of Stalingrad. Three-hundred-and-thirty thousand German men have been senselessly and irresponsibly hounded, to die and perish, on account of the brilliant strategy of that World War I corporal. Führer, we thank you!"

These observations and analyses cannot be outweighed by the few misconceptions or wrong judgments contained in those leaflets. Their authors might have been aware that it would be senseless, even counterproductive, to conjure up Goethe at a time when this quintessential German genius was appropriated (as was Beethoven)[52] to be cited when needed by Nazi ideologues and propagandists. (This was not so true of Goethe's friend Schiller, to whose universal cries for freedom, for instance in *Wilhelm Tell,* the Nazis could react phobically.)[53] The White Rose conspirators were correct in describing the plight of the

Polish intelligentsia, but their claim that noble Polish girls had been shipped to Norwegian brothels for the SS was unsubstantiated. They also assumed incorrectly that the Nazis were financing their war economy largely by printing paper money as needed, and they overestimated the slave-like labor of German industrial workers, who in fact were earning higher wages from increased armaments production. Scholl and his friends printed entreaties for "passive resistance" on the part of the entire population at a time when such resistance would be identified as active opposition punishable by death. Most naïve, and at the same time most touching, was the repeated assurance that the Third Reich was near its end, that "the war is approaching its certain finale," even that "the war is already lost." Nothing could have been further from the truth, as several more German offensives against the Allies, and a second, more diffuse and morally much less credible resistance attempt against the regime in July 1944, were yet to show.

The Munich White Rose had its support roots in Ulm, and sympathetic friends as far away as Hamburg, Freiburg, Saarbrücken, and Berlin. Otl Aicher, born in 1922 like his friend Werner Scholl, belonged to Ulm's subversive subculture. Aicher had been idiosyncratic enough never to join the Hitler Youth (and consequently had been prevented from completing Gymnasium); as a teenager, he had been repeatedly nabbed by the police on charges of vagrancy.[54] Then there was the older Inge Scholl, who had chosen not to be a student in Munich and therefore, like Werner and Otl, was not implicated in the activities of early 1943.[55] But all three were interrogated at the time by the Gestapo, although later released. Werner was reported as missing on the eastern front by that summer.[56] Sophie's close friend Susanne Hirzel, who moved between Ulm and Stuttgart, was also interrogated, and she and her brother Hans Hirzel, aged eighteen in summer 1943, were jailed for several months.[57] At the University of Hamburg, Hans Leipelt, who had a Jewish mother and who had been in 1942–43 a chemistry student in Munich, spread White Rose ideas and planned acts of sabotage in Hamburg. He acted together with his friends Traute Lafrenz, a former girlfriend of Hans Scholl, Heinz Kucharski, and

Greta Rothe, even after the death of the Scholl siblings. Lafrenz eluded the Gestapo, as did Wittenstein and Kucharski. Leipelt was executed in 1945; Rothe died in transit between prisons.[58] In Saarbrücken, Willi Bollinger, a friend of Graf, had just enough time to remove printing gear and leftover flyers before the Gestapo caught up with him, sentencing him to three months in jail in April 1943.[59] And in Berlin, university students who had received flyers in March 1943 from Wittenstein, who had smuggled them there from Munich by train, proceeded to duplicate them for shipment to Switzerland, Sweden, and England, to alert the world.[60]

At the height of the war the authorities identified other groups of youthful opponents to the regime. Most lacked the altruism of the White Rose but shared with its members important concerns on other counts. Chief among those concerns was a hatred of the monopolistic control exerted over them by the Hitler Youth. In an attempt to categorize this opposition, the judiciary, the police, and the HJ leadership came up with a range of rebellious attributes, from criminal activities to sexual promiscuity to Communism, but also including loyalty to traditional *bündische* ideals and preferences for Anglo-American values. Nevertheless, the authorities themselves realized that despite substantial distinctions between opposition groups, the Nazis had to blur these differences and pathologize and criminalize all their members, irrespective of their offenses, in order to resist and defeat them.[61]

The first of these groups, and surely the least idealistic and politically sensitive, were the cliques, bands, and gangs dispersed all over the Reich, some of whom, particularly in South Germany, liked to call themselves *Blasen,* or Bubbles. They tended to be workers or trade-shop apprentices of proletarian or lower-middle-class backgrounds, with spotty or non-existent Hitler Youth membership records and a marked predilection for petty crime. They were not particularly unique to the Third Reich; similar groups had existed in the Weimar Republic and even before then, with comparable resistance to authority. In the post-1933 context, however, anti-authority had changed to anti-authoritarian, and the cliques' transgressions assumed at least partially the dimensions of political protest. The young boys and their girl-friends of the Munich *Blasen* and similar gangs in the rest of Germany resisted the limits on their personal freedom as dictated by the Hitler Youth, and they expressed their anger not only by staying away from HJ events but also by committing acts of sabotage, theft, and some-times gross sexual indecency to protest against the society that har-bored the HJ.

It is significant that these groups, irrespective of their time of origin, became an acute threat to the regime only after the introduction of mandatory Hitler Youth service in March 1939. This was in the sum-mer before the war, when young men were being drafted in larger numbers. What the authorities characterized as unruly misfits were spotted in Breslau, Chemnitz, Hamburg, and parts of East Prussia and the Lower Danube region. In Vienna, where they had a sense of fash-ion reminiscent of the demimonde, these youths were called *Schlurfe,* or Slouches. "They let their hair grow and groomed it carefully, wore especially long jackets and long, wide pants and thin, very long neck-ties and they picked up super girls," recalls the author Ernst Jandl, "and they had switchblades and knuckledusters, and no one in HJ uniform could go to the Prater at night without the risk of being stabbed," as had been known to happen.[62] In Munich in the fall of 1941, appren-tices who belonged to an *Auerblase* (named after local wetlands) com-mitted petty theft of bicycle parts and somebody's military boots, and tried to break into telephone booths and people's homes; they were in competition with a Munich *Lidoblase* and a *Spitzblase*. Disdain for the HJ among all was de rigueur.[63]

In Hamburg, too, with its large proletarian subculture especially in suburban Harburg and Altona, attacks on HJ groups and their quar-ters were reported as early as the fall of 1939.[64] The Hamburg gang members also wore their hair long and showed off their adventurous clothes, sometimes embellished with white scarves. Their cliques, staffed with apprentices and pupils of the less exclusive schools, had names like "Jumbo Band" and "Bismarck Band" and "Death Head's Band." Petty theft, often of goods from air-raid-damaged stores, alternated with physical attacks on the Hitler Youth, particularly its police division, the universally hated Streifendienst (SRD).[65] These boys and their girlfriends were sexually active; moreover, the boys might sexually molest young women in the streets as well as carry their ill-gotten loot to the brothels of Hamburg's red-light district.[66] Even by January 1945 this phenomenon had not abated; the German youth gangs now directed their lawless activities against foreign workers, who in the face of certain Nazi defeat were moving about more defiantly and were envied for their black-market connections.[67]

Relatives of the Munich *Blasen* conducted their criminal activities also in the Bavarian hinterland, as in the provincial town of Landshut in the north. In early 1943 an "Al Capone Gang" operated in Hanover, whose prey were mostly civilians on downtown streets, and in the Pomeranian Treptow region American-gangster-style hoodlums stole goods after several break-ins; they were disenchanted apostates from the Hitler Youth.[68] In 1943 and 1944 gang activities were reported for Cottbus, Erfurt, Magdeburg, and Königsberg in East Germany, for Alfeld in central Germany, as well as for Berlin. Railway stations were favorite targets. In the capital, youths in their middle teens specialized in breaking into bakeries and grocery stores, and again stole bicycles to get around the bomb craters. National Socialist symbols such as the Hitler greeting were ignored; they counted as little for these gangs as the Hitler Youth itself.[69] In Stettin on the Baltic Sea, cliques with names such as "Violet Blue" and "Fifth Column," some fifty teenagers strong, made trouble for the HJ by loitering en masse near the post office, stealing from tobacco stores, and grabbing radios from exposed basements. Seven automobiles were stolen, and female hangers-on were forced into sex. Under the cover of darkness, the Hitler Youth's SRD suffered badly. When these fifteen- to sixteen-year-old rebels were caught, however, it was found that several were themselves leaders in the Hitler Youth.[70]

Cliques with a similar social background but with stronger ideological ties to what had once been the German political left operated in East and West Germany. In the East they were concentrated in Leipzig and known as *Meuten,* or Mobs; in the West they operated out of Cologne and Düsseldorf and cities of the industrialized Ruhr such as Duisburg, Dortmund, and Essen. The names of the western groups varied, but they were mostly known as *Edelweisspiraten* (Edelweiss Pirates). The groups' locations in East and West explain the leanings to the left, for Saxony, the Rhineland, and the Ruhr Valley had, at various times before 1933, been strongholds of Communism. But vestiges of the *bündische* groups were also visible in the clothes they wore, the songs they sang, and the names that subgroups often bore. This was especially true in the West: if the authorities tended not to criminalize the *Edelweisspiraten* as much as the *Meuten,* it was because the former were able to trace deeper roots in the comparatively less dangerous *bündisch* tradition, in contrast to the Communist roots of the *Meuten.*[71]

The *Meuten* became active around Leipzig in 1937, when military conscription was well under way and the Hitler Youth was applying greater pressure to German boys and girls to join, albeit not yet by law. Like members of the *Blasen,* they were blue-collar workers, apprentices, and shop clerks. When the *Meuten* were not congregating in cinemas, public swimming pools, or formerly Communist neighborhood pubs, where card games and talking politics were popular, they liked to hike in groups, usually with their girlfriends, who were discouraged from participating in the beer hall discussions. These discussions, innocuous as they might have been, were not surprising, since some of the older ringleaders had been active in Communist youth groups of the late republican era; a smaller number came from the youth movement camp. These not always congruent traditions were reflected in the youths' motley clothes: plaid shirts, white socks, and lederhosen in summer, slalom shirts and ski pants in winter. The girls wore the long blue skirts of the traditional youth movement. Red kerchiefs as tokens of pro-left sympathies were very popular. The *Meuten* listened to Radio Moscow and, stretching the customary *bündisch* bias for everything Russian, romanticized conditions in the Soviet Union without really knowing much about them. A vulgarized Russian greeting, "bud cadoff," a fantasy name, was used instead of "Heil Hitler." The *Meuten* were not as sexually promiscuous as the less organized petty-criminal gangs, but they were certainly no prudes. Outright criminal activity even as a form of sabotage of the regime did not interest them. The overriding concern for all was, once again, the official power and sanction of the Hitler Youth (to which some of the *Meuten* members nominally belonged); therefore they sought open confrontations with its squads. HJ members were despised as prigs and snobs, as juveniles out of touch with the lower-class society and culture of which the *Meuten* were proud. One of their slogans was: "Beat the HJ wherever you come across them!" At the height of World War II, the Leipzig *Meuten* were estimated to be about 1,500 strong.[72]

That there were *Meuten* in Dresden and other Saxon towns is certain, for they roamed even in neighboring Thuringia. But the records on this activity are scarce, probably because those *Meuten* never gave the authorities sufficient cause for prosecution, as did the large original group in Leipzig. One of the tangible grounds for prosecution by the judiciary was Marxism.[73] However, Marxist ideology was less pronounced as a motivating force behind the actions of the western German *Edelweisspiraten,* if not entirely absent. There were even fewer former Communist youth leaders in these groups than in the East. While it is true that a similar proletarian subculture served as a breeding ground for these young blue-collar workers and apprentices, influencing their self-conception, attitudes, and actions, Communism was tempered in the West by middle-of-the-road Social Democracy. Hence a workers' song, passed down through Marxist tradition, could at times be heard, but this was not necessarily evidence of doctrinaire Communism;[74] it could have been filtered through the sieve of more bourgeois Social Democracy. Most of the Edelweiss Pirates had a journeyman's pride. They were fully employed and earning their keep. They were neither Communists nor scum, as they were regarded by their contemporaries, above all those in the Hitler Youth.[75] One former HJ leader even in the 1990s described them as "from the lowest circles . . . from a milieu, in which law and order were not known," and as people whom "one did not wish to touch with a ten-foot pole."[76] The only recorded example of a direct translation of orthodox proletarian loyalties into revolutionary violence stems from the summer and fall of 1944, when six boys aged sixteen to eighteen, members of an *Edelweiss* branch in Cologne-Ehrenfeld, assisted German desperadoes who were conspiring with East European foreign workers. These teens, related to or acquainted with former KPD members, distributed antiwar flyers and derailed freight trains. Then they got themselves handguns and became involved in the illegal procurement of ration cards, as well as robberies and the killings of a guard and a local Nazi leader. They were even planning to blow up Gestapo headquarters in Cologne when they were caught and executed, along with their accomplices, in a public hanging.[77]

These western groups had several things in common with the *Meuten:* their time of origin, their intense hatred of the control exercised by the Hitler Youth even if they were members, the adventurous semi-*bündisch* outfit, the hanging-out and roaming within local and regional boundaries, and the liberal sense of sexuality.[78] What set them apart, however, were four factors: their idiosyncratic romanticism, their desire for mobility vis-à-vis the state and society, their view of girls as inferior (apart from women's sexual usefulness), and their geographic dispersion.

The romanticism of the *Edelweisspiraten* was reflected in their name alone: "Edelweiss Pirates," some of whom actually wore little Edelweiss pins. Some branches called themselves Navajos, after the North American Indian tribe; others were Kittelbach Pirates, named after a stream running north of Düsseldorf. These designations as well as the songs they favored and the nicknames they used were handed down from traditional youth movement lore. The proximity to Germany's western borders may have inspired them with fantasies connected to the United States, Mexico, and other Latin American countries. In addition to the obligatory "Cossacks," their songs featured buffalos bellowing across the prairies, where Bobby was throwing his lasso and his girl never said no, after whiskey had made the rounds with the boys. If there was no explicit political meaning in those lines, there were other ditties warning the Hitler Youth's SRD of imminent destruction: "Edelweiss is marching, watch out, clear the way!"[79] The conjuring-up of America as a representation of unlimited opportunities implicitly criticized a totalitarian society that increasingly fettered its young, and the express mention of the Hitler Youth targeted the aggressor.

The *Edelweisspiraten* disliked the HJ not so much for ideological reasons, such as its racialist world view, as for the fact that it denied them mechanisms for social advancement. They were acutely aware that the many lower and middle-level leaders in the monopolistic youth organization were usually chosen from among Gymnasium students whose parents were members of the social elite. Young Rhenish apprentices or skilled and unskilled workers with an elementary-school education felt ill at ease in a hierarchy that preserved the old order by precluding social mobility within HJ ranks. Despite Schirach's and his successor Axmann's perennial slogans in which they tried to connect to the HJ's pre-1933 lower-class tradition, such practices persisted. Thus these young workers at first avoided, then collided with the HJ, then kept to themselves. At seventeen or eighteen they preferred to join the Wehrmacht, often volunteering, which would open conventional paths of advancement.[80] In the case of the *Meuten* it was their more manifest leftist persuasion which prevented them from taking that voluntary step, even though they, too, would not resist conscription in the end. Ultimately, this implied a tacit recognition of the Hitler state by these "pirates," if never of the Hitler Youth, with whom they sought altercations whenever possible.

As a rule the *Edelweisspiraten* took the principle of exclusion of women from their private meeting places farther even than the *Meuten*, because their lower-middle-class (not Communist) understanding of society was that women were inferior to men and had to be kept in their place.[81] Ironically, this paralleled both the practices of the Hitler Youth in its placement and treatment of the BDM, and the ideology and real world of Nazi Germany, where a male-supremacist Party ruled and egocentric men took advantage of virtually all the women in their midst.

Starting from the proletarian/lower-class subculture tied to industrial structures in the greater Ruhr area from Cologne in the Southwest
to Dortmund in the Northeast, the *Edelweisspiraten* spread from their
core bases to locales as far south as Frankfurt, and places as far north as
Minden. Moreover, because of demographic changes resulting from
the bombings, such as huge evacuations from city to country and
region to region, but also as a consequence of the HJ's Kinderlandverschickung program, some *Edelweisspiraten* were swept away from western Germany entirely. In early 1945, when everything was in chaos,
some of these youths could be seen huddling together in the train station bunker of Hanover, hundreds of miles east from the Rhine and
the Ruhr.[82]

It is on record that Düsseldorf's *Edelweisspiraten* provoked clashes
with members of the Swing Youth whenever they encountered them,
although both groups shared an opposition to the HJ.[83] But the
Swings were different from the Edelweiss Pirates and the *Meuten* in
more ways than one. Most important was that, like the members of the
White Rose, the Swing Youth came from a higher social background—
upper-middle-class with more than a smattering of lower-middle-class
members, but no workers. Commensurate with their superior social
position, the Swings tended to be at the Gymnasien from which the
Hitler Youth recruited its local and regional leaders and which were
anathema to the less formally educated gangs in Saxony and the
Rhineland. The Swings, both boys and girls, ritualized their aesthetic
and economic differences from the HJ through a predilection for
Anglo-American swing and Dixieland jazz music, indulgence in the so-
called swing dance, trendy fashions, and the consumption of refined
liquors. True to their self-image as potential elites, there was not a trace
of left-wing ideology motivating them, not even in the somewhat
nominal mode of the Pirates, let alone the quasi-Communist conviction of most *Meuten.* One symbol of opposition, however, which the
Swings certainly shared with the more primitive, petty-criminal gangs
such as the South German *Blasen* was self-indulgence, whereas mem-

bers of the *Edelweisspiraten,* the *Meuten,* and especially the White Rose
were more idealistic and practiced self-denial.

It is characteristic of whatever German political opposition to Hitler
and the Nazi regime existed that it was divided into several factions
from beginning to end. Not the least of these divisions was social. For
all their commonalities, the divisions between the dissenting youth
groups, albeit at separate levels, were similar to divisions characterizing
the older and more experienced intellectuals, politicians, and military
leaders of the classical resistance. Such parallels help to explain why the
youthful dissenters ultimately had to be defeated by an unforgiving
regime, as were the older resisters.

Like the other dissenting youth groups, the Swings had originated
around 1938, in the wealthy northern port of Hamburg, and assuredly
for the same reasons. Socially privileged boys and girls who knew one
another from Gymnasien, some of them very exclusive, and from elite
sports clubs, would gather together at a major downtown skating rink.
In the words of one Hitler Youth critic, "they visited certain cafés
in droves, wore conspicuous clothes, and enthusiastically embraced
English music and English dances."[84] There were smaller groups in
Frankfurt, Kiel, Breslau, Brunswick, and Berlin, probably transplanted
there from Hamburg, although Frankfurt's swing and jazz subculture
arose independently.[85]

The Hamburg Swings came to the attention of regional authorities
in early 1940, a few months after the Hitler Youth leadership had been
authorized to utilize state agencies for the enforcement of compulsory
HJ attendance in accordance with the decree of March 1939. The well-
heeled sons and daughters of some, if by no means all, of Hamburg's
patricians rejected such force either by quitting the HJ service altogether or by attending irregularly; a few tried to sit on both sides of the
fence. In the following months until 1942–43, when the group was
suppressed, the authorities became aware of various performances and
personal practices, more or less visible to outsiders, which the Swings
of Hamburg decided to engage in. These included swing dance, based

on the American Lindy Hop of the 1920s and '30s, which was practiced at a number of semi-private and carefully chosen public venues.
The musical accompaniment was provided by indigenous German
bands playing American Benny Goodman-type swing, sometimes of
questionable amateur quality, but also by Dutch and Belgian professionals such as the John Kristel or Fud Candrix orchestras. Regarding
one large open Swing party at Hamburg's Curio-Haus in March 1940,
for which printed invitations had been sent to the cognoscenti, the
patroling HJ reported as follows: "An emcee announced the numbers
in English. English hit songs were played and crooned. Almost entirely
they were dancing swing, from the tamest to the wildest. They shoved
their upper torsos forward while shaking their lower bodies. Moreover,
many times 4–6 people danced and hopped around in circles, knock-
ing their hands together and even rolling their heads against each
other."[86]

In addition to the dance and swing music, the Hitler Youth officials
and their colleagues from the Gestapo took note of the peculiar dress,
hairstyles, and makeup of these individuals: "The male participants
were legitimized by their long hair, often reaching to their collars (hair
length up to 27 centimeters). Predominantly they wore long, frequently plaid British jackets, shoes with thick, light-colored crepe
rubber soles, eye-catching scarves, diplomats' hats on their heads, an
umbrella over the arm in every kind of weather." And, about the girls:
"They preferred their hair very long. Eyebrows were penciled in and
lips painted, and the fingernails were lacquered."[87]

The Nazis also noted the Swings' penchant for English and especially American films. Disapprovingly, they wrote: "The laid-back attitude shown in those films appealed so much to these adolescents that,
by their own admission, they consciously tried to make a derelict
impression. The 'American' element in their attitude and comportment to them constituted an ideal." Moreover, the inquisitors were
aware of the Swings' heavy trade in current swing and Dixieland
records, which allegedly were hot commodities demanding the highest
prices. Some of these records were reported to have been copied with

special appliances, changing hands for even more money. "The more fantastic and louder the disk, and the more bizarre and crazy the rhythm, the greater was the demand." The censors wrote down that non-"Aryan" members belonged to the clique, and that certain cafés and nightclubs were frequented with regularity, such as the Schiff Ahoi.[88]

More than anything, the HJ and Gestapo were intrigued by what they described in their reports as sexual practices, vibrant as they were refined, involving even fully Jewish girls between fifteen and eighteen. They observed such activity by the Swings in the nightclubs, in private homes, and during special outings in the environs of Hamburg. Alcohol was mentioned as an ever-ready stimulus. "Personal devotion usually played less of a role than the calculated choice of a partner for sexual intercourse," they quoted one of the arrested Swings as saying. "The girls kept moving around in our circle, with those partners being favored who possessed rooms safe from outside interference." At private parties in the wealthy parents' villas, it was reported that lots were drawn, "after which all participants lost their garments to the point of complete nakedness." Thereupon the boys would take turns with the girls in the available bedrooms. What was known as "French" practices would occur, pruriently described by the Nazi stenographers as "sexual deviance."[89]

Much of what the authorities took down on paper was exaggerated, but sometimes they had to fill in the gaps. Regarding the social background of the Swings, Propaganda Minister Joseph Goebbels in August 1941 spoke of Hamburg's "plutocratic youth," whose only goal was to avoid the Reich Labor Service and military conscription.[90] Although most of the fathers of the Swings were either well-off merchants or professionals such as physicians and lawyers, with residences in high-end areas like Blankenese and Harvestehude, some were master craftsmen or lower civil servants or office clerks, for example from Altona. The occupations of the Swings themselves reflected this, with probably no more than 70 percent attending Gymnasien and the rest in some practical training. And while the students received generous allowances from home, the employed white-collar workers were already earning money of their own. Girls belonged in disproportionately greater numbers to the latter group; they were accepted by the original skating-rink clique if they were attractive, showed some sense of refinement, especially in fashion, and embraced swing music and swing dance. As Robert Vogel, then the young heir to a shipping fortune, recalls: "Surely it was easier for girls to be upwardly mobile. I remember one whose father had a welding business, hence was a master tradesman. It is important to know that girls of the kind we preferred were rare. Yet girls of lower social status who were all right, meaning who were good-looking, were welcome in our midst." One such girl was Helga Rönn, a statuesque beauty whose father was a clerk and whose mother worked as a streetcar conductor; she herself was training in various shops but thought she would get into films. Another was Hanne-Lore Evers, with a retail grocer for a father, who was a trainee in the textile industry. As a result she had exquisite taste; she was pretty as well as artistic. Soon she was in the company of key members of the Swings.[91]

The elite background of the leading Swings like Vogel was determined by the social origins of the skating-rink crowd, who were members of exclusive sports clubs, especially clubs for water sports, in that world port on the Elbe River with its central Alster waterways. The Norddeutscher Regatta-Verein, for instance, produced national sailing champions and owned facilities for socializing, as did similarly exclusive clubs. Until 1940 these clubs had a rarefied atmosphere with afternoon teas, English-style, at which Dixieland or swing records would be played or live bands might perform. After spending hours of relaxation and leisure there, these privileged sons and daughters would then repair to one of several expensive cafés or nightclubs, most likely to continue their dancing to the swing of German and also foreign combos; this and the consumption of alcohol on those occasions were never questioned. In the cafés and nightclubs the boys would meet up with their (frequently lower-class) girlfriends. Hans Engel, the son of a business executive who had represented the Deutsche Reichsbahn in

New York, recalls that in the Café L'Arronge, the musicians performed "the newest American hits." Engel, whom his admirers called "Jaeggi" (in a vain attempt to pronounce "Jackie"), was knowledgeable about this music; in addition to excelling at tennis, field hockey, and ice hockey, he spoke fluent American slang and knew his Louis Armstrongs and Fats Wallers first-hand. Helga Rönn, too, went with friends to L'Arronge, but also to the Alsterpavillon (where Kristel and Candrix played), the Ex-Bar, and the less reputable Faun-Casino.[92]

A few of these watering holes were near the Dammtor railway station not far from the Alster, where the Swing crowd liked to hang out in the afternoons. Next to it was the Waterloo Cinema, which was progressive in that it featured Hollywood movies as long as that was possible, and whatever German films the Swings would deem acceptable, such as Theo Lingen's *Frau Luna* (1941).[93] Among the U.S. films was Hal Roach's sophisticated comedy *Topper* (1937) with Cary Grant and Constance Bennett, who played two wealthy, freewheeling socialites who appealed to the tastes of these young Hamburg sybarites.[94] Much loved were films with American popular music in them, preferably swing, such as the *Broadway Melody* flicks of 1936 and 1938 with Eleanor Powell, a dancer who was alluringly attractive to the Swings.[95] In *Broadway Melody* (1936) Powell impressed the lower-middle-class girls like Evers and Rönn because she got her rich and famous man in a Hollywood-type happy ending, and even more important, her character, Irene Foster, came from provincial Albany to rise to stardom in New York City. This double leitmotif of professional and social advancement was both American and modern, something which intelligent and anti-HJ teenagers in Nazi Germany could identify with.[96] Standards from Powell's films such as "You Are My Lucky Star" and "I've Got a Feelin' You're Foolin'," sung by Powell herself or by co-stars Frances Langford and a very young Judy Garland, were marketed in Germany by Brunswick and Electrola and cherished by those teenage girls, as well as their boyfriends.[97] After the German declaration of war on the United States on December 11, 1941, the Nazis wanted to alter that pro-American image by exposing American vices in a propaganda film, *Rund um die Freiheitsstatue* (Round the Statue of Liberty). They denigrated, successfully they thought, swing, sexy fashions, jazz, and other alleged American addictions. Goebbels screened this film privately for Hitler, who showed himself pleased.[98] But large numbers of young German men and women in big cities, especially in Hamburg, viewed the film as an unusual opportunity to catch those precious snippets from the glamorous American way of life.[99]

The Swings showed themselves in public in those cafés, nightclubs, and cinemas, but also on extended strolls on Hamburg's main thoroughfares and on special outings, appearing in their characteristic attire and makeup, which were diametrically opposed to the humdrum uniforms of the Hitler Youth and its BDM. And they wore those outfits conspicuously during their swing-dance fests, both in public and at private parties. They dressed expensively and ostentatiously, with much of their fashion reminiscent of American styles in the movies, but with English accents as well. The girls appeared with long, shiny hair, lipstick, painted fingernails, silk stockings, and tightly fitting short skirts or pants to show off hourglass figures: this was how Hollywood actresses looked. Often a carefully draped trench coat was the finishing touch to a casually elegant appearance. The boys, too, sported long hair and trench coats along with their thick crepe-soled shoes, and often wore a star-spangled-banner or union jack pin on their glenplaid jackets.[100]

The image of an Anglo-American life-style was reinforced by German and foreign recordings, such as those by Electrola featuring tunes from the music films, but mostly those with swing and Dixieland jazz. Even if illegal, the recordings were brought into the Reich increasingly after 1938 by soldiers from occupied countries like Holland and Denmark. The most urbane of the Swings, like Robert Vogel, had bought them on trips to New York. The Swings collected these recordings not as connoisseurs of art but mostly to dance and schmooze to. If they could not be purchased secretly or bartered, they were duplicated. One Swing girl had the audacity to suggest in school that English jazz records be played on the occasion of the 9th of November, the annual

Nazi commemoration of Hitler's Beer Hall Putsch and one of the Holy Days of the Hitler Youth.[101]

The authorities observed that the Swings were likely to go on excursions to Hamburg's outlying areas, taking records, alcohol, and portable gramophones along. Those outings might be to the banks of the Elbe, to nearby lakes, or, better, to the pricey Timmendorf resort on the Baltic Sea. The Nazis were suspicious of these customs because they resembled the roaming of the *Edelweisspiraten* or *Meuten* and, earlier, the bourgeois youth of times gone by. And even though the Swings never sought physical altercations with members of the Hitler Youth but rather haughtily ignored them, the authorities knew that whatever the Swings liked doing best was potentially contagious and could infect the State Youth where they were vulnerable. This was especially true in view of the sexual activities which were known to take place among the Swings, when they stayed overnight in small hotels or empty Army barracks or in the proverbial farmer's hay, as did Helga Rönn in June of 1941 with her clique in the lake area of Trittau.[102]

But mostly the shellac records were needed at the so-called house parties, a hallmark of the Swings, to provide the backdrop for their swing dance. These ritualized events took place at the homes of the more affluent members, sometimes when parents were nearby. When they were not, the consumption of alcohol could get out of hand, as would the sexual activities which so tantalized the Hitler Youth and Gestapo. Here anything was possible, from rather innocent affairs, where between dances the lights went out and couples were merely kissing, to group sex in the available bedrooms, although orgies seem to have been few and far between.[103]

Inga Madlung remembers that parties at the lavish flat of the Persian Oromutchi brothers on the sumptuous Bellevue promenade near the Alster featured mirrors, especially on the ceilings. She was there with blond Helga Rönn: "We young things naturally loved it."[104] This points to a characteristic of the Swings: their absolute tolerance of non-Germans and what the Nazis would define as non-Aryans. Inga and her older sister Jutta themselves had a Jewish grandparent; the cosmopolitan seaport of Hamburg had always attracted foreign export-import traders, and there was that traditional Hamburg hankering for anything British. At least two very rich young Greeks, whose fathers were in wholesale tobacco, were members of the Swing cliques; there were Swings of Dutch and Belgian origin and, until deportations began in earnest in 1942, there were Jews.[105] Hans-Joachim ("Tommie") Scheel remembers riding with his gang in a commuter train when SS men entered and chatted up two of the girls, who had their hair dyed blond. These were Jewish girls, and at the time Scheel thought it hilarious.[106]

Friendship with what were officially regarded as non-Germans or racial aliens was essential to the Swings; their life-style was a major reason why they had to dissent from the Hitler Youth to the point of neglect or withdrawal. And thus early on they denied themselves to the totalitarian regime—or they were perceived as doing so by the authorities, who sequestered and punished them. Those who escaped such a fate quietly changed over to the armed services or their affiliates such as the RAD, as did members of the *Meuten* and the *Edelweisspiraten,* volunteering or joining as soon as their number was called. But others did not escape.

The Empire Strikes Back

In order to rein in its insubordinate young, the Nazi regime employed three agencies, with their overall effectiveness in ascending order. The first of these was the Hitler Youth itself, with its various disciplinary devices. But its success was limited, because measures were directed mostly against its own HJ members, with whom the wayward youths to be targeted were not always identical. The second agency was the judiciary, which could reach beyond Hitler Youth membership, but which was still hampered by a comparatively humane legal heritage from the Weimar Republic. The judiciary sharpened its approach to wayward youth only under constant pressure from the police and SS, both of which attempted to neutralize it entirely. The third agency was Himmler's police apparatus with all its branches, which viewed itself as extra-legal and supreme and whose encroachment on the judiciary was becoming more successful with each passing year of the war. It is significant that the relatively feeble Hitler Youth profited from an early tactical alliance with the police organizations, which increasingly used inside knowledge of Schirach and Axmann's groups to insinuate themselves into the cohorts of the young. On the other hand, the judiciary, too, acquired more teeth over time, by expanding the category of youthful offenders, inventing new crimes, instituting more special political courts, and pronouncing longer and more draconian sentences. In this scenario, adolescents who were resolved to withhold their support from the Nazi regime unreservedly, not to mention those opposing it, stood little chance of escaping unscathed by the end of the Third Reich in May 1945.

These developments have to be viewed against the incidence of youth crime from 1933 to 1945. Using a yardstick of indictments and convictions from January 1933 to about 1937, at which time the authorities granted an amnesty for certain transgressions, the Nazis prided themselves on a decrease of crime in general, and of juvenile delinquency in particular. They correctly attributed this positive trend to a return to socioeconomic normalcy after the upheavals of the Great Depression (1929–1935).[107] But what they did not say was that the police presence was very much more in evidence after 1933, acting, directly or indirectly, as a powerful deterrent to social deviance.[108] After the start of the war on September 1, 1939, crimes by youths were on the increase as compared to 1937, with a brief break in convictions owing only to a short-lived amnesty issued by Hitler on the 9th of that month. This contrasted negatively with a slower increase in crimes committed by adults in the same period, as well as with a weaker pattern of youth crime for the beginning years of World War I.[109] What stood out in this statistic was a disproportionately high incidence of crimes committed by young females from 1937 to 1944. By implication, Nazi record keepers correlated such transgressions with a greater incidence of sexually motivated crimes among (male) juveniles already beginning in 1933, as if sex offenses committed by young men were the inevitable result of female promiscuity preceding them—a clear case of blaming the victims.[110] Another variable of this situation was the widening of the definition of "crime" through the creation of novel types of punishment such as Youth Arrest (*Jugendarrest*) and the promulgation of decrees like the Police Ordinance of March 9, 1940.[111] The latter identified new groups of juvenile delinquents, such as teenagers under eighteen who were seen smoking and drinking in public, those who did not heed a stringent night curfew, and those who appeared in questionable nightclubs or dance halls.[112] Now "any leisure time for youth was practically declared as hanging around the streets" and thus was punishable.[113]

Disciplinary procedures in place for the Hitler Youth could be invoked whenever any of the aberrant youths were members and proved to have absented themselves from HJ service.[114] Hence in early March 1940, when the Swing celebrations in the Hamburg Curio-Haus were uncovered, 102 of the male suspects indicted actually were HJ members, of a total of 237 culprits; 52 had left the HJ and 58 had never joined. Similar ratios obtained for the BDM.[115] In cases of individual HJ Swings, the Hamburg Hitler Youth was able to help other authorities with its judgments, as in the case of sixteen-year-old Christa Broders, who in February 1944 was said to have missed several BDM meetings, but nonetheless was judged by her local leader to be "not essentially of bad character, even though she is somewhat flighty; rather, she has suffered from a bad education."[116] At that time the Hitler Youth leadership was using Burg Stahleck, one of its service camps, to keep in line male members in the Rhineland with potentially deviant behavior.[117]

Since the lines between HJ membership and non-membership were often blurred, the Hitler Youth frequently erred on the side of injustice simply to go after its quarry successfully. In the case of Hamburg's "Tommie" Scheel, who was a Hitler Youth turned Swing and who at seventeen was grabbed by the Gestapo in 1940, even his school teachers could not say whether he was in the HJ or not.[118] Near Essen in the Ruhr, a Hitler Youth leader spotted some twenty-odd Edelweiss

Pirates wandering about in their adventurous costumes in October 1939; they were deemed to be under the jurisdiction of the HJ by virtue of illegal *bündisch* regrouping and were dispatched to a police station for questioning. These kinds of control occurred repeatedly during the war, with the HJ beating bands of Pirates into submission, pending further legal action.[119]

Because of the Reich Youth leadership's quasi-legal claim, expressed in the law of December 1936, to be responsible for *all* the youths in Germany under eighteen, Schirach and later Axmann groomed the internal surveillance service called HJ-Streifendienst or SRD for this disciplinary task. It had been established in July 1934, initially to combat "juvenile crime, delinquency, and undisciplined behavior" within the Hitler Youth itself.[120] SRD members were specially selected youths whom the HJ leadership had reliably indoctrinated. Wearing armbands resembling those of the Sicherheitsdienst (SD) of the SS, they would roam public places such as movie theaters, railroad stations, and neighborhood pubs, but also HJ youth hostels, in search of misbehaving members. With the help of the police or the SS, these youths would then be apprehended, to be disciplined inside the ranks or, in more serious cases, handed over for prosecution by the judiciary.[121] But strengthened by tighter legislation, the HJ leadership was using the SRD increasingly against lapsed or non-HJ members especially by the time of the appearance of the cliques and gangs around 1937.[122] The SRD was superfluous in the countryside, where local hostile gangs did not lurk.[123] But more often than not, in large cities the SRD tended to be outnumbered by stronger groups such as the militant *Meuten* and *Edelweisspiraten*. There were inside complaints that the Hitler Youth boys selected for the SRD (there were no girls), apart from their fanaticism, were ill suited for policing tasks, and since they could carry no handguns, they were laughed at as powerless by their often foolhardy opponents.[124] In August of 1943, with a questionable record of success, the SRD in its original form was disbanded.[125]

The very fact that the SRD, composed entirely of teenagers, was always forbidden to make arrests on its own was symptomatic of the

growing dependence of Hitler Youth discipline enforcement on the
police and SS on the one hand, and, to a lesser extent, on the bureaucracy and judiciary on the other.[126] Regional governments would con-
sult the HJ or vice versa, and after November 1941 the HJ nominally
chaired a Reich Workshop for Youth Support, to which representatives
of State, Party, and Wehrmacht also subscribed.[127] Inevitably, the discussion at such meetings would turn to the pressing issue of an increase
in youth delinquency because of the large number of fathers conscripted for the war, and a corresponding dearth of HJ leaders of
Wehrmacht age who were also at the fronts.

At the height of the war, in their persecution of rival cliques, the HJ
leadership collaborated incrementally but to dubious effect with the
judiciary. Several higher HJ leaders now possessed law degrees, serving
as *Rechtsreferenten* (legal experts); and courts of law, especially youth
courts, maintained liaisons with the HJ on a routine basis.[128] But how
weak the HJ leadership really was in suppressing disobedient youth is
demonstrated by its failure to deal with the Swing Youth phenomenon
when it was in full bloom. On January 8, 1942, HJ boss Axmann
directed the following message to Himmler, as chief of the police
forces, Gestapo, and SS: "In the upper schools of Hamburg or in the
young affluent merchant class a so-called 'Swing Youth' has developed,
which largely displays an Anglophile proclivity . . . Since the activities
of this 'Swing Youth' at the home front cause a reduction in German
national capacities, I think it essential that these people be immediately
taken to a work camp . . . I would very much appreciate an order to
your Hamburg offices to the effect that the 'Swing Youth' will be proceeded against as severely as possible."[129] Himmler subsequently
employed the concentration camp system against dissident adolescents
in Nazi Germany in such a harsh manner that Axmann, shortly before
his death in 1996, regretted ever having alerted the police chief.[130]

Although the judiciary eventually surrendered much of its power to
the police executive authorities, thereby severely afflicting German
youth, it had been on a course of radicalization of its own since the last,

authoritarian, years of the Weimar Republic. In general, this amounted to an undoing of liberal changes wrought by a reformation of the justice system under the auspices of the Weimar constitution, with the key year being 1923.[131] Some of the manifestations of this gradual regression, behind which Hitler's own hand was clearly visible, were an enlargement in the number of criminal offenses, a heightened use of the death penalty, the reduction of judges, attorneys, and especially defense lawyers to mere puppets of a totalitarian regime that eschewed due legal process, a hasty resort to "preventive police custody" (*vorbeugende Polizeihaft*), and the mutation of criminal offenses into political ones.[132] This last change brought with it the appointment and cumulative use of special political courts, where conventional courts were deemed inappropriately normative, called *Sondergerichte*. At the highest level, the Berlin-based Volksgerichtshof or People's Court, particularly under its bloodthirsty president Roland Freisler after 1941, incrementally adopted a penal philosophy of retribution rather than one of social integration.[133] This entire development was helped along by two interrelated factors. One was that three Reich Ministers of Justice, Franz Gürtner (held over from Franz von Papen's pre-fascist chancellorship of 1932), Franz Schlegelberger (Acting Minister since 1941), and Otto Georg Thierack (since 1942), showed themselves to be progressively ruthless officials at the helm of the judiciary, with Hitler's obvious approval. (It was significant that Gürtner as Bavarian Justice Minister had treated Hitler leniently after the Munich Beer Hall Putsch of 1923.)[134] The second factor was that because of the polymorphous character of the law in Germany after 1933—some pre-1933 legislation had been retained, much of it had been repealed or overridden by new ordinances and pronouncements by the Führer, and some had simply been voided by police decrees—the law was becoming ineffective as an administrative tool. Plans to reform it entirely, advanced by Hans Frank, Hitler's former lawyer, Reich Law Leader, and, as Governor General of Occupied Poland, no friend of the SS and police, never got off the ground.[135]

All of this affected German youth mainly in three ways: by making larger groups of them liable for prosecution, by creating new misdemeanors, and by introducing a greater variety and tougher forms of punishment. For example, the law reform of 1923 had "raised the age of criminal responsibility from twelve to fourteen and promoted the use of correctional education instead of punishment for juvenile offenders between the ages of fourteen and eighteen."[136] But in October 1939 correctional education in the case of capital crimes was abrogated for youths aged sixteen to eighteen, who could now be tried in adult court again and were no longer immune from judgments of indefinite detention for dangerous offenders (*Sicherungsverwahrung*), life behind bars, and even the death penalty.[137] In the autumn of 1942, the Party Chancellery under Martin Bormann, doubtless at the behest of Hitler and supported in this by the Wehrmacht, proposed to a largely pliable Justice Ministry the lowering of the limit of adult liability, in particularly severe cases, to the age of twelve.[138] Then there were the new infractions as defined by the Police Ordinance of March 1940. Not coincidentally, a few months later a novel form of Youth Arrest was instituted, placing young offenders in solitary confinement on a diet of bread and water, and under obligation of total silence, for up to four weeks. In 1941 it was observed that this form of punishment had turned out to be much more severe "than that provided by jail"; it was supposed to shock into immediate submission boys and girls who in the large majority were HJ shirkers.[139] With smirking satisfaction, HJ Leader Hische remarked in November of 1943 that up to 90 percent of all accused youths could now be sentenced, compared with a success rate of only 75 percent before the introduction of that measure.[140] And in September 1942 the Reich Justice Ministry, after particular consideration of the cliques and gangs, decided on the reintroduction of caning, which was subsequently implemented in special youth concentration camps.[141]

Insofar as the judiciary still attempted recourse to existing laws, it was most successful in cases where young Germans had committed breaches of a criminal nature. That was most evident in the case of the petty-criminal gangs like the *Blasen* in Munich, where indictments could be reached on the basis of theft or destruction of public property. The punishment would be jail or terms in youth detention centers.[142] Youth Arrest was also meted out to *Edelweisspiraten* who stole bicycles and pilfered mailboxes, and to those who beat up Hitler Youths, with resulting injuries. For all these infractions, there were paragraphs of conventional law on the books. As for "loitering in the street after 9:00 P.M.," the 1940 Police Ordinance could be invoked.[143]

But because of the shortcomings of existing criminal law in the prosecution of a greatly enlarged class of transgressions, regarded as political by Nazi standards, specially adopted political jurisprudence was resorted to. The original basis for this was the Emergency Ordinance of February 28, 1933, which was predicated on Article 48 of the Weimar constitution, the Republic's emergency law invoking presidential fiat in an assumed state of national emergency, and favored for everyday governance by the anti-democratic pre-Nazi chancellors. Subsequently, the February 1933 ordinance was combined with repeated injunctions such as the decrees of February 8, 1936, and June 20, 1939, against the *Bündische Jugend* or any of its reincarnations. In this way, members of nonspecified illegal youth groups who had even vague ties to the former *bündisch* youth could be hauled before Nazi special courts and dispatched to jail, for periods of a few months or even years.[144]

More easily recognizable gangs, like the *Edelweisspiraten* and *Meuten,* were similarly dealt with. In the case of the former, some *bündische* legacies seemed obvious, as were Communist proclivities in the case of the latter. Hence comparatively moderate court judgments against Navajos, *Edelweisspiraten,* and *Kittelbachpiraten* are documented for various parts of the Rhineland and Ruhr from 1937 well into the war.[145] The *Meuten* could be more harshly treated within the existing legislation forbidding the resurrection of any of the Weimar political parties, because being a Communist was a serious political offense.[146] At the same time, because the *Meuten*'s connection to Communism was at best tenuous, sentences against them on a charge of high treason could only be based on suspicion or conspiracy to commit this crime (sometimes bolstered by the charge of having listened to Radio Moscow), but never on its successful execution.[147] Thus a group of Leipzig *Meuten* was convicted in October 1938 and sentenced to between one and five years of incarceration.[148] Understandably, because of the more serious situation posed by the war, such sentences tended to be significantly longer after 1939.[149]

The most unequivocal and at the same time the most political jurisdiction occurred in cases where high treason against the Nazi state was actually proved. Invariably, these propagandistically useful trials were conducted before the People's Court, which could be moved from Berlin to other cities if necessary. Since Nazis viewed the accused as criminals in a time of national crisis, the death penalty was a foregone conclusion. This alone demonstrated the willingness of the judiciary after 1939 to acknowledge the stranglehold of the police and the highest Party authorities. What aided the merciless judges in their pronouncements against Josef Landgraf, Walter Klingenbeck, Helmuth Hübener, and the members of the White Rose was that charges of defeatism in wartime could also be adduced and bolstered by the fact that the defendants had listened to news from enemy stations such as Radio Moscow and the BBC and subsequently disseminated it.[150]

Against the Swing Youth, the judiciary was least successful, for lack of suitable paragraphs in the statutes to indict them.[151] And thus what ultimately proved to be abject impotence on the part of the justice administrators turned out to be a triumph for the State police, as the circumstances of the Swings well demonstrate. As a police spokesman said in 1943: "If there is no law or if it does not suffice because, due to its origins, it perhaps does not express National Socialist convictions, then the security police may, nay must, step in."[152] However, the police were in cahoots with the SS, and Himmler's racist ideology ruled both. Therefore, racialist indictments were applied against those wayward youths whose misdemeanors eluded the judicial norms.

This development had begun as early as November 1933, when preventive police custody provisions allowed all police organs to intern suspects in concentration camps without being authorized by the courts. Because the legal liability age had just been lowered, teenagers were potentially at risk.[153] In December of 1937 Reich Interior Minister Wilhelm Frick, the nominal superior of Himmler and his law enforcers, announced that the criminal police now had the right to take into preventive custody entirely new population groups defined as racially undesirable asocials, who would include vagrants, beggars, prostitutes, and chronic alcoholics—this at a time when cliques and gangs had begun to surface.[154] After the beginning of the war, at the turn of 1940, jurists came to agree with representatives of the police that the judiciary should hand over youths to them in cases where it was obvious "that it was not worth the effort at socialization."[155] Hitler himself re-emphasized the prerogative of the police when he decided in August of 1941 that unruly juveniles, incapable of reform by the justice system at the age of nineteen, should not be allowed to go free, but should be committed to a concentration camp, guarded by Himmler's SS.[156] In November 1943 the deliberations of 1940–41 were formalized when the Ordinance Regarding the Simplification of Youth Penalization stipulated that any recalcitrant youth while in indefinite detention as decreed by the courts could be transferred to the police for further treatment, to so-called youth protection camps.[157]

These youth protection camps or *Jugendschutzlager* were special concentration camps for juveniles and were the original creation and exclusive domain of Himmler's police and SS. They came to symbolize the supremacy assumed by the police apparatus in all matters of youth discipline. Ideologically, they were rooted in a key interest on the part of principal police administrators, in particular Himmler, in race biology, especially eugenics. This interest led to the establishment of a Criminal-Biological Office in Berlin police headquarters by December 1941. Institutionally, the youth protection camps represented a further triumph of the police executive in its overall struggle for total autonomy in matters of jurisprudence and the penal system; ideologically, they signified the supremacy of Nazi racist dogma in the country's educational processes.

The Police Ordinance to combat cliques of March 1940 had come about after a consensus between Hermann Göring, Goebbels, Frick, and Himmler that "very tough youth laws" would be needed, as Goebbels laconically put it in early February.[158] Thereafter SS General Arthur Nebe, the head of the criminal police under Himmler's police superintendent Reinhard Heydrich, took steps to interpret the Ordinance entirely in accordance with the law-enforcement visions of the police and SS, without any heed to the judiciary.[159] As a first result, male Swings in Hamburg considered to be racially degenerate ringleaders were arrested by the Gestapo, in collaboration with their school directors, in the fall of 1940. The Swings were brutally interrogated in the local Stadthaus jail and were sent, without intercession by the judiciary, to the municipal penal camp of Fuhlsbüttel.[160] Similar autonomous police action was initiated against the Swings of Frankfurt, the so-called Harlem Gang, shortly thereafter.[161] Subsequently, whenever a member of the Swings was not released after three weeks in investigative police custody, Heydrich's police headquarters in Berlin automatically pronounced it "protective custody," meaning arbitrary detention at the whim of the police captors.[162] As for the Edelweiss Pirates, some who had not yet been tried and sentenced by a law court were single-handedly committed by the Gestapo to a special "work and education camp" in 1941–42, one that outsiders, because of its appearance and rigorous drill routines, took to be a sort of concentration camp.[163] Socially and racially suspect offenders like Fritz Molden from Vienna were snatched from the courts and stuck into punitive SS battalions; in Molden's case it was a unit that had to explore dangerous moors on the eastern front to test their safety in partisan warfare, a mission during which several of these involuntary young scouts were sucked down to their deaths.[164]

Meanwhile, in early January 1942 Axmann had issued his plea to Himmler to make an example of the most offensive Swing members. Himmler replied on January 26 that he agreed to the need to act ruthlessly and that he had given the necessary orders. Indeed, he had already written to Heydrich that all previous actions by the police had so far constituted "half measures"—an unmistakable reference to what he considered to be the limitations dictated by the Police Ordinance of March 1940. He now wanted Heydrich to send the obvious kingpins, the most depraved boys and girls, to concentration camps for a minimum of two to three years.[165] Thus beginning in 1942, Swings over age twenty were incarcerated without trial in the camps of Auschwitz, Buchenwald, Neuengamme, Theresienstadt, Nordhausen, Bergen-Belsen, and Sachsenhausen.[166] Among them were the Madlung sisters and Helga Rönn's future sister-in-law, Ursula Nielsen.[167] Nor was Himmler only thinking of the Swings. In December 1942 the Gestapo caught 320 *Edelweisspiraten* in a dragnet, all in Düsseldorf, Duisburg, Essen, and Wuppertal, and detained 130 of them.[168] Two years later the Pirates of Cologne-Ehrenfeld, collaborators of "racially inferior" Slavic conscript workers, would be strung up by Gestapo agents without ever having been tried in a court of law.[169]

The youth protection camps of Moringen, for younger boys, and Uckermark, for teenage girls, were the brainchild of SS and Police Colonel Paul Werner; they were shaped by and became race-eugenic experimental sites for the psychiatrist Robert Ritter. Werner influenced his boss, General Nebe, and Nebe then prevailed upon Heydrich and Himmler to organize these camps. It is virtually certain that Werner himself had already been influenced by the eugenically obsessed Ritter, with whom the one-time chicken farmer Himmler saw eye to eye.[170] Born in 1901 and socialized in the fiercely nationalistic and anti-Semitic *Freikorps,* Ritter had obtained a Ph.D. with a dissertation on pedagogy at the University of Munich in 1927. His thesis, "The Sexual Problem in Education," showed an early interest in procreation and racially oriented eugenics; throughout his career the family man Ritter, who kept Eva Justin, his blond female assistant, as his mistress, was obsessed with sex and promiscuity among young women. In May 1930 Ritter's eugenic focus led him to a medical doctorate in Heidelberg, where his dissertation concentrated on heredity. Thereafter, he performed a postdoctoral practicum at the racist-oriented Burghölzli psychiatric institution near Zurich, and later in August 1932 he worked as an assistant in the psychiatric wing of the university hospital in Tübingen, where he was concerned with hereditary factors in the development of "asocial youths."[171]

By the mid-1930s Ritter, now a senior university physician grooming himself for an academic chair, had singled out Sinti and Roma and related vagrants, the so-called *Jenische,* as his new objects of study. As he laid out in his book, *Ein Menschenschlag,* the *Jenische* in Germany had historically been asocial, the "refuse of bourgeois society." Because they were congenitally of bad blood, which led to a variety of social misbehaviors, they were racial misfits and could not be reformed. Ritter intimated that sterilization of the current descendants of these groups—whom he alleged to be seeing daily as adolescents in his medical practice—by the sterilization law of July 1933 was the only solution to an obvious social evil, particularly since young *jenische* women had always exhibited an extraordinary degree of sexual promiscuity.[172] In 1936 Ritter was appointed director of the newly created Research Institute for Eugenics and Population Biology (Rassenhygienische und Bevölkerungspolitische Forschungsstelle) within the Reich Health Office under Interior Minister Frick, to research and take stock of the entire asocial, vagrant, and criminal population of the Reich. Thus Ritter became the Reich's foremost expert on the group popularly known as Gypsies and Gypsy-related bands. During the war he created what amateur eugenicist Himmler and the police would view as the scientific basis for the concentration and extermination of tens of thousands of Sinti and Roma, mostly in Auschwitz.[173]

In his capacity as a race-hygiene-oriented physician of increasing importance, Ritter became acquainted and soon collaborated with other physicians of the same scientific persuasion, as well as with criminal biologists, lawyers, and representatives of the police. All of these believed, like him, that physical or psychological disorders in certain groups of people in the Reich occurred independently of the environment, but instead were genetic and therefore irreparable. This nature-versus-nurture debate had of course been going on universally since

Darwin, but in Germany it had increasingly defined the medical *Zeitgeist* as racist, a view that held sway over all the leading National Socialists.[174]

While in Berlin, Ritter came into close contact with Professor Ferdinand von Neureiter, who was then the director of the Criminal-Biological Research Office in the Reich Health Office. Neureiter defined "criminal biology" as serving the aims of both the criminal law and hereditary race science, as Germans now understood it. The aim of criminal-biological research was to devise punitive programs, with the dual purpose of "atonement for the misdeed and removal or neutralization of criminal dispositions and tendencies." Hence this respected scholar helped to furnish the biological foundations for the retributive justice of the Nazis, which sought to protect the racial community rather than resocialize the wrongdoers. "Born criminals" were to be detected and permanently isolated from the healthy *Volksgemeinschaft*.[175] Ritter also got to know Heinrich Wilhelm Kranz, a less than credible ophthalmologist posing as a race hygienist at Giessen University. Kranz was working on a law for the permanent marginalization and isolation of *Gemeinschaftsunfähige,* or community aliens, meaning over a million persons deemed race-biologically unfit to be members of Nazi society, and suggesting their eventual liquidation.[176] Ritter's views at the time corresponded with those of an established Kiel University jurist, Professor Friedrich Schaffstein, a man much worried about the Swings, who held that while perhaps not all juvenile criminals were "biologically inferior," it was without question that "the tremendous significance of genetic factors in the criminality of youth has been corroborated by the more recent hereditary-biological research." The factor of punishment in the criminal justice system for the young, Schaffstein stated, had the important function of "removing the unworthy youths from the community."[177]

One of the higher-placed policemen in the capital who was following Ritter's exploits closely at the time and came to admire them to the point of emulation was Colonel Paul Werner, Nebe's delegate for the fight against youth crime in the Reich. Inspired by the eugenist-racist atmosphere, Werner developed into a racially motivated police extremist. Thus he came to believe that a future law for the treatment of *Gemeinschaftsunfähige* would aid the police leadership decisively in its long-standing quest for power over defendants without the cumbersome recourse to the judiciary.[178] Moreover, his extremist ideas regarding the prevention of crime before it was allowed to happen meshed with extremist views regarding the prevention of disease by some of Ritter's radical colleagues. For them, to be healthy was a duty and to be sick a crime: both concepts shared the same race-biological underpinnings.[179] In analogy to those Nazi physicians who would have liked to kill their patients in order to extinguish all diseases, Werner, who was convinced that most youth crimes were the consequence of hereditary predispositions, wished to eradicate crime by eliminating the criminals.[180] This accorded with the theories of Dr. Ritter in regard to *Jenische,* Gypsies, and wayward youth, and gained Himmler's wholehearted approval. Thus in the summer of 1941, Werner and Nebe agreed to appoint Ritter to the newly established Criminal-Biological Office in Himmler's police bureaucracy.[181]

At that time, the youth protection camp for boys in Moringen near Göttingen had already been set up. It had been established in August 1940 at the site of a former concentration camp under the guard of Death Head's units of the Waffen-SS. Male adolescents from thirteen to twenty-one could be sent there after arrest by the police, having bypassed judicial procedures. As in adult concentration camps, their stay was for an indefinite period; releases to the front lines, or, on reaching twenty-one, to regular concentration camps, were the norm; "a genuine conditional discharge is not usual." Inmates were to be tended to by "Educators," school teachers incorporated in the SS. But there was little for them to learn, for they had to slave in nearby war-related industries, including an underground munitions factory, seven days a week, with one Sunday off every month. They were subjected to a regimen of brutal punishments, including solitary confinement for extended periods as well as beatings.[182]

Of nearly 1,400 boys who were in Moringen until March 1945, close to a hundred died, many of hunger and tuberculosis. Several damaged their feet because of inadequate footwear. In August 1942 even the SS physician in charge, who had been trying to treat all kinds of infections, warned that less work would be performed and more boys would die "unless the diet is immediately improved." A number of boys were shot while trying to escape, and at least one was beaten to death during a public caning ritual. Bed wetters were concentrated in one barracks and were awakened first every two hours, then every hour during the night; they were forced to wear "penis clamps." Everyone got up at 5:00 A.M. and then worked for eleven hours. Mail could be sent out and received only twice a month.[183]

The camp for "fallen girls" was established at Uckermark in June of 1942, a stone's throw from Ravensbrück, northeast of Berlin, Himmler's concentration camp for women, where the terrible Irma Grese was then being trained. Again the guards were SS men, and the SS physician-on-duty came from Ravensbrück. Living and work conditions in Uckermark were very similar to those in Moringen, as were the hours. Some work details tried to convert swamps into meadows, while others were assisting farmers in the fields. Nutrition was so bad that some girls ate leaves from the trees; dysentery was common. Vicious guard dogs posed a particular danger here, maiming more than one girl. As one inmate remembers: "The camp commander was even worse than the Devil, this was Satan incarnate . . . I also was in Auschwitz, but for me, Uckermark was worse."[184] It was emphasized by the authorities that the main reason for the girls' incarceration was their uncontrolled sexuality, which led to immorality and endangered the biological integrity of the *Volk*.[185]

This reference provides an important clue as to why Police Colonel Werner's friend, the race- and sex-obsessed Robert Ritter, was constantly present in both camps and why in fact he helped define the various categories of inmates, of whom, altogether, less than 8 percent could ever hope to be freed.[186] Ritter was classifying youths according to the criteria of heredity versus milieu, which in the great majority of

cases meant that the suspects were judged to be socially incorrigible on genetic grounds. On the basis of the biopolitical philosophy of the proposed law against community aliens—a law constantly reconceived yet never enacted—these renegades were preordained for a lifetime of incarceration, or death. Thus they were viewed in close analogy to the Sinti and Roma whom Ritter had been studying previously and continued to examine, effectively marking them for genocide. Indeed, in Moringen Ritter was keeping "Gypsies and part-Gypsies, a few partially Jewish and even two Negro bastards." A few Sinti were also in Uckermark. The issue of sexuality was crucial, because by Ritter's reasoning it provided both the explanation for disobedient behavior among juveniles within Nazi society and the potential for those juveniles' misbegotten progeny. Once the full range of community-alien Germans from the asocial to the criminal had been defined using race-scientific techniques in the Nazi mold, criminal biology, as it was currently anchored within Himmler's police, would assist in keeping the Nazi master race wholesome and pure.[187]

Thus it is not surprising that among the individual unreformable "misfits" who were inmates in Moringen and Uckermark, such as those notoriously contemptuous of HJ membership, there also were clutches of those *Blasen* and *Edelweisspiraten* whose asocial behavior had not been legally felonious and who, by default, became prey for the police. Moreover, Swings in their teens were conspicuous in these camps after 1941, as hardly any of their crimes were legally indictable—they had not, for instance, stolen property or beaten up Hitler Youths. The Swings' sexual profligacy predestined them as candidates for detention for the sake of the racially pure community, but also as subjects for eugenic-experimental scrutiny, to serve Ritter and his expert team.[188]

The girls eventually disgorged by Uckermark would spend the rest of their lives trying to adjust to a society of Germans still ruled by views such as Schaffstein's; for decades people refused to acknowledge the evil of an institution whose mission they mistakenly understood to have been social correction. The once beautiful Helga Rönn, for instance, who like Irma Grese had wanted to become an actress,

emerged from Uckermark broken in spirit and in body. Unable to remain in Hamburg facing ordinary Germans, she married a British soldier and became a housewife in England, never realizing her dreams.[189]
Boys conscripted to the front lines from Moringen usually were exposed to direct enemy fire and did not survive for long. Ironically, that
fate in war was shared by many of their contemporaries who, until induction into the armed forces, had tried, as best they could, to live up
to the ideals of the Hitler Youth.

In retrospect, one can view the dissent and resistance of these youth,
individuals, and groups, as diverse as they were, in terms of their social
background, the effectiveness of their actions, their political motivation, and their readiness for ultimate self-sacrifice. Socially, they came
from all strata of German society—the *Blasen* from the lumpen proletariat, the *Meuten* and *Edelweisspiraten* from the proletariat and lower
middle class, and the Swings and White Rose members mostly from
the upper classes. Some individuals, like Ernst Jünger Jr., might be
elite; others, like Helmuth Hübener and Walter Klingenbeck, came
from the lower rungs of society. In that sense these dissidents reflected
the social structure of the all-inclusive Hitler Youth they were trying to
avoid. The efficacy of their activities was null, no matter what their
means of opposition—whether they only tried to elude the control of
the HJ by staying away, as did the Swings, or were more proactive like
the *Blasen*, who tried to sabotage HJ property, or whether they sought
to engage the HJ in skirmishes, a favorite pastime of the *Edelweisspiraten*. Even the mass distribution of anti-regime flyers by the White
Rose merely established a post-1945 legacy of heroism for this group,
but did not change the regime. Differences in political motivation
reflect on the moral quality of these individuals and groups and provide a better premise for historical judgments of the HJ: the higher
such a motive, the starker the relief in which the fundamentally criminal character of Hitler's youth bands would appear—as criminal as the
dictatorship that had spawned them. This issue is related to the larger
one of self-sacrifice, for the more noble the motive, the more prepared
the dissidents would be to give their own lives. In this arena, the

Swings and *Blasen* obviously have no place, for they lived by the pleasure principle and just viewed HJ members as obstacles to their desires. It was only the members of the White Rose group who undertook their disruptive actions against Nazi society with the clear prior knowledge that they might not survive. Because most of them once had been loyal HJ members, their very existence amounts to a devastating commentary on the Hitler Youth, the first Nazi body to disappoint them; the HJ was unable to retain the loyalty of what were racially exemplary young Germans, in its relentless quest to generate the Third Reich's future elite.

Hitler's Youth at War

Historical records acquaint us with the life histories of two contemporaries, Herbert Taege and Claus von Amsberg, who were HJ members and subsequently fought in the war. Herbert Taege was born in Magdeburg, a mid-size town in Saxe-Anhalt, in September 1921, the son of a minor postal official. He joined the Hitler Youth as a Gymnasium student in March 1933, six weeks after Hitler's coming to power. Before that he had been in the German Boy Scouts, under the *bündisch* label. In the Hitler Youth Taege rose through the ranks, until on the first day of World War II he became a Nazi Party member at the age of eighteen. Simultaneously, he volunteered for the field-gray Waffen-SS, the armed branch of the general, black-shirted SS. Wounded at the front in 1940, he was transferred to the SS Death Head's unit at Dachau concentration camp, where he served as a guard. By 1943 he was in an SS tank division in Warsaw, at the time when the Warsaw Ghetto was being liquidated. In December of that year, an internal review characterized the young lieutenant as "physically very able, of honest character and open, and capable of good judgment." His knowledge of tank armor was judged sufficient and his acquaintance with Nazi ideology "far above average." This verdict was reinforced in the summer of 1944, when his superiors stated that "as a leader in the Hitler Youth, SS-Untersturmführer Taege showed particularly good ideological direction. One of his strong points was to represent National

Socialist military values with candor and conviction."[1] After the war Taege settled in West Germany and founded Ascania, a neo-Nazi publishing firm, in which he printed his outpourings about the glory of the former Hitler Youth, as well as other Hitler-friendly literature.[2]

Claus von Amsberg was born in September 1926 on his parents' estate near Hamburg. Ten years later, upon entering Gymnasium, he too, like most of his peers, joined the Hitler Youth. Then in 1943, when he was sixteen, he was drafted into the ranks of the Flakhelfer, juveniles who were forced to serve as cannoneers in artillery emplacements. His artillery setup was with a Navy unit near the strategically important seaport of Kiel. Von Amsberg was fortunate not to be hit by enemy bombs, and in the summer of 1944 he was drafted into the Wehrmacht. He was trained for tank service, and from March to May 1945 fought with a panzer division in Merano, northern Italy. There the U.S. Army captured him, and he spent time as a POW in Brescia and England. By December 1945 he was a free man; as a former Hitler Youth, he had to undergo formal denazification in order to attend university. Having repeated his *Abitur,* the final Gymnasium examination, in 1947, von Amsberg studied law in Hamburg, and after graduation in 1956 he joined the West German Foreign Service. After stays in the United States, Central America, and Africa he was posted to Bonn, where in 1964 he met the Dutch Crown Princess Beatrix. They fell in love and were married in March of 1966, whereby von Amsberg became Prince Claus of the Netherlands. When his wife inherited the throne in 1980, Claus became, officially, her Prince Consort. At first the new prince had not been welcome in Holland because of his Nazi past, although the authorities had smoothed his path. Two things are noteworthy about Amsberg's new career in Holland. He dedicated all of his energies to furthering international peace and, especially, health and economic improvements in the Third World. Although this together with his personal modesty and charm soon endeared him to the Dutch public, he fell victim to severe depression. This got worse with age, and for long stretches he had to be hospitalized. Toward the end of his life, Amsberg developed heart trouble, Alzheimer's disease, and cancer. He died of pneumonia on October 6, 2002, much mourned by the people.[3]

What Herbert Taege and Claus von Amsberg have in common is their service in the Hitler Youth as teenagers and, subsequently, extended military training and active duty in the field. But what sets them apart, not counting birth and social station, is the quality of moral judgment governing their respective Nazi careers. Taege turned out to be a fanatical follower of the National Socialist creed and consequently, as a Holocaust denier, became an evil person. Von Amsberg, on the other hand, suffered from his involvement with Nazism and attempted to atone for it through his engagement with underdeveloped countries; a credible medical diagnosis at the time held that feelings of personal guilt contributed significantly to his steadily worsening melancholia.

The question of responsibility and even guilt looms large in a study of Hitler Youths, who, after years of military training, some of it initially camouflaged, were being asked to fight and kill in a real war. It is difficult to assess the individual moral guilt of young men like Taege and Amsberg and the millions of their comrades who served in the Wehrmacht and Waffen-SS. But questions of complicity do arise, and to make the task of dealing with them easier, it is helpful to have information about these youths' ideological motivations or absence thereof for war, their attitudes when training in pre-combat HJ formations, voluntarily or not, the nature of their actions and reactions when in the field, and their reflections, if any, when defeated. Taken together, these questions assume significance against the backdrop of historians' depictions of the role of German soldiers especially in the European East, and in particular where conventional military history touches on, and becomes intertwined with, the newer history of the Holocaust.

A related question is the issue of a conceptual division between the Wehrmacht and the SS, on which there have been two schools of thought. An earlier view maintained that the Waffen-SS fighting at the eastern front was almost exclusively responsible for any and all of the atrocities one heard about, against Jews or Soviet partisans, and that the Wehrmacht was not. A second, more recent school has held that such a distinction is specious, in that—as one American historian maintains—virtually every young German was brought up through premilitary training to view Slavs and Jews as subhumans to be mercilessly killed, and this was the one thing that propelled them at the fronts.[4]

With qualifications, there is much to be said for the arguments of this second school. Today we know that the Wehrmacht was considerably more in accord with the SS's lethal objectives toward Jews than its postwar representatives cared to acknowledge for years, and that its cruel treatment of partisans, prisoners of war, or hostages was dictated by contempt for, if not abject hatred of, humans other than those of "Nordic" blood.[5] Only recently, the German public was again reminded that in September 1943 ordinary German troops executed approximately 5,000 Italians who had been cornered on the Greek island of Kephallenia. This was a Nazi reprisal after Mussolini's fall in July of that year and the refusal by Italian General Antonio Gandin to follow German orders to disarm his troops.[6]

On the other hand, despite the millions who cheered on their armies' advance, there is evidence that young German soldiers, even in the SS, were horrified by what they saw and what they were ordered to do. And indeed, in the Wehrmacht, it is unlikely that *every* recruit fought with enthusiasm for the Nazi goals the way he had been instructed beforehand in the Hitler Youth. Especially in the later years of mounting defeat, many soldiers fought desperately, once they were at the front, because in the face of disaster all around them, they became afraid for their lives; they just wanted to get out and survive. "We have to meet again, I just cannot imagine that I will have to die so soon," wrote a desperate ex-HJ leader to his girlfriend from the Hungarian front.[7] That did not necessarily make their fight more humane or their responsibility less grave.[8] Still, even in view of the enthusiasm of all their dyed-in-the-wool Nazi comrades, a number of factors warn us not to engage in quick generalizations regarding trigger-happy post-HJ youths. One is that a horror of being sent to the eastern front evidently caused an increase in suicides among young soldiers after 1941.[9] Second, Himmler and his staff, in a progressively uncoordinated Nazi administration, experienced ever greater difficulties in the recruitment of Hitler Youth candidates for service in the Waffen-SS, a service that was becoming less popular as the war dragged on. Third, in order to embed National Socialist dogma more deeply in the Wehrmacht at the fronts, special Nazi indoctrination officers (NS-Führungsoffiziere) had to be employed—mirror images of the Red Army political commissars.[10] Finally, there were young Wehrmacht officers who attempted to stem the tide, as did the members of the White Rose on the home front. One officer who tried and eventually remained in Russian captivity was Wilm Hosenfeld, the Wehrmacht captain who allowed Jewish Warsaw Ghetto escapee Wladyslaw Szpilman to go free after hearing him play Chopin's Nocturne in C-sharp minor, as Roman Polanski's film *The Pianist* so movingly portrays.[11]

The corollary to an over-reporting of the criminality of young soldiers at the fronts is an under-exposure of the suffering of civilian young people back home in the Reich, as the war theater closed in on them and many were expelled from Germany's eastern provinces. In the shadow of the Holocaust, such suffering is a delicate subject, especially because reactionary postwar German historians used it as a counterweight to the pain inflicted on the Jews, thus attempting to exonerate Germans.[12] But in 2002 when Nobel laureate Günter Grass, himself a HJ Pimpf at ten, a Flakhelfer at fifteen, and a tank gunner at seventeen, memorialized thousands of German casualties resulting from the advance of the Russians, the majority of them young people, in East Prussia in early 1945, he had a different purpose in mind. Because he wished to help in "documenting these terrible, barbaric expulsions," he wrote about the torpedoing and sinking of the *Wilhelm Gustloff* by Russians near Gotenhafen (Gdynia) on January 30, 1945, with a loss of approximately 8,000 lives. Among the fatalities were hundreds of young Wehrmacht female helpers (Wehrmachtshelferinnen) and a thousand young sailors en route to Kiel for new submarine duty.[13] As the judicious South African J. M. Coetzee, a more recent

Nobel Prize winner, has observed, the Social Democrat Grass, long a critic of Nazism, felt freer than most to enter the ongoing debate about silence and silencing. For Grass was assuming, "in a characteristically cautious and nuanced way, a position that until recently only the radical right has dared to champion in public: that ordinary Germans—not just those who perished in the camps or died opposing Hitler—have a claim to be numbered among the victims of World War II."[14] In agreement with this, John Updike has written that Grass laudably called attention "to assaults on the reeling Third Reich that neither the victors nor the defeated victims were motivated to publicize."[15]

Elation and Disenchantment

When war broke out in early September 1939, former Hitler Youths aged eighteen or older found themselves as members of the Wehrmacht, helping to advance the German front against Poland. Their attitude was characterized by a boundless optimism that Germany would achieve quick victory, the view of an external enemy deserving of defeat as inferiors—as ideology in the Hitler Youth had dictated for years—and a sense of attachment to the younger HJ comrades whom they had left behind. This initial enthusiasm was so powerful as to stifle a sense of their own loss—the sudden death of a comrade or their own war injuries. The long-held images of the enemy were corroborated for these young soldiers—in the case of the Poles as slovenly and cruel, often civilians caught red-handed and shot as the accused prewar killers of ethnic Germans on Polish soil, and in the case of Jews as subhuman, with their beards and caftans and their dwellings in cramped, unsightly *shtetl* or large-town ghettos.[16] As Karl Kreutzer, a corporal and former local HJ leader from Heidelberg, wrote home in November to a friend, then still serving in the Hitler Youth and aching to rush to the front: "I am overjoyed that you believe in the proud Wehrmacht." For "a soldier's faith in victory is always fortified whenever he sees that the loved ones at home believe in him, he who is out there day and night in order to protect us all."[17]

This pattern was repeated during the campaigns in Norway and Denmark in April and May of 1940, although the enemy here, with their blond and "Germanic" appearance, was thought to be so respectable as to be worthy of assimilation.[18] The darker-haired French, however, uprooted by the Wehrmacht a few weeks later, fared worse by the Germans' racial standards, if still better than the eastern foes. Young soldiers conditioned in the HJ as recently as a few months earlier were apt to describe the French as a derelict people, "indifferent, deferential and dumb" in the countryside, yet morally decadent and sexually depraved in the cities, especially Paris.[19] In the capital, the epitome of corruption was observed, for example "Negroes who walk arm-in-arm with white French women and who sit with them in the street cafés," to the point where, as one enlisted youth insisted, he couldn't "approve of that!"[20] To a greater or lesser degree, such self-righteousness extended to other areas and populations, giving these adolescents the certitude of being masters of a vanquished land, whether it be Denmark or France, let alone Poland. They felt organically bonded to a master race and, in the occupied countries and after intermittent bursts of fighting, thought they were entitled to a "master's life."[21] In this Manichean world view, they were at the summit, and at the nadir were the Jews, who were said to have no right to life: "As one watches these people one gets the impression that they really have no justification whatsoever to exist on God's earth."[22]

Fueled by easy Blitzkrieg victories and agreeable occupation tasks in northern and western Europe during 1939–40, the German euphoria continued after the Nazi surprise attack on the Soviet Union on June 22, 1941. As more than three million Wehrmacht soldiers moved rapidly into Russia on three broad fronts—a northern, a central, and a southern one—the dynamics of easy conquest during the summer and autumn heightened the sense of superiority even of Hitler's youngest soldiers. In these naïve young men's minds, fighting for an early "Final

Victory" in what was originally conceived as yet another lightning war was an article of faith.[23] "Since 2 o'clock in the morning we are at war with the Russians," wrote former Hitler Youth Hellmut to his parents on June 22, "and I am proud to be a part of this."[24]

Certain obstacles tended to dampen this conqueror mentality, but they were either suppressed in a state of denial or compensated for with the simple yet tangible rewards that war booty afforded. The most common palliatives were satisfying food and drink obtained from farmsteads or occupied estates, at a time when feasts were rare, but also clothing, especially as the Russians were discovered to have the more effective winter gear.[25]

By far the most serious impediment to an optimistic soldier's fortune was the figure of the Russian fighter himself, whose vitality and supremacy in numbers had not been expected but were soon palpable. In defeating this peril, psychological crutches helped. Hitler publicly called the Russians "swamp humans."[26] The HJ's own inbred stereotype of the racially inferior, primitive "Iwans," said to be Slavs mixed with Jewish and Asiatic elements (the Germans soon learned to conflate anything Russian with "Mongol"), helped to temper the fear of the enemy. This was reinforced by the wretched-looking Red Army POWs the Germans encountered early in the campaign; more than three million of them were captured already in the fall.[27] Even dead Russians spotted in a ditch presented a picture of "most miserable soldiers," wrote one of the former HJ boys in June; they reminded him of "croaked cattle." Another one observed about the Russian POWs, "Hardly ever do you see the face of a person who seems rational and intelligent. They all look emaciated and the wild, half-crazy look in their eyes makes them appear like imbeciles."[28] A young officer seeing starving, thirsty prisoners trying to lap up rainwater from the street pavement viewed this as proof of some lower form of life.[29] Almost from the start of "Operation Barbarossa"—the Nazi code name for the Russian campaign—many of the youthful soldiers would guard thousands of these Slavs at a time, cooped up in vast prisoner-of-war camps, where the Russians were left to themselves to die, usually of hunger and thirst and sometimes after acts of cannibalism.[30] (During the entire eastern campaign, the Wehrmacht would capture 5.7 million Red Army soldiers, of whom 3.3 million perished.)[31] Hence the very comparison of the lives of the Russian adversaries with their own convinced young German soldiers of their superiority and furnished them with a raison d'être for continued conquest. They adhered to the official mantra "that one German infantry soldier was worth ten or twelve Russians," or that Russians expected to be treated brutally because they were the product of a brutal environment.[32] The alleged brutality of Russians was typically substantiated after German comrades had been found mutilated, "hands tied, their ears, tongues, noses and genitalia cut off," as was observed in Tarnopol.[33] Members of a cultured, morally superior nation like Germany, it was implied after such gruesome finds, would not stoop to commit such deeds. Indeed, for most young men this belief was a fantasy they preferred to uphold even after they had witnessed and perhaps participated in the torture and murder of partisans and Jews.

Jews could be Soviet soldiers, and at the beginning of the Russian campaign Hitler proclaimed the "Commissar Order," stipulating that any Red Army political commissar, all of whom were automatically assumed to be Jews, should be summarily shot when captured.[34] But Jews could also be cunning partisans, in keeping with the image of the racial enemy par excellence, who were chased and killed by the SS-Einsatzgruppen, often with the regular Army's cooperation and as a weirdly attractive spectacle for young conscripted soldiers. Eyewitnesses have reported some form of "execution tourism," where enlisted men would congregate to watch and sometimes ask to be allowed to assist in the murder of Jewish men, women, and children.[35] Among the Jewish men (but also some women), many were suspected of partisan activity, and since Stalin relied heavily on them in his defense of the motherland, it gave ex-Hitler Youth warriors great satisfaction in helping to destroy them.[36] This spurred their ideas about eventually assuming high German office in the vanquished East, in particular becoming the lords of expansive *Wehrbauern* settlements.[37]

But despite all the success and satisfaction in the first campaigns—including one in North Africa and another in the Balkans—things were beginning to become undone for Germany's young soldiers, as new cohorts from the Hitler Youth entered the armed forces until early 1945, some as young as sixteen.[38] One source of discontent was a duplication of the pre-combat drill they had experienced in the HJ and had engaged in again for years during regular service as well as in specialty institutions such as the Adolf Hitler Schools. The premilitary training in the armed forces endured until the very end of the Third Reich, even though the HJ had stepped up its own training after 1935, with the introduction of conscription, and in 1938, several months before the war. During all this time there was no coordination between HJ leaders and Army officers as to which military exercises would make sense at the HJ level up to age eighteen, thereafter to be intensified and complemented by Army trainers prior to actual war duty. Moreover, apart from the necessary technical routines, such as learning how to scale walls and to use various firearms, the HJ recruits were unhappy with the psychological torture drills indulged in by Army sergeants and the nasty peer hazing for the sake of "character building"; they had already come to resent these insults under Schirach and Axmann. Such experiences began to erode morale in the Wehrmacht, apart from incrementally discrediting the legacy of the Hitler Youth in these young men's minds.

Wehrmacht inductees like the eighteen-year-old Erich Albertsen, who had already had more than his share of a punishing regimen in the Hitler Youth, had to march for long stretches in a heavy uniform, often wearing a gas mask as well. He and others had to scrub the barracks floors with toothbrushes and clean up lockers repeatedly, after they had been soiled with ashes by their drill sergeants. Any small oversight would lead to punitive exercises.[39] Jürgen Peiffer had to climb up trees with his gas mask on, and then sing, "It is so nice to be a Soldier." Often these chores had to be senselessly repeated when the men were on sick leave.[40] As had been the practice in the HJ, Ralf Roland

Ringler, training to become an officer, was forced to jump into the water from a 10-meter board; others who could not swim, rather than being taught that skill, were ousted in disgrace.[41] Hermann Melcher remembers the "Masked Ball," when for an hour or so Army recruits had to appear for roll call, only to be dismissed and told to reappear in a different outfit, always within three minutes.[42] In a drill as vicious as it was senseless, young soldiers had to dig holes in the ground to hide in, minutes before tanks would move over them, liable to crush them if the holes were dug badly. That was a form of chicanery not in the HJ's training arsenal.[43] Some of these exercises continued for weeks, even months on end, for soldiers who were eager to get to the fronts to defend their country.[44]

Moreover, the fortunes of war itself were changing, starting with September of 1941. It was then that the Wehrmacht's advances in Russia were slowed by an unexpectedly early rainfall, followed by a harsh and sudden winter, which created mud and then ice and snow for which the German soldiers and their armor were ill prepared. Now the numerical and technical inferiority of the German tanks as opposed to the Soviet ones was acutely felt.[45] In November, the German troops were stopped some thirty miles outside of Moscow. By December it was clear that the Red Army was able to hold its own and actually launch a counter-offensive. Whereas Hitler's allies—Romania, Hungary, Italy—remained impotent, the United States, foolishly challenged by Hitler after Pearl Harbor, became an ally to the British and the Free French, strengthening them militarily and morally. On December 16, Britain itself forged a difficult but tactically effective alliance agreement with the Soviet Union. Three days later Hitler accepted the resignation of his commander-in-chief of the Army, General Walther von Brauchitsch, and assumed this role himself, to his ultimate detriment. One month earlier, General Erwin Rommel had been defeated for the first time by the British near Tobruk, North Africa, despite the fact that the Germans had diverted two hundred extra bombers to the African theater in 1940. As Gerhard L. Weinberg, the foremost expert on the subject, has judged, by January 1942 the Germans' martial specialty, "the whole concept of a Blitzkrieg, a lightning war, had failed"— irrevocably as it turned out, and on all fronts.[46]

These setbacks and the ensuing more serious defeats had severe consequences for all of Nazi Germany's soldiers and caused particularly grave harm and disillusionment for the younger ones among them, who almost without exception had come from the Hitler Youth, where the tone had been nothing but optimistic right into the high war years. Even while marching into battle, the young soldiers were extraordinarily taxed. One former Hitler Youth wrote of marching forty-five miles every day from Finland toward the northern Russian front, for several days on end: "Day and night. No sleep. Hardly a crust of bread." This occurred during July with its short nights, "in wilderness, jungle, swamp and desert sand, under a scorching sun."[47] Food was frequently scarce, so that soldiers soon ate nearly everything, including potatoes fried in motor oil, which led to dysentery.[48] Other scourges were mosquitoes, especially in eastern and southeast Europe, and blood-sucking lice, which never disappeared.[49] Helmut Nielsen from Kiel noted in May of 1940, advancing into Russia: "We are tired to the point of falling down. The only things keeping us awake are alcohol, nicotine and the never-ceasing, ear-shattering rage and roar of the flak." All this had a numbing effect: "You can only act mechanically, you can't think any more."[50] Shell shock and battle horror reduced many young soldiers to automatons, and this got worse as the war progressed. One of them wrote home about a friend who had been in North Africa for twenty-three months without leave, always in the desert. During this time, his parents were killed in an air raid, his bride had betrayed him, and his brother had fallen at the eastern front.[51]

Actual battle for many former Hitler Youths, even with grueling war games behind them, turned out to be a rude awakening. When Friedrich Grupe had to join a dangerous advance detail in Russia in June 1941, he realized that this experience was rather different from the stories of World War I which he had read to his charges around the campfire; this was now "tough reality." His commander had sent him on a mission to find out whether the enemy was at the edge of the forest and what weapons they possessed. During this mission, many men were lost.[52] Also at the Russian front from 1942 to 1944 was Kurt Meyer-Grell, a pilot in a Luftwaffe Special Operations Wing which dropped agents over enemy territory. "Every time I was shot down behind Russian lines I was prepared to shoot myself," he recalls; "I had seen the remains of *Stuka* fliers who had been massacred by Russian soldiers, their stomachs slit open, and so on."[53] His comrade Hans-Ulrich Greffrath, who was wounded for the fourth time in the spring of 1944 fighting Russian tanks hand-to-hand, had come across mutilated Wehrmacht soldiers captured by the Russians, "without ears, without noses, without eyes. One of them was a very good friend of mine."[54]

Indeed, no Hitler Youth war games could have prepared these young soldiers for the death and destruction they would now help to cause on a daily basis and would often fall victim to themselves. When Hitler spoke in his Reichstag address of October 6, 1939, of 10,572 men who had fallen during the Polish campaign, 314 of these had been full-time HJ leaders.[55] Seeing the first dead or wounded of one's own battalion was always a major jolt, until one became inured, although that only occurred after a multitude of terrors. A former Hitler Youth assigned to a tank division still has stark memories from the Russian front: "We are lying flat on the ground. All around us is a raging inferno. Those who have already been wounded once are being hit a second and third time. You can hear their whimpering. The commander of the tank in front of me has taken a bullet in the head, and his brains are running down his face. He's running around in grotesque circles crying, 'mother, mother.' Finally, and almost mercifully, he is hit again by shrapnel and falls to the ground."[56] The lack of anonymity for these soldiers, fighting alongside their own friends, only increased the horror; this is what made partisan warfare so threatening, for it was always small bands of German soldiers who would be lured into an ambush, to be killed in the most gruesome manner, and then to be discovered by close comrades. The feeling of complete impotence in the face of omnipresent partisans was all-pervasive. Horst Lange tells of an incident near Gshatsk on the south Russian front in November 1941, when five partisans were caught and hanged. The next morning, a German soldier was found hanging right beside them.[57] Nor was the carnage limited to Russia. In Greece, partisans specialized in killing members of the Wehrmacht occupation forces by throttling them from behind with steel wire.[58] And such experiences were happening to ever-younger Hitler Youths who were drafted by 1944. When the invasion of Normandy by the western Allies occurred in June of that year, it was the tanks of the Hitler Youth division "Hitlerjugend" that tried to stop them; these tanks then became coffins for thousands of young soldiers, often after they had been burned alive.[59]

Apart from physical injuries and death, there were psychological factors that compounded the misery of these young soldiers and threatened to reduce their efficacy as cogs in Hitler's war machine. As is true of soldiers at all times, worries about young wives and girlfriends back home did much to undermine front-line morale. With young German women feeling lonely and deserted, and sexually tempted by the conscripted laborers at home, their fidelity could be in doubt. Thus young Hermann wrote to his sweetheart Rosl to ask whether she, too, was betraying him. "Dear Rosl, you have to love me. If I were with you I would have no fear, for then I could fight for you to the last, but this way I am far away from you and cannot see you."[60] Another soldier wrote to his girlfriend Herta that, surely, she had not forgotten him— or did she now have another lover?[61] Some of these doubts led to tragic results. One young conscripted man, suspecting that his wife had betrayed him, asked the opinion of a sergeant, who was renowned as a sage. The sage took the wedding band, fixed it to a human hair and, as it swung slowly across the photograph of the woman, divined that she was unfaithful. Desperate, the soldier sought death the next day.[62]

Entirely different, but equally damaging to the morale, were rising doubts about the truth of the Nazis' image of the enemy, especially in regard to the Russians. After several months the former Hitler Youths found that many of the Russian soldiers were open and valiant fighters, rather than the beastly cowards that Nazi propaganda had projected. "The Russians are extraordinarily tough soldiers," wrote one, "and if you call them subhuman, that's nonsense. Some who were captured looked as if they could easily have been in the HJ."[63] Already in the fall of 1941, the superiority of Soviet air power was conspicuous; after an early Nazi rout in June 1941, the Red Army once again had more planes than the Wehrmacht.[64] The partisans were, on the whole, deemed effective, and German soldiers had to admit grudgingly that their Soviet counterparts were humans like themselves.[65] Not surprisingly, many young German soldiers fell in love with Russian girls, who, contrary to the teachings of Schirach and Goebbels, were often found to be blond and blue-eyed.[66]

For the Germans, the defeat at Stalingrad on February 2, 1943, turned out to be a watershed in more ways than one, and it significantly affected Schirach and Axmann's erstwhile charges. Within his larger strategic scheme, Hitler needed this industrial city on the Volga River in the Southeast of Russia because it was to be instrumental in salvaging the area already conquered beyond the Crimea and was a key post for further expansion in the East. It was in this entire region and further east into the Donets Basin and the Caucasus that the German armed *Wehrbauern* settlement would be started, so that agricultural staples, heavy industry, and valuable oil would be secured. Beyond these immediate goals, Hitler was hoping to move his armies into Iraq and Iran for the control of oil in those regions. Thereafter, joining up with Rommel's forces who would push east from North Africa, the aim was to unite with the Japanese and expel the British from South Asia.[67]

After the Wehrmacht's setback on three extended Russian fronts in late 1941, Hitler's Army groups in the South were making headway again in the new year, conquering Sevastopol on the southern Crimea in early July, 1942. By the end of that month three German armies were moving east and southeast, and in early August they occupied the first of several rich oil fields near Maikop in the northern Caucasus. Further to the northeast, General Friedrich Paulus ordered the attack on Stalingrad on August 19. Paulus was assisted by Luftwaffe General

Wolfram von Richthofen, who flew 1,600 attacks against the city, bombing it into a field of ruins. Forty thousand civilians died. "Stalingrad was important not only as a major industrial center and as a place where the Germans could halt all shipping on the Volga but as the major connecting point to any operations in the Caucasus," writes Weinberg. It also possessed valuable armament factories. However, it soon became obvious that the city would be hard to conquer completely, in the face of continuing Soviet resistance. Until November, there was house-to-house combat. "Streams of blood in the streets," noted Nobel laureate Thomas Mann in his diary, who from his exile in Los Angeles was keenly following the war, "much of it German." When the Germans finally controlled most of the nearly destroyed city, their army had suffered huge losses. Having regrouped, the Russians began a concerted attack on the Wehrmacht in Stalingrad on November 19, and three days later, after a successful pincer operation by three Russian Army groups, Stalingrad was encircled. This came on the heels of the Soviet relief of Leningrad in the North, which had been besieged by the Germans for seventeen months. By January 1943, after three months of winter fighting, the Wehrmacht in southern Russia had lost more than half a million men in killed and wounded. Hitler, who refused General Paulus and his 6th Army permission to break out of the city, was still building on Göring's promise that Stalingrad could be well supplied from the air, with 300 tons of provisions per day, but the enfeebled Luftwaffe managed merely a third of that. And even then the Führer could not make good on his promise to send relief troops under General Erich von Manstein, but still he forbade Paulus to capitulate. The Soviets started to invade the city on January 10, 1943, and the German forces inside were split in two. On February 2 Paulus, having just been promoted to field marshal, capitulated of his own volition, surrendering 90,000 men to the Russians, of an army originally up to 250,000 strong. The rest had fallen or died of disease and hunger. Of those taken prisoner, most perished soon after; only 5,000 eventually made it back to Germany.[68]

The disillusionment and desperation experienced by the young soldiers before their certain doom is evident from their diaries and letters, as well as from the memoirs of the few wounded soldiers who were flown out by the Luftwaffe or those who eventually returned from captivity. They stand in grotesque contrast to Hitler's and Goebbels's decision to recast what was a major disaster for the nation as a giant heroic sacrifice. Instead of owning up to egregious military blunders and a deplorable defeat culminating in dishonorable unconditional surrender, as Paulus himself had been too cowardly to stand up to Hitler, Nazi propaganda proclaimed the event to have been a valiant action, in which every single German soldier in the cauldron of Stalingrad willingly laid down his life for Germany and its Führer.[69]

As part of this larger deception, German families on Christmas 1942 were linked to a radio broadcast from Stalingrad, so that they could join the soldiers in singing "Silent Night." Those families did not know that the link-up was a fake; 1,280 soldiers died in Stalingrad on Christmas Day alone.[70] Two separate reports on Christmas in and around Stalingrad tell us that one group of German soldiers had to dig themselves a new hole with a makeshift roof on Holy Night, during a snowstorm at minus 30 degrees Celsius. Lacking bread or potatoes, they made hamburgers out of horsemeat; there were no parcels or letters from home. The other group huddled nearby did have a bit of chocolate and candy, a few pieces of meat and bread. They consumed this an hour after Russian artillery had torn a comrade to shreds.[71]

Although there was hope against hope to the very day of surrender, a growing sense of despair had begun during the advance on the city in the late fall of 1942, especially among the young soldiers just out of the HJ and still dependent on home. The lack of mail delivery seemed incomprehensible to the younger men, particularly at Christmas.[72] And then there was hunger. Because of constant air-supply interruptions, rations of bread and meat had to be incrementally decreased, until by Christmas Eve sixty-four soldiers had died of undernourishment. Around this time, meat from the dying horses and the stray cats, dogs, and rats was becoming the sole staple, with minuscule portions at that. The men made soup from sawdust. Because of the lack of fresh water,

thirst added to the agony of famine. Göring's planes were still drop-
ping supply bags, but they often missed their targets, falling to the
enemy instead. During January the German soldiers were drinking
machine oil and cannibalizing dead comrades. Many of those taken
prisoner on February 2 had not eaten anything for about a week.[73]

The infamous Russian cold, setting in by early November, compounded the nutrition problem. The steppe in front of Stalingrad contained no wood for burning, and inside the city's walls combustible
material was scarce, as was gasoline. Garments were deemed to be sufficiently warm only after several dead soldiers had been stripped of their
uniforms; even then hypothermia proved endemic.[74]

The cold did not destroy lice and fleas, which carried diseases such
as typhus. One of the most common causes of death in the Stalingrad
area apart from malnutrition was freezing. Sheer exhaustion after days
and nights of sleeplessness was also widespread, weakening a soldier's
will to live. Having been wounded would prolong his agony, unless he
was lucky enough to be flown out of the encircled area. At one of two
functioning airports, the lightly wounded kept stepping over more
serious cases in an effort to reach a plane; they had to be restrained
with pistols. A doctor reported in January that on the roads around
Stalingrad lay the wounded, as well as those frozen to death and still
freezing, who were blocking his car with their bodies. "Their screams
begging to be run over or be rescued repeated themselves with variations over the entire route. Many were lifting their hands entreatingly,
hidden in soaked bandages, some were shaking their fists, and others
did not stir at all." By the end of the month approximately 40,000
wounded German soldiers were staggering from one field hospital to
the next, never finding entry and finally collapsing in the city's ruins.
The Russians bombed one of the central sickbays, resulting in 3,000
patients being burned to death.[75]

In both the civilian population and the armed forces, when the scale
of the catastrophe became apparent, the results were dread and discouragement. Contemporaries were not good judges of the past, nor
could they divine the future. Therefore, they could not adequately

gauge the significance of the defeat at Stalingrad as a turning point in the fortunes of Nazi Germany. As we now know, a string of serious reversals ensued: German manpower much reduced in the East; the tide of war turning in North Africa; the landing of the western Allies in Sicily; Mussolini's deposition; Hamburg's fire-bombing; D-Day in June and the attempt on Hitler's life in July 1944—all of these represented a major chain of disasters leading up to German capitulation in May 1945, virtually a mirror image of the string of successes the Nazis had taken for granted from September 1939 to February 1943. In hindsight, Stalingrad symbolizes the false security in which Hitler's young warriors had lived since the beginning of the war. To prescient minds even then, Stalingrad appeared as just punishment for past follies and as a bad omen for the future of generations younger than the ones who had moved into battle in September 1939. Among those who harbored such sobering thoughts were the Wehrmacht soldiers Hans Scholl, Alexander Schmorell, and Willi Graf of the Munich White Rose resistance cell, who would pay for voicing their conscience with their lives.

Problems encountered by young German soldiers even before Stalingrad led to doubts about their function in the Nazi regime and its expanding war in particular. For many, they also led to questions regarding the value of the Hitler Youth, insofar as it had been instrumental in landing them in what more often than not turned out to be physically and morally compromising situations. By the nature of the police state they were serving, any criticism had to remain muted—of the regime, the Army, the Party and its affiliates, including the HJ, if not of Hitler himself, whose charisma consistently rendered him immune to criticism; instead Germans generally thought he was being deceived by his entourage.[76] These widespread negative feelings belie the optimism that Goebbels displayed publicly when in December 1941 he visited more than a hundred men blinded during the recent campaigns, the oldest of whom was just twenty-four. After he had given each of them a radio set, "they were overjoyed like children," he claimed, "as they were already starting to pick up their lives again."

Goebbels was fooling himself and others when he concluded that from this field hospital, "doom and gloom" had been banished.[77]

Memoirs and even diaries and letters from the front, though censored by the Nazi authorities, suggest that some young soldiers, despite their indoctrination in the HJ regarding the enemy, were beginning to watch certain practices by their superiors with misgivings. They felt ill at ease when SS and police squads accompanying their units burned down whole villages or employed Wehrmacht comrades in the execution of prisoners.[78] Disillusionment could also set in whenever the Army ordered young men barely out of their teens to officiate at or participate in the ceremonial execution of deserters.[79] Not surprisingly, by late 1941 as the war was starting to go badly, more and more young soldiers developed doubts about it, and questions about the competence of the higher leadership arose. Such feelings intensified at the time of the assassination attempt on the Führer in July 1944; even diehard young Nazis were wondering what it was that could motivate Prussian officers to murder their commander-in-chief, whose inviolability was still being taken for granted.[80]

Seeing comrades around them die and be maimed, but also watching with barely concealed horror a similar fate befalling their adversaries at the front, young soldiers became more introspective, starting to think about their lives as a very expendable commodity. Despite the many Hitler Youth idealists, whose unchanging fanaticism remained a mystery to some of the more seasoned officers such as Army physician Curt Emmrich, who thought their idealism totally distorted, pessimism among some was palpable.[81] A few of these young men resolved to seek action at the front lines, looking for a speedy death; others kept bullets for a suicide in reserve, full of doubts that this war could ever be won.[82]

Another source of disenchantment especially in the last phases of the war was an increasing distance between conscripted soldiers and their commissioned officers, who, in order to drown out their own frustrations, were often observed amusing themselves at the expense of their subordinates. These amusements were sexual as well as involving all sorts of corruption such as hoarding and squandering liquor. In early 1944 the SD, the security service of the SS, reported that behind the lines officers were organizing parties with various women, for whose enjoyment the rank and file had to provide live entertainment. While the common soldiers were suffering from hunger, officers were feasting and even sending packets home. "The higher the rank, the better the good life," the SD cited one disappointed soldier as saying.[83] The longer the war lasted, the more frequently even married officers were taking French or Russian girls as lovers and unabashedly displaying them in their company even during official functions, to the disgruntlement of the lower ranks. Even as promiscuous a man as Goebbels was complaining about this—presumably not the fact as such, but rather the lack of discretion with which it occurred.[84] "Almost all of us, the veteran youth leaders, experienced an inner cleansing process," recalls Ralf Roland Ringler for the period after 1943, "in that progressively we damned this war, although we did not have a clue how to carry on ourselves once it was over."[85]

Today one may doubt the intensity of this "cleansing process," since most former HJ leaders possessed neither the maturity nor any guidance other than the horrors of the war to recognize the fundamental wrongs. They had also been too thoroughly conditioned in the HJ ranks. But under the impact of this awful conflict, many were gradually impelled to doubt its rationale, their own role in carrying out its aims, and the overall integrity of their superiors. It was dawning on them that unheard-of injustices were being perpetrated. After Warsaw had been bombed to bits in October 1939, one eighteen-year-old soldier wrote home that "the population is terribly starved and without shelter . . . we often share our own modest provisions, because the misery of the children and women touches our hearts."[86] Fraternization with, even sympathy for the enemy was of course forbidden, but especially during the murderous Russian advance some compassionate German soldiers tried to alleviate needless suffering by preventing acts of arson and calming down the peasants. Others visibly distanced themselves from the indiscriminate looting.[87] "The barbarism is becoming obvious," observed one young German soldier at the Russian front in the late summer of 1941, while another thought nothing of helping out wounded POWs with drinks of water.[88] In November 1941 a former Hitler Youth was devastated by the execution of some twenty Soviet female soldiers: they had to lie down in the dirt next to each other and then were flattened by panzers.[89] The moral indignation of many of his comrades increased after witnessing the front-line shooting of Jews; in one case a woman fell on her knees begging for her life, while the soldier could not help her.[90] Even at the risk of court-martial, by 1944 criticism of the regime voiced in the censored letters from the front became louder and more frequent; the war itself and the July attempt on Hitler were openly discussed.[91] Increasingly, as the war was drawing to a close, German soldiers refused to kill the enemy, especially in hand-to-hand combat, and one of them tells of defying an order to execute Italian partisans, thereby risking his own life.[92] The Hitler Youth was no moral compass in such situations; hence it was out of mind for many of these soldiers at that time. "I do not feel drawn to the HJ," stated one former member from a mountain division in 1943, for it "does not give a hoot about me any more."[93]

This comportment, however infrequent, approached not heroism but decency, as these soldiers watched the majority of their former comrades in the HJ continuing the vicious treatment of the enemy or participating without qualms in the killing of innocent civilians, partisans, and Jews. Others, however, were driven not by desperation motivated by high-mindedness, but by selfishness. They had concern merely for their own suffering, and thus they sought suicide or self-inflicted battle death, self-mutilation for the sake of being sent home, or outright desertion. How many desperate young men killed themselves or willingly tried to end their lives in the front lines is not known, because every casualty of this kind was officially declared a hero's death. (Attempted suicide was treated as self-mutilation.)[94] But desertions were accelerating, especially after Stalingrad, with various ordinances from 1934, 1938, and 1940 providing for incremental punishment.[95] More and more, prison sentences were replaced by the death penalty, the most honorable of which was death by shooting, which, after Stalingrad, had to be done as a deterring ritual, in public view of the troops.[96] In March 1943 Hitler as the new commander-in-chief of the Army stipulated that military and civil courts should carefully weigh the type of death penalty to be meted out. Next to shooting, dishonorable guillotining and, worse, hanging were to be decreed for especially shameful behavior, such as repeat offenses or having caused harm to others.[97] The staggering statistics pertaining to desertions between 1939 and 1945, with a steep increase from 1943 to 1945, reflect the worsening erosion of the Wehrmacht's morale. Whereas during World War I merely 150 German soldiers had been condemned to death and only 50 actually executed, during World War II nearly 23,000 death sentences were pronounced, of which up to 16,000 were also carried out. These death verdicts do not include the smaller number of cases in which deserters were successful or those where they tried and then gave up in the middle of the act.[98]

Today it is chilling to read the stories of those young German soldiers who actually made it. In early 1945 Horst Krüger along with a buddy crossed the Dortmund-Ems-Kanal at night to the American lines. When the GIs detected them at dawn, the Americans at first held up their hands in a gesture of surrender, believing the two to be part of a German advance platoon.[99] Twenty-year-old Heinz Brenner planned his escape meticulously. Wearing his old HJ outfit underneath the Wehrmacht uniform, in October 1944 he absented himself from his barracks, still in Germany, changed his clothes in the forest, and then boarded the train as the youth leader he had once been. Until the end of the war he hid with friends in a remote rural area near Ulm.[100] Albert R., an eighteen-year-old soldier, deserted from the elite "Grossdeutschland" division after only three weeks in early 1945. He was caught and sentenced to death, but during an air raid he managed to escape. Initially trying to reach the Russians, he then gradually drifted westward until he met up with U.S. troops.[101]

More disturbing is the fate of those who were killed. The military court procedures were juridically correct, punishing even brief unexcused absences from the troops but still allowing for pardons at an appeals court. Most often, these were denied.[102] A nineteen-year-old deserter from Berlin, blond, the picture of a Hitler Youth and German soldier, was executed in December 1942. A comrade remembers: "He stood straight like a candle and looked directly at the rifles. He did not scream, nothing. They aimed at his heart, toward his chest. And then there was a bang. He had been shackled, his hands tied behind him. Now his entire chest was ripped open, because eight soldiers shot at it. The poor fellow got the full load into his chest and then slumped down, but he was still alive. He was alive. And moaning terribly. We could hear this fifteen meters away. Finally the master sergeant appeared with his 08, approached him and—this was the most terrible thing—knocked two, three bullets into his head."[103] Indeed, even after several shots, some delinquents were still stirring and then had to be finished off with a coup de grâce.[104] At the end of the war, in early May, many German soldiers were tried, sentenced, and shot even when they had assumed—often correctly—that the Third Reich had surrendered and they just wanted to avoid falling into the hands of the enemy. In a particularly tragic case, two sailors, Bruno Dörfer and Rainer Beck, who while in Holland had deserted and joined the Dutch resistance, were delivered to a Canadian POW camp, where the captured Wehrmacht sub-commandant, who still had internal jurisdiction, tried them for treason. The Canadians thereupon delivered rifles to the Germans, so that both men could be executed, a week after capitulation.[105]

These executions degenerated to veritable lynchings in the last desperate German retreats of the war. Because desertion had become endemic, and the more so the younger a soldier was, the military police and SS exercised what was cynically termed "emergency justice" on the spot and hanged, on trees, lamp posts, or anything that could support a rope, any man who could not produce proper marching papers. Hitler Youth boys as young as fifteen and just drafted became ensnared in these actions because, children that they were, their nerves were giving out; they started crying and just wanted to go home to their mother. Some were thrown from the balconies of houses where they had sought shelter, with ropes around their necks. Others were given enough time to write big letters on a piece of cardboard, which was then fixed to their bodies. As the German film actress Ingrid van Bergen recalls it, fleeing East Prussia as a child of thirteen, one such sign read: "I am a deserter. I was a coward in the face of the enemy."[106]

Self-mutilation, which was defined as a punishable offense in the law of 1938, was somewhat less dangerous than desertion.[107] If done properly, it could go totally undetected by Army physicians and the "war-wounded" man might then be sent home, out of fighting commission for the balance of the war. The fact that what officially was an act of cowardice often worked as a ruse was due not least to sympathetic physicians who decided to shield the patients by not reporting them and nursing them back to health.[108] Still, at the eastern front, where soldiers were particularly prone to inflict wounds on themselves, the Army maintained special institutions in which suspicious candidates were subject to expert examinations and legal proof of defeatism could be collected.[109] Even if proved, however, self-mutilation led to fewer arrests than those for desertion, because in practice it was deemed less serious than running away from the war zone.[110] Nonetheless, there were no guarantees. These soldiers could still be shot, hanged, or guillotined, as was the case with twenty-five-year-old Berlin draftsman Heinrich Pryswitt in Brandenburg penitentiary in June of 1944, who was decapitated.[111]

The most common type of mutilation, sometimes with the help of comrades, who also were liable to punishment, was damaging a part of one's body, usually with a shot through the hand or by hacking off parts of a limb. One might also induce commonly recognized sickness symptoms by ingesting some chemical, or, especially at the eastern front and notably at Stalingrad, purposely freezing one's extremities.[112] Some of these war shirkers endured odysseys of self-injury. Josef Sch. from Bavaria was seventeen when in June of 1943 he injured his left foot with an ax, after having been called up to fight. Recovered, he was conscripted again in November, and this time he severed his left index finger. He was tried in July of 1944 and received eight years in penitentiary.[113] Also faced with conscription in 1944, Claus B. from Munich simulated abdominal pain, getting nowhere with physicians. He then smoked aspirin all night until he trembled, but the hoped-for neurological inflammation failed to appear. Finally he injected himself with turpentine, which destroyed the tendons in his arm. The doctor treating him saw through the ruse but kept his composure, and Claus then survived the end of the war by rubbing salt into his wound to keep it open.[114]

Hamburg's Wolfgang Borchert was able to combine the effects of a self-inflicted wound with true illness in order to survive, albeit in a pitiable state, beyond 1945. A sensitive young man and former reluctant Hitler Youth, at the age of twenty and just having seen action at the eastern front in 1942, he too cut one of his fingers off, claiming later, most implausibly, that he had lost it in close combat with a Russian. With the help of a skilled defense lawyer Borchert was sentenced to only six weeks' incarceration and subsequent probation at the front, during which he contracted a terminal liver disease. He returned to Hamburg a wreck; until he died in 1947, his life was a constant balancing act between mental exhaustion and illness, the terribly persistent memories of war, and unpleasant reactions to an unsettled postwar society.[115]

Detours, Duplications, and Alternatives

Subsequent to entering the armed forces by September 1939 and fighting at the fronts, German adolescents reared in the Hitler Youth experienced several changes, most often in close correlation with Germany's fortunes in war. As time went on, this had the effect of robbing many of them of their former faith in the Hitler Youth as a disciplinary and ideological training opportunity. But it could also render them less effective as soldiers: the duplication of training and drill in the Wehrmacht, vis-à-vis the HJ, seemed thoughtless and demeaning. Such counter-productive measures, apart from hurting the efficacy of the Wehrmacht in battle as well as the legacy of the Hitler Youth, ulti-mately caused much frustration and anger among the young soldiers, who saw their acquired skills ignored or treated contemptuously by non-HJ-related NCOs and officers alike.

The redundancy of training in the transition from Hitler Youth to Wehrmacht was repeated in other instances, resulting in additional duties and multiple chains of command, which further demoralized Germany's fighting youth, in addition to detracting from their effec-tiveness in the Third Reich's war machine. The first experience of this kind occurred through the Reichsarbeitsdienst (RAD), or Reich Labor Service, which most veteran Hitler Youths were enrolled in after 1935 as RAD Workmen, a step between HJ and Wehrmacht. It was one of the many rival organizations of Party and State clamoring for the total control of Hitler's subjects at various age, occupation, and gender levels after January 1933, in which institutional Darwinism determined the ultimate winners—often, but not always, with the Führer's final judg-ment weighing in.[116]

The RAD resulted from the Freiwilliger Arbeitsdienst (FAD), or voluntary labor service, which was created during the austere Brüning regime of the Great Depression in July 1931. It was the long-term product of conservative planners within right-of-center political par-ties, including the NSDAP, several Weimar youth leagues such as the *Artamanen,* and the national universities' student bodies, which by that time had been largely right-radicalized. Chancellor Heinrich Brüning had adopted the labor service as part of a national policy to get unemployed youths off the streets and provide them with mini-mum wages for performing public works such as draining swamps and building roads, but there was also a nationalistic pedagogical agenda.

When Hitler took over the government, there was a multitude of FAD groups, often involved in internecine fights against each other. The Nazis, interpreting this situation as just another sign of the hated pluralistic system of Weimar, consolidated these groups in 1933 under retired Army Colonel Konstantin Hierl, a dependable follower of Hitler, and created the state-monopolist Reichsarbeitsdienst. Its membership remained voluntary (although the consolidation of diverse groups had not been) until the introduction of re-armament and two-year conscription after March 1935, when it became obligatory for each young man past age eighteen to serve in it for six months. A variation of this service, which fit more appropriately into their educational program, was prescribed for adolescent females.[117] For young male Nazis, the Reichsarbeitsdienst became mandatory after service in the HJ. At all times the RAD was considered a stepping-stone to conscription. When the war broke out, RAD duty remained compulsory, wedged between HJ and the armed-forces branches, but now that service in the Wehrmacht was indefinite, the RAD duty came with a reduced term of three months.[118]

The RAD was not an ancillary to the Party, as was the Hitler Youth, nor of the Wehrmacht, which first reported to the War Ministry and after February 1938 directly to Hitler; instead, it came under the Reich Minister of the Interior, with its own disciplinary jurisdiction.[119] As such, the RAD existed in a separate space beyond the HJ and Wehrmacht and was not coordinated with the duties of either in any practical way. Since the RAD's original economic purpose had been fulfilled by the time Germany had conquered joblessness and had in fact reached under-employment in 1937, it had only two major objectives until the end of the Third Reich, either of which could have been, or actually was, assumed by the Hitler Youth and armed forces as well. In the prewar years both objectives were symbolized by the spade, which as the emblem of the RAD had to be obsessively polished by its bearers until it looked like a mirror.[120] This was demanded by RAD personnel, often unsophisticated men shunned by the Wehrmacht and SS, who erected a small empire of their own within which they were free to torment their Arbeitsmänner (Workmen) at will. The first of these objectives was National Socialist indoctrination in the tradition of "Blood and Soil," which the *Artamanen* youth league had held high, with its aggressive vision of eventually settling in armed camps in a conquered

East. Indeed, RAD leaders expressly acknowledged the ideologically grounded imperialist settlement aims of the *Artamanen* with their reference to Blood and Soil.[121] The spade, as the chief instrument for working the soil, was supposed to point the way to such a future. The second objective was military training, in which the spade, with its sharp blade and the heft of its long wooden handle, was a substitute rifle. Indeed, it would be presented like a rifle, repeatedly during endless roll calls, on the order of the RAD leaders, who were responsible neither to the HJ, from which their young charges had just emerged, nor to the Wehrmacht, where they were headed. But the spade signified humiliation in those camps where spadework was employed solely for Sisyphean tasks, such as building a camp road for a camp that was then dissolved.[122] The cult of the spade persisted until well into the war. After the introduction of rifle, revolver, and grenade training, RAD exercises anticipated those in the Wehrmacht.

In most ways, war-preparation activities and their accompanying circumstances in the RAD resembled those either in the Hitler-Jugend or the Wehrmacht, or both. RAD Workmen wore simple uniforms of a drab brown color and were housed in far-off barracks. Their basic training, involving first the spade and then increasingly firearms, was exacting but often redundant in relation to earlier courses in the HJ and subsequent ones in the Wehrmacht. Nutrition was substandard, often based on tripe and other offal. Freezing temperatures afflicted recruits in winter as much as excessive heat stifled them in summer; the mass latrines were humiliating and conducive to ailments. These consisted of rheumatism and scurvy, along with high fever, as well as the occasional frozen limb. The repetitive communal singing was unnerving, as were the various spade and flag rituals. The schadenfreude of the tormenting staff was ubiquitous. Apart from occasional real work such as reconstruction jobs in Occupied Poland, draining swamps, digging ditches, or helping farmers with the harvest, the primitive staff's designs for mindless drill ruled the work days, with the Nazi-specific purpose of numbing the Arbeitsmänner into a state of physical and mental submission, the better for them to function in the killing fields. More often than not, veteran Hitler Youths found these redundant drills demeaning and complained about them. Discouraged and disappointed, they would leave the RAD after three arduous months to join the Wehrmacht, hopeful that conditions would improve.[123]

The system of Wehrertüchtigungslager (WE), or armed-preparedness camps, existed alongside the RAD and operated on the same theme. The Hitler Youth, Wehrmacht, and sometimes also the SS organized these camps jointly. The WE camps were a new form of what had been the HJ's own paramilitary training for senior members, those from sixteen to eighteen, involving more rigorous, concentrated training exercises after 1941. Those of age fifteen and younger continued to receive junior military instruction locally, in the HJ's own ranks. This new idea for condensed stationary exercises, from initially three weeks to twelve in the end, was Artur Axmann's. It enjoyed a closeness to the military that the would-be poet Schirach never understood. When Axmann, in collaboration with Army General Hans Friessner, approached Hitler about this plan at the Berchtesgaden *Berghof* in April 1942, the Führer agreed to the founding of boot camps for older Hitler Youths, generally at installations owned by the Wehrmacht, RAD, or HJ.[124] It is likely that Axmann, who had lost an arm in 1941 while intermittently fighting on the eastern front, was hoping for a revaluation of his office in a more military mold, perhaps with a promotion to General for himself. He knew that many former HJ leaders were now front-line officers, and some intermittently returned from combat to continue in the Hitler Youth leadership as well. If they enjoyed dual status, why couldn't he? Indeed, when the camps were established by the summer of 1942, their commandants were always HJ leaders with Wehrmacht officer ranks, with the military coaching being done by seasoned NCOs who had been wounded in the field.[125] By the end of 1943, 226 WE sites had been set up, servicing almost 515,000 Hitler Youths aged sixteen and up; in 1944–45, with longer training terms to accommodate, fifteen-year-olds were also called up.[126] Among the boys, this service was deeply unpopular, because those already gainfully employed had to sacrifice their vacation time to attend, and secondary-school pupils, who were drafted as class units, had to forgo summer or fall holidays.[127]

In a positive description of the WE camps, one American historian has recently characterized them as "a successful way to implement universal paramilitary training for Germany's adolescent population."[128] However, this service represented yet another duplication of the training which youths had received in the HJ, and which would be experienced again in the RAD and then in the Wehrmacht recruitment drill. The WE camps complicated further the entire premilitary exercise regimen, exacerbating difficulties resulting from overlaps of organization or gaps in logistics, resource allocation, personnel deployment, and institutional jurisdiction. As was typical of his governmental style, Hitler had probably authorized the project with the knowledge that, so long as it did not threaten the center of his universe, the more chaos developed around him and the more decisively he could act as the final arbiter, the stronger he would emerge. Holding out promises to underlings that might never be fulfilled or doling out empty honors was a favorite personnel ploy of his (as in his futile promotion of Paulus to field marshal at Stalingrad); in this case he could rely on the venal Axmann's bolstered loyalty, at a time when Vienna Gauleiter Schirach's allegiance to the Berlin political leadership was already very much in doubt.[129] As for the type and quality of training in the WE camps, it differed only by degree from that of the HJ, or of the RAD and the Wehrmacht itself, with the same brutal terrain and mindless weapons drill.[130] All told, the forces of counterproduction triumphed, to the further detriment of overall military efficiency and the erosion of the will of the recruits.

Both factors were even more in evidence after the establishment of the Flakhelfer or auxiliary anti-aircraft emplacement program in early 1943. This was the direct consequence of the events surrounding the defeat at Stalingrad, which had cost the regime several hundred thousand men, and the stepped-up bombardments of German cities and industrial or strategic sites, by British planes at night and American ones during the day. Throughout 1940 and 1941, the Luftwaffe had still been able to ward off most air attacks, although British bombs, for example, had hit Berlin as early as August 1940.[131] In 1942 it became obvious that the industrial centers of the Ruhr were prime targets, followed by Berlin and the strategic northern ports. Three weeks after Germany's humiliation at Stalingrad, Air Marshal Arthur Harris took over the RAF bomber command and introduced "areal bombing." That meant the intensive shelling of densely settled urban areas and concentrated industrial sites, such as those between the Rhine and Ruhr rivers.[132] As a trial target with many flammable wood-frame houses, one of them Thomas Mann's paternal home, the Baltic port of Lübeck was pounded at the end of March. Rostock was next a month later, and at the end of May one thousand planes rained 1,455 tons of bombs on Cologne for ninety minutes, at a loss of only thirty-nine RAF planes.[133] After this bombing, there were 480 people dead, 5,000 wounded, and 3,300 buildings destroyed.[134] Yet while this called for stronger German air defenses, by the fall of 1942 the necessity of diverting more planes to the eastern front had become equally obvious. This meant fortifying artillery emplacements to be manned by soldiers rather than using fighter planes. However, those soldiers were also increasingly needed for combat. Thus in September Hitler ordered 120,000 ground specialists of the Luftwaffe to be redeployed in active fighting, at the same time authorizing the use of flak personnel to be drawn from civilians. Later in the year, to reinforce the replacement measures, Göring asked the Reich Education Ministry for permission to recruit teenagers from the schools. Reich Education Minister Bernhard Rust's bureaucracy, already weakened by much regime infighting, agreed to the measures after perfunctory protests, and they were implemented early in 1943.[135]

On January 26, 1943, one week before Paulus's surrender at Stalingrad and after Rust's and Nazi Party chief Bormann's grudging acquiescence, Göring conspired with Axmann to conscript male pupils in secondary schools from age fifteen up to and including age seventeen as auxiliary artillery personnel, or flak helpers in colloquial language. The pupils were to be stationed in bunkers near their flak emplacements, and since virtually all of them belonged to the Hitler Youth, they nominally were under its supervision, with their regular teachers giving them eighteen hours of instruction per week. Those attending occupational schools and employed in industry, now all considered to be war-related and controlled by Göring, were to be exempt at first, but they too were drafted by 1944. From early 1943 to the end of the Third Reich, then, a total of 200,000 teenagers came to serve as cannoneers. After a stretch of indeterminate duration, they were to join the RAD, and subsequently the regular armed forces. They were spared the trying weeks in the WE camps.[136]

Once on duty, these youngsters were ordered to assist in the destruction of a variety of enemy planes: the heavy British Lancaster and Halifax bombers, as well as the nimble fighter and reconnaissance Mosquito aircraft. Increasingly in 1943, the American B-24 Liberators and the B-17 Flying Fortresses became a target as well. In its time, the B-17 was the most advanced bomber in the world. Although it was susceptible to catching fire after shelling, it managed the farthest distances and could take a maximum of two thousand hits per mission, some planes returning to their English bases with only one of their four engines intact.[137]

From the middle of February 1943, in order to turn these children into soldiers—the youngest of World War II—the Luftwaffe gave them four weeks of training near their artillery sites, before they actually manned the guns. At first, these were situated as close as possible to their hometowns, schools, and original HJ commands. In 1944–45 some boys were sent farther afield, for instance from Bavaria to East Prussia or the northern coast, as the moving-front situation required and as new emplacements were established.[138] The boys' trainers and immediate supervisors were NCOs who would instruct them in the use of varied-gauge ground-implanted guns, from the lightest 2.2 to the heaviest 12.8-centimeter type, and then fight alongside them. The artillery with the 2.2 and 8.8-cm gauges soon became the norm. Flak helpers had to learn how to lug around the heavy ammunition, to load the guns, and then to fire. They had to detect enemy aircraft with a form of radar less developed than that of the Allies,[139] and had to shine huge searchlights on approaching aircraft at night so these could be targeted. They memorized complicated codes and were taught to service the equipment, which, even when inactive, could be dangerous. Usually an artillery battery consisted of four standard cannon systems known as Emil, Dora, Caesar, and Würzburg; later there were six. Not surprisingly, the Ruhr area in striking distance from the Channel and with Münster as the Luftwaffe command, along with the capital of Berlin, usually received the largest contingent of flak helpers, followed by Hamburg for the northern flank. There were special marine flak emplacements, for instance in Kiel and Heligoland, staffed by the naval HJ.[140]

The Flakhelfer experience beginning in February 1943 represented the first time in the history of the Third Reich that boys as young as fifteen were fighting as soldiers in active combat. Helping to shoot down enemy planes was a harrowing task for them and marked them psychologically in their development to adulthood, aside from the fact that it killed hundreds of them and wounded thousands.[141] Although the boy soldiers fought valiantly, the Reich-stationed artillery did not have a chance from the start because of enemy air superiority, which turned this venture into a considerable tragedy by the spring of 1945.[142] "To hit anything up there was like a lottery," as Ottmar Mantz, today an internist, sums it up; "not to be hit ourselves was sheer luck."[143]

One reason the flak helpers did not have better luck was that, young as they were, they never received the hours of sleep they needed even under normal circumstances. Frequently they had to fight at night and then again the following day. To compound the effects of sleeplessness, they were haunted by fright and became prone to nervous breakdowns on the eve of an attack.[144] They refrained from putting cotton in their ears, to protect them from the deafening raids, because they did not want to be despised as weaklings.[145] One flak helper remembers indelible impressions of these assaults. "Bombs were whistling and howling down on us. After crashing with a thump and a screaming explosion, bomb splinters whirred into the walls of our barracks and the earthwork of our embankments. We tried to claw ourselves into the ground, but were constantly thrown into the air, with every new bomb impact. Some were praying aloud. And then came the air mines . . . they made no noise and caused no shocks, but almost unbearable air pressure, which threatened to destroy eardrums and lungs . . . the pressure was followed by suction that appeared to pull us out of the embankment. About a meter into the air, we were thrown from one corner into another, hurting our heads and backs on the tubing."[146]

Casualties were severe. As early as March 1, 1943, six flak helpers died in Berlin; four days later, four were killed in Essen.[147] A few months after that a 1,000-kilogram bomb swept an entire team of seven students and their corporal off their platform in Berlin; no one survived.[148] Often the boys attempted to dig out their comrades trapped by earth and debris, as in April 1944 near Brunswick. "Here a body, there an arm and over here another limb. A terrible chore! After two hours we give up. Total casualties for our battery tonight: two dead, four critically injured, and six lightly wounded."[149] Time and again these boys, who had been drafted, about a dozen per battery, straight from the school benches, found that their best friends had died.[150] This was especially traumatic when they were forced to search for them, holding body bags with which to retrieve severed limbs.[151] These searches also occurred whenever a cannon malfunctioned and exploded—every flak helper's nightmare—tearing everyone around to shreds.[152] Probably the worst mishap in Falkhelfer history occurred toward the end of the war, on the North Sea island of Heligoland, when on April 18, 1945, the British dropped 1,000 bombs on what was considered a strategic platform to the German mainland. A hundred and fifty pupils from as far away as East Prussia and Silesia had been stationed at several emplacements. The concerted bombing lasted for two hours and killed at least a third of the boys. Entire batteries were seen sliding from the rocks into the sea, taking everybody with them.[153]

Apart from the ineffectiveness of their military prowess, the adolescent Flakhelfer soon found themselves in an uncertain situation, between the Hitler Youth on the one side and the armed forces on the other. More precisely, they were escaping the HJ's purview before they had been properly received into the Wehrmacht. Whereas this anomalous position tended to undermine their self-confidence, which they compensated for by overemphasizing military paraphernalia and comportment, it further weakened the authority of the Hitler Youth toward the end of the war as the national keeper of youth, while burdening the Wehrmacht with the responsibility for not having properly integrated Hitler's youngest soldiers into the armed forces.

As they were summoned to serve in the flak positions, the teenagers were proud to be able to leave behind the Hitler Youth, which they associated more with boyhood than manhood, and instead to link their fate to the Wehrmacht's, which, they thought, brought them closer to manhood and to serving the Third Reich. This started with the uniform they were ordered to wear—one that was vaguely gray-blue in color like the Luftwaffe's, but cut in the HJ style.[154] Even though it resembled Wehrmacht attire on the street, it was still marred in the view of the boys by two of the HJ's insignia: HJ regalia affixed to the cap, and the HJ armband. So, in order to bolster their self-esteem as soldiers, the Flakhelfer, at a safe distance from their emplacements, would hide the armband and fold away the cap emblem.[155] Although this was forbidden, it gave them advantages in the nearby towns such as attending adult-only films, staying up late in pubs, smoking and drinking alcohol—all against the Police Ordinance of March 1940, but guaranteed to impress the girls. Fortunately, such recreation could now be financed by military, albeit modest, pay.[156] The Flakhelfer justified such liberties to senior HJ critics with the argument that if they were old enough to give up their lives, they should also be ceded soldiers' rights. The HJ was an impediment on a fast road to adult status, which service in the artillery teams seemed to guarantee. To further prop up their self-esteem and new status, the flak helpers would avoid greeting HJ leaders outside their compounds. They chanted soldiers' rather than Hitler Youth songs, and in some locales they took delight in beating HJ teams in competitive sports such as soccer.[157]

After 1945, former flak helpers went to great lengths to emphasize that they rejected the Hitler Youth not because it was more National Socialist than the Wehrmacht, but because it stood for infancy and immaturity, despite all the war games and premilitary training they had undergone as boys there since age ten.[158] Indeed, forced into pseudo-adulthood by a totalitarian regime early on, these juveniles felt that living a Flakhelfer life was a logical next step; they seized on it as a way to speed up the growing-up process and to achieve a more significant status in the Nazi hierarchy. Still, by denying themselves natural steps in the development from childhood to adolescence and artificially forcing rites of passage, which, for their age cohort, were decidedly premature, they suffered an aborted youth.

This became apparent to them as soon as the flak helpers experienced the arrogant welcome they received from the entrenched Wehrmacht soldiers. This took the form of several weeks of preliminary exercise and drill, similar to what they had gone through in the Hitler Youth and anticipating what they would endure again in the RAD and in regular Wehrmacht front duty. "All of us, since the age of ten, had not only learned and executed all orders but many of us had taught and supervised basic training routines for more than four years," complains one veteran flak helper in retrospect. Now the familiar indignities were exacerbated.[159] One aspect of Flakhelfer basic training was especially distasteful as the boys, still not grown to their full height, had to wear adult uniforms (until they received their specially made outfits); their heads disappeared under helmets that were too large, and oversized underwear had to be tucked into ill-fitting Army boots. Some of them looked like scarecrows.[160] To add insult to injury, insensitive non-commissioned officers refused to give them shaving cream, because only a few of them displayed what could at best be described as downy facial hair.[161]

Those corporals wanted to deny these youths the very symbols of maturity for which they had embraced the Wehrmacht after turning their backs on the HJ. But in this case the age difference between the corporals and the flak helpers was significant, in contrast to veteran Hitler Youths over eighteen who had already been through the RAD and now were regular soldiers. These NCOs were rough and resented the superior education, dexterity, and often higher social backgrounds of the young draftees, most of whom later opted for officer training. In the words of Field Marshal Rommel's son Manfred, sixteen at the time, the best one could do was learning to "endure their insults." The NCOs reveled in off-color jokes that disturbed the mostly sexually innocent boys, and being themselves rather low in the military hierarchy, they delighted in bullying youngsters who sometimes could have been their sons. Nor was there any more sympathy expressed by the (often younger) commanding officers. As a rule, they were haughty, frequently as a result of rivalry for the affection of local girls, and, what was worse, they were slow to protect the flak helpers against encroaching HJ leaders who wished to reassert their authority.[162]

Although this was incomprehensible from a practical point of view, it was officially stipulated that Flakhelfer should continue to come under the jurisdiction of the HJ, and that one HJ leader per emplacement should act as "corps leader." There was even talk of regular Hitler Youth service to be maintained within the framework of the old formations, as if the new and all-consuming objectives did not matter.[163] Not surprisingly, however, even the former HJ leaders in the ranks of the flak helpers not only could not care less about their former functions, but also simply paid no heed to any call for HJ duty.[164] (Because of an overall lack of communication, they did not know that a particular regulation of the Luftwaffe backed them in this.)[165] Consequently, whenever a higher Hitler-Jugend functionary put in an appearance at a flak battery, he was resented and ignored by boys who now considered themselves above the HJ. In some cases, flak helpers threw their nominal bosses out of the compound, lest they show up a second time.[166] In September 1944, the Hitler Youth leadership urged its regional chiefs to visit the emplacements more regularly and pay more attention to ideological training, as well as insisting on the execution of HJ service, including, unrealistically, sports and rifle drill. "The guidance of the

Air Force and Navy helpers must take place much more strongly and more intensively than has previously been the case," the HJ leadership insisted, only to add: "Hitler-Jugend service has to be conducted in such a way that the Air Force and Navy helpers look forward to it, rather than rejecting it as a nuisance."[167]

In addition to manning the batteries, dealing with their Wehrmacht superiors, and trying to ward off HJ interference, the flak helpers still had to see their families, who usually lived in the nearby towns they were defending, as well as some teachers from their old schools. This applied only to Gymnasium students, for instruction in lesser secondary schools such as Mittelschulen had ceased.[168] Unlikely as it may sound, the Flakhelfer still had to undergo schooling of eighteen hours a week, instead of the regular thirty-six, in a reduced number of subjects, usually not more than four, with German and History topping the curriculum.[169] These exercises had very little benefit for anyone involved. Because only a small number of teachers, never more than three per week, were able to visit the flak compounds to teach their charges irregularly (after visits by the students to the school buildings had become impossible), the quality of instruction was minimal. The teachers themselves were old and often uninspired, generally over sixty-five and recalled after normal retirement. Having made these arduous trips to the emplacements, they found no proper teaching facilities there and felt that they were needlessly endangering themselves.[170] At the end of term, all classmates received indifferent, uniform grades; some passed a final examination or were handed school-leaving certificates, which later were not worth the paper they were printed on.[171] With most of the regular school instruction truncated, and what was left of it militarized, "the period spent as a flak helper was as good as lost for school study," recalls former cannoneer Rolf Schörken.[172] What was worse, and ultimately detrimental in civilian life, was that the wastes and losses incurred in formal education were not even regretted at the time by most pupils, either because of sheer exhaustion or because excitement now derived from weapons rather than the pen.[173]

Flakhelfer service also changed the relationship between the boy soldiers and their homes, and usually for the worse. The same insecurity
was at play here as when facing other authority figures: these teenagers wanted to be adults but had not yet mastered necessary hurdles
in their ongoing adolescence. To the same degree that they admired
soldiers and their officers—sometimes an experience that resembled
unrequited love—they somewhat unsuccessfully dismissed traditional
schoolteachers and regime-sanctioned youth leaders, thinking themselves almost adults. This mentality entered into their relationship with
older members of their families as well. With fathers or older brothers
mostly at the fronts or already killed, it was easy to ignore the authority
of concerned mothers, aunts, or grandparents.[174] While the boys, frequently close to their towns, were allowed home leave several times a
month, they used this opportunity to get home-cooked meals and a
good night's rest and for posturing, but hardly to return to the bosom
of the family. The boys felt uneasy at home, as a result of doubts about
their newly acquired status; they knew that something was out of
sync.[175] They especially resented it when mothers came to visit them in
their compounds, because this gave the older soldiers more grounds for
sarcasm.[176] Because of their ambivalence about maternal affection,
another childhood support was torn away from these teenagers.

The entire Flakhelfer interlude resulted in changes in these boys'
collective persona that set them apart from the world around them,
alienating them from their conventional peers and superiors, while not
yet amalgamating them with the new soldier class they craved to belong to. This gave them a strange new sense of identity as a group unto
itself; they developed their own rituals and taboos, where feelings of
negativity and self-doubt, but also the tremendous fear of instant
death, were turned into a subjective sense of being part of an elite. And
that brought with it certain entitlements. Because it just was not done,
Flakhelfer would enter into conversations with Soviet POWs who had
been commandeered to assist in artillery service, finding them quite
human (contrary to what Nazi propaganda made them out to be).[177]
While hardly wavering from the standard belief in Germany's "Final

Victory," they would also interest themselves in some of the enemy soldiers they shot down—British, Canadian, and particularly American pilots and their crews—whose uniforms or haircuts intrigued them and inspired their own budding sense of fashion.[178] America was, after all, an interesting phenomenon despite being the enemy; the flak helpers were impressed by the power of their superior planes. And Allied Forces pilots were held in awe, even in Nazi Germany, where in the worst of cases angry crowds in the country might lynch them as "terror fliers."[179] But fleeting encounters with these western enemies, as they were observed falling from the skies suspended from parachutes or found as casualties in crashed planes, also led to curiosity about their life-style and popular culture as gleaned through enemy radio stations, which those elderly teachers did not talk about. Therefore, like the Swings of Hamburg or Frankfurt, flak helpers soon took to listening to Dixieland jazz and swing, though clandestinely, trying to heat up the HJ hymns and wearing their hair a bit longer, as signs of mutual recognition among themselves and symbols of being different from the world around them.[180]

It is important to emphasize that the Flakhelfers' unusual situation—wanting to outgrow the HJ and being ill served by teachers, yet not accepted as full-fledged soldiers and hence developing certain idiosyncrasies like wearing their hair longer—did not translate for them into a rejection of the Nazi system. On the contrary: whatever had been abstract dogma or preliminary drill and training in the Hitler Youth, could now be put to the test of hands-on practice in the flak emplacements. The memoirs of former Flakhelfer attest to the fact that differences between them and the HJ were not over ideology, but over their status as juveniles or adults. The war itself, during which they were attempting to shoot down enemy planes, for most of them reinforced pre-existing notions that they were fighting a justified war for Adolf Hitler and his Third Reich.

The final factor that interfered with a smooth transition from the Hitler Youth to the armed forces was the SS. Its armed wing, the Waffen-SS, had been in existence since August 1938. Always beyond the Wehrmacht but ideologically and institutionally tied to Himmler, it was routinely staffed by conscripting members of the black-shirted General SS, by Death Head's squads from the concentration camps, and by regular police units, as well as by enticing volunteers from the HJ.[181] The HJ youth were drawn to it for several reasons: the SS's reputation for hardness, its well-tailored uniforms, the prestige that Hitler's Praetorian Guards enjoyed among all of the Party cadres, and, not least, its status as the personification and embodiment of Nazi ideology and superiority. The SS claimed to be the elite of the renewed German nation, and as such was idolized by many young people. As soon as fighting began in September 1939, the standing of the field-gray-uniformed Waffen-SS was enhanced by its emphasis on the toughest discipline and order as well as resourcefulness and resilience in battle; it was said to be supported by superior apparatus such as fully motorized battalions. The fact that within its officer ranks the SS paid much less attention to social class than did the traditional formations of the Wehrmacht worked to its benefit. The truly fanatical members of the HJ who had embraced the racialist ideology revolving around the German master race, and especially the role of males in guarding core values, regarded the Waffen-SS with high enthusiasm, feeling that incorporation in its ranks was a natural complement to a fulfilling HJ tour of duty.[182]

Ideally, from the vantage point of Himmler and his insiders, every year starting from 1938 the top graduates of the HJ at age eighteen were to enter the Waffen-SS as volunteers. This claim was supported by a well-functioning relationship between the HJ and SS dating back to 1933, especially after the creation of the youth police, the HJ-Streifendienst (SRD), in 1934.[183] If anything, Axmann's relationship with high SS leaders such as Himmler and Reinhard Heydrich was even closer than that of his predecessor, von Schirach. But as time was to show, there were limits to the number of recruits the Waffen-SS could claim for itself from the ranks of senior HJ members, despite various ruses that Himmler and the deferential Axmann employed to get around the difficulties.

Primary among these limitations was the statutory advantage the traditional Wehrmacht branches held over the SS in that the Wehrmacht High Command had been assigned an official ratio for its forces, which it had to fill by conscription or through volunteers. With slight variations from year to year, until 1942, this consisted of 66 percent for the Army, 9 for the Navy, and 25 for the Air Force. The Waffen-SS, of whom the Wehrmacht had been suspicious as an upstart since its inception, was too small to be specifically included in this distribution scheme. Hitler had granted it a few armed divisions, leaving the details to be worked out by the Wehrmacht and SS.[184] Thus the Führer had once again seen to it that a potentially chaotic situation could be resolved ultimately only by himself. In effect, this meant that Himmler was permitted to induct a generous contingent of men from his General SS for his Waffen-SS, but that the number of volunteers he could court for the Waffen-SS from other sources would be limited. The Wehrmacht thus exercised a recruiting monopoly until the second half of 1942, when Himmler, too, was permitted to conscript recruits because Hitler wanted more and younger troops.

Another limitation on SS recruiting was that the Wehrmacht— apart from its official liaison with the HJ since 1935—made full use of its privilege of visiting the Reich's Gymnasien for the sake of courting future officers from among the pupils, who were of course also Hitler Youth. This was based on the rationale that when candidates joined the Wehrmacht as volunteers before being drafted, they could elect whatever armed branch suited their taste. On the other hand, if they waited until their name was called, they would be assigned to a branch they might not like.[185] Aiding the Wehrmacht in this quest was the fact that in the youths' eyes, the conventional military was legitimized by German history. Moreover, as a result of general conscription from March 1935 to 1938, the Wehrmacht was ahead of the SS by a full three years in actually possessing operational combat units. It reflects on the HJ as a prime conveyor of Nazi ideology that it could not motivate a critical mass of its graduates to choose the Waffen-SS over the Wehrmacht, despite the fact that originally both the HJ and SS were creations of the

Nazi Party. When faced with the choice, unlike their more enthusiastic comrades, many HJ leaders and ordinary members tended to pass up Himmler's revolutionary corps in favor of the Army, Air Force, or Navy.

This was the predominant trend from 1938 until capitulation in spring 1945. Within its limits, the SS was determined to recruit as many HJ youths as possible, by trying to outwit the Wehrmacht and availing itself of its good relations with Axmann. At first it was taken for granted that enough pressure could be exerted on veteran SRD members, with the result that they would join the Waffen-SS to a man, perhaps after first having joined the General SS. But despite constant exhortations, even those youths who were awed by the SS often did not feel up to it; it was precisely the elitist reputation of physical toughness and ideological rigor in the SS that induced them to consider the Wehrmacht's safer and less demanding alternatives.[186] It is true that there were SRD members who did join the Waffen-SS, accompanied by fellows from the general HJ, many of them flocking to Himmler's troops in their early stages.[187] Before long, however, quite a few of them, when home on furlough, warned their younger comrades not only of the excessive harshness in these Nazi elite troops, whose standards were much tougher than those in the Wehrmacht, but also of SS pressure to shed Christian church ties. As well, they told of atrocities against partisans, POWs, and Jews by the SS that they had witnessed in the field, often as accomplices.[188] Nor was the higher casualty rate among the Waffen-SS lost on HJ teenagers.[189] Although many were intrigued by it, others were repulsed by the blood-group tattoo that every SS man received near his armpit, for they saw it as a stigma betraying its bearers as a sworn group, a group whose purpose was dubious.[190]

As soon as the Waffen-SS recruiting teams realized that adverse news from the fronts was beginning to dampen the enthusiasm of potential SS candidates, they began to operate with a mixture of flattery and pressure. By 1941, recruiters were approaching senior Hitler Youths, complimenting them on their looks ("You two tall fellows, what are you looking for in the Navy? Come to the SS! That's an honor!") and then prompting them to sign their names. It took strength of will not to be seduced by the SS aura of power and virility.[191] Soon the Waffen-SS perfected a tactic that critics from the Wehrmacht termed "the categorical demand to join voluntarily," with the HJ leadership abetting. It instructed its local leaders to call in the boys for regular service, there to meet SS recruiters, but "without telling them what it is all about."[192]

During 1942, the SS was complaining about how little headway it was making in comparison with Wehrmacht recruiters.[193] Meanwhile, Hitler was approaching his manpower impasse in the months before the fall of Stalingrad. Impressed by the brutality and military successes of Himmler's squads thus far, Hitler allowed him to modify in his favor the recruitment allotment ratio set earlier, thereby facilitating enlargement of the Waffen-SS by conscription. The Führer did this duplicitously in order not to upset the Wehrmacht, and Himmler wisely commenced the SS draft not in the German Reich, but among ethnic Germans in the Balkans.[194] At the same time, the Waffen-SS intensified its recruitment efforts in local HJ stations by stepping up its pressure; sixteen-year-old Hitler Youths like Erhard Eppler could barely escape through quick pre-registration with one of the Wehrmacht's proprietary enlistment offices.[195] Wehrmacht pre-enlistment also became a favorite line of defense for Flakhelfer after the capitulation at Stalingrad in February 1943, because even in the face of the daily friction with superiors in the battery emplacements they had immediate recourse to a traditional armed-forces branch.[196]

By 1942, then, the SS was concentrating its efforts to recruit youth in three areas: in the newly established WE camps, the RAD camps, and the regular HJ stomping grounds. The WE camps offered great potential because out of 120 of them, about 40 were run by the SS, to which 90,000 HJ members were assigned. Here the SS was grossly over-represented, given that its stake in the combined Nazi armed forces was merely 3 percent. But the problem was that although the SS furnished 700 trainers for the WE centers, the great majority of their charges, including promising SRD veterans, still opted for Wehrmacht service, not least because of the cruelty of their SS warders. Ironically,

of those who did apply, many had to be rejected because they did not
meet Himmler's elite racial standards, as they were either too short or
their skull measurements were not right.[197]

Himmler's next chance arrived when after the Stalingrad debacle
Hitler relaxed the stern conscription rules for SS recruitment within
Germany, to be initially attempted in the RAD camps.[198] But trying to
press already discouraged RAD trainees into the Waffen-SS, a process
during which SS recruiters would use all the physical and psychological force at their disposal, proved disastrous. Since there was still no
official SS draft ordinance, only a tacit understanding between Hitler
and Himmler, the RAD draftees resisted the bullying. This was not
easy; the SS worked on some candidates for many hours without inter-
ruption, while others were physically assaulted. In at least one Reich
Labor Service camp the SS pretended to sign up candidates only generally, specifically crossing out, in pencil, the name of the Waffen-SS.
Only later did the HJ boys learn that the pencil lines had been erased.[199]

Understandably, Himmler was not too happy with the overall
results. Even among those who had signed up, whether by the carrot or
the stick, many were either physically unacceptable or mentally not
ready, for example if they refused to renounce their Christian faith.
Blaming the HJ, Himmler found many of the inductees to be afraid.
"It was reported that the candidates were crying and that those who
did not pass muster were rejoicing," he complained to Bormann in
May 1943.[200] But until the spring of 1945, the pied pipers from the
Waffen-SS had no choice but to continue their fiendish combination
of persuasion and terror in every part of the HJ leadership's realm. By
paying lip service to the principle of voluntarism, the SS extorted more
signatures, sometimes after the visit of a dashing SS officer showing off
his Iron Cross, on other occasions after screening a fascinating SS film
from the front. But tricks and traps still abounded. In one case the
boys were X-rayed for tuberculosis by Himmler's mobile radiation unit
headed by an SS Colonel, Professor Hans Holfelder. When they confirmed the examination in writing, they also confirmed the small print,
containing their consent to be drafted. As late as March 1945 in the

countryside east of Munich, the SS was still using scare tactics: explod-ing grenades behind sixteen-year-old boys to shock them (they in-stantly wet their pants), or threatening others with handguns.[201] These dubious methods brought few rewards. The SS's own quotas could never be met, since juveniles from the Hitler Youth kept showing a marked predilection for "tank divisions, Navy, mountain troops, motorized units," but not those of the SS.[202]

It was in collaboration with Axmann that the Waffen-SS eventually attained a triumph, short-lived as it was, with a tank division manned almost entirely by Hitler Youths—the highlight of the laborious collu-sion between the HJ and SS. Overly ambitious and in craven devotion to Himmler, Axmann in early February of 1943 exploited the defeat at Stalingrad and, in search of a military legacy for himself, approached the highest SS echelons with a plan of creating HJ panzer troops. He knew this might be successful because he was familiar with the pen-chant of his charges for military rolling stock, especially tanks, which so far HJ trainees had only admired from a distance. Axmann used to his advantage the instinct for play in every Hitler Youth, who in the case of action in the field would be between sixteen and eighteen years old. In many ways they were still children, "in love with their vehicles," as one of their field commanders, SS General Hubert Meyer, remem-bers.[203] It is both significant and touching that when they were trained for combat in 1943 and early 1944, the panzer recruits did not receive cigarettes like mature soldiers, but candy.[204] Yet as with the Flakhelfer, in the acute situations of warfare, the fight was no game.

Himmler, backed in this by Hitler, was immediately attracted to the idea and decided that a HJ tank division, to be modeled on the classic "SS-Panzerdivision Leibstandarte Adolf Hitler," the first of several SS tank units, had to have around 20,000 men and 4,000 leaders. They were to be screened from among 30,000 current Hitler Youths as well as seasoned veterans of other SS divisions, but also from former HJ al-ready in the Wehrmacht as NCOs and officers.[205] Nevertheless, Axmann soon had to concede that it would be difficult to recruit a youth con-tingent of that strength, especially since he did not have sufficient experts to train them.[206] The redoubled recruiting efforts of the SS especially in RAD camps that so bothered the HJ boys after 1942 was being done with these tank divisions in mind.[207] In the end, large numbers of youths were trained for many months in Wehrertüchtigungslager staffed by the SS as well as in Beverloo in Belgium, until they were ready for battle on the western front in the early summer of 1944.[208]

Their first encounter with the enemy was a day after D-Day, on June 7, 1944, near Caen, just off the beach in Normandy, as they faced Canadian, American, and British assault craft. There appear to have been close to 20,000 boys, and during one of their first attacks they promptly knocked out twenty-eight Canadian tanks.[209] A former HJ, in retrospect, has said, "our division fought valiantly."[210] With the ingenuousness and resilience of youth, but also fully conscious of being in an SS division known for murderous onslaught, the boys battled so tenaciously that by the middle of July they had lost 3,000 soldiers, and Himmler and Axmann were desperate for replacements.[211] Some of these youthful soldiers engaged in suicide missions that seasoned Wehrmacht soldiers would never have dared to attempt, such as allowing tanks to roll over them and then detonating a grenade.[212] German Army commanders like Rommel and Heinz Guderian got to be as much in awe of them as their enemies were.[213] Their fanatical faith in their cause and in themselves led them to commit war crimes, however; in the late summer of 1944 they shot sixty-four British and Canadian prisoners-of-war, for which their commanding officer, Kurt Meyer, was eventually sentenced to death by a Canadian court.[214] In keeping with the character of this tank division, Meyer had been the youngest divisional commander in the entire Nazi forces at the time of his appointment. Meyer was already the second commander after the first one had fallen during the invasion, and after his capture, he was followed by two more leaders.[215] Effective leadership could not be depended upon.

After many cataclysmic events at the fronts, the most disastrous for the HJ panzer division and also the most sobering for its survivors in the end was its defeat of September 1944. Faced with insuperable enemy forces and never-ceasing Allied air attacks, the 12th SS Panzer Division "Hitlerjugend" got caught in the encircled area near Falaise, some twenty miles south of Caen (which it had taken on July 9). With only 600 men remaining and no tanks breaking free and returning to the Reich, they regrouped as part of the 6th SS-Panzer Army under Hitler's favorite warrior Sepp Dietrich, a butcher's apprentice turned SS general, known for his desperate but unsuccessful attempt to save the regime.[216]

The Final Victory

When the ultimate defeat began to descend upon Nazi Germany in late 1944, its leaders had no choice but to husband their last resources in both manpower and materials. By this time the Allied air forces had attained total control of the skies, and the German Navy was losing its grip in the Atlantic, the North Sea, and the Baltic, the last of which had been crucial for the safe conduct of Swedish iron ore to German shores. Vital industrial installations in the Ruhr Valley were bombarded decisively in early 1944, as were the Schweinfurt ball-bearing works in northern Bavaria. The German synthetic oil industry was being knocked out, and Romanian crude oil was no longer available to the Nazis after successful British and U.S. long-range planes had staged their last raid on Ploesti in August 1944.[217]

All the while, after the successful invasion of Sicily in July 1943 and Normandy in June 1944, the western Allies were inching up to the Reich from the edges of Europe in the South and West, and the Soviets were preparing to take the capital of Berlin from the East. In September 1944 the U.S. First Army crossed over the German frontier for the first time, near Eupen in Belgium, occupying Reich territory north of Trier. By early February 1945, the western armies, consisting altogether of two million Americans, British, Canadians, and Free French, were poised to move from France into Germany. They reached the area west of the Upper Rhine on February 9. By the beginning of March

the entire left bank of the Rhine River was in Allied hands, and on March 7 U.S. troops crossed the last remaining bridge over the Rhine at Remagen, some fifteen miles south of Bonn. The northern part of the heavily industrialized Ruhr area was subdued at the end of that month, as the Allies were now advancing toward the North Sea and Baltic coasts. Bremen and Lübeck fell to Field Marshall Bernard Montgomery's Army just before the Americans were able to take Hamburg on May 3. By early April the entire Ruhr had surrendered to the American Ninth Army, with over 300,000 German prisoners being taken. At that point Hitler's formerly unflinching vassal, Field Marshall Walter Model, put a bullet through his head.[218]

Having collected soldiers who had lost contact with their units, flak emplacement personnel as well as inmates of officer training schools and WE camps, Field Marshall Albert Kesselring had formed an Army Group South for the defense of southern Germany. Despite his efforts, General Alexander Patch's American tanks entered Nuremberg, an important shrine of Nazidom, which was theirs on April 20. Ironically, it was Hitler's birthday and the traditional day of initiation for new Hitler Youth recruits. Patch and his colleague George Patton continued into the Alpine region, Patton eventually to meet up with the Red Army, which had invaded Vienna on April 6th, conquering it on the 13th.[219] This happened after Budapest had been taken by the Russians in February, with a loss of almost 30,000 German men.[220]

Meanwhile, in the East, the White Russian Front of General Ivan Tscherniakovsky had plunged into East Prussia in October 1944, touching Gumbinnen, not far from Königsberg or, for that matter, Rastenburg, home to the Führer's command post Wolf's Lair. Even though the Soviet general had to beat a retreat for the time being, huge numbers of Wehrmacht soldiers had already been surrendering to the Red Army for some time. The conquest of East Prussia, bordering on the Baltic Sea, was essential for the march on Berlin from the North; in January 1945 Stalin knew the capital would be included in the future Soviet occupation zone. By the end of that month Königsberg was surrounded, with German forces driven onto Pillau, the Baltic peninsula somewhat northwest of the East Prussian capital. Further to the south, the Oder River—the last major impediment before Berlin—had been crossed and almost all of Silesia to the east of it occupied. February saw the Soviets pushing fiercely westward in a broad front from East Prussia and Pomerania down to Silesia. Small German counter-offensives such as the one at Pomeranian Pyritz-Stargard were soon quelled. The Russian advance was indirectly helped by a series of Anglo-American air raids against the Saxon capital of Dresden, a strategically important railway hub, on February 14–15. The death toll there of "tens of thousands" of civilians who were fire-bombed, many of them fugitives en route from the East, had a similarly devastating effect on German morale as the fire-bombing of Hamburg had had in the summer of 1943. From West Prussian Danzig (Gdańsk), a great many fugitives could still escape from the Russians by sea, until at the end of March that port too fell to the Red Army. As the Battle of Berlin was beginning by mid-April, Lower Silesian Breslau was still holding out and did so until early May, and so was Prague in the Protectorate, until on May 5 it was captured by Czech resistance fighters, who, however, had to surrender control to the Russians later in the month. By that time, countless "inhuman acts of cruelty," in the words of the German historian Lothar Gruchmann, had already been perpetrated on Prague's remaining Sudeten and Reich German population.[221]

The Russians could have captured Hitler earlier when he was at Wolf's Lair in October 1944, but by January 16, 1945, he had repaired to his bunker below the Berlin Reich Chancellery. By the middle of April Marshal Georgi Zhukov with his 1st Belorussian Front was moving against the northern outskirts of Berlin from the Oder River, while Marshal Ivan Koniev's Ukrainian forces were closing in on the city's southern environs, after having traversed the Neisse, a tributary of the Oder. Hitler briefly considered opening up a new German front under SS General Felix Steiner and Wehrmacht General Walther Wenck; Wenck's 12th Army division stationed near Wittenberge in Brandenburg on the Elbe and Stepenitz rivers, like Kesselring's to the southwest, was staffed by an assortment of young, inexperienced soldiers, including hastily drafted RAD Workmen and members of the Hitler Youth. Parts of these contingents were then set in motion to march eastward on Berlin, but were unable to get there before the end of April. U.S. forces too were moving east during this last month in the Third Reich's history, encountering heavy German opposition in the Harz Mountains east of Brunswick, where Himmler had addressed the Hitler Youth nine years earlier. On April 25, when the capital was completely encircled by Zhukov's and Koniev's armies, the Americans met up with Russian troops near Saxon Torgau on the Elbe, tentatively celebrating their hard-won victory. For seven days thereafter, until Berlin as a city surrendered on May 2, Russian tanks and foot soldiers waged ferocious street and house-to-house battles, winning territory inch by inch against disorganized squads of straggling Wehrmacht soldiers, motley Waffen-SS crews, and clutches of poorly armed Hitler Youths. Those desperate boys did not know they were defending a moribund tyrant who, shielded in his bunker by his cronies, married his mistress, Eva Braun, on April 29, only to commit suicide a day later.[222]

The increasing demands on men and matériel were raising important questions regarding ever-greater deficits in the Third Reich's overall resources. There had been problems ever since the invasion of the Soviet Union in June 1941, but after the disaster of Stalingrad in February 1943 and with enemy invasions looming, it had become clear that the Nazi regime had to redouble its efforts in the marshaling of economic and manpower potential. On the matériel side, the new Reich Armaments Minister Albert Speer, along with Reich Marshal Göring and Plenipotentiary for the Work Force Fritz Sauckel, took firmer control.[223] On the personnel side, Sauckel had insisted, a week before the fall of Stalingrad, that he needed all males from age sixteen to sixty-five to join the war economy.[224] However, as was typical of the confusion that had already infected all bureaucracies in the Third Reich, this would conflict with Goebbels's widely publicized Sportpalast speech of February 18, 1943, in which the Propaganda Minister asked the German people to agree to the new extraordinary demands of total war. Goebbels required "operative reserves," meaning the military deployment of hitherto non-draftable men, including adolescents.[225] Potential contradictions between the needs of the economy and those of the military were not removed when Goebbels became Plenipotentiary for the Total War Effort (yet another grandiose title signifying a parasitical office) on July 25, 1944, in which capacity he could scout for manpower additions to the war economy, thus assisting Speer and Sauckel, while at the same time helping to find new soldiers, in this way counteracting them.[226]

Hitler himself, as usual trying to have the last word in situations of disorder, appeared to cast his lot with the advocates of armed forces expansion when he decreed the establishment of the Volkssturm, a sort of last-ditch people's militia for the defense of the home front, to be recruited from among men aged sixteen to sixty, on September 25, 1944. Civilians by the Geneva conventions, and therefore in danger of being treated as partisans when caught, they would wear armbands over mufti to indicate combatant status and would be instructed in the use of whatever arms could be found.[227] In early October Himmler, freshly installed as Supreme Commander of the Replacement Army, decided that a new batch of fighters could be made available by declaring younger cohorts of Hitler Youths eligible for this service than had been the rule before: all those of age sixteen were to be trained in WE camps of six weeks' duration, and those of age fifteen in camps of four weeks' duration. A few days later, in conjunction with Bormann, Himmler ruled that anyone now in RAD camps—the stage just prior to Wehrmacht induction—could also be sent into immediate combat, within the framework of the Volkssturm. Newly organized HJ training courses would acquaint the youthful warriors with high-power weapons, such as machine guns, bazookas, and carbines, in only four days. Specifically mentioned were future encounters with enemy tanks.[228]

As the Allied invasions proceeded that year, it became clear how important the tank was as a weapon. Tanks were the land armament of choice for the Americans and the Russians, as they had been, indeed, for the only regular division ever set up under the banner of the Hitler Youth. To be conquered by Americans may have been bad enough, but

there existed a mortal fear of the Russians among the German civilians living close to the eastern borders and among the Wehrmacht and
Waffen-SS fighting near the Soviet lines. It dawned increasingly on the
Germans that "as an incentive for the soldiers of the Red Army, now
that the prewar territory of the U.S.S.R. had been freed of German
occupation, the internal propaganda was concentrated on the theme of
vengeance as a replacement for the earlier theme of defending the
homeland."[229]

Hence by January 1945 at the latest, anti-tank weapons became part
of the munitions arsenal of every HJ branch of the Volkssturm that was
now organized and lying in wait, especially for Russians about to tread
on German soil.[230] At that time Reich Youth Leader Axmann asked
Hitler for permission to create special HJ anti-tank brigades, to prevent the Soviets from crossing the Oder. After some hesitation, Hitler,
grasping at every last straw, welcomed the idea. From January on, the
enrollment of fifteen-year-old boys for active combat, through special
Hitler Youth, WE, or RAD camps, was further encouraged. Beginning
in February, the possibility of combat for fourteen-year-olds (those
born in late 1930) was not excluded.[231] And if until March the lines
between voluntarism and compulsion in the various forms of the
armed service by these youths—all under nineteen—had still been
blurred, that uncertainty was removed when on the third of that
month Hitler's Wehrmacht Chief of Staff, Field Marshal Wilhelm Kei-
tel, ordered conscription for any male born in 1929 or earlier.[232] Moreover, Hitler planned to pull out all those born in 1928 from the
Volkssturm and have them thrown in with troops at the regular fronts,
however close those fronts may already have been to German towns
and cities.[233] Those boys born in 1929 and 1930 were to serve in
Volkssturm brigades or in Axmann's special anti-tank divisions, stationed in or near endangered German settlements.[234]

By the end of March those brigades were often staffed by boys who
had already done much fighting elsewhere and, exhausted and sometimes wounded, represented reserves of the last resort. "Here they are,"
wrote Vienna HJ leader Ringler in his diary on March 28, "Willi with

his artificial lower leg, Hubert with his shot-off thigh, Hannes with his damaged foot, Schorschi with a prosthesis and head bandage, Karl with his empty sleeve, and all the others, those already recuperated or barely so."[235] At the beginning of April, there were similar troops all over Hitler's Reich—Munich, Nuremberg, Berlin.[236]

Already in the fall of 1944 Goebbels was full of admiration for HJ squads that were rushing to the western front to help with heavy fortifications.[237] Later in the year and in early 1945, Hitler Youth troops of various sizes and provenance were specializing in halting the tanks of Americans pushing to the Northwest and South of Germany. In some locations, such as Nuremberg until April 20, the HJ troops also carried anti-tank rockets and rifles, typically older French and Italian models, because new ordnance was scarce. Usually, these HJ formations, whatever their size, were fighting in conjunction with the Wehrmacht or Waffen-SS.[238] Sometimes they informally attached themselves to individual officers, content to follow their orders, thereby sealing their own fates. Near Einbeck, between Göttingen and Hanover, four local Hitler Youths met up with Heinz Neupert, a fanatical Luftwaffe lieutenant, who was recuperating from a war injury. On Sunday, April 8, as American troops were moving east across the northern half of Germany, the four schoolboys loaded their bazookas into a small Opel car and under Neupert's guidance drove to the village of Lüthorst, close to the U.S. line of fire. They hid behind a pile of boulders and recklessly began to shoot at the Americans. According to a local witness, "one tank positioned itself in front of the village and shelled the quarry until nothing was moving any more. The boys were hit mostly in the abdomen. They were still screaming, but nobody dared to go in there."[239]

In the East, by the middle of January 1945 Königsberg had become the first important target of the Red Army. There were Hitler Youth troops on the East Prussian front, in defense of that one-time bastion of the Teutonic Knights. One squad consisted of the cadets of a glider school that had been transferred there from the West, sixteen and seventeen years old, who were now manning machine guns. However, some of them had only old rifles that froze and kept stalling in the cold. The Russians got dangerously close and totally overran this group. As Joe Volkmar later recalled, "out of 90 proud glider pilots, we lost 20 killed or missing in our four-hour combat experience that fateful morning of January 25th."[240] Hitler Youths were everywhere in the defense of Königsberg and its surroundings, but no sooner did Soviet soldiers come across them than they treated them brutally, often by beheading them with bayonets.[241]

Whereas Königsberg held out until April 10, Danzig in West Prussia had already surrendered on March 27.[242] In the spring of 1945 the entire eastern front, now being pushed steadily to the West, was sustained in large part by those newly created Hitler Youth battalions, with some interruptions, right down to Vienna.[243] In Pyritz, south of Pomeranian Stettin, there were many who had been trucked there as part of the last-ditch Volkssturm, holding the German lines against the assaults of the Soviet 9th Guard Tank Corps moving in from eastern Lippehne. Among them were former flak helpers who had been rushed there from elsewhere in the Reich and granted the status of soldiers (their dream of former months) to protect them under the Geneva conventions. When recalling this time, Rolf Noll can name comrades as young as thirteen, and he remembers how Russian tank drivers specialized in spotting youths in hastily created dugouts, then moving their vehicles over them and turning on the spot, thus crushing the boys underneath.[244] Further south in provincial Brandenburg, on the Oder River near Frankfurt and Küstrin, a specially called-up Hitler Youth regiment "Frankfurt/Oder" was fighting under HJ commander Kiesgen, trying to halt the Russian onslaught on the capital.[245] And in Silesia, too, there were such regiments, in particular one in Breslau called "Regimentsgruppe Hitlerjugend," under HJ leader Herbert Hirsch and several Wehrmacht NCOs. Altogether, 1,000 boys were fighting there in two battalions, as they retook from the Russians a railway station and a factory, mostly with hand grenades. At least half of those child soldiers perished.[246] Breslau fell in early May, as did Prague, where armed Hitler Youths had also been holding their ground. When the Czech insurgents took control of the city center, they—who were now drowning, hanging, and burning German civilians by the hundreds—singled out these boys. "Approximately forty Hitler Youths, blood-stained and with swollen, beat-up faces, were driven into the human square. In front of the assembled prisoners, after unspeakable cruelties, they were finished off with knives and clubs."[247]

Many if not most of these young German soldiers, out of desperation but also because they had been brainwashed in prior training sessions to show no mercy especially to Slavic enemy soldiers, were equally cruel. In order to boost their morale, but also for Goebbels's newsreels, Hitler received a contingent of twenty of them in his Reich Chancellery bunker on March 19. They had been brought in from Pomerania and Silesia, and each of them was presented as a little hero, having knocked out a tank single-handedly or having taken Russian prisoners. The youngest of them was Alfred Czech, twelve years old and from Upper-Silesian Oppeln, who had been decorated for rescuing twelve wounded Wehrmacht soldiers and catching a "Soviet spy." Some had knocked out tanks with bazookas; others served as couriers. All wore the Iron Cross. "You already know what battle is like from your own experience," said the gray, hunched-over Führer, "and you know that this struggle is for the German people, to be or not to be. In spite of all the hardships of our times, I am completely convinced that we shall emerge victorious from this battle, especially as I am looking at German youth and at you, my boys." Hitler could not have expressed it better in his *Mein Kampf.* "Heil, mein Führer!" shouted the boys, with their eyes agleam.[248]

By the end of March more and more Hitler Youths were being concentrated in clusters around Berlin, moved from places like Brandenburg an der Havel, Luckenwalde, and Oranienburg to locations inside the capital's suburbs, such as Spandau and Tegel in the North, and from there closer to the center. In mid-April nearly 6,000 of them were in the city, under the nominal command of Reich Youth Leader Axmann and his deputy, WE inspector Ernst Schlünder, awaiting the invasion of the Soviet troops. The youths were only supposed to assist regular Wehrmacht and Waffen-SS detachments, as well as firemen, police, and the old men of the Volkssturm. But as it turned out, when the Russians got inside Berlin on April 25, the older fighters, under town commandant General Helmuth Weidling, were sadly deficient and totally dependent on the reserves of Wenck, which were never to materialize.[249]

Axmann himself was safe in the bunker, next to his Führer, "one of those devoted believers, a blind idealist," as Hitler's private secretary Traudl Junge remembers him.[250] The young fighters, on the other hand, temporarily buoyed by prospects of fame and glory, took positions in dangerous places not immediately accessible to the invading Soviets, many of whom were relatively immobile in tanks and trucks. But they came, of course, in huge numbers. Armed mostly with bazookas, hand grenades, and some firearms, and now with only rudimentary training, the HJ bands proved to be flexible and fleet-footed. Especially for the younger ones, it was like playing cops and robbers, as they moved around in underground passageways and subway tunnels, hid behind ruins, and lay in wait in basements, cellars, and bombed-out shops. Their specialty was holding still until a tank was only a few yards away and then hurling their grenades. Some would lie on the sidewalk playing dead until a tank arrived, and then they would fire. As the Russians became more ubiquitous, engaging in house-to-house combat with soldiers, Hitler Youths jumped onto rooftops, sneaking up behind Red Army snipers and pushing them into the street.[251]

For lack of regular troops, thousands of Hitler Youths were charged by Hitler's and Axmann's orders with securing strategic bridges, particularly those across the Havel River, to safeguard the Wenck Army's crossing. (For his part in this, the "incitement of youth for war," Axmann was later to be condemned by a West German denazification court.)[252] About six hundred of them were at the Havel Pichelsdorf Bridge in Berlin-Spandau. Not only did Hitler expect Wenck in just that area, but high-placed Nazis themselves used that bridge to facilitate their escape from the capital.[253] When the Russians took the bastion, however, almost all the Hitler Youths were killed. The same fate befell those holed up in the Olympia stadium and those sniping from

bunkers in the Tiergarten, the large zoo in the middle of town.[254] In
the end, after Hitler had committed suicide on April 30, Axmann in
the company of Bormann made his own getaway, passing hundreds of
dead HJ boys as he did so. Bormann was killed by Soviet gunfire, but
Axmann was able to reach safety in South Germany. He had abused
mere children in order to save his own skin.[255]

There can be no doubt that the few Hitler Youths received by the
Führer on March 19, 1945, were ecstatic. Inspired by their personal
successes against the enemy, they were being upheld as the paragons of
a picture-book HJ career as it had been advertised by Nazi propaganda
since 1933. And to meet Hitler in person was the fulfillment of a
dream that virtually all HJ boys and girls had harbored (as did most
German adults until late 1944), no matter how many reasons they may
have had to complain about the conditions of their political and paramilitary socialization, especially in recent times. But the exigencies of
this critical last phase of the war, which had truly turned into the
struggle of survival their political leadership had always conjured up,
made these young boys, who like their older peers had routinely been
told that they would be male warriors and protectors of the Reich, particularly fanatical. In 1945 they were too young to have had the opportunity to evaluate the situation in the Reich in general, and their own,
potentially highly perilous circumstances in particular. Hastily drafted
and with superficial military training, they were thrown into the fighting by leaders spouting slogans of easy victory, which their older and
more mature peers might have treated much more skeptically. Looking
back, a fifteen-year-old with a bazooka on his shoulder fighting Russian tanks at close range on the Oder River in late 1944 probably
would have been aghast, had he been told as a ten-year-old HJ novice
at the war's beginning that he would end up at the front while still a
teenager. In the face of imminent defeat, the majority of young boys
who were forced to take up arms during the last phase of the Third
Reich were demoralized, disillusioned, and scared for their lives, no
matter what youthful ambitions and energies were still driving them.
They had become desperate. In terrible skirmishes they had seen their

comrades fall to the left and right of them and were hoping only to be lucky enough to survive. All they really wanted to do now was go home.

It is not surprising that with the radicalization of warfare, accompanied by an intensified Nazi indoctrination of youth in the last years of the war, there was, in its final weeks, a very small number of Hitler Youths who engaged in extreme activities unquestionably condemned by the Geneva conventions. First, there were some boys who were driven to commit crimes against humanity which at the beginning of the war they would only have committed as young adults, for example as concentration camp guards or as members of SS or Army death squads. Second, there were Hitler Youths who volunteered as members of what in postwar sensationalist literature has sometimes been falsely romanticized as the "Werewolves," a Nazi resistance movement.[256]

In order to inure HJ adolescents to inhuman acts, to make them complicit in the crimes of the Third Reich, and to bond them to its murderous reputation, its leaders ordered them to commit atrocities. For example, in mid-March 1945 a seventeen-year-old serving in a Volkssturm batallion was told to execute a Ukrainian conscript worker found guilty of looting. The Soviet lad was fetched from a bunker, and when attempting to flee he was gunned down by the HJ rifleman at close range.[257] Later that month a HJ-Bannführer commanded seven subordinates aged sixteen and seventeen near Austrian Deutsch-Schützen to escort sixty Jews into the woods. They then had to close off the area before two SS men executed the Jews. The HJ members had to bury them, only to notice that in one of the shallow graves a mortally wounded man was still stirring. After the SS had fired into the head of the victim, his burial began anew.[258] Also in Austria, fourteen-to seventeen-year-old Hitler Youths had to execute a deserter, one of their own from a flak emplacement. Barely over five feet tall and afraid of the advancing Russians, he had wanted to go home.[259] Further north near Soltau and close to Bergen-Belsen concentration camp, some fifty Hitler Youths were ordered to catch dozens of inmates who had fled. The hapless victims were lined up at dusk on the edge of town and then shot by the boys who had hunted them. One of them who witnessed this scene, but was spared the shooting, broke down in the face of such evil. His father took him to the local Party office, asking why children had to perform these traumatizing tasks. Characteristically, two high-placed functionaries answered: "We wish to educate the young people so that they become even tougher and will not shrink from any cruelty."[260] Still, whether on orders or not, Hitler's youths served and perpetrated the deadly racial ideology of the Third Reich. The issue of culpability is made exceedingly difficult by their youth, but the issue of complicity remains.

The Werewolves, by the more narrow and technically correct definition, were small suicide commandos of boys and sometimes even girls who were dropped behind enemy lines on what was already foreign-occupied German soil, to reverse the conquest—in itself an insane task. But in a wider sense the HJ leadership would have liked every one of its charges to become saboteurs, causing destruction among occupation forces in every way possible, in a casual rather than organized manner. This is apparent from a flyer dropped over North Germany in April with a request to "pass it on." It would not take much schooling or mechanical know-how to harm the enemy—merely a hammer, a pair of pliers, a knife, a screwdriver, and some basic skills could be enough to stall the enemy's war machine significantly. The flyer also contained suggestions for destroying army vehicles by throwing sugar into gas tanks or suspending invisible wires across roads, to cause decapitation. Instructions for derailing trains looked as foolproof as they were simple. And telephone lines could be rendered obsolete using heavy stones.[261]

The few Werewolf commandos of the HJ were organized and trained in conjunction with the SS. In fact, these activities signaled the finale in the unsavory collaboration between Himmler's and Schirach's formations since 1935. In the most notorious case, the new German anti-Nazi lord mayor of Aachen, Franz Oppenhoff, after having been installed by U.S. Forces, was successfully assassinated by an SS man, two HJ boys, and a BDM girl in March 1945. (After the Allied armies had penetrated Germany west of the Rhine, Aachen was the first major city to fall to them, in late October 1944.) The sworn group of young killers landed on Belgian territory near the Dutch border, having been dropped from the skies by a captured B-17 Flying Fortress. They immediately killed Josef Saive, a Dutch border guard. They then made their way into Aachen, shot Oppenhoff in his own house, and managed to flee, with the Americans in hot pursuit. In the end, they all perished on their way back to German-held territory, after having stepped on land mines.[262]

The event was played up in the German media for the best possible effect, but there were no others like this one. Armed with weapons and in possession of cyanide capsules for quick suicide, Werewolves tried to wreak havoc in Vienna during April but got nowhere.[263] In one instance a posse of Berlin Hitler Youths, again joined by the SS, were dropped behind Russian lines for suicide missions, but at least one of them gave up and made his way back to the capital, in good enough shape to tell about it.[264] Three days before the Reich's capitulation, two Hitler Youths were again parachuted behind American lines in the West, only to be caught. They were taken to Brunswick, put on trial as spies, and condemned to death. Sixteen and seventeen years old, they were executed on June 1.[265] The last Werewolves to make any impression at all were inmates of a WE camp who, when caught by the Russians in Berlin, were found to have signed their names on a list, promising to become active after the occupation of the Fatherland. Although they allowed the occasion to lapse, this did not help them much. Only one of them seems to have been immediately released; the others were taken prisoner. They lingered in Soviet camps for years, except for one who went missing.[266]

The march into captivity constituted the last episode in the history of Hitler's youths from 1933 to 1945. The figures vary; according to one account, at the end of World War II close to 12 million Germans were in the custody of the victor nations, which would represent more than 10 percent of the Reich's total population in 1933. We can estimate that of those captured, at least half had been in the Hitler Youth at one time or another, and that would include females.[267] The most credible sources maintain that over 3 million men had been captured by the Red Army. Of those in Soviet captivity, nearly 2 million were sent home by 1950, but an unknown number remained in Stalin's camps. Even in 1955, almost one-third of the German population was affected by this state of affairs. When Konrad Adenauer, the Chancellor of the Federal Republic, traveled to Moscow in June of that year, he was promised the release of 10,000 prisoners. By January 1956, after holding back some prisoners, the Soviet Union had returned the remaining 4,150 POWs still alive.[268]

More German soldiers suffered and died in Soviet captivity than under the supervision of any of the other Allies. One aggravating circumstance here was that in 1949 the Soviet Union, not bound by the Hague Laws of Land Warfare nor the Geneva conventions specific to POWs, sentenced 30,000 prisoners, randomly and after mock trials, to twenty-five years of hard labor for supposed war crimes, thus removing them from the comparatively privileged category of war prisoners to that of common (native) criminals and launching them into the notorious Gulag. This was predicated on Stalin's decision that Russia needed laborers.[269] Predictably, life even in the POW camps was onerous, marked by dangerous chores, starvation, pests, and disease, among which hunger edemas and dysentery were endemic. There was cruelty on the part of the guards and Soviet-appointed German capos. Hitler Youths who had been pressed into the Waffen-SS and received the blood-group tattoo were singled out for special treatment, as were voluntary members of the SS (hence they often tried to remove the stigma by burning or cutting it out, but the scar gave them away like a mark of Cain).[270] All told, however, these hardships scarcely measured up to the levels of sadistic abuse and murder which the SS had inflicted on their victims in the concentration camps, or which the Wehrmacht, for that matter, had practiced in camps for Soviet POWs. Indeed, bad as they were, the conditions in the Soviet POW camps were perhaps not unexpected in view of the Nazis' long-time propaganda against the allegedly subhuman Russians and their vicious campaign of material and human exploitation after June 1941, to say nothing of the outright destruction of Soviet Jews. However demoralized and ineffective they became, German soldiers had anticipated long before the final catastrophe that falling into Soviet hands would be tantamount to a life sentence or death, and had therefore tried to get moved away from the eastern front as soon and as far as possible. But especially in the final weeks of the war, anybody caught by the SS or military police attempting this on their own without proper identification would be shot on the spot or strung up on the nearest pole.

The United States was the other major Allied nation responsible for German POWs. The Americans kept prisoners on occupied German soil and in Belgium, France, and Britain, as well as state-side. Experiences in those camps varied widely. Those Germans who were eventually brought to America fared best, being fed on normal American rations.[271] The most devastating conditions obtained, for hundreds of thousands of German soldiers, in camps near the Rhine River, all of them in the open. In Worms across from a U.S. Army base in picturesque Heidelberg, there was a former Wehrmacht barracks where up to 40,000 men were fenced in at any one time. For the majority, little food was on hand, and the latrine for all of them consisted of a huge square dug into the ground, where some men would drown during the night.[272] When inmates from this camp, which was not far from the French border, were handed over to camps in the south of France, the German POWs, fearing French revenge, despaired and many mutilated or killed themselves. (Whereas the Free French had not captured even a quarter of a million Germans, under the command of Charles de Gaulle they came to guard over a million of them.) In those camps POWs tried to survive in open cages in situations as bad as the worst American ones.[273] Meanwhile, the U.S. Forces had established unsheltered camps on the swampy banks of the Lower Rhine, the so-called *Rheinwiesen-Lager,* which acquired a terrible reputation for the way inmates were treated there. Especially notorious were the camps near Wickrath, Rheinberg, and Remagen. During the spring and summer of 1945, left virtually to themselves, the German men vegetated in earth pits under open skies. Scores suffocated in water and mud after heavy rainfalls, while others starved to death on meager rations; some had only tree bark and clover to eat.[274] It was clear that the Final Victory had eluded them.

Hitler's Young Women Deceived

From the beginning of the Nazi regime, girls and young women were told by the political leadership that they were eugenically valuable because they were the biological complement to men whose helpmates in the home they would be, as well as the mothers of their children, in order to perpetuate the German master race. They were conditioned in this manner by parents of Nazi persuasion, in most schools, and, unequivocally, in the Bund Deutscher Mädel of the Hitler Youth, after age ten and often far into their twenties. They were trained for female-specific occupations—caregiving and homemaking—while being discouraged from politics, male-centered activities, intellectual pursuits, and large-scale decision-making. They would have to submit to males without question in every respect, in particular sexually, and in return, they were told, men would protect them. All this meant that young women did not have to shoulder important responsibilities in the industrial and agricultural processes of the nation; above all, it meant that they would never have to bear arms.

However, because at many levels Hitler's dictatorship was dysfunctional and, as such, ultimately not able to defend itself against the external foes it had conjured up, beginning in the mid-1930s, young women were gradually compromised to the same extent that the Nazis were compelled to compromise their ideology, in order to survive. In both farming and industry all women had to assume ever-heavier work loads (although without the attendant benefits in status or earnings that usually accrued to men in comparable positions), until during the war they were standing in for males in stop-gap, transitory capacities.[275] After 1938, the girls were engaged more and more with war-related work, in theory and practice, through the Hitler Youth and its affiliates such as the RAD and, less commonly, the elite racist program

"Glaube und Schönheit." At the height of the war, tens of thousands of women were serving in semi-military circumstances, which became more life-threatening to them as more of the menfolk perished and Hitler's inevitable military defeat drew near. Even after the Reich's capitulation on May 8, 1945, German adolescent females continued to be victimized as the wrath of the conquerors turned against them especially in the eastern provinces, where they were raped, mutilated, killed, or deported to long terms of captivity.

However, insofar as many young and older women had assisted their male superiors in creating a system that facilitated ever-greater human abuses, including their own continuous exploitation, German women were by no means without blame. Although they may have lived after 1933 in a male-supremacist society in which policy decisions affecting them were made largely above their heads, still their own responsibility for their misfortune by 1945 was hardly negligible. After all, some women like Gertrud Scholtz-Klink, the Nazi women's leader, and Jutta Rüdiger, the BDM leader, even while under the supreme control of males had wielded power and perpetrated cruelty on others. In the BDM, many had accepted the racial theories constantly propounded to them, and a few, like Irma Grese, had taken these to their farthest terrible extreme. The adage concerning the survival of the fittest had influenced the behavior of girls who bore down on the minority of those in their ranks who showed little enthusiasm for sports, who were physically weaker or in appearance did not conform to the Aryan ideal, or who tended to stay away from Hitler Youth functions. Older girls in the "Glaube und Schönheit" program were willing participants as their immaculate racial countenance was complimented by the regime leaders; they knew they would be coveted as wives by the highest Nazis and thus would rule over Slavs in eastern European zones that had been cleansed of Jews.[276]

The Nazi leadership called up young females to serve in auxiliary military situations by 1940, when clerical personnel were increasingly needed in the occupied countries. Senior graduates of the BDM and members of the female RAD were at first voluntarily called and later seconded or conscripted to do tours of duty as "helpers" (Helferinnen) for the various branches of the armed forces, including the Waffen-SS. Thus there were staff helpers, Navy helpers, nurses, and Luftwaffe helpers, as well as communication (telegraph or telephone operator) helpers for the Army, who were known as Nachrichtenhelferinnen. While so-called staff helpers, usually for the Army, took care of clerical work, interpreting, accounting, and some chauffeuring and horse-handling, Luftwaffe helpers assisted in running alarm and warning systems and in measurements and other technical tasks. Some men had also been carrying out these functions, but when more of them were sent into combat with the attack on the Soviet Union in June 1941, more girls were called up to replace them. This became a recurring theme for the rest of the war, as—with the Blitzkrieg concept abandoned—increasing numbers of men were needed to face the enemy in action rather than for occupation and home-front duties. The ages of these girls ranged at the beginning of the war from eighteen to about twenty-two, but toward the end of the conflict it widened to between sixteen and well into the mid-twenties. More young women had been newly inducted after Stalingrad, so that by the spring of 1945, when the armed forces comprised approximately 10 million male soldiers, there were nearly half a million Wehrmachtshelferinnen.[277]

How close were these young women to combat, injury, capture, and death, and, as auxiliaries to soldiers, how much harm did they inflict themselves? Until the end, at least theoretically, the government held fast to its dogma that women should not bear arms. Reichsreferentin Jutta Rüdiger of the BDM after 1945 prided herself on the fact that her girls, having been forbidden, never had to fight like soldiers.[278] But the reality was quite different. The armed-forces helpers were exposed to partisan attacks in the occupied territories, and even on the home front they could undergo air raids and then, after the multiple invasions, near-combat situations, for instance in heavy bunkers, as the fronts were being pushed inward. When they were surprised, along with the male soldiers they were serving, by the furious onslaught of the Red Army in the East, they often took up arms and joined in battle, fighting quite ferociously and undoubtedly killing many. This alone made them complicit in Hitler's aggressive warfare since 1939. Some of them received decorations for this fighting, such as the Iron Cross. These women all came under German military jurisdiction and in case of capture were theoretically protected by formal combatant status according to the Hague (1907) and Geneva (1929) conventions.[279]

But even though toward the end of the war the Wehrmacht had special orders to see to the timely evacuation of these young women from front zones in the face of imminent danger, many were captured by the Allies, especially in the East. Nobody knows how many were ultimately lost; some 25,000 German women are said to have been carted off to Stalin's Gulag—not as POWs, which would have eased their lot, but as civilians, who could be more brutally treated and held indefinitely. The Czechs and Yugoslavs acted particularly viciously against those who had not been able to save themselves in time; in Prague, during the mêlées of early May 1945, many nurses were shot point-blank, while other helpers were stripped naked, and, with their tendons cut, were forced to crawl across Wenzel's Square, with an enraged crowd kicking them, until they all succumbed.[280]

In colloquial German the armed forces helpers were called *Blitzmädel,* or lightning girls. This term was ambivalent. Originally it derived from "Blitzkrieg," lightning war, for the first helpers had been sent to assist in the occupation of countries conquered by lightning warfare, such as France. The second meaning was derogatory, for *Blitzmädel* soon became known as adventure-loving girls who were quick in dispensing sexual favors.[281] Since they were usually over eighteen, this was undoubtedly an extension of the culture of sexual license that had characterized the over-fifteen echelons of the Hitler Youth in all of Germany since the mid-1930s, and from which, of course, these girls had graduated.[282] In the armed forces they got to know men who were often older and more experienced than themselves; bent on seduction, these soldiers were generous with flattery, money, and unambiguous presents such as lingerie, perfume, and liquor, particularly in France. As one soldier wrote home from Rennes: "Recently this has been all we care about: what do you eat, who do you lay, where do you go on Sundays?"[283] Officers in handsome uniforms especially knew how to take advantage of these circumstances, although officially liaisons were discouraged.[284] The girls themselves often were eager for pleasure and love affairs, since fraternization with the enemy was forbidden, whereas German Wehrmacht soldiers took ample advantage from their superior positions in starting relationships with young women in the occupied countries.[285] To the extent that these foreign women became rivals to the *Blitzmädel,* the German girls often found themselves in situations where they practically had to offer themselves to soldiers, even for the sake of normal social intercourse.[286] These scenarios in 1940–41 in France, Scandinavia, and to a lesser degree Poland and Greece foreshadowed what would happen at much lower ranks of the BDM and with distinctly younger girls toward the end of the war in most German towns and cities.[287] On the one hand, therefore, one might say that the exigencies of the war themselves created conditions in which girls lost decorum and self-discipline beyond what sexual mores would have allowed in peacetime back home. On the other hand, these were additional signs of victimization of young females in situations where, vis-à-vis more powerful males sanctioned by the Nazi system, they were coerced into settings in which sex became unavoidable, whether the official excuse of "giving a child to the Führer" or plain libido was a factor.[288]

When the fronts moved closer and the *Blitzmädel* were on longer tours of duty with less time off, such sexual activity ceased. This became the rule for all the other groups of young women militarily employed after Stalingrad, when the mood was more somber and defensive chores multiplied. In 1944, for example, many of the female helpers who had worked for the Luftwaffe were deployed to artillery emplacements, for service alongside male Flakhelfer. No sooner had they arrived on the scene than they were augmented by members of the female RAD and even the BDM, some of them as young as sixteen.[289] Hitler, in conjunction with Luftwaffe generals, had authorized the use of female adolescents in this way in July 1943, and Göring had supported it that fall.[290] After the defeat of Stalingrad this had become necessary, as the conscription age of male Flakhelfer for service in the Wehrmacht was gradually being lowered and large numbers of them were removed to the fronts. In their stead, by the spring of 1945 tens of thousands of female Flakhelfer were stationed in approximately 350 artillery emplacements at the key strategic centers of the Reich— chiefly the Rhineland, the northern coasts, and Berlin. Before being sent there, they had been specially trained not on site by rough NCOs, as the boys had been, but, for four weeks and more sparingly, in a unique facility in Rendsburg, close to the North German entry zone for many Allied airplanes.[291]

In 1943, when they were first assigned, it had been expressly stated that female flak helpers were not to be engaged with the actual use of firing equipment aimed at aircraft. However, even having to put young women close to armory bothered the Nazi leaders. They betrayed their uneasy conscience when they declared, in November 1944, that "the question whether such a service for women is fitting is moot. Assuredly we would like to see our girls performing other tasks."[292] In fact, during 1944, these girls were also employed as anti-aircraft gunners, as the boys had been from the beginning.[293] In addition to learning how to fire the cannons, some were instructed in the use of machine guns, grenades, and small firearms. One troop of female Flakhelfer who had been assigned to a Waffen-SS artillery unit in the center of Prague shot their way out of town, pursued by Czech snipers, until they landed, west of the city, in U.S. captivity. As handmaidens of the SS, they knowingly killed Czech civilians who might have been merciless in trying to recapture Prague, but who as patriots had moral justice on their side.[294] The fact that girls were now firing weapons proved even more embarrassing to the Nazi leadership. "The Nazis were hiding from the German public the fact that women were being used to shoot down planes," former flak helper Erna Tietz told an American author in the 1980s, adding that she was given a special identification, z.b.V., short for *zur besonderen Verwendung* or "for special use." This meant that "maybe I could have been active in news gathering for the Wehrmacht, or in the secretarial pool, or distribution of clothing, or so on. One wanted to avoid that the public learn that women were assigned to weapons."[295]

In the pursuit of these non-feminine tasks, the flak girls, who like the boys used their skills to down enemy planes, came to much harm. Totally exposed to air raids and especially targeted by enemy aircraft in the emplacements, many lost their lives, although complete statistics are not available.[296] Some girls saw others die and were unable to cope with the calamity. Lisa was a sixteen-year-old BDM girl when in January 1945 her battery took a hit from an RAF plane. "I felt the blood on my face, it came from my left temple. My thigh was full of grenade splinters." That was bad enough. "But the corporal had his stomach ripped open, so that his guts were hanging out. I stood in front of him without being able to move. 'Lisa, take the pistol, kill me!' I could not do it."[297] Others were bombed on treks, in an attempt to flee.[298] Elisabeth Zimmer witnessed how a group of girls cracked under the strain; those who had run for cover without expressly being told to do so were later pulled out and shot for cowardice.[299] At the very end of the war, under reasonably compassionate superiors, female flak helpers were allowed to disband, but many ended up in captivity—American or British if they were lucky, or Russian if they had been stationed too far east.[300]

At the beginning of November 1944 Bormann conveyed a final decision by Hitler that German females, flak helpers or otherwise, were not to be utilized in any organized combat.[301] But—another contradiction in a regime full of paradoxes—exactly one month later Jutta Rüdiger, the chief of the BDM, linked up with Reich Women's Leader Gertrud Scholtz-Klink in a general call for arms. "German women and girls" aged eighteen and over were implored to join the armed forces anywhere in the Reich and "render the kind of service which they may be asked to undertake within these ranks in accordance with their aptitude, in lieu of soldiers."[302]

Although Axmann later argued that this did not constitute an order since any such assignment was voluntary, the pressure even on BDM girls was great, because that appeal also affected girls under the age of eighteen.[303] In fact, from December 1944 to May 1945, BDM girls as young as fourteen joined the Volkssturm and other military facilities that provided instruction in the use of hand grenades, bazookas, machine guns, and lesser firearms.[304] Forthwith, in small detachments, they integrated themselves into whatever regional front was battling the invading enemy, mostly in the East and the capital. At the Oder front they fought with anti-tank weapons and some, freshly inducted from the RAD, in hand-to-hand skirmishes, wielding spades against the bayonets of Russians.[305] In the defense of Berlin they specialized, like their male cohorts, in hurling anti-tank grenades from short distances.[306] There was also a "death squad" of young girls commanded by the Waffen-SS, who had red-painted lips and fought with abandon, but the documentation about what exactly they did is missing. Since the SS was involved, it is likely that by the terms of the Geneva conventions they overstepped their bounds.[307] After all, there were SS-directed female Werewolves, like the BDM girl in Aachen, who from Berlin were dropped behind the Russian lines, each with a poison pill.[308] It may be assumed that those girls who fought alongside the SS were sufficiently faithful to fit the Nazi ideal for boys, but as young girls transformed into Amazons they were the most extreme embodiment of Hitler's ideological sellout. For the average BDM girl in those final months, it was a combination of love for the Führer and hatred of the noxious invaders that motivated her actions. Doris Schmid-Gewinner, who, fourteen in 1945, was trained in Stuttgart on bazookas and was waiting for the Americans, wrote later: "I don't believe I thought: I am dying for Hitler. No, we have to go against those who are hurting us so. Just imagine how much I hated the bomb throwers at that time—and now they were supposed to come to Stuttgart. I would have fired any number of bazookas against them."[309] It is likely that in her memoirs Schmid-Gewinner suppressed the fact that she had also been prepared to die for her Führer, because over the years she had invested too much in him to see his world, and her own with it, tumble down in the end.

While many German teenage girls were exposed to the enemy in large numbers, to the point of being embroiled in active and perhaps morally questionable combat in the last four months of the "Thousand-Year Reich," a much greater number of them were placed in harm's way as non-combatants. Their fate was to become entrapped by invading troops, especially in the East, and to have a very uncertain future to look forward to. All girls over ten years old were nominally members of either the BDM or the female RAD until Germany's capitulation on May 8, 1945.

The events in East Prussia in October 1944 were a foreshadowing of what was to follow. The Red Army had advanced to a line east of Königsberg, including Gumbinnen, Nemmersdorf, and Goldap, towns that were easily captured. Until the Wehrmacht retook the area, atrocities were committed by Russians against the civilian population, just as atrocities had been committed by German troops in Russia, which prompted an exodus to the West, swelling to a flood in early 1945.[310] By January, large numbers of women, children, and old men were departing from East Prussia, some on ships supplied by the Wehrmacht. One of these, the *Wilhelm Gustloff,* was sunk by Russian torpedos off Gotenhafen on January 30 with its 8,000 passengers, among them 400 female flak helpers. To this day, this remains the greatest disaster in maritime history.[311] Many other civilians from the countryside fled by wagon treks, the last express train having pulled out of Königsberg's main station on January 23. On that day the Red Army was in Elbing, down the Baltic coast halfway between Königsberg and Danzig (which was not occupied until March 27), attempting to block all roads and rail traffic. By public loudspeakers, the Wehrmacht under General Otto Lasch urged Königsberg's citizens to leave the city on January 27, and the flood of fugitives increased.[312]

More refugees tried to flee East and West Prussia, Pomerania, and Silesia during the winter and spring until May of 1945, "plagued by icy cold and hunger, pursued by the enemy, shot at, sometimes overtaken and leaving countless victims on the way." Historians have counted these episodes among "the most terrible tragedies that Hitler's war visited upon the German people."[313] Eventually, a total of more than 10 million Germans managed to escape from the Russians.[314] During these harrowing journeys, the young girls suffered more than most, and for the least of reasons. Thirteen-year-old BDM trooper Ingrid van Bergen, her father killed at the front, fled with her mother and their new baby from Danzig west to Oliva, but then turned around. They reached a refugee ship that was supposed to take them to Holstein. Clambering onto it, soldiers with passes tried to push past them. "For the first time I was being confronted with the cowardice and recklessness of men," notes the actress; "if they could find a better spot they brutally shoved women and children aside." The vessel was bombed by Russian planes, but without consequences. However, a neighboring ship carrying wounded soldiers was hit. Van Bergen remembers seeing the boat listing to one side, and "how the stretchers with the wounded on them slid from the deck into the ice-cold sea. The terrifying thing was that from where we were, you could not hear a sound."[315] How many veterans of the Hitler Youth were on that Red Cross carrier, we shall never know. Hannelore Sch., finally released from the RAD, moved west to fetch her siblings in Mecklenburg and continued on foot to Holstein, where she learned of the suicide of her parents, who had stayed behind.[316] Others were trying to abandon the Protectorate. Ingeborg P., like Hannelore Sch. not yet twenty, fled with her mother, sister, and twelve-year-old brother, but lost both mother and brother to Czech violence just before reaching East German soil. What followed were months of pillage and much worse under Red Army occupation, until the Poles took over.[317]

There were other and worse forms of suffering for young German females during this period: rape, torture, and murder. To be sure, the injuries suffered even by blameless young people during the Nazi period are often overlooked or downplayed, in light of the towering injustices perpetrated by the Nazis on their foreign enemies. However, the chronicle of this suffering must also find its place in the history of youth under Hitler.

Many details regarding the rape of girls and women by Red Army soldiers in the eastern provinces of the Reich, as the Russians were advancing, and especially in Berlin, as they occupied the city between April 24 and May 5, have already surfaced. But in order to see the whole picture, some considerations have to be kept in mind. Although the total number of injured can hardly be doubted—up to half a million in Berlin alone (which would mean every third female)—this treatment of women, as Atina Grossmann has said, was in some ways like a self-fulfilling prophecy in that Hitler and Goebbels had for years excoriated the evil image of the "Mongols" who, beast-like, were on the prowl for rape and murder.[318] The fact that not just the Russians did the raping, although they certainly stood out, provides further perspective: all the victor armies engaged in it, as triumphant armies throughout history have always done. In the Stuttgart region, for example, over a thousand cases of rape of women by invading French troops, involving females from ages fourteen to seventy-four, were placed on record.[319] In the village of Merklingen alone, on the road to Ulm, by the end of April, 152 girls and women needed medical attention, some with pregnancies, the youngest twelve years old.[320] Indeed, rapes by French occupation soldiers, in addition to the Russians, were notorious, whereas in American and British zones of influence the borderline between rape and consensual sex became blurred, since the use of chocolate, lingerie, and cigarettes as barter encouraged covert prostitution.[321]

When the Red Army had first invaded East Prussia in the fall of 1944, its soldiers raped and murdered many women who were subsequently discovered by the Wehrmacht when they arrived to reclaim the territory.[322] The Germans charged that the Russians were following repeated exhortations by the Soviet writer Ilya Ehrenburg, sanctioned by Stalin, that to exact revenge on German fascists by killing every man and raping every woman was a Red Army soldier's duty.[323] It is true that in almost daily articles for its newspaper Ehrenburg had aimed to teach the Army "how to hate," urging it to kill as many German soldiers as possible. But he never called for raping German women. This was a lie, planted personally by Goebbels.[324] On the contrary, during the entire invasion of the Reich, Russian officers kept insisting that the

Red Army was forbidden to abuse women (which did not stop them from actually doing it themselves); Ehrenburg himself reinforced the official position against rape when visiting with Red Army troops in East Prussia in the spring of 1945.[325]

In any event, after December 1944 no order could stop sexually frustrated Russian soldiers from going on a furious rampage against the women whose men had killed thousands in Stalingrad, had besieged Leningrad for over a year, and had conquered the suburbs of Moscow.[326] In 1945, at the end of January, the Russians were back in the hinterland of Königsberg and close to the coast northwest of it, where they occupied the villages of Metgethen and Gross Heydekrug. Here they raped every female in sight, no matter what age, and killed some with bayonets or rifle butts. Teenage girls, all rightly suspected of being in the BDM, were crucified on barn doors after their violation or dragged behind Army trucks until dead. When the Germans briefly recovered the area in February, they found not only every former inhabitant killed, but two piles of bodies, close to three thousand adults, children, and infants—all female.[327] In Fuchsberg, fifteen miles southeast of Königsberg, the Soviet artillery officer Yuri Uspanski noted in his diary: "In the house of the divisional staff, evacuated women and children stayed overnight. Then came the drunken soldiers, one after the other, to select their women, to take them aside and abuse them. Several men to one woman. The soldiers said that 13–15-year-old girls were also abused. Oh, how they fought it!"[328]

On April 10 Königsberg itself was surrendered to the Russians, who now began to lead General Lasch's Wehrmacht soldiers away to captivity, but not without committing cruelties against the civilian population. One German POW on his way out later reported seeing "girls and women, being pulled into houses protesting and crying, children calling out for their parents . . . The ditches were filled with bodies, which showed the traces of unimaginable maltreatment and rape. Dead youngsters were lying around in masses, there were people hanging from the trees, their ears cut off, their eyes gouged out, German women were being led in both directions, drunk Russians were fighting for a German nurse, with an old woman sitting near a tree, both her legs squeezed off by vehicles."[329]

As the Russians swooped down on East Prussia, and thereafter adjoining West Prussia and Mecklenburg, as well as, to the south, Pomerania, Silesia, and then Brandenburg surrounding Berlin, an orgy of destruction, rape, torture, and killings swept over these provinces. Among potential victims, females were in the majority, because many males were gone or fighting somewhere else; the younger and more attractive the girls, the more endangered they were. In one village in Pomerania, all the young women were gathered together, and after being forced to shed their clothes, they were driven into a barn to be gang-raped.[330] Girls scarcely in their teens were being violated, with their mothers having to watch and even to assist the Russians.[331] No matter what assurances had been given, Russian officers often hand-picked the most attractive teenagers for their own use, then handing them down to the men. Suicides, including those of many girls, multiplied.[332] Using ashes and old sackcloth to make oneself look older seldom worked, but because Russians were extremely afraid of contagious diseases, pretending that some girls had typhoid fever sometimes helped, as it did in the village of Eichenau, Upper Silesia, in early May.[333] In Berlin, young women sometimes had the chance to say "I syphilis" when asked, by Russians, "you healthy?"[334] Others painted their inner thighs red, in order to feign menstruation.[335] But often even this did nothing to stop the rapes. The Russians would enter hospital wards looking for nurses, and after finishing with them (as they did in one clinic every night) would search patients' beds for more girls.[336]

There are hardly any known cases of teenagers who were not raped by Red Army troops after the invasion of Greater Berlin on April 25, especially during the first terrible week lasting to about May 3.[337] Those who escaped this fate must have been completely hidden, crippled, or otherwise been perceived as ill.[338] When the fighting was over and they were finally victorious, Russian soldiers went about Berlin with four pleasures in their mind: stealing watches, consuming food and alcohol, joy-riding on bicycles, and having sex with women.

They would stuff their pockets with watches no matter how many they had already. They would requisition food and especially wine and schnapps and would feast in people's homes to the limit. When drunk, they would try to get on bicycles and, unaccustomed to their use, would usually wreck them quickly. Then they would look for women, and although they preferred young ones, neither old age nor lack of physical attraction was protection for this particular prey.[339]

Acts of rape occurred during any time of day or night and in full private or public view; the rape victims were often infected with venereal disease. If girls refused, they could be killed outright, as were two acting students, whose torsos had been sliced open.[340] Often girls were murdered after multiple rapes (if they had not died from them already), and as news of this spread around, the fear of being violated became endemic.[341]

In some cases, virtually entire families perished. In the outskirts of the capital a mother had lost one of her daughters and had made a pact with the remaining one to shoot the daughter once the Russians approached her. When the Russians arrived, she fired at her daughter twice and missed, only to be shot by the soldiers in turn.[342] In the upper-class section of Dahlem, a drunken Russian violated two women and five daughters, aged eight to fourteen, in a basement. He had killed them all during the sex act and then hung them from the walls.[343] Of course, there were no longer any men to shield these unfortunates, except perhaps for a liberated, compassionate Jew or a lone courageous cleric. The Lutheran pastor Heinrich Grüber, for example, who had had ties to the Resistance, had helped Jews and been in Nazi concentration camps. When young girls were in his care he locked them into a room, blocked the threshold with his body, and then used his holy office to some effect. If the common soldiers did not understand him, the commandants, who frequently spoke German, might listen. But his was an isolated stand.[344]

The ultimate humiliation for young women was deportation to the camps of eastern Russia. They were not alone in this; any German deemed able to perform hard work was chosen, sometimes even children under ten, but often the choice was made arbitrarily. These measures, which also involved German POWs, occurred as part of the grand scheme by Stalin to secure cheap labor for the Soviet economy, after the land had suffered from German invasion, occupation, and the extraordinary exertions by Soviet citizens for home defense. Tens of thousands of civilians had been driven out of Stalingrad alone by the marauding Wehrmacht.[345] The Russians selected for these actions the provinces immediately adjacent to them (and those where they would not be interfered with by western Allies), the first of which, East Prussia, was scheduled to become theirs by annexation and hence had to be totally depopulated. "East Prussia," wrote Ehrenburg, was "the most reactionary part of Germany."[346] West Prussia, Pomerania, East Brandenburg, and Silesia, next to the Generalgouvernement and Wartheland, were to be claimed by the Poles and thus could also be emptied of Germans, with many being deported to the Soviet Union and others expelled by the Poles to Germany later.[347] Major collection points for evacuation were Insterburg in East Prussia and Beuthen in Upper Silesia, where more indignities were suffered. Altogether, the entire German territory east of the rivers Oder and Neisse was at risk. How many girls disappeared in these population transfers is not exactly known, but the figure is in the tens of thousands.[348]

The transportation of girls and young women by the Russians to the East, by forced marches, trucks, and cattle trains, was always preceded and accompanied by beatings and rapes at the hands of guards—Red Army soldiers or members of the Soviet secret service NKVD—of the kind already described. Rape and sometimes pregnancies—in a further ironic twist of Nazi eugenics—were also a part of the daily lives of the captured women in the camps, albeit less frequently.[349]

During transport, teenagers were routinely asked whether they belonged to the BDM or RAD. Most of them did and admitted it, which is what the Russians wanted to hear. Those who were still too young or had really not been members were threatened and beaten until they signed something in Cyrillic, which they could not read, and that sealed their fate.[350] The journey to a Soviet camp—civilians were sent to the Gulag—took many weeks; there was little food or water and an absence of sanitary facilities. "Almost all of us had diarrhea," remembers Erna B., who was twenty-four when she was carted out of Pomerania; "the truck convoy stopped only once a day. And then there was the thirst, so that in the mornings we licked the dew from the truck walls."[351] On one rail transport, the dead were collected every day from the cattle wagons and stacked on top of the coal piles in the fuel car behind the engine.[352]

The names of the Gulag camps have not all been recorded. One was Karpinsk in western Siberia; another was Chelyabinsk, further to the southeast. Two others were Nogatka in the Urals and Anthrazyd in the Don River region, where coal was mined. Here typhoid fever broke out already in May.[353] The food was unmentionable, sometimes consisting only of strongly salted herring or a horse's head boiled in water.[354] Young women had to do dangerous work, some being crushed by huge logs or perishing in unsafe coal mines; there was dysentery; and many went insane or died of malnutrition or other ailments. But there were fewer rapes, no systematic beatings, no medical experiments, and no mass liquidations; on the whole, conditions were much better than they had ever been in Nazi concentration camps.[355]

In the end, it is impossible to weigh the inhumanities perpetrated by Nazis on the one side and Soviets on the other. Both of them were murderous regimes. However, there is an element of bitter irony in this, the unintended finale of Adolf Hitler's youth policy, for it turned out to be the inversion of his original goals. The Führer had wanted to see his young men and women as masters in an expansive foreign land to colonize it: tilling its soil, reaping its fruits, harvesting its mineral wealth, all the while lording it over the indigenous population, who were to be the slaves. Now the young Germans were there, but they had become the slaves. While some returned to the land of their birth decades later, most of them never came back.

The Responsibility of Youth

In the play *The Man Outside* Sergeant Beckmann, having returned in tatters from the lost war, tries to find acceptance from the people he encounters in his home town of Hamburg. He has just found his wife in bed with another man. With his unshaven face and haggard look, his gas-mask eye goggles held together by a rubber band, and his shabby Wehrmacht coat, he makes a terrible impression. The young woman who finds him near the Elbe River, where Beckmann has attempted suicide, takes him to her room, but Beckmann has to leave in a hurry when her husband suddenly returns from the front. Next Beckmann visits his former Colonel, a jolly schnapps-drinking fellow who does not even remember him. "What do you want from me?" he asks. "I am returning it to you," says Beckmann. "Returning what?" the Colonel wants to know. Quietly, Beckmann says: "Responsibility. I am returning the responsibility to you." Beckmann reminds the Colonel that near Gorodok on the Russian front, on February 14 in subzero temperatures, the Colonel had given him responsibility for twenty men. This was for reconnaissance purposes, and to take a few prisoners. And then they had moved on and there was shooting in the night. "And when we returned to our position, eleven men were missing. And I had the responsibility. Yes, this is all, Colonel. But now the war is over and I want to get some sleep and I am returning the responsibility, Colonel, I don't want it any more, I am giving it back to you, Colonel."[1]

This haunting scene from what became the first successful German postwar play depicts its author, Wolfgang Borchert, who himself is Beckmann. He is the former reluctant Hitler Youth who as a soldier at the Russian front tried to maim himself so he could get away from the horrors of the war, and who escaped from the Nazi courts only with difficulty.[2] Borchert had returned from the front a sick and injured man. During the first few years after the German catastrophe he had found some work with Hamburg theater groups and moved in the newly reviving literary circles. But his liver disease was incurable, and he became more and more emaciated until he died in a sanatorium in Basel, one day before his play was premiered, on November 21, 1947. He was twenty-five.[3]

Beginning in May 1945, there were many Beckmanns who made their way back from the fronts, equally desperate and equally confused.[4] What they found in post-Hitlerian Germany was a devastated land under foreign occupation, in which even the most obvious survival techniques often could not save a person's life. Family members were dead or displaced, dwellings destroyed, food scarce or nonexistent and, during the dreadful winters of 1945–46 and especially 1946–47, the cold lethal. People's health was at risk, and work was hard to find in an economy that was barely functioning. Black Market conditions ruled; the fertility rate decreased. Cologne had lost 75 percent of its housing. In Hamburg in 1946, twelve men, women, and children were dying of malnutrition every ten days. As in the period before the Third Reich, young people were again disproportionately represented among the growing mass of unemployed.[5] One factor contributing to this, in the U.S. Zone of occupation for instance, was an employment embargo by the summer of 1945 against anybody who had ever held a leadership position in the Hitler Youth (as had most), no matter how nominal or inferior.[6]

The question is whether in all of this chaos young HJ and war veterans like Borchert really had any responsibility to return, responsibility for subordinates they had commanded, or responsibility for the crimes committed by the Third Reich. Among the many records and testimonials of the postwar era, there are only a few from individuals who admit to any responsibility or even guilt for Hitler's regime or who promise to atone for it.[7] By far the majority of young people claim to have been victims, in the sense of having been seduced by the Nazi regime, then used and thrown away, and thus having been cheated out of youth. They admit to a feeling of shock shortly after capitulation on May 8, 1945, when it became clear that they had been deceived by a criminal regime whose nature they had been unable to comprehend.[8] One young person cried that he could not bear to watch his ideals "sink into the mud"; another claimed that he had "lost my belief in humankind."[9] Nine out of ten juveniles had been in the Hitler Youth, and most expressed relief about having made it through the final hostilities alive. Apart from acute peril to life and limb, they claimed to have hated the increasing militarization in all Nazi formations most, with its attendant reduction of personal freedom. But such hatred had been balanced by promises of future leadership in the Third Reich.[10]

Resocialization of youths was first attempted in the Allied prisoner-of-war camps. The Free French were the least active in this effort because they had not had enough time to work on political re-education concepts, and there were not enough French POW camps to begin with. They also subscribed to the cynical belief that according to past experience, German nature was immutably fascist unless there was forced "degermanization," and that in daily life it was better to deal with Germans on an ad hoc basis.[11] As for the Soviets, they had distributed an appeal by 250 captured former Hitler Youths as early as October 1942, which attempted to make youths in the Reich aware of certain facts: Before conscription, they had been trained in special skills, yet this was not for the sake of jobs but for the military use of handguns, tanks, and planes. As Hitler Youths, they had been sent camping not for the enjoyment of nature but to learn how to march. They had engaged in sports not to strengthen their health but to train for even longer marches.[12] Because quick releases from Soviet POW camps were not forthcoming, German soldiers there were never aware of the preparations for citizenship in a newly reconstructed Germany.

Instead, once in the eastern Soviet-occupied Zone, if they ever got there, boys and girls were brought under the control of the FDJ, the Free German Youth, which, totalitarian in its own right, was Communist-controlled and anything but free. Others, deemed recalcitrant by the Soviet occupiers, were held in special youth internment camps; girls and young women were always at risk of being raped.[13]

The Americans and British, schooled in democracy, were much more conscientious. Great Britain began broadcasting messages to German soldiers during the war about the value of democracy as opposed to the scourge of tyranny. On the BBC, one of Thomas Mann's pre-recorded addresses from Los Angeles ridiculed Baldur von Schirach in October 1942 as a "poetry-dabbling fat-boy of advanced age" and belittled his claim to lead a united youth front in Europe.[14] "Re-education" became a formulaic answer to the problem of eradicating the Nazi weltan-schauung in British POW camps; the British were careful to introduce new ideas about democracy and tolerance slowly and tactfully. They co-opted captured Germans who had high levels of education and ideals beyond suspicion to help them in the educational process, thereby attempting to dispel doubts and resistance among the fenced-in troops. Still, as Chancellor Emeritus Helmut Schmidt remembers from his own POW camp, there were always those, especially among the younger Wehrmacht officers, who thought that, in collaborating with the former enemy, they had "fouled their own nest."[15]

The British extended these efforts, less successfully, in special intern-ment camps on German soil, and later carried "re-education" into Ger-many's youth population by way of "youth officers." They arranged orientation and cultural meetings and organized social clubs, where reconciliation was to be preached and practiced. Here, too, the results were mixed, if only because the target groups were from the higher German social classes: Gymnasium and university students. Willy Schumann, who would end up teaching German literature at Smith College, recalls an instance of kindness that must have done more than all the theoretical lectures put together. In the British Zone near Ham-burg, on a very hot summer day when he and his friends were working in the field trying to harvest some produce, they noticed a small group of British soldiers passing by, who stopped to put something on the edge of the field, waved, and walked on. Because of non-fraternization orders, speaking was forbidden. As it turned out, they had left their lunch boxes for the emaciated-looking Germans. "This small human gesture," writes Schumann, "made an enormous, positive impression on all of us, even on my father, who was not an Anglophile."[16]

Once in Germany, American re-educators were just as likely to engage in such acts of mercy, as they would prove with their care packages under the Marshall Plan.[17] But they had much larger groups of POWs, and later, youths on German soil to deal with. Early on, their re-education policy was guided by theorists who were often exiled German Jews and knew the enemy country's background well, but were not always on the mark. Kurt Lewin, who had been a professor of psychology at the University of Berlin and in 1943 was teaching at the University of Iowa, held that Nazism was "deeply rooted, particularly in the youth on whom the future depends." Contrary to the evidence, he believed that a streamlined Nazi educational system had made an egoistic, uninhibitedly aggressive and destructive individual out of every German juvenile. He thought it absolutely necessary to change "a group atmosphere from autocracy toward democracy through a democratic leadership," by turning autocratic followers into democratic ones. But Lewin was pessimistic about the ability of German youths to do this, for he also believed that they, as a "lost generation," had the potential to go underground and "prepare the next world war."[18]

After German capitulation, further position papers were published by representatives of the Pentagon and the U.S. State Department, aided by other Central European emigrants. In 1946 German teenagers located in camps in Hesse and Bavaria were questioned, as were groups of POWs around the age of seventeen, held in northern France. It was concluded that they were "still totalitarian youth in search of leadership," who now echo "what they consider to be the official views of their current masters," thereby revealing "their totalitarian attitude of implicit and uncritical submission to authority, ingrained by Nazi education and German tradition." Untrained in democratic procedures, "German youth appear to presume that the American leaders will now solve their problems in an authoritarian fashion just as the Nazi leaders proposed to do."[19] Around the same time, Department of State Research Analyst Henry J. Kellermann concluded, more affirmatively and realistically, that the current nihilism of German youth was "largely the result of the breakdown of the Nazi system." Under arms-length American supervision and with German authorities more directly in control, indigenous youth organizations should be created for the purposes of recreation, culture, and religion, "as instrumental to democratic education."[20]

In the months that followed, many other American control officers would work along such positive lines. They could make use of the information they had gathered in their POW camps, located in the United States years before the war was over, and later also in England, France, and western Germany. It is true that often German resistance to re-education was considerable, grounded not only in a persistent idealization of the Führer, but also in clumsy indoctrination methods by the victors.[21] The initial lack of depth in reschooling methodology, however, in time gave way to more effective persuasion, and this was particularly true with regard to youth. By the summer of 1945, for example, approximately 7,000 German boys aged twelve to seventeen were "taught democracy" by Americans in a camp at Attichy in France. They were all captured soldiers and had been purposely separated from their more hardened older comrades. In the camp they studied trades and farming and took commercial courses. School subjects they had long ago been forced to give up were reintroduced to them, with geography by far the most popular. Their instructors were 144 carefully screened non-Nazi prisoners of war. In order to stamp out behavioral patterns of militarism, the boys did not salute, but tipped their caps. Instead of bugle calls, there was Brahms's Lullaby. Military band music was prohibited in favor of orchestral concerts.[22] The Americans were less successful when they mistook groups of former opponents to the Hitler Youth, such as the *Edelweisspiraten,* for hoodlums, dismissing them or placing them in camps without giving them the hearing they deserved. Out of ignorance or spite, local German administrators did nothing to correct this injustice. One such administrator was Professor Friedrich Schaffstein, who continued in a position of juridical authority, inveighing against *Edelweisspiraten* and other Nazi-incriminated groups as he had done before 1945.[23]

General Dwight D. Eisenhower had nullified the Hitler Youth Law of March 25, 1939, requiring total membership in the HJ, on September 28, 1944.[24] This constituted the beginning of political re-education as a program for the Americans, which continued later within the tight occupational framework of OMGUS (Office of Military Government of the United States for Germany). Until the late 1940s even for young people this took place against the intimidating backdrop of the Nuremberg Trials, which were often experienced as an undeserved manifestation of "the right of the victor."[25] The consequences of those trials for Germans from all walks of life were interrogations, endless questionnaires, internment, and regional denazification proceedings. These caused more resentment, for instance when politically suspect students were prevented from registering in the universities.[26] But "re-education" was soon overlapping with and then superseded by "re-orientation," which had been facilitated by a general youth amnesty for political infractions, as early as August 1946 for the U.S. Zone (to be emulated shortly by the British and in May 1947 also by the French authorities, for their respective jurisdictions).[27] In pronouncing their amnesty, the Americans admitted that they wished to concentrate on prosecuting older Nazis, for whom it was easier to prove that they were guilty for the crimes of the Third Reich.[28]

During the process of re-orientation, at the end of which Americans visualized re-integration into a Western value system and full democratization on the parliamentary model, German youths were able to benefit from cultural stimuli which were coming their way through various media.[29] One was the phenomenon of the *Amerika-Häuser*, institutes sponsored by the State Department where young people could go to read in libraries, view films, listen to recordings and the

occasional lecture, and take in exhibitions. Although there was an elitist quality to these activities, because ideally the young people had to
know English and thus probably came from from the higher social
strata, the administrative staff were Germans and one-quarter of the
literature was in German. In 1946 the first *Amerika-Haus* was established in Frankfurt; by early 1951 there were already twenty-seven in
the largest towns, most of them in the American Zone.[30] The one in
Kaiserslautern, founded in 1952 and featuring a bookmobile for the
outlying country, sponsored 2,560 events in that city in its first year
alone, when close to 300,000 German locals from all walks of life
attended.[31]

Since music knows no language barriers, American radio stations
became even more important. First and foremost there was the American Forces Network (AFN) run by the Pentagon, which broadcast in
English for the military only, delivering U.S.-generated news and programs reflecting American culture. But precisely because the network
was not specifically directed toward Germans, they became interested
in it like forbidden fruit, and eventually they formed a huge "shadow
audience." AFN turned into a cult vehicle for introducing the American way of life all over Europe (wherever GIs were stationed), but particularly in Germany, which already had a strong pre-1933 history of
adopting American popular culture. AFN featured cowboy music
(which in the 1950s was to evolve into the genre of country and western music) and items from the American hit parade, and these were
increasingly cherished by ordinary Germans in their teens and twenties.[32] The more educated and eclectic among them would listen to
late-night jazz shows—programs which the British emulated in their
region with their own BFN.[33] New German stations influenced by
American culture, especially popular-culture programming, were
Radio Frankfurt, Radio Stuttgart, Radio Munich, and RIAS Berlin, all
in the American Sector.[34] These stations were also obliged to rebroad-
cast programs from the Voice of America in Washington, D.C., which
sponsored overtly political content, and therefore, despite Willis
Conover's jazz offerings, they were less frequently listened to, particu-

larly with the commencement of the Cold War in 1947, by which time German youth in the western half of the country was fully on the way to re-orientation.[35]

But things were different at the beginning of the occupation period. The relatively early amnesty for the politically tainted among the youth in the three western zones in 1946–47 could have been viewed as an olive branch extended by former enemies willing to forgive. Yet not all adolescents wished to see it this way. Right after the war, many still professed their admiration for the Führer. National Socialism had not been such a bad idea, if only it had been executed right.[36] Denazification and the Nuremberg Trials caused much resentment. Many remained impervious to the idea, as did Manfred Rommel, the ex-Flakhelfer, that democracy of the Western type could work with Germans.[37] In the first few postwar years, an appreciable number of adolescents were still exhibiting racist patterns of prejudice, as when a boy with a KLV background found himself spitting at a displaced Polish worker in Hanover, a captured nurse resented having to work side by side with American Jews, and the physical proximity of black soldiers was reported as being offensive.[38] Abject hatred was reserved for the Soviets, who were thought to have murdered Polish officers in a forest near Katyn—a crime for which many Western occupiers still held the Nazis responsible, wrongly as it later turned out.[39] With cynicism, German boys and girls in the so-called Tri-Zone looked across the unfortified border with eastern Germany, where the blue-shirted FDJ was being built up, so it seemed, on the fascist model of the Hitler Youth. They had merely changed their shirts.[40] Others smarted under the stigma of former SS incorporation, especially when, toward the end of the war, they had been conscripted against their will.[41]

Unreconstructed university students were a special problem, for they could use sophistry in anti-West arguments. In Bonn, still in 1945, Stephen Spender encountered Herr Haecker, a student who claimed to be not a Nazi, but a nationalist. Although Hitler's anti-Semitism was a great mistake, he said, there was no denying that the Jews were an "inferior section of the population." Haecker rushed to explain: "Race is real. We Germans really do belong to a Nordic stock which is different from and superior to the Southern and, especially, the Eastern peoples."[42] In Heidelberg, lectures given by the philosopher Karl Jaspers on German collective guilt were greeted with hostile responses, and when a medical professor mentioned a disease affecting only Jews and said that one could not observe this disease any more, he was interrupted by raucous laughter and the pounding of feet.[43] In 1946 U.S. Research Analyst Kellermann, too, found that there were hotbeds of student chauvinism in the universities of Erlangen, Hamburg, Jena, Göttingen, and Aachen—largely senior HJ graduates and frustrated veterans of the armed forces.[44] It was in Göttingen that a fascist Wiking Youth group was started in 1947, as an adjunct to the neo-Nazi Deutsche Reichspartei led by Adolf von Thadden, because here the British had allowed the re-establishment of new youth groups, politically oriented ones included. But other, democratic-minded youth leaders were alarmed, and on their urging the British authorities had the Wiking Youth dissolved.[45]

Since these events occurred at the very beginning of the military occupation phase and had no lasting consequences, it is fair to conclude that the resurgence of Nazism was not a major problem in the country at least during the second half of the 1940s, and certainly as far as German youth was concerned. By 1951, when the newly charted Federal Republic was set on its democratic course, an American-conducted opinion poll of the population found that in the new polity, only 10 percent would applaud the rise of a new Nazi Party, while 4 percent would actively support it. Even though youths appear to have been pushing these percentages upward, they still did not constitute a danger to the new democratic order.[46]

In 1945, the youngest members of the "Nazi Regime Youth Cohort" were eleven years old, and the oldest twenty-nine. In 1950, when conditions in Germany were settling down and these youths along with them, they were sixteen and thirty-four respectively.[47] Within this crucial five-year period, these children and young adults, shattered morale aside, adjusted to a German society which was initially shaken by the

effects of destruction, the loss of loved ones, unsteady political governance, economic disruptions, and a breakdown in the public health-
care system. In the late 1940s and throughout the 1950s, a number of
American and German social scientists held that youths in Germany
were apathetic and, in regard to society and politics, "passive and usually still uninterested."[48] Dismissing the community around them
completely, they maintained an interest only in themselves, in their
immediate "personal and economic problems."[49] Because they had
been misled and disappointed by an older generation, they mistrusted
any authority other than their own, even if they knew that to be shaky.
"The great majority is still waiting and watching—not so much out of
indecision as because of the fact that they don't want to be 'wrong'
again in three, five or ten years. German youth is still in the transient
stage between yesterday and tomorrow."[50]

One German scholar who pursued this thesis relentlessly was the
sociologist Helmut Schelsky. To describe youths well into the 1960s,
he coined the catchy phrase "The Skeptical Generation," popularized
in articles, lectures, and a book with that title published originally in
1957.[51] Schelsky wrote that this skepticism of youth was paired with a
crass egotism that was practical, realistic, and totally centered on materialism. These youths were not interested in community, although they
constantly worked out and revised clever schemes of social adaptation
for the sake of everyday survival. Taking a cue from the Flakhelfer generation included in his target group, Schelsky denied these young Germans maturity, which, he alleged, they had lost by being forced to
grow into adulthood too fast. According to him, there reigned a "skepticism against and repudiation of the politics of the past as well as the
present, a distrust of political ideologies and theories, a 'without us'
attitude toward all public and societal demands, so as to be able to concentrate on the private and professional, on areas manageable in terms
of one's own powers of judgment and responsibility."[52] In writing this,
Schelsky had his own ax to grind, for as a former Nazi Party member
(1937) who once officiated at the SS University in Strasbourg, he
viewed the Third Reich in retrospect as the structural monolith the

Nazi leadership had claimed it to be, implying the highest degree of totalitarian pressure on youth. The result, he held fatalistically, was that they as a group were stultified and stunned.[53]

To a certain extent, contemporary examples seem to prove Schelsky right.[54] In its first issue, on February 21, 1946, the soon-to-be-prominent German weekly *Die Zeit* printed a statement authored by Ernst Samhaber, which contained a collective vote of non-confidence in the newly founded United Nations: "We do not trust the powers which constitute the U.N. They have faced us in war for six years . . . Neither do we trust the men who represent the U.N. They are human beings who are subject to human weaknesses, to fear, suspicion, passions, and to error."[55] At a political forum at Munich University shortly thereafter, attended by outside observers such as André Gide and the historian Walter L. Dorn of OMGUS, students voiced their ongoing pessimism. One in particular, the fine arts major Annemarie Krapp, who claimed to have left the BDM voluntarily, was so outspoken that she incurred the anger of many in the audience. She said, "I would gladly say to you that I believe in democracy, but I would be lying. It is not that I reject democratic ideas; on the contrary, not only do I have the best intentions, but I even wish to be convinced." But how could she form an opinion? "Are we sure today that perhaps in a few years we will not again be called criminals, because we are now supporting one of the existing political parties?"[56] These sentiments were shared by many other students, one of whom, Jost Hermand, now at the University of Wisconsin, admits to never tuning in to the radio for news or reading political commentaries in the papers at the time because of his total mistrust of politics.[57] But young people outside of Gymnasien and universities were equally guarded. Subjects of indifference ranged from politics to the military to moral guilt to human rights; some downplayed the media, others shunned social bonds; man was assumed to be evil.[58]

Concurring with Schelsky in 1958, a female observer from Hamburg agreed that German young people were "indolent, superficial, weary of government and materialistic."[59] However, beyond an otherwise pessimistic verdict, this analyst was one of the few who attempted to differentiate, in this case in terms of a division of the generational cohorts. She argued that those youths born before 1930, having been exposed to National Socialism the longest, were the ones most likely to have been drawn into the line of fire at the front, or used in dangerous home defenses. Hence their level of consciousness about social or political matters was thought to be higher than that of the generation born after 1930, who had also been infected by National Socialism, but, since they were still children, not as seminally.[60]

Such a qualifying view was supported by others, notably Helmut Schmidt, who maintained that all those who had been children before the Third Reich were, of necessity, lacking "any education toward democracy."[61] Some pointed out that one reason this older HJ cohort seemed so indifferent to the world around it was that unlike the members of the younger HJ cohort, who were still or again being taken care of by parents and teachers, they had had to fend for themselves in largely adverse circumstances, to the point where nothing else could matter.[62] In the immediate aftermath of May 1945, the older HJ cohort's attitude was based not on global disinterest, but, as many were claiming, on feelings of shock which had rendered them furtive and jaded. However, as young people found their way back into a society that was being newly anchored in democracy and, eventually, economic stability, they began to find time and opportunity to make up for the losses and disruptions of their adolescence, and in time they became mature citizens.[63]

Moreover, when questioned further, young veterans admitted to being disinterested not so much in matters of politics in the widest sense as in anything having to do with *party* politics, as in the Nazi Party. Having grown up mostly in a one-party system, they regarded politics as synonymous with the rule of a single autocratic party, and they had to be taught the values of multi-party pluralism. That of course was the essence of parliamentary democracy of the Western type, something which had been tried in the Weimar Republic and which, as some of the oldest ex-Hitler Youths might still remember, had often been vilified in Hitler's speeches.[64]

One interesting barometer of this gradual change toward normal social and political awareness among youth was membership in new post-1945 youth organizations, at least in the western zones, as they were gradually authorized by the Allied Forces. Even in the short period from April 1946, when youth clubs were again permitted, to February 1948, when the founding of the Federal Republic was near, membership in them increased six-fold, reaching just under a million and a half in the U.S. Zone. Sports clubs drew the majority of young people, even more than religious ones; trade union groups were next; and the *Falken*, hiking groups supported by the reborn Social Democratic Party (SPD), constituted the largest outright political formation.[65] That a left-wing youth group would be the foremost political band in a West German landscape gradually dominated by Konrad Adenauer's home-grown conservatives, spoke well for former Hitler Youths as future guarantors of democracy.

Yet contrary to what the new Federal German President, Theodor Heuss, said publicly in 1950, the overwhelming majority of the newly constituted youth leagues held no connections to the moribund Weimar youth groups, which had been largely anti-democratic and thus had sold out so easily to Schirach.[66] Baldur von Schirach, Artur Axmann, and Adolf Hitler played critical roles in what happened to German youth between 1933 and 1950. Even though they could not convince all youths, they had made a credible start in generating a functional elite for a totalitarian Reich of a thousand years, despite many inconsistencies in their regime structure. The regime's lethal power was proved during a war of aggression of nearly six years, when it was obvious that without the recruits that Schirach, Axmann, Rommel, and Himmler had trained, however haphazardly, they would not have had an army of many millions of men and hundreds of thousands of women to subjugate and kill persons they considered aliens on a grand scale. No lack of prior planning, no contradictions in a heteroge-

neous governing structure could prevent those crimes from being insti-
gated or stop them once they were under way. And the increasing dis-
comfort of a youth generation that was placed inside this structure
and, on the whole, performed as expected almost to the end, likewise
could do nothing to stop those crimes.

In the end, Hitler made short shrift of youth. One day before he
killed himself, despite the fulsome words of praise for youth he had
spoken many times before, he wrote simply in his political testament
that he was about to die happy with the thought of youth on his mind,
a youth that had carried his name and had not shied away from
action.[67] Axmann did not even bother with such a commonplace
before or during his selfish retreat from Berlin, which was shielded by
hundreds of his charges. Instead, he went into hiding, only to start one
of the earliest neo-Nazi groups by 1946.[68] The BDM's chief, Jutta
Rüdiger, also remained an unreconstructed Nazi after internment.[69]
Hitler neglected to mention either Axmann or Rüdiger in his will.

Nor did he mention Baldur von Schirach. The pompous founder of
the Nazi youth organizations, and their mentor until the end, at first
wanted to defend Vienna as its Gauleiter. But unlike many of his
young lieutenants he despaired early and, disguised with glasses and a
moustache, fled to Schwaz in the Austrian Tyrol. He called himself
Richard Falk, pretending to be an author. Always a spinner of phrases,
he was now working on a novel called "The Mysteries of Mira Loy."
But in early June he thought better of this and surrendered to the
Americans, whom he addressed in a southern drawl.[70]

It was at the Nuremberg Trials in 1946 where Schirach, as one of the
main Nazi defendants, decided to do what the Colonel in Wolfgang
Borchert's play had trouble comprehending: to accept the sole responsibility. "It is my fault to have educated youth in the service of a man
who was a murderer of millions," he confessed. "I believed in this man.
This is all I can say in my defense, or to explain my actions. I bore the
responsibility for youth, I held it in my charge, and hence I alone bear
the guilt for these juveniles. The young generation is guiltless."[71]
Schirach's rhetoric was disingenuous, calculated to persuade the High

Court to decide not to condemn him on charges of having misled German youth, because he appeared to be contrite. His calculation bore fruit, for he did not suffer the death sentence. Instead he received twenty years of incarceration, not for any crimes against or on behalf of youth, but for having assisted in the deportation of Jews from Vienna.[72] His words, however, only compounded the central problem regarding the responsibility or guilt of German youth from 1933 to 1945. The responsibility that Schirach wanted to claim for himself to exonerate youth did not exist as the kind of moral issue he made it out to be. Schirach had his own responsibility, which he could never shed; there was no way for him to assume the collective responsibility of his charges.

For Schirach's underlings were answerable on their own behalf. In the case of the younger and older generations of Hitler Youth and the young armed forces veterans who now found themselves adrift, however, guilt could not be apportioned that easily. This is not to say that most of them were not complicit in the tragedies they helped to cause as members of the Hitler Youth and Hitler's armies, including the SS. Even if they were merely small cogs in the huge war machinery, or in the intricate system of persecution and mass liquidation, they had become a part of these systems, helping to guarantee their terrible functionality. That most of them knew this after May 1945 is demonstrated by their attitudes of shock and their refusal, at least at first, to become engaged in any civic matters. Their own discussion, insofar as it happened, of their possible status as "victims" was strongly indicative of a bad conscience, of wishing to explain away any part of their biographies dating from before the Nazis' humiliating surrender.

While the issue of complicity for all youth in the Third Reich is one the historian can have little doubt about, the question of moral guilt is harder to come to grips with. The degree of guilt that any Hitler Youths possessed, whether boys or girls in HJ camps, whether young men or women fighting at the fronts, depended on their age, their hierarchical position in Nazi governance, and, ultimately, on the sum total of activities of a criminal nature they became engaged in. These activities would have included the Nazi indoctrination of their peers for imperialistic ends or what later would be subsumed under war crimes, or, with reference to Hitler's specific annihilation warfare, "crimes against humanity": serving in concentration camps; setting Polish villages ablaze; guarding Soviet prisoners in starvation camps; undue cruelty against enemies in hand-to-hand combat; and, the worst atrocity of all, assisting in the genocide of Gypsies and Jews. It is clear that many actions in this category could not have been undertaken by some, as they were still too young or were physically removed from the scenes of crime—for example, a sixteen-year-old Hitler Youth who was drafted in 1944 and never saw combat, or a young woman who served as an auxiliary telegrapher in her home town. But in a martial society where the entire youth culture was systematically contaminated with concepts of intolerance and oppression of the physically weak and hatred against those who were of a different "race," there could hardly have been a Hitler Youth who had not learned to adopt notions of power over those below him, since he was emulating those above him powerful enough to have taught him. Such was the chain of command, militarily, mentally, and morally. Hence there was many an eleven-year-old Pimpf who in 1934, after only one year in the Hitler Youth, had learned to humiliate the ten-year-olds who had just joined, and there were large numbers of flak helpers of both genders at the fronts who in the spring of 1945 made sure to take no prisoners. In 1943, there existed tens of thousands of Waffen-SS soldiers who were breaking universal laws of humanity; they had been indoctrinated in the Hitler Youth as juveniles and, through its racist tenets, now became guilty. And there were many HJ judges who officiated while still in their twenties, after having moved through the HJ ranks and then obtained a law degree; they used as their yardstick the perverted legal code of a criminal regime, for example when they were condemning youthful dissenters to solitary confinement, and thus they themselves became criminal. By 1945, among the surviving youths, Nazi ideology often was still so prevalent that, as in the encounter between Spender and the Bonn student Haecker, a sense of German racial superiority was unshakable. For others, like the Munich student Annemarie Krapp, it was the knowledge of having been misled not without their own complicity that caused them to experience a feeling of guilt, while cautioning, at the same time, against any further commitment to future German politics.

Thus Wolfgang Borchert, who knew about these liabilities, was portraying a psychological truth when he pictured the Colonel in his play as a man who just did not understand. According to the Colonel, by the military as well as the Nazi leadership principle, responsibility toward subordinates or for actions taken was something that everyone in the hierarchy had to bear for himself; it could not be passed back. This is why Borchert himself, through his play's character Sergeant Beckmann, in the final analysis could not shake off his own responsibility or perhaps even his guilt for the death of the men he had led in a sortie against the Russians (or for other deeds he might have committed in war). He himself bore this burden. As Borchert rightly saw, all of this had been the consequence of children not having been taught to ask the right questions beforehand, and of their superiors, including parents, teachers, and politicians, not ever feeling motivated to offer appropriate answers.[73] Indeed, some of those questions were at least as old as the Weimar Republic, which in its last stages had caused young people to wonder about their own and their parents' role in the midst of psychological tension, political turmoil, and economic misery, many of these generated by the First World War.

Eventually, German youth, partly guilt-ridden and partly disenchanted but hardly innocent, resolved to help in the reconstruction of democracy in West Germany, thereby also building a sound new economic base for the state and for themselves. The mechanisms by which this happened within a relatively short time span still call for more explanation. What is clear, however, is that much of the democratic government under Konrad Adenauer, himself a former sufferer under the Nazi regime yet a politial reactionary, was compromised, since not only his own party, the Christian Democratic Union (CDU), but also the so-called Free Democrats (FDP) and, especially, smaller right-wing groupings harbored many old Nazis. It goes without saying that Hitler Youth veterans and one-time Wehrmacht soldiers constituted majorities in all of these parties, even the oppositional SPD.[74] Possibly because questions about complicity or guilt were just too vexing and detracted from the path of economic progress, but also because they wanted to erase the memory of often joyful, but later more bitter, days under Nazi rule, middle-aged Germans in the 1960s not only became successful at their jobs but even helped to maintain a viable democracy on the British, French, or American model.

In the early postwar phase, the silence of the younger generation about the past had served an anesthetizing purpose. But by the late 1970s, when these former Hitler boys and Hitler girls were becoming grandparents and their past appeared less threatening, they started to recollect, and many sat down to write their memoirs—a process that is still ongoing. It was the trauma of their knowledge, about the rule of force and the intolerance engendered by a totalitarian dictatorship, that had kept them from remembering earlier, when they had still been much too close to shame and disaster. As they grew older and looked back, they found it easier to face the memories of their place in this dictatorship, including the contributions that they themselves had made—a dictatorship which oppressed, maimed, and killed millions, and, if they were honest enough to admit it, had damaged their own souls.

Abbreviations

ADJ	Archiv der Deutschen Jugendbewegung, Burg Ludwigstein
AFN	American Forces Network
AHS	Adolf-Hitler-Schulen
Antifa	*Antifaschistische Junge Garde*
APA	Author's Private Archive
ARL	Institut für Rechtswissenschaften, Arbeitsgruppe Jugend und Strafrecht, Universität Lüneburg
BA	Bundesarchiv Koblenz
BAB	Bundesarchiv Berlin (records from the former Berlin Document Center)
BAF	Bundesarchiv Freiburg—Militärarchiv
BBC	British Broadcasting Corporation
BDM	Bund Deutscher Mädel (League of German Girls in the HJ)
BFN	British Forces Network
BHSAM	Bayerisches Hauptstaatsarchiv München
CDU	Christlich-Demokratische Union (Christian Democratic Union)
CM	Allgemeine Korrespondenz, Carl Orff-Zentrum, München
DAF	Deutsche Arbeitsfront (German Labor Front)
DAOW	Dokumentationsstelle des Österreichischen Widerstandes, Wien
DNVP	Deutschnationale Volkspartei (German National People's Party)
FAD	Freiwilliger Arbeitsdienst (Voluntary Labor Service)

FDJ	Freie Deutsche Jugend (Free German Youth)
FDP	Freie Demokratische Partei (Free Democratic Party)
Gestapo	Geheime Staatspolizei (Secret State Police)
GStAM	Geheimes Staatsarchiv München
HHSAW	Hessisches Hauptstaatsarchiv Wiesbaden
HIS	Hoover Institution, Stanford
Hiwis	*Hilfswillige*
HJ	Hitler-Jugend (Hitler Youth)
IfZ	Institut für Zeitgeschichte München
KJVD	*Kommunistischer Jugendverband Deutschlands* (German Communist Youth League)
KLV	Kinderlandverschickung (Save the Children in the Country program)
KPD	Kommunistische Partei Deutschlands (German Communist Party)
NHSA	Niedersächsisches Hauptstaatsarchiv Hannover
NPEA	Nationalpolitische Erziehungsanstalten (National Political Educational Institutions)
NS	*Nationalsozialistisch* (National Socialist)
NSAO	Niedersächsisches Staatsarchiv Oldenburg
NSAW	Niedersächsisches Staatsarchiv Wolfenbüttel
NSDAP	Nationalsozialistische Deutsche Arbeiterpartei (Nazi Party)
NSF	Nationalsozialistische Frauenschaft (Nazi Women's League)
NSKK	Nationalsozialistisches Kraftfahrkorps (Nazi Motor League)
NSLB	Nationalsozialistischer Lehrerbund (Nazi Teachers' League)
OLA	Oberösterreichisches Landesarchiv Linz
OMGUS	Office of Military Government of the United States for Germany
RAD	Reichsarbeitsdienst (Reich Labor Service)
RIAS	Radio im Amerikanischen Sektor [Berlin]
SA	Sturmabteilungen (storm troopers/Brown Shirts)
SAB	Staatsarchiv Bremen
SAF	Staatsarchiv Freiburg
SAG	Staatliches Archivlager Göttingen, Gauarchiv Ostpreussen (Niedersächsisches Staatsarchiv Bückeburg)

SAH	Staatsarchiv Hamburg
SAL	Staatsarchiv Ludwigsburg
SAM	Staatsarchiv München
SAMs	Staatsarchiv Münster
SAN	Staatsarchiv Nürnberg
SAND	Staatsarchiv Neuburg an der Donau
SD	Sicherheitsdienst (Security Service of the SS)
SPD	Sozialdemokratische Partei Deutschlands (German Social Democratic Party)
SRD	HJ-Streifendienst (Security Service of the HJ)
SS	Schutzstaffel (Black Shirts)
StAM	Stadtarchiv München
Stuka	*Sturzkampf-Flugzeug*
TGI	Elke Föhlich, ed., *Die Tagebücher von Joseph Goebbels: Sämtliche Fragmente*, 5 vols. (Munich, 1987)
TGII	Elke Fröhlich, ed., *Die Tagebücher von Joseph Goebbels, Teil II: Diktate, 1941–1945*, 16 vols. (Munich, 1993–1996)
Ufa	Universum Film-Aktiengesellschaft
U.N.	United Nations
WE	Wehrertüchtigungslager

Notes

1. "Make Way, You Old Ones!"

1. Hermann Graml, "Integration und Entfremdung: Inanspruchnahme durch Staatsjugend und Dienstpflicht," in Ute Benz and Wolfgang Benz, eds., *Sozialisation und Traumatisierung: Kinder in der Zeit des Nationalsozialismus* (Frankfurt am Main, 1992), 74–79. (All translations from German-language sources are those of the author.)
2. Margarete Hannsmann, *Der helle Tag bricht an: Ein Kind wird Nazi* (Munich, 1984).
3. Melita Maschmann, *Fazit: Kein Rechtfertigungsversuch,* 5th ed. (Stuttgart, 1964); Edgar Gielsdorf, *Vom Christkind eine Landsknechtstrommel* (Cologne, 1994); Renate Finckh, *Mit uns zieht die neue Zeit* (Baden-Baden, 1979).
4. Ian Kershaw, *Popular Opinion and Political Dissent in the Third Reich: Bavaria, 1933–1945* (Oxford, 1983); Kershaw, *The "Hitler Myth": Image and Reality in the Third Reich* (Oxford, 1987).
5. Michael H. Kater, *Studentenschaft und Rechtsradikalismus in Deutschland, 1918–1933: Eine sozialgeschichtliche Studie zur Bildungskrise in der Weimarer Republik* (Hamburg, 1975), 108; Ursula Baumann, *Vom Recht auf den eigenen Tod: Die Geschichte des Suizids vom 18. bis zum 20. Jahrhundert* (Weimar, 2001), 326, 330; Reinhold Schairer, *Die akademische Berufsnot: Tatsachen und Auswege* (Jena, [1932]), 6.
6. Peter Loewenberg, *Decoding the Past: The Psychohistorical Approach* (Berkeley, 1985), 251.
7. For an example involving a very young child, toward the end of the Republic, see Hildegard Morgenthal, *"Rotkopf, die Ecke brennt, Feuerwehr kommt angerennt": Leben in der NS-Zeit und zwei Leben danach* (Frankfurt am Main, 2000), 88.

8. Ute Frevert, *Women in German History: From Bourgeois Emancipation to Sexual Liberation* (New York, 1989), 198.

9. On the economic upheavals, see Gerald D. Feldman, *The Great Disorder: Politics, Economics, and Society in the German Inflation, 1914–1924* (New York, 1997); Harold James, *The German Slump: Politics and Economics, 1924–1936* (New York, 1986); and the articles in Ian Kershaw, ed., *Weimar: Why Did German Democracy Fail?* (London, 1990). On unemployment especially among youth, see Manfred Hermanns, *Jugendarbeitslosigkeit seit der Weimarer Republik: Ein sozialgeschichtlicher und soziologischer Vergleich* (Opladen, 1990), 16–21, 77–80, and the report of social worker Albert Lamm, *Betrogene Jugend: Aus einem Erwerbslosenheim* (Berlin, 1932).

10. Loewenberg, 249, 254–62, 268, 270, 278–79; Kater, 43–73; Kater, "Generationskonflikt als Entwicklungsfaktor in der NS-Bewegung vor 1933," *Geschichte und Gesellschaft* 11 (1985): 224–229. See also a contemporary source, Leopold Dingräve, *Wo steht die junge Generation?* (Jena, 1931).

11. See Peter Suhrkamp, "Söhne ohne Väter und Lehrer: Die Situation der bürgerlichen Jugend," *Neue Rundschau* 43 (1932): 681–696.

12. Peter Gay, *Weimar Culture: The Outsider as Insider* (New York, 1968). See also Werner Hasenclever, *Der Sohn: Ein Drama in fünf Akten* (Leipzig, 1914); Franz Werfel, *Nicht der Mörder, der Ermordete ist schuldig: Eine Novelle* (Munich, 1920); Ernst Glaeser, *Jahrgang 1902* (Potsdam, 1928). Otto Dix and George Grosz caricatured many of the power mongers of the older generations who were blocking the path to progress for the younger ones. See M. Kay Flavell, *George Grosz: A Biography* (New Haven, 1988). For this theme in the music establishment of the Weimar Republic, see my article "The Revenge of the Fathers: The Demise of Modern Music at the End of the Weimar Republic," *German Studies Review* 15 (1992): 295–315.

13. Rudolf Kneip, *Jugend der Weimarer Zeit: Handbuch der Jugendverbände, 1919–1938* (Frankfurt am Main, 1974), 157–158, 215; Peter D. Stachura, *The German Youth Movement, 1900–1945: An Interpretative and Documentary History* (London, 1981), 64, 111.

14. Walter Z. Laqueur, *Young Germany: A History of the German Youth Movement* (New York, 1962), 10–83 (quotes, 3–4).

15. See Modris Eksteins's trenchant analyses in *Rites of Spring: The Great War and the Birth of the Modern Age* (Boston, 1989), 95–207. On England, see also Paul Fussell, *The Great War and Modern Memory* (London, 1977).

16. Laqueur, 87–98; Stachura, 34–37.

17. Karl Unruh, *Langemarck: Legende und Wirklichkeit* (Koblenz, 1986); Werner Kindt, ed., *Die deutsche Jugendbewegung, 1920 bis 1933: Die bündische Zeit* (Düsseldorf, 1974), 74–75, 139–144, 159, 288, 352, 423–424.

18. Bernhard Schneider, *Daten zur Geschichte der Jugendbewegung* (Bad Godesberg, 1965), 36.

19. An excellent overview can be found in Felix Raabe, *Die Bündische Jugend: Ein Beitrag zur Geschichte der Weimarer Republik* (Stuttgart, 1961).

20. Stachura, 40, 42, 105–108.

21. Kneip, 39, 136–137.

22. Laqueur, 144.

23. Howard Becker, *Vom Barette schwankt die Feder: Die Geschichte der deutschen Jugendbewegung* (Wiesbaden, 1949), 109; Michael H. Kater, "Bürgerliche Jugendbewegung und Hitlerjugend in Deutschland von 1926 bis 1939," *Archiv für Sozialgeschichte* 17 (1977): 149–150.

24. Gregor Strasser quoted in Loewenberg, 250.

25. Gottfried Neesse, "Der Jugendführer des Deutschen Reiches," *Archiv des öffentlichen Rechts* 26 (1935): 203; *Hitler-Jugend, 1933–1943: Die Chronik eines Jahrzehnts* (Berlin, [1943]), 13–14; Kater, "Generationskonflikt," 239–240.

26. Peter D. Stachura, *Nazi Youth in the Weimar Republic* (Santa Barbara, Calif., 1975); Kater, "Jugendbewegung," 146–148; Kater, "Generationskonflikt," 237.

27. Loewenberg, 478–479; Kater, "Generationskonflikt," 232, 240; Kater, *Studentenschaft,* 111–205.

28. Hans Gerth, "The Nazi Party: Its Leadership and Composition," *American Journal of Sociology* 45 (1940): 529–530; Michael H. Kater, *The Nazi Party: A Social Profile of Members and Leaders, 1919–1945* (Cambridge, Mass., 1983), 139–144, 230–231, 233–236.

29. Jürgen Falter, *Hitlers Wähler* (Munich, 1991), 152–154.

30. The detailed explanation of Hitler's entire pre-1933 political strategy is still unsurpassed in Dietrich Orlow, *The History of the Nazi Party: 1919–1933* (Pittsburgh, 1969). Also see Michael H. Kater, "Der NS-Studentenbund von 1926 bis 1928: Randgruppe zwischen Hitler und Strasser," *Vierteljahrshefte für Zeitgeschichte* 22 (1974): 173–174.

31. Hitler cited in Kater, *Studentenschaft,* 118.

32. Albert Speer, *Erinnerungen,* 8th ed. (Berlin, 1970), 137. For September 1933, see Dietrich Orlow, *The History of the Nazi Party: 1933–1945* (Pittsburgh, 1973), 81.

33. Kater, *Nazi Party,* 235; Martin Broszat, *Der Staat Hitlers: Grundlegung und Entwicklung seiner inneren Verfassung* (Munich, 1969), 56; Peter Hüttenberger, *Die Gauleiter: Studie zum Wandel des Machtgefüges in der NSDAP* (Stuttgart, 1969), 200–201. For Nazi dread of this, see entry for May 24, 1942, *TGII,* vol. 4, 354; and for April 19, 1943, *TGII,* vol. 8, 131.

34. For a Nazi voice, see Hans Spethmann, ed., *Die Stadt Essen: Das Werden und Wirken einer Grossstadt an der Ruhr* (Berlin, 1938), 312. Critically: John E. Knodel, *The Decline of Fertility in Germany, 1871–1939* (Princeton, 1974).

35. Joseph Goebbels, "Erziehung und Führerschicht," *Nationalsozialistisches Jahrbuch* (1930): 179.

36. Gregor Strasser cited in Jürgen Reulecke, "Jugendprotest—Ein Kennzeichen des 20. Jahrhunderts?" in Dieter Dowe, ed., *Jugendprotest und Generationenkonflikt in Europa im 20. Jahrhundert: Deutschland, England, Frankreich und Italien im Vergleich* (Bonn, 1986), 2.

37. Karl Mannheim, "Das Problem der Generationen," *Kölner Vierteljahrshefte für Soziologie* 7 (1928): 157–185, 309–330. Cf. Alan B. Spitzer, "The Historical Problem of Generations," *American Historical Review* 78 (1973): 1353–1385; Walter Jaide, *Eine neue Generation? Eine Untersuchung über Werthaltungen und Leitbilder der Jugendlichen* (Munich, 1961); Michael Mitterauer, *Sozialgeschichte der Jugend* (Frankfurt am Main, 1986), 48–50, 247; Christopher Hausmann, "Heranwachsen im 'Dritten Reich': Möglichkeiten und Besonderheiten jugendlicher Sozialisation im Spiegel autobiographischer Zeugnisse," *Geschichte in Wissenschaft und Unterricht* 13 (1990): 607–618.

38. Erhard Eppler, *Als Wahrheit verordnet wurde: Briefe an meine Enkelin,* 3rd ed. (Frankfurt am Main, 1995), 104.

2. Serving in the Hitler Youth

1. *Deutsches Lesebuch für Volksschulen: 3. und 4. Schuljahr,* 2nd ed. (Lahr, 1938), 264–265.

2. For improvisation as a rule of governance in the Third Reich, see the representative essays in Christian Leitz, ed., *The Third Reich: The Essential Readings* (Oxford, 1999).

3. Peter D. Stachura, *Nazi Youth in the Weimar Republic* (Santa Barbara, Calif., 1975); Heinz Boberach, *Jugend unter Hitler* (Düsseldorf, 1982), 19.

4. Stachura; Baldur von Schirach, *Ich glaubte an Hitler* (Hamburg, 1967), 101–102, 153.

5. Von Schirach, 153; Arno Klönne, *Hitlerjugend: Die Jugend und ihre Organisation im Dritten Reich* (Hanover, 1960), 11.
6. Von Schirach, 7–8, 11–12. On Weimar at the turn of the century, see Laird M. Easton, *The Red Count: The Life and Times of Harry Kessler* (Berkeley, 2002), 145–156.
7. Von Schirach, 18–22, 28 (quotes).
8. Ibid., 33, 40–61 (quote, 59).
9. Ibid., 101–102; 159; Boberach, 21. In Nuremberg Schirach mentioned 100,000 youths (Schirach cited for May 23, 1946, in *Der Prozess gegen die Hauptkriegsverbrecher vor dem Internationalen Militärgerichtshof Nürnberg, 14. November 1945 – 1. Oktober 1946* [Munich, 1984], vol. 13, 412).
10. Werner Klose, *Generation im Gleichschritt: Ein Dokumentarbericht* (Oldenburg, 1964), 19.
11. Boberach, 21; Jay W. Baird, *To Die for Germany: Heroes in the Nazi Pantheon* (Bloomington, 1990), 108–129.
12. Von Schirach, 190, 264–265, 269–271; Harald Scholtz, *NS-Ausleseschulen: Internatsschulen als Herrschaftsmittel des Führerstaates* (Göttingen, 1973), 285. On Axmann, see Robert Wistrich, *Who's Who in Nazi Germany* (New York, 1982), 7.
13. Klönne, 15; Von Schirach, 193, 232; Matthias von Hellfeld and Arno Klönne, *Die betrogene Generation: Jugend in Deutschland unter dem Faschismus* (Cologne, 1985), 35.
14. Harry Pross, *Vor und nach Hitler: Zur deutschen Sozialpathologie* (Olten, 1962), 127–128.
15. Helmut Schmidt in Schmidt et al., *Kindheit und Jugend unter Hitler,* 2nd ed. (Berlin, 1992), 203.
16. Winfried Speitkamp, *Jugend in der Neuzeit: Deutschland vom 16. bis zum 20. Jahrhundert* (Göttingen, 1998), 229.
17. *Das junge Volk* (Aug. 6, 1933): 2; ibid. (Sept. 15, 1933): 2.
18. Report, [July 1934], IfZ, MA-1190/1, FN 1505861-64.
19. Hans-Christian Brandenburg, *Die Geschichte der HJ: Wege und Irrwege einer Generation* (Cologne, 1968), 195–196, 202–203; Matthias von Hellfeld, *Bündische Jugend und Hitlerjugend: Zur Geschichte von Anpassung und Widerstand, 1930–1939* (Cologne, 1987), 169–170.
20. Rietzel to Janssen, July 11, 1934, IfZ, MA-1190/1, FN 1505872-73; Brandenburg, 196.
21. *Vorschriftenhandbuch der Hitler-Jugend (VHB.HJ)* (Jan. 1, 1942), 2: 1068–1070, (IfZ, Db/44.01).
22. ADJ, A166/1.

23. Jürgen W. Falter and Michael H. Kater, "Wähler und Mitglieder der NSDAP: Neue Forschungsergebnisse zur Soziographie des Nationalsozialismus, 1925 bis 1933," *Geschichte und Gesellschaft* 19 (1993): 155–177.

24. "Verordnungsblatt der Reichsjugendführung," Dec. 19, 1933, BA, NSD/43/1; Detlev Peukert, "Protest und Widerstand von Jugendlichen im Dritten Reich," in Richard Löwenthal and Patrick von zur Mühlen, eds., *Widerstand und Verweigerung in Deutschland, 1933 bis 1945* (Bonn, 1982), 191.

25. Manfred Priepke, *Die evangelische Jugend im Dritten Reich, 1933–1936* (Hanover, 1960).

26. Report, [July 1934], as cited in n. 18; Speitkamp, 230–231.

27. Heinrich Roth, *Katholische Jugend in der NS-Zeit unter besonderer Berücksichtigung des Katholischen Jungmännerverbandes: Daten und Dokumente* (Düsseldorf, 1959); Lawrence D. Walker, *Hitler Youth and Catholic Youth, 1933–1936: A Study in Totalitarian Conquest* (Washington, D.C., 1970).

28. Weichinger to Bezirksaussenstelle Bad Reichenhall, May 23, 1934, SAM, LRA/30655. See also the material in SAM, NSDAP/361.

29. Peukert, 192–193.

30. Von Schirach, 232; Gerhard Klemer, *Jugendstrafrecht und Hitler-Jugend: Stellung und Aufgaben der Hitler-Jugend in der Jugendstrafsrechtspflege,* 2nd ed. (Berlin, 1941), 24–25; Franz Baaden, *Jugendverfassung und Jugenddienstpflicht* (Berlin, 1943), 23, 25, 32–33.

31. See Von Schirach, 190–191.

32. "Gesetz über die Hitlerjugend," in Heinrich Schönfelder, ed., *Deutsche Reichsgesetze: Sammlung des Verfassungs-, Gemein-, Straf- und Verfahrensrechts für den täglichen Gebrauch,* 13th ed. (Munich, 1943), 1a: 1.

33. Ibid., 2.

34. Calculations based on figures in Von Hellfeld and Klönne, 35.

35. Statistics for Vechta, July 28, 1934, NSAO, 134/1157.

36. Peter Pahmeyer and Lutz van Spankeren, *Die Hitlerjugend in Lippe (1933–1939): Totalitäre Erziehung zwischen Anspruch und Wirklichkeit* (Bielefeld, 1998), 124.

37. *Deutschland-Berichte der Sozialdemokratischen Partei Deutschlands (Sopade), 1934–1940* (Salzhausen, 1980), vol. 2 (1935), 698.

38. Pressenotiz, [Oct. 1935], NSAW, 12 A Neu, 13 h/19596.

39. List of pupils in the HJ, [Brunswick . . . Bad Harzburg], Feb. 15, 1936, NSAW, 12 A Neu, 13/19598; HJ statistics for Bavarian elementary and trade schools, [spring 1936], NSAO, 134/1158.

40. Mergenthaler, "Stärke der Hitlerjugend in den Schulen Württembergs am 1. Juni 1938," NSAW, 12 A Neu, 13 h/19596.

41. Michael Wortmann, *Baldur von Schirach: Hitlers Jugendführer* (Cologne, 1982), 145.

42. Böll cited in Marcel Reich-Ranicki, ed., *Meine Schulzeit im Dritten Reich: Erinnerungen deutscher Schriftsteller* (Munich, 1984), 12.

43. Günter De Bruyn, *Zwischenbilanz: Eine Jugend in Berlin* (Frankfurt am Main, 1995), 92; Jörg Schadt, ed., *Verfolgung und Widerstand unter dem Nationalsozialismus in Baden: Die Lageberichte der Gestapo und des General-staatsanwalts Karlsruhe, 1933–1940* (Stuttgart, 1976), 58.

44. Weildorf Schuljugendwalterin report, [Fall 1936], SAM, NSDAP/348.

45. Activity report Jörschke, for Saxony, Dec. 1934, HIS, 13/250; Barbara Königs testimony in Reich-Ranicki, 128; Alfons Kenkmann, *Wilde Jugend: Lebenswelt grossstädtischer Jugendlicher zwischen Weltwirtschaftskrise, Nationalsozialismus und Währungsreform* (Essen, 1996), 73.

46. Edith Müller, *Ursel und ihre Mädel* (Reutlingen, [1939]), 70–73.

47. Quotation from Baaden, 79. See also *Jugend im nationalsozialistischen Frankfurt: Ausstellungsdokumentation, Zeitzeugenerinnerungen, Publikum* (Frankfurt am Main, 1987), 52, and Kenkmann, 67, 70.

48. Hermann Melcher, *Die Gefolgschaft: Jugendjahre im Dritten Reich in Hei-delberg, 1933–1945* (Berg, 1990), 44; Carola Kuhlmann, *Erbkrank oder er-ziehbar? Jugendhilfe als Vorsorge und Aussonderung in der Fürsorgeerziehung in Westfalen von 1933–1945* (Weinheim, 1989), 101.

49. *Hitler-Jugend, 1933–1943: Die Chronik eines Jahrzehnts* (Berlin, [1943]), 47.

50. Böhmer to police stations et al., Feb. 10, 1940, BA, Schumacher/239.

51. Landrat Landsberg to Regierungspräsident Munich, Nov. 26, 1940; Klein to Landrat Landsberg, Dec. 12, 1940; Fischer to Landrat Landsberg, Apr. 8, 1941, SAM, LRA/45157.

52. Hindelang to Landräte et al., Aug. 13, 1941, BA, Schumacher/239.

53. Leinfelder to Landrat Wertingen, Apr. 29, 1941, BA, NS28/27.

54. "Der Hitler-Jugend-Richter" 4 (June 1941): 7–8; ibid., 5 (Feb. 1942): 9, (BA, R22/1176); *Das Junge Deutschland* (1942): 183.

55. Helgemeir to Landrat Landsberg, May 22, 1942, SAM, LRA/45157 (quote); Hans Scherer, *Ich war Oberschüler und Luftwaffenhelfer, 1927–1948* (Staffelstein, 1996), vol. 2, 62.

56. Himmler, "Erzwingung der Jugenddienstpflicht," Nov. 24, 1942, BA, R22/1176.

57. "Richterbriefe" 14 (Nov. 1, 1943), (BA, R22/1177); Stumpf to Löfflath, Nov. 8, 1944, BA, NS28/25.

58. See Kreisleitung Darmstadt memo, Feb. 17, 1944, HHSAW, 483/5538, and the evidence for 1942–1944 in BA, NS28/25.

59. For HJ and leadership claim, see Gerhart Wehner, "Die rechtliche Stellung der Hitler-Jugend," Ph.D. dissertation, Dresden, 1939, 55.

60. Maili Hochhuth, *Schulzeit auf dem Lande, 1933–1945: Gespräche und Untersuchungen über die Jahre 1933–1945 in Wattenbach* (Kassel, 1985), 162.

61. Albrecht Möller, *Wir werden das Volk: Wesen und Forderung der Hitlerjugend* (Breslau, 1935), 76; Schirach's speech of September 14, 1942, partially printed in Wortmann, 211–213.

62. Schaar to HJ-Führer Nordmark, May 12, 1944; Peters to Gauhaus Kiel, July 12, 1944, BA, R22/1190.

63. Max von der Grün, *Howl like the Wolves: Growing up in Nazi Germany* (New York, 1980), 219–220; Wapnewski's testimony in Reich-Ranicki, 98–101.

64. *Jugend . . . Frankfurt*, 262.

65. Inge Stolten, *Das alltägliche Exil: Leben zwischen Hakenkreuz und Währungsreform* (Berlin, 1982), 30–31.

66. Rauhut's testimony in Alison Owings, *Frauen: German Women Recall the Third Reich* (New Brunswick, N.J., 1993), 344–345; Rosemarie Heise, "Aufbruch in die Illusion? Eine Jugend in der SBZ/DDR," in Franz-Werner Kersting, ed., *Jugend vor einer Welt in Trümmern: Erfahrungen und Verhältnisse der Jugend zwischen Hitler- und Nachkriegsdeutschland* (Weinheim, 1998), 193.

67. Fest's testimony in Reich-Ranicki, 188–191.

68. Von Schirach on May 23, 1946, in Nuremberg (*Der Prozess*, 419); Artur Axmann, *"Das kann doch nicht das Ende sein": Hitlers letzter Reichsjugendführer erinnert sich*, 2nd ed. (Koblenz, 1995), 230; Hubert Meyer, *Kriegsgeschichte der 12. Panzerdivision "Hitlerjugend"* (Osnabrück, 1982), vol. 1, 17.

69. Hans Volz, *Daten der Geschichte der NSDAP*, 9th ed. (Berlin, 1939), 66; Blomberg quoted in doc. 39 (Apr. 16, 1935), in Karl Heinz Jahnke and Michael Buddrus, eds., *Deutsche Jugend, 1933–1945: Eine Dokumentation* (Hamburg, 1989), 92.

70. *Volksaufklärung und Schule* (no. 29, 1936) (quote), facs. in Von Hellfeld and Klönne, 129; Wortmann, 158.

71. Hein Stünke, "Die Hitlerjugend," in Rudolf Benze and Gustav Gräfer, eds., *Erziehungsmächte und Erziehungshoheit im Grossdeutschen Reich als gestaltende Kräfte im Leben des Deutschen* (Leipzig, 1940), 88–89; Linstow draft, July 8, 1943, BA, Schumacher/239.

72. Hermann Graml, "Integation und Entfremdung: Inanspruchnahme durch Staatsjugend und Dienstpflicht," in Ute Benz and Wolfgang Benz, eds.,

Sozialisation und Traumatisierung: Kinder in der Zeit des Nationalsozialismus (Frankfurt am Main, 1992), 73.

73. Martin Cranz, *Ich, ein Deutscher* (Dülmen, 1987), 63–66; Willy Schumann, *Being Present: Growing up in Hitler's Germany* (Kent, Ohio, 1991), 35–36, 45; Jürgen Peiffer, *Vergangenheit, gebrochener Spiegel: Erinnerungen* (Tübingen, 2000), 47.

74. Camp agendas printed in *HJ erlebt Deutschland: Die Grossfahrten der sächsischen Hitlerjugend* (Leipzig, n.d.), 64; Elke Nyssen, *Schule im Nationalsozialismus* (Heidelberg, 1979), 51; Karl-Heinz Huber, *Jugend unterm Hakenkreuz* (Berlin, 1982), 107–110.

75. Günter Kaufmann, "Die deutsche Jugend im Zeltlager," *Das Junge Deutschland* (1937), 360–365; *Pimpf im Dienst: Ein Handbuch für das Deutsche Jungvolk in der HJ* (Potsdam, 1938), 175–179, 194–197, 204–223.

76. *HJ erlebt Deutschland*, 24, 59; Gottfried Neesse, *Reichsjugendführung* (Berlin, n.d.), 35–39.

77. *Hitler-Jugend . . . Chronik*, 51; Friedrich Grupe, *Jahrgang 1916: Die Fahne war mehr als der Tod* (Munich, 1989), 309–313.

78. Adolf Hitler, *Mein Kampf,* 26th ed. (Munich, 1933), 453–455.

79. Kurt Abels, *Ein Held war ich nicht: Als Kind und Jugendlicher in Hitlers Krieg* (Cologne, 1998), 13; Hans Heinz Pollack, *Verschleppt und verschollen: Geschichte einer Deportation aus Ostpreussen* (Frankfurt am Main, 1990), 30.

80. Möller, 92.

81. Neesse, 28–30; *Hitlerjugend und NS-Reichsbund für Leibesübungen: Richtlinien für die Zusammenarbeit* (n.p., 1940), 37–38; *Hitler-Jugend . . . Chronik*, 20–21, 24.

82. Roman Schnabl, *Das Hitler-Jugend-Schibuch: Grundschule und Leistungssport* (Munich, 1943); Günter Kaufmann, *Das kommende Deutschland: Die Erziehung der Jugend im Reich Adolf Hitlers,* 3rd ed. (Berlin, 1943), 328–329.

83. Dieter Galinski et al., *Nazis und Nachbarn: Schüler erforschen den Alltag im Nationalsozialismus* (Reinbek, 1982), 62, 80–81; Christoph Schubert-Weller, *Hitler-Jugend: Vom "Jungsturm Adolf Hitler" zur Staatsjugend des Dritten Reiches* (Weinheim, 1993), 163–164.

84. Lenz quoted in Reich-Ranicki, 165.

85. Ralf Roland Ringler, *Illusion einer Jugend: Lieder, Fahnen und das bittere Ende: Hitlerjugend in Österreich: Ein Erlebnisbericht* (St. Pölten, 1977), 78 (first quote); Bertram Otto, *"Wussten wir auch nicht, wohin es geht . . .": Erinnerungen, 1927–1947* (Munich, 2000), 77 (second quote).

86. Cranz, 67; Guido Knopp, *Hitlers Kinder,* 2nd ed. (Munich, 2000), 28; Walter Kempowski, *Tadellöser und Wolff: Ein bürgerlicher Roman,* 2nd ed. (Munich, 1975), 406–415; Henry Metelmann, *A Hitler Youth: Growing up in Germany in the 1930s* (London, 1997), 129.

87. *Pimpf im Dienst,* 234–242; *HJ im Dienst: Ausbildungsvorschrift für die Ertüchtigung der deutschen Jugend,* 6th ed. (Berlin, 1940), 200–231; Galinski et al., 67.

88. Bernhard Haupert and Franz Josef Schäfer, *Jugend zwischen Kreuz und Hakenkreuz: Biographische Rekonstruktion als Alltagsgeschichte des Faschismus* (Frankfurt am Main, 1991), 153; Edgar Gielsdorf, *Vom Christkind eine Landsknechtstrommel* (Cologne, 1994), 102.

89. Kaufmann, *Deutschland,* 329; Brandenburg, 230; Huber, 231–233; Boberach, 104.

90. Amtsgericht München, judgment against Rudolf Stimmel, May 16, 1941, ARL, Lü 6.1.2 (München).

91. Alfons Heck, *A Child of Hitler: Germany in the Days when God Wore a Swastika* (Frederick, Colo., 1985), 57; Gabriele Rosenthal, ed., *Die Hitlerjugend-Generation: Biographische Thematisierung als Vergangenheitsbewältigung* (Essen, 1986), 289; Fred Borth, *Nicht zu jung zum Sterben: Die "Hitler-Jugend" im Kampf um Wien, 1945* (Vienna, 1988), 37–38; Schumann, 86–87. On German youth and flying, see Peter Fritzsche, *A Nation of Fliers: German Aviation and the Popular Imagination* (Cambridge, Mass., 1992), esp. 120–124.

92. NSKK-Korpsführer to Reichsjugendführung, Jan. 5, 1940, BA, Schumacher/239; Huber, 167; Haupert and Schäfer, 152; Pahmeyer and Van Spankeren, 194–199.

93. Alfons Heck, *The Burden of Hitler's Legacy* (Frederick, Colo., 1988), 80; Pahmeyer and Van Spankeren, 200.

94. Gielsdorf, 105; Axmann, 329.

95. Peiffer, 64.

96. *Hitler-Jugend . . . Chronik,* 25; Otto Zander, ed., *Weimar: Bekenntnis und Tat: Kulturpolitisches Arbeitslager der Reichsjugendführung, 1938* (Berlin, 1938), 74.

97. Horst Rumpf in Wolfgang Klafki, ed., *Verführung, Distanzierung, Ernüchterung: Kindheit und Jugend im Nationalsozialismus* (Weinheim, 1988), 231; Cranz, 61.

98. Stünke, 86; *Hitler-Jugend . . . Chronik,* 38–39; Zander, 65–67; Michael H. Kater, *The Twisted Muse: Musicians and Their Music in the Third Reich* (New York, 1997), 135–150; Kater, *Composers of the Nazi Era: Eight Portraits* (New York, 2000), 120–121.

99. Wolfgang Klafki in Klafki, 155.

100. Erwin Schwarz-Reiflingen, ed., *HJ Singt: Die schönsten Lieder der Hitler-Jugend: Landsknechts-, Soldaten-, Reiter- und Wanderlieder mit den vollständigen Texten für Klavier in leichter Spielbarkeit* (Mainz, [1933]), 5. See also Cranz, 62; Eva Sternheim-Peters, *Die Zeit der grossen Täuschungen: Eine Jugend im Nationalsozialismus* (Bielefeld, 1992), 38. An excellent analysis of the uses of music in the Hitler Youth toward ideological ends can be found in Baird, 155–171.

101. Cranz, 64.

102. *Das Junge Deutschland* (1939): 137; Gustav Gräfer, "Die Deutsche Schule," in Benze and Gräfer, 55.

103. Stünke, 91.

104. Neesse, 41–42; "Landdienst der Hitler-Jugend," [1942], BA, Schumacher/239; Edith Niehuis, *Das Landjahr: Eine Jugenderziehungseinrichtung in der Zeit des Nationalsozialismus* (Nörten-Hardenberg, 1984).

105. *Hitler-Jugend . . . Chronik*, 22; Erich Blohm, *Hitler-Jugend: Soziale Tatgemeinschaft*, 2nd ed. (Vlotho, 1979), 226–231; Michael H. Kater, "Die Artamanen—Völkische Jugend in der Weimarer Republik," *Historische Zeitschrift* 213 (1971): 577–638.

106. Axmann, 261–265.

107. *Hitler-Jugend . . . Chronik*, 49–50, 59–60.

108. Kaufmann, *Deutschland*, 202.

109. Tritschler report, Oct. 5, 1943, SAG, SF6827, GA/110; Axmann, 324–325.

110. Cranz, 33–36.

111. Example from Katowice (Kattowitz, Silesia) in Jurgen Herbst, *Requiem for a German Past: A Boyhood among the Nazis* (Madison, 1999), 101–102, 107–109.

112. "Die Hitler-Jugend im Kriege," [1944], HIS, 19/358; Heinz Höhne, *Der Orden unter dem Totenkopf: Die Geschichte der SS* (Gütersloh, 1967), 270–273.

113. *Hitler-Jugend . . . Chronik*, 42–43; Horst Rumpf in Klafki, 246–248; Blohm, 302; Axmann, 256–257.

114. Axmann, 257, 330–331.

115. Otto, 128 (quote); Grupe, 304–305; Axmann, 328.

116. Testimony in Johannes Steinhoff et al., eds., *Voices from the Third Reich: An Oral History* (New York, 1994), 212 (quote); *Jungen im Einsatz 1944: Kriegsjahrbuch der Hitler-Jugend* (Munich, n.d.), 22–24; Axmann, 344–346.

117. Hitler, 452.

118. Speech of December 2, 1938, partially printed in Jahnke and Buddrus, 155.

119. Baldur von Schirach, *Die Hitler-Jugend: Idee und Gestalt* (Leipzig, 1934), 165; Hans-Helmut Dietze, *Die Rechtsgestalt der Hitler-Jugend: Eine verfassungsrechtliche Studie* (Berlin, 1939), 221; Pahmeyer and Van Spankeren, 99–100.

120. Neesse, 19–20.

121. Dietze, 218–219; *Das Junge Deutschland* (1937): 47 (quote).

122. Wilhelm Möller-Crivitz, "Das Elternhaus (Vorschulzeit)," in Benze and Gräfer, 34.

123. Act 10, "Der Spitzel," in Bertolt Brecht, *Furcht und Elend des III. Reiches: 24 Szenen* (New York, 1945), 61–70.

124. Heck, *Burden,* 83. See also Pahmeyer and Van Spankeren, 98.

125. Galinski et al., 102; *Jugend . . . Frankfurt,* 133.

126. Robert Gellately, *Backing Hitler: Consent and Coercion in Nazi Germany* (Oxford, 2002), 198.

127. Case of Manfred Sommer in Rosenthal, 234; Gielsdorf, 50.

128. Hüttig memo, June 1, 1934, HIS, 13/248.

129. Gielsdorf, 58; case of Manfred Sommer in Rosenthal, 233; Speitkamp, 212, 225.

130. Melita Maschmann, *Fazit: Keine Rechtfertigung,* 5th ed. (Stuttgart, 1964), 35.

131. Peiffer, 44.

132. *Deutschland-Berichte,* vol. 3 (1936), 174.

133. Speitkamp, 240.

134. Wortmann, 127–130.

135. Von Schirach, *Revolution der Erziehung: Reden aus den Jahren des Aufbaus,* 2nd ed. (Munich, 1939), 110–111 (quote, 111).

136. Alfred Andersch, *Der Vater eines Mörders: Erzählung* (Zurich, 1980). A description of Studienrat Gebhard Himmler from an earlier time is in George W. F. Hallgarten, *Als die Schatten fielen: Erinnerungen vom Jahrhundertbeginn zur Jahrtausendwende* (Frankfurt am Main, 1969), 34–36.

137. Hans-Günter Zmarzlik, *Wieviel Zukunft hat unsere Vergangenheit? Aufsätze und Überlegungen eines Historikers vom Jahrgang 1922* (Munich, 1970), 20–22; De Bruyn, 104–105; Abels, 15; Peiffer, 45–46.

138. Huber, 83; Hans R. Queiser, *"Du gehörst dem Führer!" Vom Hitlerjungen zum Kriegsberichter: Ein autobiographischer Bericht* (Cologne, 1993), 66–67.

139. Entry for March 22, 1933, in Victor Klemperer, *Tagebücher 1933–34,* ed. Walter Nowojski (Berlin, 1999), 14; Ralf Giordano in Geert Platner

et al., eds., *Schule im Dritten Reich—Erziehung zum Tod? Eine Dokumentation,* 2nd ed. (Munich, 1984), 73; Hans Scheuerl in Klafki, 68–69; Wolfgang Klafki in Klafki, 149–150.

140. De Bruyn, 106–107 (quote, 106).

141. Heinrich Böll, *Was soll aus dem Jungen bloss werden? Oder: Irgendwas mit Büchern,* ed. J. H. Reid (Manchester, 1991), 56.

142. Von der Grün, 180–181. See Stefan Zweig, *Decisive Moments in History: Twelve Miniatures* (Riverside, Calif., 1999 [German publ., 1927]).

143. De Bruyn, 106; Hans Scheuerl in Klafki, 67; Hochhuth, 93, 100; Speitkamp, 243.

144. See the text of this chapter at nn. 281f.

145. Otto, 88; Queiser, 69; Ulrich Popplow, "Schulalltag im Dritten Reich: Fallstudie über ein Göttinger Gymnasium," *Aus Politik und Zeitgeschichte: Beilage zur Wochenzeitung Das Parlament,* B18, 80 (1980): 35.

146. Popplow, 35; Harald Buss in Platner et al., 93; Benjamin Ortmeyer, *Schulzeit unterm Hitlerbild: Analysen, Berichte, Dokumente* (Frankfurt am Main, 1996), 63; Peiffer, 45.

147. Albert Böhme and Werner Piutti, eds., *Schulkind im Dritten Reich: Eine Handreichung für Eltern und Erzieher* (Wuppertal-Barmen, [1936]), 41–42; Dietze, 222; A. Kluger, ed., *Die Deutsche Volksschule im Grossdeutschen Reich: Handbuch der Gesetze, Verordnungen und Richtlinien für Erziehung und Unterricht in Volksschulen nebst den einschlägigen Bestimmungen über Hitler-Jugend und Nationalpolitische Erziehungsanstalten* (Breslau, 1940), 387–388.

148. Manfred Rommel in Platner, 62; Schumann, 62; Otto, 88.

149. Maschmann, 31; Huber speech, [early 1939], SAL, PL 512/II, N, 98, 2; Gräfer, 57, 60; Wortmann, 169–173.

150. Nygaard to Kohlmeyer, March 7, 1940, SAH, Jugendbehörde I, 343e; Reichsjugendführung, "Cliquen- und Bandenbildung unter Jugendlichen," Sept. 1942, BA, R22/1177.

151. Möller-Crivitz, 29, 32.

152. Martin Greiffenhagen, *Jahrgang 1928: Aus einem unruhigen Leben* (Munich, 1988), 39; Von der Grün, 247; Karl-Heinz Janssen in Hermann Glaser and Axel Silenius, eds., *Jugend im Dritten Reich* (Frankfurt am Main, 1975), 93; Schumann, 77; Friedrich Juchter, *Formeln, Fahnen, Flakgeschütze: Eine deutsche Jugend zwischen Schule und Kriegsdienst (1934–1947),* 2nd ed. (Oldenburg, 1999), 108–109.

153. "Aufgaben und Leistungen des NS.-Lehrerbundes im Kriege," [1941/ 42], HIS, 12/243; Schumann, 73, 115; De Bruyn, 102–103; Harald

Scholtz, *Erziehung und Unterricht unterm Hakenkreuz* (Göttingen, 1985), 105.

154. Grevemühl to Bade, Sept. 18, 1942, NSAW, 12 A Neu, 13 h/19597.

155. De Bruyn, 103.

156. Bormann circular, Sept. 27, 1940, printed in Gerhard Dabel, *KLV: Die erweiterte Kinder-Land-Verschickung: KLV-Lager, 1940–1945* (Freiburg, 1981), 7; "Disziplinarbestimmungen für die Lager der Erweiterten Kinderlandverschickung," in "Der Hitler–Jugend–Richter," no. 5 (Feb. 1942), (BA, R22/1176); Baaden, 120, 123–124; Kaufmann, *Deutschland*, 358.

157. See Gerhard Kock, *"Der Führer sorgt für unsere Kinder . . .": Die Kinderlandverschickung im Zweiten Weltkrieg* (Paderborn, 1997), 178–188; Juchter, 54, 114.

158. Claus Larass, *Der Zug der Kinder: KLV—Die Evakuierung 5 Millionen deutscher Kinder im 2. Weltkrieg* (Munich, 1983), 9, 15; Axmann, 348.

159. Alfred Ehrentreich, *Pädagogische Odyssee: Im Wandel der Erziehungsformen* (Weinheim, 1967), 219; Jost Hermand, *Als Pimpf in Polen: Erweiterte Kinderlandverschickung, 1940–1945* (Frankfurt am Main, 1993), 39; Kock, 192; Ilse Koehn, *Mischling zweiten Grades: Kindheit in der Nazi-Zeit* (Reinbek, 1980), 145.

160. Ehrentreich, 213; Koehn, 51–52; De Bruyn, 109; Knopp, 245.

161. Juchter, 81.

162. Ehrentreich, 211, 237; Koehn, 99–101.

163. Scholtz, *Erziehung*, 104.

164. Koehn, 120–121; Larass, 27, 73–74.

165. De Bruyn, 109; Ehrentreich, 207, 214; Knopp, 245.

166. Koehn, 56, 91–97; Ehrentreich, 208, 237; Juchter, 80, 84, 119; Sigrid Bremer, *Muckefuck und Kameradschaft: Mädchenzeit im Dritten Reich: Von der Kinderlandverschickung 1940 bis zum Studium 1946* (Frankfurt am Main, 1988), 15–17.

167. Kock, 205; Larass, 58–59, 74; De Bruyn, 113; Koehn, 54–55, 91, 116–118.

168. De Bruyn, 111; Ehrentreich, 216; Hermand, 72–73.

169. Dahrendorf quoted in Larass, 166.

170. De Bruyn, 112; Hermand, 73–74.

171. Larass, 63.

172. Hermand, 85; Koehn, 57–60, 99–100.

173. Ehrentreich, 207–208, 210, 216–217; Larass, 211, 223; Koehn, 54, 61, 145; De Bruyn, 112–113.

174. "Die Adolf-Hitler-Schulen," [1944], HIS, 19/358; Wortmann, 146–147; Knopp, 168–170.

175. Gaupersonalamtsleiter to Gauleiter et al., Feb. 20, 1937, BA, Schumacher/270I; "Auslese für den Besuch der Adolf-Hitler-Schule Jahrgang 1940," Gaupersonalamt, BA, Schmacher/372; Durchführungsbestimmungen Härtel, Oct. 2, 1944, SAM, NSDAP/31; Gräfer, 72.

176. Albert Speer, *Erinnerungen,* 8th ed. (Frankfurt am Main, 1970), 137.

177. Dietrich Orlow, "Die Adolf-Hitler-Schulen," *Vierteljahrshefte für Zeitgeschichte* 13 (1965): 278; Scholtz, *NS–Ausleseschulen,* 251–253.

178. Scholtz, *NS–Ausleseschulen,* 175, 210; Blohm, 134.

179. Kaufmann, *Deutschland,* 165; Rolf Eilers, *Die nationalsozialistische Schulpolitik: Eine Studie zur Funktion der Erziehung im totalitären Staat* (Cologne, 1963), 47.

180. Grundmann quoted in Knopp, 196.

181. Baldur von Schirach, *Revolution,* 112.

182. Testimony of Peter E. in Kurt Hass, ed., *Jugend unterm Schicksal: Lebensberichte junger Deutscher, 1946–1949* (Hamburg, 1950), 50, Speitkamp, 247–248.

183. Orlow, 276.

184. Ibid., 280 (quote); Knopp, 176, 190, 192.

185. Kaufmann, *Deutschland,* 170; Knopp, 207, 210–211.

186. Grundmann quoted in Knopp, 176.

187. Hitler quoted for January 1, 1942, in Henry Picker, ed., *Hitlers Tischgespräche im Führerhauptquartier, 1941–42* (Bonn, 1951), 200.

188. Blohm, 133–134; Orlow, 274.

189. David Schoenbaum, *Hitler's Social Revolution: Class and Status in Nazi Germany, 1933–1939* (Garden City, 1967), 268; Orlow, 277; Scholtz, *NS–Ausleseschulen,* 133, 245.

190. Jennes circular, March 24, 1939, BA, NS22/2023; Schoenbaum, 269–271; Dietrich Orlow, *The History of the Nazi Party, 1933–1945* (Pittsburgh, 1973), 188–190.

191. Reinhard Bollmus, "Zum Projekt einer nationalsozialistischen Alternativ-Universität: Alfred Rosenbergs 'Hohe Schule,'" in Manfred Heinemann, ed., *Erziehung und Schulung im Dritten Reich* (Stuttgart, 1980), vol. 2, 125–152.

192. *Verfügungen/Anordnungen Bekanntgaben,* ed. Partei-Kanzlei (Munich, n.d.), 6: 41–43; Schoenbaum, 265–267; Scholtz, *NS–Ausleseschulen,* 299–324; Knopp, 174, 203.

193. Gräfer, 70–71.

194. Christian Schneider et al., *Das Erbe der NAPOLA: Versuch einer Generationengeschichte des Nationalsozialismus* (Hamburg, 1996), 42, 45.

195. Schoenbaum, 268; Scholtz, *NS–Ausleseschulen,* 80, 110, 132–133; Schneider et al., 109.

196. Schneider et al., 55–62 (quote, 57); 161–163; Winfried Maass, *Die Fünfzigjährigen: Portrait einer verratenen Generation* (Hamburg, 1980), 33–37; Knopp, 180–181, 186, 188–189, 194, 208.

197. Eilers, 44; Schneider et al., 54.

198. Heinz W. Kämmer, *Von arm bis braun: Eine Kindheit in der Mitte Deutschlands von den "goldenen" 20ern in die "braunen" 30er* (Essen, 1996), 119.

199. Hitler quoted in Von Schirach, *Ich glaubte,* 180.

200. Hackländer to Oldigs, Wolfsee, Nov. 8, 1933, BA, NS22/342; Veiner to Kommandant, July 15, 1934, BAF, R W6/V67/1; situation report for Lower Franconia, Sept. 7, 1934, GStAM, RE/450; situation report for Wilhelmshaven, May 1938, NSAO, 320/2,2; Martin Broszat et al., eds., *Bayern in der NS-Zeit: Soziale Lage und politisches Verhalten der Bevölkerung im Spiegel vertraulicher Berichte* (Munich, 1977), 83; Von der Grün, 161.

201. Reichsjugendführung circular, June 16, 1934, HIS, 19/360.

202. Jahnke and Buddrus, 88; *Deutschland-Berichte,* vol. 3 (1936), 227.

203. Von Flotow file (1938–39), ARL, Lü 6.1.7 (Jugendgericht Berlin).

204. Situation report for Süd-Hannover-Braunschweig, May 1933, NHSA, Hann. 310I, B13; "Reichs-Jugend-Pressedienst," June 1, 1934, HIS, 19/355; Rabenhofer file (June 1934), SAM, NSDAP/117; Blomquist to Klagges, May 8, 1939, NSAW, 12 A Neu, 13h/16198; *Deutschland-Berichte,* vol. 2 (1935), 969; Broszat et al., 524; Robert Thévoz et al., eds., *Pommern 1934/35 im Spiegel von Gestapo-Lageberichten und Sachakten* (Cologne, 1974), 59.

205. Gendarmerieposten Windischgarsten to Landrat, Sept. 23, 1940, OLA, Pol. Akten/15; Munich Oberlandesgerichtspräsident report, Apr. 30, 1942, BA, R22/1176a; Popp to Weber, Nov. 9, 1942, SAM, LRA/45157; NSDAP "Befehlsblatt," Nov. 1943, BA, NS28/41; Grolmann to Amt für Volkswohlfahrt, Dec. 28, 1943, SAMs, Polit. Polizei, 3. Reich/408.

206. Abelein to Kreisleitung, Jan. 12, 1943, SAL, PL 512/II, 98, 5.

207. Landgericht Berlin, case against Wichmann (1943–44), ARL, Lü 6.1.8 (Jugendgericht Berlin); Kreisamtsleiter Minden to Amt für Volkswohl-

fahrt, Dec. 27, 1943, SAMs, Polit. Polizei, 3. Reich/408; Hermann Stresau, *Von Jahr zu Jahr* (Berlin, 1948), 344.

208. Von Schirach in *Das Junge Deutschland* (1937), 45 (quote); Neesse, 204.
209. Wortmann, 152.
210. Klein, "Jugendführung und politische Leitung," Dec. 15, 1938, SAM, NSDAP/532; Speitkamp, 222.
211. Arno Klönne, "Widersprüche der HJ-Sozialisation," in Ulrich Herrmann, ed., *"Die Formung des Volksgenossen": Der "Erziehungsstaat" des Dritten Reiches* (Weinheim, 1985), 207–208.
212. Activity report Klein, March–Oct. 1933, GStAM, RE/450.
213. Von Schirach, *Revolution,* 19–20; Jahnke and Buddrus, 107–108; Huber, 120.
214. Gabriele Kinz, *Der Bund Deutscher Mädel: Ein Beitrag über die ausserschulische Mädchenerziehung im Nationalsozialismus,* 2nd ed. (Frankfurt am Main, 1991), 33.
215. Von Schirach, *Revolution,* 19–20.
216. Minutes, Jugendrechtsausschuss meeting, Berlin, Dec. 10/11, 1937, BA, R22/1180.
217. Riegraf to Spiess, Feb. 8, 1938, SAL, PL 509/1/3.
218. Entry for March 19, 1943, in Dieter Borkowski, *Wer weiss, ob wir uns wiedersehen: Erinnerungen an eine Berliner Jugend* (Frankfurt am Main, 1980), 28–29.
219. Ringler, 116.
220. Jürgen Schultz, *Die Akademie für Jugendführung der Hitlerjugend in Braunschweig* (Brunswick, 1978), 43; Von Schirach (Dec. 1936) in *Das Junge Deutschland* (1937), 44; Von Schirach, *Revolution,* 11; Dietze, 217.
221. Schultz, *Akademie,* 164, 206; Jahnke and Buddrus, 137–138; Stünke, 84.
222. Scholtz, *Erziehung,* 97.
223. Axmann, 229 (quote); Gielsdorf, 128.
224. Ringler, 79–80.
225. Gielsdorf, 128–131.
226. Ibid., 121.
227. Activity report Klein, March–Oct. 1933, GStAM, RE/450; activity report for Süd-Hannover-Braunschweig, Oct. 1933, NSHA, Hann. 310I, B 13; Galinski et al., 55.
228. Zinsmeier to Bannführer, Apr. 6, 1937, BA, NS28/25; Broszat et al., 93; Von Hellfeld and Klönne, 130.
229. Von Schirach, *Revolution,* 57.

230. Kinz, 63–64; Mahlmann report, Nov. 11, 1940, NSAW, 12 A Neu, 13 h/19596.

231. Voss application, May 19, 1941, NSAW, 12 A Neu, 13h/16123; Silvester Lechner, ed., *Die "Hitlerjugend" am Beispiel der Region Ulm/Neu-Ulm: Ein Aspekt im Umfeld der "Weissen Rose,"* 1942/43 (Ulm, 1993), 68; Munich Oberlandesgerichtspräsident report, Apr. 30, 1942, BA, R22/1176a.

232. Leiter Wohlfahrtspflege to Hauptamt für Volkswohlfahrt, SAMs, Polit. Polizei, 3. Reich/408; Gielsdorf, 120, 130; Heck, *Child,* 161.

233. Helmut Heiber, ed., *Reichsführer!* . . . *Briefe an und von Himmler* (Stuttgart, 1968), 270–271.

234. Osterfelt activity report, March 14, 1935, HIS, 13/251; Sieverts, "Jugendgefährdung im Kriege," Oct. 20, 1942, BA, NL/289; K-Führer to Schwarz, June 16, 1944, BA, NS28/25.

235. Galinski et al., 56; political situation report for Party chapter Rothenburg, Feb. 1939, BA, Schumacher/372; Haug to Bannführer, Oct. 9, 1940, BA, NS28/25.

236. Bormann ordinance, March 12, 1940, BA, NS22/856; Pfundtner to Oberste Reichsbehörden et al., Nov. 30, 1942, BA, R18/2958; Kreisleiter Gross-Frankfurt circular, Feb. 2, 1943, HHSAW, 483/5541; Mauer/Schenke memo, Oct. 5, 1943, BA, Schumacher/368; Walkenhorst memo, Feb. 24, 1945, BA, Schumacher/239; Broszat et al., 588.

237. Entry for Sept. 27, 1934, in Klemperer, *Tagebücher 1933–1934,* 146.

238. Köhler to Ley, Feb. 9, 1937, BA, NS22/739; Oberlandesgerichtspräsident Danzig, situation report, Apr. 10, 1943, BA, R22/1176a.

239. Riegraf to Spiess, Nov. 21, 1938, SAL, PL 509/1/3.

240. Ringler, 80 (quote); Queiser, 63; Koehn, 44–45.

241. Axmann, 370–371; Maschmann, 150–151.

242. Ringler, 123, 134–135 (quote).

243. Ley/Von Schirach agreement, June 1, 1934, BA, NS22/342; *Bremer Nachrichten,* March 3, 1934.

244. Jahnke and Buddrus, 104–105; "Arbeitsanweisung Nr. 13/1938," BA, NS22/2022; Hess ordinance draft, Sept. 9, 1940; Hess to Ley, Sept. 29, 1940, BA, NS22/856.

245. Entry for Aug. 23, 1941, in *TGII,* vol. 1, 299.

246. Entry for Dec. 17, 1941, in *TGII,* vol. 2, 525.

247. Entry for May 5, 1942, in Picker, 238. See also entry for June 23, 1942, in *TGII,* vol. 4, 583; Heiber, 142–143.

248. Bormann to Sauckel, May 27, 1943, BA, Schumacher/378. See also Hitler ordinance A 26/43, April 7, 1943, BA, Schumacher/239.

249. Orlow, *History,* 342; Mauer/Schenke memo, Oct. 5, 1943, BA, Schumacher/368.

250. Maschmann, 153.

251. Ian Kershaw, *The "Hitler Myth": Image and Reality in the Third Reich* (Oxford, 1987).

252. Lauterbacher "Eilbefehl," June 27, 1934, HIS, 18/339; Höhne, 53, 90–124.

253. Lauterbacher memo, Dec. 8, 1934, BA, NSD43/1.

254. Jahnke and Buddrus, 116; *Berliner Zeitung,* May 23, 1936.

255. Jahnke and Buddrus, 124–125, 144–146. See text at n. 120 in Chapter 4.

256. Himmler/Von Schirach memo, Dec. 17, 1938, BA, Schumacher/239; Schindlmayr to Landrat Grafenau, Nov. 30, 1939, BA, Schumacher/239.

257. Jahnke and Buddrus, 327.

258. Files in SAND, unsign. Best., EAP 221-b-20/9; anon. testimony [Feb. 1939] in Huber, 212–213 (quote); *Aschaffenburger Zeitung,* Aug. 16, 1939.

259. See Wolfgang Neuber in Hans Wienicke, ed., *"Schon damals fingen viele an zu schweigen . . .": Quellensammlung zur Geschichte Charlottenburgs von 1933–1945* (Berlin–Charlottenburg, 1986), 158; Queiser, 63, 79.

260. Von Schirach on May 24, 1946, in Nuremberg (*Der Prozess,* 566); Schirach, *Ich glaubte,* 244, 246, 285; Axmann, 220; Herbert Reinecker, *Ein Zeitbericht unter Zuhilfenahme des eigenen Lebenslaufs* (Erlangen, 1990), 98. Critically, see Gisela Miller-Kipp, ed., *"Auch Du gehörst dem Führer": Die Geschichte des Bundes Deutscher Mädel (BDM) in Quellen und Dokumenten* (Weinheim, 2001), 245.

261. Lore Walb, *Ich, die Alte—ich, die Junge: Konfrontation mit meinen Tagebüchern, 1933–1945,* 2nd ed. (Berlin, 1997), 120.

262. Jahnke and Buddrus, 148–151. For HJ action in Vienna, see George E. Berkley, *Vienna and Its Jews: The Tragedy of Success, 1880s–1980s* (Cambridge, Mass., 1988), 311.

263. Albert Bastian in Steinhoff et al., 14–15; Klaus Tischler in Rosenthal, 264; Horst Fuchs Richardson, ed., *Sieg Heil! War Letters of Tank Gunner Karl Fuchs, 1937–1941* (Hamden, Conn., 1987), 36–37.

264. Reinhold Kerstan, *Blood and Honor* (Elgin, Ill., 1980), 34–36; Erhard Eppler, *Als Wahrheit verordnet wurde: Briefe an meine Enkelin,* 3rd. ed. (Frankfurt am Main, 1995), 93–94.

265. Dietrich Strothmann in Glaser and Silenius, 46; Helge Pross, *Memoiren eines Inländers, 1923–1993* (Munich, 1993), 68–70; Peiffer, 73.

266. Rosenthal, 263; Wolfgang Klafki in Klafki, 163; Eppler, 75.

267. Melcher, 199.

268. Neesse, 31; Huber, 91, 108; Schumann, 24, 26, 29.

269. Entry for Feb. 9, 1943, in Borkowski, 21.

270. Funk cited in Jahnke and Buddrus, 141.

271. Otto, 77; entry for May 31, 1943, in Borkowski, 42–43.

272. Wolfgang Hempel, "'Ein kleiner Nazi bis zum letzten Tag': Meine frühe Jugend in der Nazizeit und das Kriegsende," in Kersting, 265.

273. See Stefan Zweig, *Die Welt von Gestern: Erinnerungen eines Europäers* (Berlin, 1965), 367; Berkley, 259–260.

274. Ian Kershaw, *Hitler, 1936–1945: Nemesis* (New York, 2000), 351; Gerhard Botz, *Wohnungspolitik und Judendeportation in Wien, 1938 bis 1945: Zur Funktion des Antisemitismus als Ersatz nationalsozialistischer Sozialpolitik* (Vienna, 1975).

275. Cranz, 105–108.

276. Entries for Aug. 21, 1942, in Klemperer, *Tagebuch 1942,* 217, Feb. 14, 1943, *Tagebuch 1943,* 32, and Oct. 16, 1944, *Tagebuch 1944,* 141.

277. Entry for May 17, 1943, in Borkowski, 40–41; entry for June 23, 1943, in Klemperer, *Tagebuch 1943,* 100; Cranz, 87; Queiser, 79.

278. Kerstan, 32–36; Albert Bastian in Steinhoff et al., 15.

279. Scherer, vol. 1, 51; Karl-Heinz Janssen in Glaser and Silenius, 92; Gielsdorf, 49.

280. Example quoted in Huber, 87. See also Möller, 104–105.

281. Peter Gay, *My German Question: Growing up in Nazi Berlin* (New Haven, 1998), 64 (quote); Gay in *Der Spiegel* (July 21, 2003): 161.

282. Kerstan, 32.

283. Klaus E. quoted in Lothar Steinbach, *Ein Volk, ein Reich, ein Glaube? Ehemalige Nationalsozialisten und Zeitzeugen berichten über ihr Leben im Dritten Reich* (Berlin, 1983), 125.

284. Thea Mandowsky quoted in Platner, 157.

285. Peiffer, 81; Michael Wieck, *Zeugnis vom Untergang Königsbergs: Ein "Geltungsjude" berichtet* (Heidelberg, 1990), 120; Herz quoted in Steinhoff et al., 48.

286. Entry for May 14, 1943, in Borkowski, 40.

287. See Heinz Knobloch, *Eine Berliner Kindheit: Zwischen Olympia und Luftschutzkeller* (Berlin, 1999), 53–54.

288. See the fictionalized chapter, "Adolf Hitler, a Boy, Quick, Tough and

Tenacious," in Hermine Morgenroth and Maria Schmidt, *Kinder, was wisst ihr vom Führer?* (Leipzig, 1933), 25–29; Peiffer, 46; Schumann, 24; Juchter, 93–94; Huber, 110.

289. Janssen in Glaser and Silenius, 88; Klaus E. in Steinbach, 123; Ferdinand B. in *Jugend . . . Frankfurt*, 263; Wolfgang Klafki in Klafki, 152.

290. Klaus Tischler in Rosenthal, 261; Knopp, 29.

291. *Der Kongress zu Nürnberg vom 5. bis 10. September 1934: Offizieller Bericht über den Verlauf des Reichsparteitages mit sämtlichen Reden* (Munich, 1934), 165–167.

292. Otto, 80.

293. Von Schirach's dedication for Horst Kerutt, ed., *Adolf-Hitler-Marsch der deutschen Jugend* (Munich, 1939), n.p.

3. German Girls for Matrimony and Motherhood

1. Raymond Phillips, ed., *Trial of Josef Kramer and Forty-four Others (The Belsen Trial)* (London, 1949), 247–261 (first quote, 260; third quote, 256), 531, 601, 615–616, 641, 644, 711–712, 747; Gisella Perl, *I was a Doctor in Auschwitz* (New York, 1979), 61–65 (second quote, 61); Daniel Patrick Brown, *The Beautiful Beast: The Life and Crimes of SS-Aufseherin Irma Grese* (Venture, Calif., 1996), (fourth quote, 85); Giles Playfair and Derrick Sington, *The Offenders: Society and the Atrocious Crime* (London, 1957), 154–185; Martina Ehlert, "Umerziehung zur Demokratie: Der erste Bergen-Belsen-Prozess in Zeitungsberichten," in Claus Füllberg-Stolberg et al., eds., *Frauen in Konzentrationslagern: Bergen-Belsen, Ravensbrück* (Bremen, 1994), 256–257; Wieslar Kielar, *Anus Mundi: Fünf Jahre Auschwitz* (Frankfurt am Main, 1984), 298–299; Olga Lengyel, *Five Chimneys: The Story of Auschwitz* (Chicago, 1947), 147–150, 186–189.

2. The most vocal exponent of this view has been Claudia Koonz. See her *Mothers in the Fatherland: Women, the Family, and Nazi Politics* (New York, 1987).

3. The victim status has been most aptly portrayed in Gisela Bock's study of females as the most prominent targets of forced sterilizations perpetrated upon them by males: *Zwangssterilisation im Nationalsozialismus: Studien zur Rassenpolitik und Frauenpolitik* (Opladen, 1986). See also Bock, "Die Frauen und der Nationalsozialismus: Bemerkungen zu einem Buch von Claudia Koonz," *Geschichte und Gesellschaft* 15 (1989): 563–579; Atina Grossmann, "Feminist Debates about Women and National Socialism,"

Gender and History 3 (1991): 350–358; Adelheid von Saldern, "Victims or Perpetrators? Controversies about the Role of Women in the Nazi State," in David F. Crew, ed., *Nazism and German Society, 1933–1945* (London, 1994), 141–165.

4. That was NSDAP-Amtsleiter Erich Hilgenfeldt. On the larger issue, see Michael H. Kater, "Frauen in der NS-Bewegung," *Vierteljahrshefte für Zeitgeschichte* 31 (1983): 218–224.

5. Ute Frevert, *Women in German History: From Bourgeois Emancipation to Sexual Liberation* (New York, 1989), 202–203.

6. Personal communication by Annemarie Gensichen to the author, Marbella, June 2, 1993. She herself fit just such a model.

7. See the work of Ute Frevert, Jill Stephenson, and Adelheid von Saldern.

8. For the latter, see Frevert, 171–172, 179–180, 198–199, 208–209; Robert Gellately, *Backing Hitler: Consent and Coercion in Nazi Germany* (Oxford, 2002), 10.

9. Adolf Hitler, *Mein Kampf*, 26th ed. (Munich, 1933), 74, 455 (quote).

10. Schemm as quoted in Bernd Lembeck, *Hans Schemm: Ein Leben für Deutschland* (Munich, 1936), 35.

11. Guida Diehl, *Die Deutsche Frau und der Nationalsozialismus* (Eisenach, 1933), 11, 43, 70, 80; "Nationalsozialistische Frauenschaft," in Paul Meier-Benneckenstein, ed., *Das Dritte Reich im Aufbau: Übersichten und Leistungsberichte* (Berlin, 1939), vol. 2, 361; Michael H. Kater, *The Nazi Party: A Social Profile of Members and Leaders, 1919–1945* (Cambridge, Mass., 1983), 151.

12. Hermann Okrass, *Das Ende einer Parole: "Hamburg bleibt rot,"* 2nd ed. (Hamburg, 1935), 243; Jill Stephenson, *Women in Nazi Germany* (Harlow, 2001), 83–84.

13. Hess speech, 1938 Reich Party rally, SAG, SF 6815, GA/6.

14. Nuremberg-Fürth police report, March 3, 1925, SAN, Rep. 503/99.

15. Report [Aug. 1927] quoted in Ernst Deuerlein, ed., *Der Aufstieg der NSDAP in Augenzeugenberichten* (Munich, 1974), 279.

16. Heinrich Hoffmann, *Hitler Was My Friend* (London, 1955), 142; Ernst Hanfstaengl, *Unheard Witness* (Philadelphia, 1957), 36.

17. NSF-Gauaubteilungsleiterin Sachsen to NSDAP-Reichsschulungsamt, June 1, 1935, HIS, 13/254.

18. Joachim C. Fest, *Hitler: Eine Biographie,* 3rd ed. (Frankfurt am Main, 1973), 288; Hitler to Frau Vorsitzende, Nov. 15, 1924, HIS, 13/256 (quote).

19. Albert Speer, *Erinnerungen,* 8th ed. (Frankfurt am Main, 1970), 59.

20. "Nationalsozialistische Frauenschaft," 363; NS-Frauengruppe Leipzig to Doktor, Feb. 1927; Goebbels to NS-Frauengruppe, Feb. 16, 1927, HIS, 13/256 (quote).

21. Jay W. Baird, *To Die for Germany: Heroes in the Nazi Pantheon* (Bloomington, 1990), 73–107.

22. Strasser, "Die Organisation der nationalsozialistischen Frauen in der NS-Frauenschaft," Nov. 1, 1931, BA, Schumacher/230; Rees-Fawerdes to Party archive, Oct. 22, 1936, HIS, 13/254; Friedrich Alfred Beck, *Kampf und Sieg: Geschichte der Nationalsozialistischen Deutschen Arbeiterpartei im Gau Westfalen-Süd von den Anfängen bis zur Machtübernahme* (Dortmund, 1938), 327, 371, 517.

23. Munich police memo, Jan. 27, 1931, BHSAM, Sonderabgabe I/1545; circular no. 3, Oct. 7, 1931, BA, Schumacher/230.

24. "Die Frauenarbeit in der Göttinger Ortsgruppe der NSDAP, 1922–35," HIS, 13/254.

25. Baden police report, Jan. 1, 1928, SAF, 317/1257d; Stein to Gau Brandenburg, Oct. 13, 1932, BA, NS22/1046; Heidrich, "Richtlinien für die Organisation und Arbeit der Frauengruppen," May 1, 1930, SAG, SF6818, GA/31.

26. Diehl, 100–101.

27. Hans-Christian Brandenburg, *Die Geschichte der HJ: Wege und Irrwege einer Generation* (Cologne, 1968), 51; Gisela Miller-Kipp, *"Auch Du gehörst dem Führer": Die Geschichte des Bundes Deutscher Mädel (BDM) in Quellen und Dokumenten* (Weinheim, 2001), 17; Lotte Becker, "Der Bund Deutscher Mädel," in Rudolf Benze and Gustav Gräfer, eds., *Erziehungsmächte und Erziehungshoheit im Grossdeutschen Reich als gestaltende Kräfte im Leben des Deutschen* (Leipzig, 1940), 94 (quote).

28. Okrass, 243; Miller-Kipp, 18, 26; Koonz, 129; Schirach to [Strasser], Nov. 11, 1932, BA, Schumacher/230.

29. Hoffmann, *Hitler,* 142; Hartmann Lauterbacher, *Erlebt und mitgestaltet: Kronzeuge einer Epoche, 1923–1945: Zu neuen Ufern nach Kriegsende* (Preussisch Oldendorf, 1984), 124; Miller-Kipp, 293.

30. Becker, 95 (quote); Artur Axmann, *"Das kann doch nicht das Ende sein": Hitlers letzter Reichsjugendführer erinnert sich,* 2nd ed. (Koblenz, 1995), 81; Dagmar Reese, *Straff, aber nicht stramm—herb, aber nicht derb: Zur Vergesellschaftung von Mädchen durch den Bund Deutscher Mädel im soziokulturellen Vergleich zweier Milieus* (Weinheim, 1989), 40.

31. Personal file, Jutta Rüdiger, BAB; Axmann, 249.

32. Husfeld as quoted in Axmann, 249.

33. See Geoffrey Cocks, *Psychotherapy in the Third Reich: The Göring Institute,*
     2nd ed. (New Brunswick, N.J., 1997) and, for the HJ, Ludwig Hemm, *Die
     unteren Führer in der HJ: Versuch ihrer psychologischen Typengliederung*
     (Leipzig, 1940).

34. Jutta Rüdiger, "Der Bund Deutscher Mädel in der Hitler-Jugend," in
     Meier-Benneckenstein, 402; Matthias von Hellfeld and Arno Klönne,
     Die betrogene Generation: Jugend in Deutschland unter dem Faschismus
     (Cologne, 1985), 35; Gabriele Kinz, *Der Bund Deutscher Mädel: Ein
     Beitrag über die ausserschulische Mädchenerziehung im Nationalsozialismus,*
     2nd ed. (Frankfurt am Main, 1991), 25; Reese, 37.

35. Becker, 109–110; Rüdiger, 398, 412; Waltraut Rath in Wolfgang Klafki,
     ed., *Verführung, Distanzierung, Ernüchterung: Kindheit und Jugend im
     Nationalsozialismus: Autobiographisches aus erziehungswissenschaftlicher Sicht*
     (Weinheim, 1988), 194.

36. Gisela Miller-Kipp, "Der Bund Deutscher Mädel in der Hitler-Jugend:
     Erziehung zwischen Ideologie und Herrschaftsprozess," *Pädagogische Rund-
     schau* (1982): 88.

37. Lydia Schürer-Stolle, "Jungmädel im BDM," in Hilde Munske, ed., *Mädel
     im Dritten Reich* (Berlin, [1936]), 46; Karin K. in Kurt Hass, ed., *Jugend
     unterm Schicksal: Lebensberichte junger Deutscher, 1946–1949* (Hamburg,
     1950), 35; Mathilde Mundt, Ellen Frey, and Anna Fest in Alison Owings,
     Frauen: German Women Recall the Third Reich (New Brunswick, N.J.,
     1993), 88, 174, 314; Elfriede Schuster in Gabriele Rosenthal, ed., *Die
     Hitlerjugend-Generation: Biographische Thematisierung als Vergangenheits-
     bewältigung* (Essen, 1986), 163; Eva Sternheim-Peters, *Die Zeit der grossen
     Täuschungen: Eine Jugend im Nationalsozialismus* (Bielefeld, 1992), 182.

38. Baldur von Schirach, *Revolution der Erziehung: Reden aus den Jahren des
     Aufbaus,* 2nd ed. (Munich, 1939), 47 (quote); Doris K. in Lothar Stein-
     bach, *Ein Volk, ein Reich, ein Glaube? Ehemalige Nationalsozialisten und
     Zeitzeugen berichten über ihr Leben im Dritten Reich* (Berlin, 1983), 86.

39. Waltraut Rath in Klafki, 190; Doris K. in Steinbach, 88; Maili Hochhuth,
     *Schulzeit auf dem Lande, 1933–1945: Gespräche und Untersuchungen über
     die Jahre 1933–1945 in Wattenbach* (Kassel, 1985), 154; Peter Pahmeyer
     and Lutz van Spankeren, *Die Hitlerjugend in Lippe (1933–1939): Total-
     itäre Erziehung zwischen Anspruch und Wirklichkeit* (Bielefeld, 1998), 195,
     n. 170; Miller-Kipp, *Auch,* 101.

40. Ilse McKee, *Tomorrow the World* (London, 1960), 8 (quote); Silvester Lech-
     ner, *Das KZ Oberer Kuhberg und die NS-Zeit in der Region Ulm/Neu-Ulm*
     (Stuttgart, 1988), 83–87; *HJ erlebt Deutschland: Die Grossfahrten der sächs-*

ischen Hitlerjugend (Leipzig, n.d.), 41–41; Sternheim-Peters, 183, 197; Reese, 135–136; Miller-Kipp, *Auch,* 129–130.

41. Kinz, 215–228.
42. Elisabeth K. and Karin K. in Hass, 103, 126; Reese, 135; Anna Fest in Owings, 314; Eva Amann in Lechner, 111. See the analysis in Rosenthal, 59.
43. Hochhuth, 203; Sternheim-Peters, 178; Reese, 206; Ursula Krezschmar in Owings, 186.
44. Quoted in Reese, 205. See also Roswitha Koslowski in Lutz Niethammer, "Privat-Wirtschaft: Erinnerungsfragmente einer anderen Umerziehung," in Niethammer, ed., *"Hinterher merkt man, dass es richtig war, dass es schiefgegangen ist": Nachkriegserfahrungen im Ruhrgebiet* (Berlin, 1983), 30.
45. Marie Mulde in Rosenthal, 128.
46. Sternheim-Peters, 173.
47. Becker, 104, 112; *Hitler-Jugend, 1933–1945: Die Chronik eines Jahrzehnts* (Berlin, [1943]), 24; Rosenthal, 130.
48. Elfriede Zill, "Die körperliche Schulung im BDM.," in Munske, 24–28; *HJ erlebt Deutschland,* 42–43; Trude Bürkner, *Der Bund Deutscher Mädel in der Hitler-Jugend* (Berlin, 1937), 13–14; Axmann, 175–176.
49. Guido Knopp, *Hitlers Kinder,* 2nd ed. (Munich, 2000), 104.
50. Leni Riefenstahl, *Olympia* (1938); Cooper C. Graham, *Leni Riefenstahl and Olympia* (Metuchen, N.J., 1986).
51. Schirach quoted in Michael Wortmann, *Baldur von Schirach: Hitlers Jugendführer* (Cologne, 1982), 162.
52. Maria Kramarz, *Dies Mädel ist Hanne—später bist Du es* (Berlin-Lichterfelde, 1937), 113; Helmut Stellrecht, *Neue Erziehung* (Berlin, 1942), 160; Sternheim-Peters, 270.
53. Sternheim-Peters, 195; Robert Proctor, *The Nazi War on Cancer* (Princeton, 1999), 218–219.
54. *Mädel im Dienst: Ein Handbuch* (Potsdam, 1934), 78; Edelgard Seidel, entry for March 8, 1944, in Heinrich Breloer, ed., *Mein Tagebuch: Geschichten vom Überleben, 1939–1947* (Cologne, 1984), 218; Reese, 62; Sternheim-Peters, 194.
55. Entry for Aug. 27, 1944, in Ingrid Hammer and Susanne zur Nieden, eds., *Sehr selten habe ich geweint: Briefe und Tagebücher aus dem Zweiten Weltkrieg von Menschen aus Berlin* (Zurich, 1992), 298–299; Sternheim-Peters, 196.
56. Hitler quoted in Stephenson, 141. See also Hitler quoted for May 1936 in Reese, 43.

57. Ulla Kuhlo, "Gesundheitsdienst im Bund deutscher Mädel," *Die Ärztin* 17 (1941): 193–200.

58. Bürkner, 21; Sternheim-Peters, 70.

59. Becker, 115; Bürkner, 16; Kinz, 202; Anne Niessen, *"Die Lieder waren die eigentlichen Verführer!": Mädchen und Musik im Nationalsozialismus* (Mainz, 1999).

60. *Mädel im Dienst,* 97, 183–184, 192, 194, 215 (quote). See also Kinz, 213.

61. Kinz, 267; Frevert, 232–233. Michael Burleigh persuasively exposes Mother's Day as the manipulative Nazi instrument it was: see *The Third Reich: A New History* (New York, 2001), 230.

62. Albrecht Möller, *Wir werden das Volk: Wesen und Forderung der Hitlerjugend* (Breslau, 1935), 120; Reinhold Sautter, *Hitlerjugend: Das Erlebnis einer grossen Kameradschaft* (Munich, 1942), 191; Rosenthal, 61.

63. Frevert, 217–218.

64. Günter Kaufmann, *Das kommende Deutschland: Die Erziehung der Jugend im Reich Adolf Hitlers,* 3rd ed. (Berlin, 1943), 290–292; Axmann, 319; testimony in Erich Blohm, *Hitler-Jugend: Soziale Tatgemeinschaft,* 2nd ed. (Vlotho, 1979), 242; *Jugend im nationalsozialistischen Frankfurt: Ausstellungsdokumentation, Zeitzeugenerinnerungen, Publikum* (Frankfurt am Main, 1987), 118.

65. *Das Junge Deutschland* (1937): 560–562; Bürkner, 19; Rüdiger, 401; Hochhuth, 219–220, 224–225, 228, 232–234. On the issue of proper Nazi "female" occupations, see Jill Stephenson, *Women in Nazi Society* (London, 1975).

66. Miller-Kipp, *Auch,* 175–179.

67. Ibid., 180.

68. Stephenson, *Women in Nazi Germany,* 65–66, 81.

69. Bürkner, 18; Rüdiger, 400; Kaufmann, 288; Miller-Kipp, *Auch,* 168–173.

70. Margarete Hannsmann, *Der helle Tag bricht an: Ein Kind wird Nazi* (Munich, 1984), 157–164; Erika S., entry for Apr. 2, 1943, in Breloer, 157; *Jugend . . . Frankfurt,* 273.

71. For the pre-1939 origins, see Stephan Bajohr, "Weiblicher Arbeitsdienst im 'Dritten Reich': Konflikt zwischen Ideologie und Ökonomie," *Vierteljahrshefte für Zeitgeschichte* 28 (1980): 331–350.

72. Frieda Sopp, *Der Arbeitsdienst der deutschen Mädchen* (Berlin, n.d.); Franz W. Seidler, *Frauen zu den Waffen? Marketenderinnen—Helferinnen—Soldatinnen* (Bonn, 1978) 39; Stephenson, *Women in Nazi Germany,* 89; Manfred Seifert, *Kulturarbeit im Reichsarbeitsdienst: Theorie und Praxis nationalsozialistischer Kulturpflege im Kontext historisch-politischer, organisatorischer und ideologischer Einflüsse* (Münster, 1996), 98.

73. Regina Maria Shelton, *To Lose a War: Memoirs of a German Girl* (Carbondale, Ill., 1982), 52–54; *Frauen im Wehrdienst: Erinnerungen von Ingeborg Hecht, Ruth Henry, Christa Meves* (Freiburg, 1989), 10–20; Ingeborg P. in Hass, 79.

74. See the text of Chapter 5 at nn. 116f.

75. Seidler, 47–50, 64; Gerda Szepansky, ed., *"Blitzmädel," "Heldenmutter," "Kriegerwitwe": Frauenleben im Zweiten Weltkrieg* (Frankfurt am Main, 1986), 93–98; Sigrid Bremer, *Muckefuck und Kameradschaft: Mädchenzeit im Dritten Reich: Von der Kinderlandverschickung 1940 bis zum Studium 1946* (Frankfurt am Main, 1988), 78–79; Ursula von Gersdorff, *Frauen im Kriegsdienst, 1914–1945* (Stuttgart, 1969), 68, 339–340.

76. See the text of Chapter 5 at nn. 276f.

77. Gersdorff, 400, 439–440; Maruta Schmidt and Gabi Dietz, eds., *Frauen unterm Hakenkreuz* (Berlin, 1983), 46.

78. Martin Broszat et al., eds., *Bayern in der NS-Zeit: Soziale Lage und politisches Verhalten der Bevölkerung im Spiegel vertraulicher Berichte* (Munich, 1977), 614; Gersdorff, 68; Szepansky, 95; Seifert, 100.

79. Seifert, 102.

80. Burleigh, 446–450; Martin Broszat, *Nationalsozialistische Polenpolitik, 1939–1945* (Stuttgart, 1961); Robert L. Koehl, *RKFDV: German Resettlement and Population Policy, 1939–1945: A History of the Reich Commission for the Strengthening of Germandom* (Cambridge, Mass., 1957); Gellately, 153–154; Knopp, 247.

81. *Hitler-Jugend . . . Chronik,* 49–50, 57–58; Axmann, 325; Kinz, 82; Knopp, 247; Melita Maschmann, *Fazit: Kein Rechtfertigungsversuch,* 5th ed. (Stuttgart, 1964), 121–123.

82. Maschmann, 121; Renate Finckh, *Mit uns zieht die neue Zeit* (Baden-Baden, 1979), 145.

83. Fridel Pauls, "Einsatz in den neuen Ostgebieten," [Aug. 1943], SAG, SF6827, GA/110.

84. Ibid. (quotes); Finkh, 146.

85. Maschmann, 78.

86. Erna Stahl, *Jugend im Schatten von gestern: Aufsätze Jugendlicher zur Zeit* (Hamburg, 1948), 53–57.

87. Fridel Pauls, "Einsatz in den neuen Ostgebieten," [Aug. 1943], SAG, SF6827, GA/110; Finkh, 145.

88. Finkh, 144. Similarly, see Margarethe Eichberger, *Endlich ehrlich erinnern: Jugend unter Hitler, Kriegs- und Nachkriegszeit* (Frankfurt am Main, 1997), 73–74.

89. Finkh, 145.

90. Ibid., 147–148.

91. Stahl, 55–57.

92. Cited in Martin Klaus, *Mädchen im 3. Reich: Der Bund Deutscher Mädel* (Cologne, 1998), 37–38.

93. See Karl-Heinz Huber, *Jugend unterm Hakenkreuz* (Berlin, 1982), 305.

94. On the boys, see Chapters 2 and 5.

95. "Kriegseinsätze der Hitler-Jugend: Gesamteinsatz der Mädel im 1. Kriegsjahr," [1940], HIS, 19/358; "Aufstellung . . . Gau Mecklenburg," [1943], BA, NS26/150.

96. Hildegard Morgenthal, *"Rotkopf, die Ecke brennt, Feuerwehr kommt angerennt": Leben in der NS-Zeit und zwei Leben danach* (Frankfurt am Main, 2000), 17; Sautter, 199; "Mädelerziehung im Kriege," [1944], HIS, 19/358.

97. Sautter, 307, 312; illustration no. 47 in Huber; "Kriegseinsätze der Hitler-Jugend: Gesamteinsatz der Mädel im 1. Kriegsjahr," [1940], HIS, 19/358.

98. "Kriegseinsätze der Hitler-Jugend: Gesamteinsatz der Mädel im 1. Kriegsjahr," [1940], HIS, 19/358; Kauffmann, 315; "Bannbefehl HJ," HJ-Bann Lech (478), [Fall 1942], BA, NS28/27; Kinz, 243–245.

99. "Kriegseinsätze der Hitler-Jugend: Gesamteinsatz der Mädel im 1. Kriegsjahr," [1940], HIS, 19/358; *Hitler-Jugend . . . Chronik*, 43–44.

100. Kreisleitung Darmstadt memo, Feb. 17, 1944, HHSAW, 483/5538.

101. Blohm, 313–314.

102. Ilse Koehn, *Mischling zweiten Grades: Kindheit in der NS-Zeit* (Reinbek, 1980), 106.

103. Venter, report on journey to Angermünde and Prenzlau, Dec. 29, 1943, HIS, 13/260.

104. "Kriegseinsätze der Hitler-Jugend: Gesamteinsatz der Mädel im 1. Kriegsjahr," [1940], HIS, 19/358.

105. Karl Heinz Jahnke, *Hitlers letztes Aufgebot: Deutsche Jugend im sechsten Kriegsjahr, 1944/45* (Essen, 1993), 146–147.

106. Shelton, 36; Schmidt and Dietz, 41.

107. Marie Mulde in Rosenthal, 135; Martin Cranz, *Ich, ein Deutscher* (Dülmen, 1987), 203–204; Friedrich Grupe, *Jahrgang 1916: Die Fahne war mehr als der Tod* (Munich, 1989), 301–302; Bremer, 29.

108. Shelton, 35.

109. Eisenecker quoted in Knopp, 144.

110. Inge Stolten, *Das alltägliche Exil: Leben zwischen Hakenkreuz und Währungsreform* (Berlin, 1982), 88 (quote); Szepansky, 97; Frevert, 249–250; Stephenson, *Women in Nazi Germany*, 112–113; Knopp, 142.

111. *Hitler-Jugend . . . Chronik,* 38.
112. Speer, 73–74; Leni Riefenstahl, *The Sieve of Time: The Memoirs of Leni Riefenstahl* (London, 1992), 131–306; Anna Maria Sigmund, *Die Frauen der Nazis,* 12th ed. (Munich, 2003), 145–171.
113. Her successor was Annemarie Kaspar who got married in 1943, at which time the organization came under Rüdiger directly (Reese, 27–28).
114. See the photograph in Knopp, 111.
115. Sternheim-Peters, 216.
116. Gustav Memminger, ed., *Die Jugend des Führers Adolf Hitler: Bildbuch über die grossdeutsche Jugend* (Leipzig, 1942), 72–73; Axmann, 250; Kinz, 232; Miller-Kipp, *Auch,* 300.
117. Kinz, 229–231; Blohm, 273.
118. Quoted in Miller-Kipp, *Auch,* 78.
119. Becker, 108 (first two quotes); *Hitler-Jugend . . . Chronik,* 38 (third quote).
120. Erna Benze, "Nationalsozialistische Frauenschaft und das Deutsche Frauenwerk," in Benze and Gräfer, 301; Doris K. in Steinbach, 78; *Jugend . . . Frankfurt,* 110.
121. Felix Kersten, *Totenkopf und Treue: Heinrich Himmler ohne Uniform* (Hamburg, n.d.), 92–104.
122. Maschmann, 151–152.
123. Georg Lilienthal, *Der "Lebensborn e.V.": Ein Instrument national-sozialistischer Rassenpolitik* (Stuttgart, 1985); Dorothee Schmitz-Köster, *"Deutsche Mutter, bist Du bereit . . .": Alltag im Lebensborn* (Berlin, 1997), esp. 10–15; Stephenson, *Women in Nazi Germany,* 39, 150–151. Perhaps not surprisingly, the old myth of the Lebensborn as a stud farm still haunts even the most up-to-date literature. See Miller-Kipp, *Auch,* 194. For an earlier sensationalist version see Louis Hagen, *Follow My Leader* (London, 1951), 263–265.
124. See Himmler's remarks regarding "questions about illegitimate motherhood," June 15, 1937, BA, R18/5518; Sybille Hübner-Funk, *Loyalität und Verblendung: Hitlers Garanten der Zukunft als Träger der zweiten deutschen Demokratie* (Potsdam, 1998), 259–260; Carola Kuhlmann, *Erbkrank oder erziehbar? Jugendhilfe als Vorsorge und Aussonderung in der Fürsorgeerziehung in Westfalen von 1933–1945* (Weinheim, 1989), 197; Brandt to Frank, Dec. 12, 1944, in Helmut Heiber, ed., *Reichsführer! . . .: Briefe an und von Himmler* (Stuttgart, 1968), 297 (also 196, 198, 219–220), and the case of Sigmund Rascher in Michael H. Kater, *Das "Ahnenerbe" der SS: Ein Beitrag zur Kulturpolitik des Dritten Reiches,* 3rd ed. (Munich, 2001), 239–245.

125. J. Mayerhofer, "Liebe und Ehe," *SS-Leitheft* 9, no. 8 (Aug. 1943): 17.

126. Himmler to all SS and Police, Apr. 6, 1942, BA, R43II/512.

127. Kersten, 92–104 (quotes, 93, 94).

128. "Das BDM-Werk 'Glaube und Schönheit,'" May 1938, in Miller-Kipp, *Auch*, 79.

129. Kater, *Das "Ahnenerbe" der SS;* Sautter, 222.

130. Sautter, 223.

131. Kersten, 156–171 (quote, 157).

132. See Hugh R. Trevor-Roper, ed., *The Bormann Letters* (London, 1954); Anna Maria Sigmund, *Die Frauen der Nazis II* (Munich, 2002), 7–60.

133. Heinz Höhne, *Der Orden unter dem Totenkopf: Die Geschichte der SS* (Gütersloh, 1967), 388.

134. Kersten, 223–236; Stephenson, *Women in Nazi Society*, 69–70; Stephenson, *Women in Nazi Germany*, 43.

135. Reich Ministry of Justice, "Der Frauenüberschuss nach dem Kriege," [1944], BA, R22/4003.

136. Sautter, 223; Rüdiger, 407.

137. Sautter, 197; Edith Müller, *Ursel und ihre Mädel* (Reutlingen, [1939]), 54; *Mädel im Dienst*, 243–246; Miller-Kipp, *Auch*, 130.

138. *Mädel im Dienst*, 241 (quote); Maschmann, 41.

139. *Mädel im Dienst*, 198.

140. Quoted in Knopp, 117.

141. Quoted in Finkh, 168.

142. Bürkner, 24; Hannsmann, 75.

143. *Mädel im Dienst*, 249.

144. Becker, 105–106; Finckh, 120.

145. *Mädel im Dienst*, 198–199, 246–248 (quotes, 246, 248).

146. Entry for Feb. 5, 1940, by Charlotte L. in Breloer, 414.

147. Sternheim-Peters, 144.

148. Bürkner, 15; Becker, 103; Miller-Kipp, *Auch*, 258–259.

149. "Das Raubtier," *Der Stürmer* 13 (1935), reproduced in Walter Wuttke-Groneberg, ed., *Medizin im Nationalsozialismus: Ein Arbeitsbuch* (Tübingen, 1980), 353. On the effect of *Stürmer*, see also Sternheim-Peters, 146.

150. Marie Mulde quoted in Rosenthal, 132.

151. See Knopp, 108.

152. *Mädel im Dienst*, 255.

153. Hannsmann, 164.

154. Friedrichs speech, March 23, 1944, BA, Schumacher/368.

155. *Mädel im Dienst*, 253.

156. *Wir Mädel singen: Liederbuch des Bundes Deutscher Mädel* (Wolfenbüttel, 1938), 172–175; today's recollection of Christa Thorau in Hans Wienicke, ed., *"Schon damals fingen viele an zu schweigen . . .": Quellensammlung zur Geschichte Charlottenburgs von 1933–1945* (Berlin-Charlottenburg, 1986), 157.

157. Möller, quotes on 118 and 119.

158. Ibid., 116–119 (quotes, 118); Rüdiger, 396; Bürkner, 22.

159. Stephenson, *Women in Nazi Germany*, 19.

160. Ibid.

161. "Der Führer spricht zu den deutschen Frauen," in *Der Kongress zu Nürnberg vom 5. bis 10. September 1934: Offizieller Bericht über den Verlauf des Reichsparteitages mit sämtlichen Reden* (Munich, 1934), 168–173 (quote, 169).

162. Rosenthal, 62; Charlotte L. in Breloer, 415.

163. Axmann, 229; Reese, 34; Stephenson, *Women in Nazi Germany*, 74; Miller-Kipp, "Bund," 90; Jürgen Schultz, *Die Akademie für Jugendführung der Hitlerjugend in Braunschweig* (Brunswick, 1978), 171–174.

164. Alfons Heck, *A Child of Hitler: Germany in the Days when God wore a Swastika* (Frederick, Colo., 1985), 131.

165. See the examples in Rosenthal, 112–113; Koehn, 107; Knopp, 106.

166. Sternheim-Peters, (quote, 174), 180; Müller, 50; *Mädel im Dienst*, 219–220; Rosenthal, 60.

167. Quoted in Knopp, 122–123. Also see Doris K. in Steinbach, 96.

168. Stephenson, *Women in Nazi Germany*, 55, 65; Michael H. Kater, *Doctors Under Hitler* (Chapel Hill, N.C., 1989), 87–110.

169. Sternheim-Peters, 215; Reese, 41; Rosenthal, 111.

170. Edith Niehuis, *Das Landjahr: Eine Jugenderziehungseinrichtung in der Zeit des Nationalsozialismus* (Nörten-Hardenberg, 1984), 67.

171. Maschmann, 160.

172. Jürgen Falter, *Hitlers Wähler* (Munich, 1991), 143–144; Ian Kershaw, *Hitler, 1889–1936: Hubris* (New York, 1999); Kershaw, *Hitler, 1936–1945: Nemesis* (New York, 2000).

173. See Gisela Otmar in Rosenthal, 107; Gertraude Wortmann in Knopp, 101.

174. *Mädel im Dienst*, 187, 220 (first quote); *Wir Mädel singen*, 31 (second quote).

175. Liselotte G. in Hammer and Zur Nieden, 278; Sternheim-Peters, 186.

176. Lore Walb, *Ich, die Alte—ich, die Junge: Konfrontation mit meinen Tage-büchern, 1933–1945,* 2nd ed. (Berlin, 1997), 35–36.

177. Doris K. in Steinbach, 85–86.

178. Helga Giessel in Winfried Maass, *Die Fünfzigjährigen: Portrait einer ver-ratenen Generation* (Hamburg, 1980), 59.

179. See *Deutschland-Berichte der Sozialdemokratischen Partei Deutschlands (Sopade),* vol. 3 (1936), 1317–18; partial report of Oberlandesgericht-spräsident Munich, Apr. 30, 1942, BA, R22/1176a. Schirach's quote is from his book *Die Hitler-Jugend: Idee und Gestalt* (Leipzig, 1934), 62.

180. On the freedom, see the remarks of former Hitler Youth Hermann Graml, "Integration und Entfremdung: Inanspruchnahme durch Staatsjugend und Dienstpflicht," in Ute Benz and Wolfgang Benz, eds., *Sozialisation und Traumatisierung: Kinder in der Zeit des Nationalsozialismus* (Frankfurt am Main, 1992), 78–79.

181. Ian Buruma and Avishai Margalit, "Occidentalism," *New York Review of Books* (Jan. 17, 2002): 7.

182. Frevert, 64, 134, 186; Elizabeth Heineman, "Sexuality and Nazism: The Doubly Unspeakable?", *Journal of the History of Sexuality* 11 (2002): 30–31. Note the moralizing in Peter Paul Pauquet, *Gespräche mit der Ju-gend einer zerschlagenen Nation* (Nuremberg, 1947), 114–115.

183. Brauer to Parteigenossin, March 16, 1934, BA, NS22/342.

184. *Deutschland-Berichte,* vol. 2 (1935), 694–696 (quote, 695).

185. Ibid., vol. 3 (1936), 359; Huber, 185.

186. Miller-Kipp, "Bund," 100 (n. 57).

187. Kinz, 42.

188. Von Saldern, 144.

189. Entry for Dec. 13, 1943, in Heinz Boberach, ed., *Meldungen aus dem Reich: Die geheimen Lageberichte des Sicherheitsdienstes der SS, 1938–1945* (Herrsching, 1984), vol. 15, 6145–6147; entry for Jan. 24, 1944, ibid., vol. 16, 6279; monthly report of Regierungspräsident Regensburg, June 11, 1943, BA, Schumacher/483; Ulrich Herbert, *Hitler's Foreign Workers: Enforced Foreign Labor in Germany under the Third Reich* (Cambridge, 1997), 64–66, 70–77, 96–100, 109, 125–127, 133, 269; Michael Bur-leigh and Wolfgang Wippermann, *The Racial State: Germany, 1933–1945* (Cambridge, 1991), 264–266.

190. Erhard Eppler, *Als Wahrheit verordnet wurde: Briefe an meine Enkelin,* 3rd ed. (Frankfurt am Main, 1995), 84–85; Lechner, 85.

191. Stephenson, *Women in Nazi Germany,* 29, 171–172.

192. Gellately, 157–158.

193. Huber, 268.

194. Entry for Jan. 22, 1942, in Boberach, vol. 9, 3202.

195. Amtsgericht München, judgment against Moser and Nusskern, Sept. 2, 1942, ARL, Lü 6.1.5 (München).

196. Amtsgericht München, judgment against Krammer, Jan. 26, 1943, ARL, Lü 6.1.5 (München).

197. Friedrichs speech, March 23, 1944, BA, Schumacher/368.

198. Amtsgericht München, judgment against Kreitmeier, May 18, 1943, ARL, Lü 6.1.5 (München); entry for June 6, 1943, in Boberach, vol. 14, 5341 (quote).

199. Testimonies of Dieter Wellershoff and Martin Gregor-Dellin in Marcel Reich-Ranicki, ed., *Meine Schulzeit im Dritten Reich: Erinnerungen deutscher Schriftsteller* (Munich, 1984), 146–147, 179. This is corroborated from a girl's point of view in Sternheim-Peters, 356.

200. W. Knopp, "Kriminalität und Gefährdung der Jugend: Lagebericht bis zum Stande vom 1. Januar 1941," BA, NSD43/96 (p. 165); youth court to Reich justice minister, Apr. 5, 1944, BA, R22/1165.

201. Walb, 151.

202. Entry for Nov. 3, 1939, in Boberach, vol. 2, 416; monthly report of SRD Augsburg, Nov. 1, 1940, SAND, unsign. Bestand, EAP 221-b-20/9; W. Knopp, "Kriminalität und Gefährdung der Jugend" (pp. 164–166); excerpt, report of attorney-general Celle, Apr. 4, 1942, BA, R22/1176a; youth court to Reich justice minister, Apr. 5, 1944, BA, R22/1165.

203. Entry for Nov. 3, 1939, in Boberach, vol. 2, 416 (quote); Ungereiter to Reich interior minister, July 26, 1944, BA, R22/3364.

204. Munding to Scheffelt, Feb. 23, 1941, in Friedrich Munding, *Dass ich nur noch selten schreibe: Briefe aus Berlin, 1940–1943*, ed. Werner Trapp (Berlin, 1985), 18; Howard K. Smith, *Feind schreibt mit: Ein amerikanischer Korrespondent erlebt Nazi-Deutschland* (Frankfurt am Main, 1986), 131. See also entry for March 18, 1943, in Ursula von Kardorff, *Berliner Aufzeichnungen: Aus den Jahren 1942 bis 1945,* 3rd ed. (Munich, 1962), 35.

205. Quoted in Huber, 265.

206. Monthly report, Regierungspräsident Regensburg, March 10, 1943, BA, Schumacher/483; Heck, 133–134.

207. Hoffmeister to Reich justice minister, June 30, 1942; situation report of attorney-general Frankfurt, Jan. 28, 1943; excerpt, situation report Oberlandesgerichtspräsident Nuremberg, March 31, 1943, BA, R22/

1176a; Edelgard Seidel, entry for Nov. 27, 1944, in Breloer, 225; entry for Apr. 13, 1944, in Boberach, vol. 16, 6484; Klaus Tischler's testimony in Rosenthal, 266–267; Helmut Altner, *Totentanz Berlin: Tagebuchblätter eines Achtzehnjährigen* (Offenbach, 1947), 32; Walter Kempowski, *Tadellöser and Wolff: Ein bürgerlicher Roman,* 2nd ed. (Munich, 1975), 456.

208. Winfried Süss, *Der "Volkskörper" im Krieg: Gesundheitspolitik, Gesundheitsverhältnisse und Krankenmord im nationalsozialistischen Deutschland, 1939–1945* (Munich, 2003), 396–397.

209. Nazi Party proceedings against Balnus, Oct. 10, 1942, personal file Balnus, BAB; Edelgard Seidel, entry for Sept. 23, 1944, in Breloer, 223–224; Finckh, 146–147.

4. Dissidents and Rebels

1. Hans Rothfels, *The German Opposition to Hitler: An Appraisal* (Hinsdale, Ill., 1948), 12. On Weimar, see Rothfels, "Deutschlands Krise," in Alfred Bozi and Alfred Niemann, eds., *Die Einheit der Nationalen Politik* (Stuttgart, 1925), 1–15; Rothfels, "Wolfgang Kapp," *Deutsches biographisches Jahrbuch* 4 (1922): 132–143. On Rothfels's (eastern-expansionist) politics and historiography, personal biography, and the resistance book, see, preeminently, Ingo Haar, *Historiker im Nationalsozialismus: Deutsche Geschichtswissenschaft und der "Volkstumskampf" im Osten* (Göttingen, 2000), 86–90; Hans Mommsen, "Geschichtsschreibung und Humanität—Zum Gedenken an Hans Rothfels," in Wolfgang Benz and Hermann Graml, eds., *Aspekte deutscher Aussenpolitik im 20. Jahrhundert: Aufsätze Hans Rothfels zum Gedächtnis* (Stuttgart, 1976), 9–27; Hans-Ulrich Wehler, "Historiography in Germany Today," in Jürgen Habermas, ed., *Observations on "The Spiritual Situation of the Age": Contemporary German Perspectives* (Cambridge, Mass., 1984), 229 (quote). On Rothfels as a Jew, see the seminal article by Peter Loewenberg, "Antisemitismus und jüdischer Selbsthass: Eine sich wechselseitig verstärkende sozialpsychologische Doppelbeziehung," *Geschichte und Gesellschaft* 5 (1979): 455–475. Wehler's plight in 1943–44 is documented in *Der Spiegel* (Jan. 6, 2003): 51. In contrast to Rothfels, compare the almost contemporaneous, more inclusive approach to anti-Nazi resistance by Annedore Leber, ed., *Das Gewissen steht auf: 64 Lebensbilder aus dem deutschen Widerstand, 1933–1945* (Berlin, 1954), esp. 22–24.

2. Robert Gellately, *The Gestapo and German Society: Enforcing Racial Policy, 1933–1945* (Oxford, 1991).

3. George (Jürgen) Wittenstein, "The White Rose: Memories and Reflections," paper presented at the International Conference entitled "CONFRONT! Resistance in Nazi Germany," Boston College, Apr. 17, 2002 (APA).

4. Rohlfing memo, June 7, 1935, SAB, 4,65-II, E, 3, a/13.

5. Andreas von Hellfeld, *Bündische Jugend und Hitlerjugend: Zur Geschichte von Anpassung und Widerstand, 1930–1939* (Cologne, 1987), 121–126.

6. Kurt Schilde, *Jugendorganisationen und Jugendopposition in Berlin-Kreuzberg, 1933–45: Eine Dokumentation* (Berlin, 1983), 92–97; Karl Heinz Jahnke and Michael Buddrus, eds., *Deutsche Jugend, 1933–1945: Eine Dokumentation* (Hamburg, 1989), 239–243.

7. Beck to Landräte et al., May 24, 1939, SAM, LRA/47093.

8. Fritz Molden, *Fepolinski und Waschlapski auf dem berstenden Stern: Bericht einer unruhigen Jugend* (Vienna, 1976), 151–152, 158–159.

9. Von Hellfeld, 140–141.

10. Otto B. Roegele, *Gestapo gegen Schüler: Die Gruppe "Christopher" in Bruchsal* (Constance, 1994), 35–51, 85–101.

11. Karl Heinz Jahnke, *Jugend im Widerstand, 1933–1945,* 2nd ed. (Frankfurt am Main, 1985), 127–132.

12. "Politischer Lagebericht," Ortsgruppe Rothenburg, Feb. 1939, BA, Schumacher/372.

13. "SRD-Monatsbericht Oktober," Nov. 4, 1940, SAND, unsign. Best., EAP 221-b-20/9.

14. Jahnke and Buddrus, 284–285.

15. Von Hellfeld, 162–165.

16. Volksgerichtshof Berlin, judgment against Landgraf et al., Sept. 23, 1942, ARL, Parteikanzlei/Mikrofiches (quotes); Landgraf, "Jugend im Kampf für Freiheit und Vaterland," Vienna, n.d., DAOW, 2542.

17. Christine E. King, *The Nazi State and the New Religions: Five Case Studies in Non-Conformity* (New York, 1982), 63–87.

18. Detlev Peukert, "Protest und Widerstand von Jugendlichen im Dritten Reich," in Richard Löwenthal and Patrick von zur Mühlen, eds., *Widerstand und Verweigerung in Deutschland, 1933 bis 1945* (Bonn, 1982), 194 (quote); Ursula Prückner and Axel Waldhier, "Verweigerung—Opposition—Widerstand: Einblicke in das Leben dreier Nicht-Faschisten," in Brigitte Abramowski et al., *"Ohne uns hätten sie das gar nicht machen können": Nazi-Zeit und Nachkrieg in Altona und Ottensen* (Hamburg, 1985), 51; Blair R. Holmes and Alan F. Keele, eds., *When Truth Was Treason: German Youth against Hitler: The Story of the Helmuth Hübener Group* (Urbana, Ill., 1995).

19. Guido Knopp, *Hitlers Kinder,* 2nd ed. (Munich, 2000), 202.

20. Michael Burleigh, *The Third Reich: A New History* (New York, 2001), 411.

21. Wolf Jobst Siedler in Johannes Steinhoff et al., eds., *Voices from the Third Reich: An Oral History* (New York, 1994), 358 (quotes); Gunter Fahle, *Verweigern—Weglaufen—Zersetzen: Deutsche Militärjustiz und ungehorsame Soldaten, 1939–1945: Das Beispiel Ems-Jade* (Bremen, 1990), 170–176; Hans-Dietrich Nicolaisen, *Die Flakhelfer: Luftwaffenhelfer und Marinehelfer im Zweiten Weltkrieg* (Berlin, 1981), 155–156.

22. Eva Amann's testimony is in Silvester Lechner, *Das KZ Oberer Kuhberg und die NS-Zeit in der Region Ulm/Neu-Ulm* (Stuttgart, 1988), 110–111.

23. Otl Aicher, *Innenseiten des Kriegs* (Frankfurt am Main, 1985), 57, 60, 130.

24. Hartnagel to Sophie Scholl, Sept. 14, 1942, quoted in *Spiegel Online,* Jan. 31, 2003.

25. Christian Petry, *Studenten aufs Schafott: Die Weisse Rose und ihr Scheitern* (Munich, 1968), 28; Scholl quoted on p. 30.

26. Personal communication by George Wittenstein to the author, Santa Barbara, May 4, 2003 (quote); Detlef Bald, *Die "Weisse Rose": Von der Front in den Widerstand* (Berlin, 2003), 130.

27. Aicher, 83. On Inge: personal communication by George Wittenstein to the author, Santa Barbara, May 4, 2003.

28. See the text of Chapter 2 at n. 19.

29. Petry, 25–28 (quotes, 27); Lechner, 97–100; Inge Scholl, *Die Weisse Rose* (Frankfurt am Main, 1965), 18–21, 26–30. Scholl's book has become a virtual bible on the White Rose, in several commercially successful editions, heightening the cachet of the Scholl siblings in the conspiracy immeasurably. But since the author was never personally involved in it, the book's information, as George Wittenstein rightly points out, is only second-hand and, as I have been able to ascertain, frequently skewed or incorrect. Obviously, for self-serving reasons, Inge Scholl placed herself at a point in the movement where she had never been, and gave herself an aura of authority that she had never possessed. It is significant that in the latest book on the White Rose, by Detlef Bald, she is not mentioned at all. See Wittenstein, "The White Rose," as in n. 3.

30. Wittenstein, "The White Rose," as in n. 3.

31. Petry, 21–25 (quote, 24); Gerhard Paul, *Ungehorsame Soldaten: Dissens, Verweigerung und Widerstand deutscher Soldaten (1939–1945)* (St. Ingbert, 1994), 96–97.

32. Wittenstein, "The White Rose," as in n. 3.

33. Petry, 19–21.

34. Heinz A. Brenner, *Dagegen: Bericht über den Widerstand von Schülern des Humanistischen Gymnasiums Ulm/Donau gegen die deutsche national-sozialistische Diktatur* (Leutkirch, [1992]), 22–25, 37; Lechner, 98; Scholl, 33–38, 71–72; Petry, 50–51.

35. Lechner, 101; Scholl, 58.

36. Wittenstein, "The White Rose," as in n. 3 (quotes); Petry, 65–73.

37. Petry, 36–42 (quote, 41).

38. "Denkschrift zur Neugründung und Angliederung der deutschen Schule für Volksmusik und Tanz am Trapp'schen Konservatorium der Musik" [1935], StAM, Kulturamt/480.

39. Kurt Huber, "Der Aufbau deutscher Volksliedforschung und Volks-sliedpflege," *Deutsche Musikkultur* 1 (1936): 66, 68–69.

40. Petry, 42–47; Maria Bruckbauer, *". . . und sei es gegen eine Welt von Feinden!": Kurt Hubers Volksliedsammlung und -pflege in Bayern* (Munich, 1991), 13–15, 99–204.

   Huber's friend, the Munich composer Carl Orff, claimed in 1945–46 that he, too, had been mentoring, had even co-founded, the White Rose in partnership with Huber. He told this to the U.S. authorities in an effort to get easy denazification clearance, since he knew he was guilty of collaboration with the Nazi regime, although he himself had never been a Nazi. Although his scam worked at the time, it has recently been exposed through research. See Clara Huber to the author, Munich, Sept. 30, 1993; Gertrud Orff to the author, Munich, Nov. 12, 1993; George Wittenstein to the author, Santa Barbara, Oct. 21, 1997, APA; Michael H. Kater, *Composers of the Nazi Era: Eight Portraits* (New York, 2000), 111–143; Kater, "In Answer to Hans Jörg Jans," *Musical Quarterly* 84 (2000): 711–712; Richard Taruskin, "Orff's Musical and Moral Failings," *New York Times,* May 6, 2001.

41. Wittenstein, "The White Rose," as in n. 3.

42. Bald, 18–21, 145; Petry, 92–100 (quote, 99).

43. Petry, 100–106 (quotes, 102); Wittenstein, "The White Rose," as in n. 3.

44. Scheibe to anon., [March 1943], SAM, NSDAP/11.

45. Wittenstein, "The White Rose," as in n. 3.

46. Petry, 107–111; Bald, 154–155.

47. Wittenstein, "The White Rose," as in n. 3.

48. Petry, 175–183, 195–211.

49. Scholl, 112, 114.

50. Facs. of leaflets I–VI in Lechner, 7–17.

51. Ian Kershaw, *Hitler, 1880–1936: Hubris* (New York, 1999); Kershaw, *Hitler, 1936–45: Nemesis* (New York, 2000), esp. 751f.

52. Albrecht Riethmüller, "Wunschbild: Beethoven als Chauvinist," *Archiv für Musikwissenschaft* 58 (2001): 91–109; Michael H. Kater, "Introduction," in Kater and Albrecht Riethmüller, eds., *Music and Nazism: Art under Tyranny, 1933–1945* (Laaber, 2003), 1–2.

53. See Günter De Bruyn, *Zwischenbilanz: Eine Jugend in Berlin* (Frankfurt am Main, 1995), 107; Jahnke and Buddrus, 334.

54. Aicher, 10, 14, 28, 36, 81.

55. Ibid., 61, 80, 82; Scholl.

56. Aicher, 88, 154; Lechner, 104.

57. Lechner, 108, 115.

58. Petry, 138–145; Jahnke, 180–186; Inge Stolten, *Das alltägliche Exil: Leben zwischen Hakenkreuz und Währungsreform* (Berlin, 1982), 64, 69.

59. Paul, 97, 99.

60. Wittenstein, "The White Rose," as in n. 3; Ruth Andreas-Friedrich, *Der Schattenmann: Tagebuchaufzeichnungen, 1938–1945* (Berlin, 1947), 110–116.

61. "Anhang: Einzelbeispiele für die Cliquen- und Bandenbildung neuerer Zeit," Sept. 1942; Reichsjugendführung, "Entwurf: Bekämpfung jugendlicher Cliquen," May 11, 1943; Reichsführer-SS, "Betrifft: Bekämpfung jugendlicher Cliquen," Oct. 1943, BA, R22/1177. See Matthias von Hellfeld and Arno Klönne, *Die betrogene Generation: Jugend in Deutschland unter dem Faschismus* (Cologne, 1985), 268–269; Alfons Kenkmann, *Wilde Jugend: Lebenswelt grossstädtischer Jugendlicher zwischen Weltwirtschaftskrise, Nationalsozialismus und Währungsreform* (Essen, 1996), 342; Winfried Speitkamp, *Jugend in der Neuzeit: Deutschland vom 16. bis zum 20. Jahrhundert* (Göttingen, 1998), 234–237.

62. Jandl in Marcel Reich-Ranicki, ed., *Meine Schulzeit im Dritten Reich: Erinnerungen deutscher Schriftsteller* (Munich, 1984), 120–121.

63. Amtsgericht München, judgment against Hüttner et al., March 7, 1941; minutes of youth courts at Amtsgericht München, March 14, 1941, ARL, Lü 6.1.2. and 6.1.3. (München).

64. Heinz Boberach, ed., *Meldungen aus dem Reich: Die geheimen Lageberichte des Sicherheitsdienstes der SS, 1938–1945* (Herrsching, 1984), vol. 3, 477; "Bericht zur innenpolitischen Lage," Nov. 22, 1939, BA, R58/145.

65. "Anhang: Einzelbeispiele . . . ," Sept. 1942 (as in n. 61); Sieverts, "Jugendgefährdung im Kriege," Oct. 20, 1942, BA, NL/289; Studt to Schulverwaltung Hamburg, Dec. 5, 1941 and Jan. 1, 1942, SAH, Oberschulbehörde VI, 2 F VIII a 2/3/1.

66. "Die Jugendkriminalität in Hamburg seit Beginn des Krieges," [May 1943], BA, NL/289.

67. Gernet to Präsident Hanseatisches Oberlandesgericht, Feb. 2, 1945, SAH, 213-1, OLG Hamburg.

68. Eschenbacher to K-Gebietsführer et al., Oct. 18, 1942, SAM, OLG München/278; Kümmerlein, "Auszug," Feb. 1, 1943; "Tagesmeldung des GenStA in Stettin," Feb. 18, 1943, BA, R22/1177.

69. Venter report, Dec. 29, 1943, HIS, 13/260; "Jugendliche Cliquen und Banden," enclosed with Reich justice minister to Oberlandesgerichtspräsidenten, June 10, 1944, BA, R22/1177.

70. Stedtnitz report, Nov. 30, 1944, in Karl Heinz Jahnke, *Hitlers letztes Aufgebot: Deutsche Jugend im sechsten Kriegsjahr, 1944/45* (Essen, 1993), 104–105.

71. See Detlev Peukert, "Edelweissspiraten, Meuten, Swing: Jugendsubkulturen im Dritten Reich," in Ulrich Herrmann, ed., *"Die Formung des Volksgenossen": Der "Erziehungsstaat" des Dritten Reiches* (Weinheim, 1985), 223.

72. Von Hellfeld and Klönne, 86–89; "Anhang: Einzelbeispiele . . .," Sept. 1942 (as in n. 61) (quote); minutes of judgment against Pflocksch et al., June 15, 1942, BA, R22/1177.

73. "Anhang: Einzelbeispiele . . .," Sept. 1942 (as in n. 61).

74. Detlev Peukert and Michael Winter, " 'Edelweissspiraten' in Duisburg: Eine Fallstudie zum subkulturellen Verhalten von Arbeiterjugendlichen unter dem Nationalsozialismus," *Duisburger Forschungen* 31 (1982): 259–260; Kenkmann, 161–163, 182.

75. Peukert and Winter, 268.

76. Edgar Gielsdorf, *Vom Christkind eine Landsknechtstrommel* (Cologne, 1994), 125–127.

77. Jahnke, *Jugend,* 169–170; Ulrich Herbert, *Hitler's Foreign Workers: Enforced Foreign Labor in Germany under the Third Reich* (Cambridge, 1997), 366–367.

78. "Anhang: Einzelbeispiele . . .," Sept. 1942 (as in n. 61); Albath, "Wilde Jugendgruppen—Edelweissspiraten," [spring 1943]; Pastor to Amtsgerichtspräsident, Nov. 7, 1943, BA, R22/1177.

79. SS-Reichssicherheitshauptamt memo, March 15, 1943, BA, R22/1177.

80. Albath, "Wilde Jugendgruppen—Edelweissspiraten," [spring 1943], BA, R22/1177; Kenkmann, 256–257; Peukert and Winter, 264.

81. Peukert and Winter, 260.

82. Gieseking, minutes of interrogation, Nov. 1, 1943, SAMs, Polit. Polizei, 3. Reich/408; Pastor to Amtsgerichtspräsident, Nov. 7, 1943, BA, R22/1177; *Jugend im nationalsozialistischen Frankfurt: Ausstellungsdokumentation, Zeitzeugenerinnerungen, Publikum* (Frankfurt am Main, 1987), 179–180;

Jurgen Herbst, *Requiem for a German Past: A Boyhood among the Nazis* (Madison, 1999), 175.

83. Kenkmann, 298.

84. "Anhang: Einzelbeispiele . . .," Sept. 1942 (as in n. 61).

85. "Auszug aus einem Lagebericht des GenStA. in Braunschweig v. 26.5.1943," BA, R22/1176a; Anderegg to Schlüter, Apr. 27, 1944, BA, R36/2021; Herbert Koleczek interview, Rüdesheim, June 25, 1988; Kenkmann, 297–298. On Frankfurt's youthful jazz and swing scene, which, in contrast to Hamburg's, was predominantly lower-middle-class, see Wassermann to Reich justice minister, June 3, 1943, BA, R22/3364; Cornelia Rühlig and Jürgen Steen, eds., *Walter: *1926, +1945 an der Ostfront: Leben und Lebensbedingungen eines Frankfurter Jungen im III. Reich* (Frankfurt am Main, 1983), 116–118, 121, 123; *Jugend . . . Frankfurt,* 157–160, 181–186, 297, 300–304; Michael H. Kater, *Different Drummers: Jazz in the Culture of Nazi Germany* (New York, 1992), 148–151, 196–198. For Berlin, see Heinrich Kupffer, *Swingtime: Chronik einer Jugend in Deutschland, 1937–1951* (Berlin, 1987), 44–46, 49, 54–57.

86. "Bericht über eine Veranstaltung am 2.3.40 im Curio-Haus," SAH, Jugendbehörde I, 343 e.

87. "Anhang: Einzelbeispiele . . .," Sept. 1942 (as in n. 61).

88. Ibid.

89. Ibid.

90. Entry for Aug. 21, 1941, *TGII* 1: 284.

91. Interrogation protocol of A.v.d.E., Oct. 16, 1941, SAH, Oberschulbehörde VI, 2 F VIII a 2/40/1; Grell to Amtsgericht Hamburg, July 16, 1942, SAH, Amtsgericht Hamburg, Abtlg. Vormundschaftswesen, 115 XI, R 1886, 1653/Rönn; Kruse memo, [1942], BA, NL/289; Hannelore Evers-Frauboes and Robert Vogel (quote) recorded interviews, Hamburg, June 18 and 21, 1988; Hans-Joachim Scheel recorded interview, Toronto, March 29, 1988.

92. Pereira report, Febr. 28, 1941, BA, NL/289; interrogation protocol of Helga Rönn, Sept. 10, 1941, SAH, Amtsgericht Hamburg, Abtlg. Vormundschaftswesen, 115 XI, R 1886, 1653/Rönn; Hans Engel recorded interview, Mamaroneck, N.Y., March 5, 1988; Evers-Frauboes and Vogel recorded interviews.

93. Interrogation protocol of Helga Rönn, Sept. 9, 1941, SAH, Amtsgericht Hamburg, Abtlg. Vormundschaftswesen, 115 XI, R 1886, 1653/Rönn; Vogel recorded interview. See Gerd Albrecht, *Nationalsozialistische Filmpolitik: Eine soziologische Untersuchung über die Spielfilme des Dritten Reichs* (Stuttgart, 1969), 109, 383, 434, 547.

94. Engel recorded interview.
95. Evers-Frauboes recorded interview.
96. Karsten Witte, "Gehemmte Schaulust: Momente des deutschen Revue-films," in Helga Belach, ed., *Wir tanzen um die Welt: Deutsche Revuefilme, 1933–1945* (Munich, 1979), 24.
97. *Skizzen* (June/July 1938): 20; German Brunswick record catalogs for March and Apr. 1936, and Apr. 1938, APA.
98. Entry for Feb. 10, 1942, *TGII* 3: 282.
99. Günter Lust in Bernd Polster, ed., *"Swing Heil": Jazz im Nationalsozialis-mus* (Berlin, 1989), 166; Werner Burkhardt, "Musik der Stunde Null (II)," *Zeitmagazin* (Nov. 18, 1983): 42.
100. Interrogation protocol of Heinrich Fey, Oct. 13, 1941; of A.v.d.E., Oct. 16, 1941; of H.P., Oct. 18, 1941, SAH, Oberschulbehörde VI, 2 F VIII a 2/40/1; Uhlenhorst Oberschule für Jungen memo, Dec. 16, 1941, SAH, Oberschulbehörde VI, 2 F VIII a 2/3/1; Kruse memo, [n.d.], BA, NL/289; Scheel, Vogel, Evers-Frauboes, and Engel (quote) recorded interviews.
101. Crepon report, Nov. 10, 1941, SAH, Oberschulbehörde VI, 2 F VIII a 2/3/1; Kruse memo, [1942], BA, NL/289; interrogation protocol of Heinrich Fey, Oct. 13, 1941; of A.v.d.E., Oct. 16, 1941; of O.S., Oct. 18, 1941; of W.D., Oct. 18, 1941; of W.R., Oct. 21, 1941, SAH, Oberschul-behörde VI, 2 F VIII a 2/40/1; Engel, Vogel, and Evers-Frauboes recorded interviews; Hans-Joachim Scheel to the author, Toronto, Apr. 7, 1988, APA (quote).
102. Gestapo Hamburg to Gemeindeverwaltung Hamburg, Nov. 13, 1940, SAH, Oberschulbehörde VI, 2 F VIII a 2/3/1; Wege memo, Sept. 10, 1941, SAH, Amtsgericht Hamburg, Abtlg. Vormundschaftswesen, 115 XI, R 1886, 1653/Rönn; interrogation protocol of A.v.d.E., Oct. 16, 1941, SAH, Oberschulbehörde VI, 2 F VIII a 2/40/1; Engel and Vogel recorded interviews.
103. Gestapo Hamburg to Gemeindeverwaltung Hamburg, Nov. 13, 1940, SAH, Oberschulbehörde VI, 2 F VIII a 2/3/1; interrogation protocol of A.v.d.E., Oct. 16, 1941, SAH, Oberschulbehörde VI, 2 F VIII a 2/40/1; interrogation protocols of Helga Rönn, Sept. 9, 10, and 11, 1941, SAH, Amtsgericht Hamburg, Abtlg. Vormundschaftswesen, 115 XI, R 1886, 1653 Rönn; Prinzhorn memo, Dec. 12, 1942, SAH, Oberschulbehörde VI, 2 F VIII a 2/40/1.
104. Inga Madlung-Shelton recorded interview, London, May 9, 1988 (quote); Grell to Amtsgericht Hamburg, July 16, 1942, SAH, Amts-gericht Hamburg, Abtlg. Vormundschaftswesen, 115 XI, R 1886, 1653/Rönn.

105. Interrogation protocol of W.D., Oct. 18, 1941, SAH, Oberschulbehörde VI, 2 F VIII a 2/40/1; Pereira report, Feb. 28, 1941, BA, NL/289; Madlung-Shelton recorded interview; Andreas Panagopoulos recorded interview, Hamburg, June 16, 1988; Harry Stephens (Demitrius Georgiadis), *Swing Threatens Third Reich* (Nicosia, 1988); photograph in Kater, *Drummers,* 97, also 109.

106. Scheel recorded interview.

107. *Das Junge Deutschland* (1937): 441–443; *Deutsches Ärzteblatt* 66 (1936): 541.

108. See Gellately.

109. "Die Entwicklung der Kriminalität, namentlich der Jugendkriminalität während des Krieges," [1942]; Bormann, "Bekanntgabe 204/44 g.," Aug. 29, 1944, BA, R22/1165.

110. See *Das Junge Deutschland* (1937): 443–444; "Die Entwicklung der Kriminalität, namentlich der Jugendkriminalität während des Krieges," [1942], BA, R22/1165; "Die Struktur der Jugendkriminalität im ersten und zweiten Weltkrieg," 1943, BA, R22/1159. See also the text of Chapter 3 at n. 182.

111. "Die Entwicklung der Kriminalität im Deutschen Reich vom Kriegsbeginn bis Mitte 1943," BA, R22/1159.

112. Kenkmann, 151; Von Hellfeld and Klönne, 296.

113. Kenkmann, 151.

114. Hanns Anderlahn, "Führung—Erziehung—Strafe," *Das Junge Deutschland* (1937): 54.

115. HJ-Gebiet Hamburg memo, March 12, 1940, SAH, Jugendbehörde I, 343 c.

116. Stark memo, Feb. 2, 1944 (quote); see also Ofterdinger to Schrewe, Jan. 14, 1944, SAH, Oberschulbehörde VI, 2 F VIII a 2/40/1.

117. Amtsgericht Abteilung 28 (Jugendgericht) to Reich justice minister, Apr. 5, 1944, BA, R22/1165.

118. Oberstudiendirektor to Hitler-Jugend Gebiet Hamburg 26, Nov. 27, 1940, SAH, Oberschulbehörde VI, 2 F VIII a 2/3/1.

119. Kenkmann, 130–131, 211.

120. Gerhard Rempel, *Hitler's Children: The Hitler Youth and the SS* (Chapel Hill, N.C., 1989), 52.

121. Ibid., 52–55; "Vorläufige Dienstvorschrift für den HJ-Streifendienst," May 15, 1936, HIS, 13/338.

122. Jahnke and Buddrus, 311–312.

123. Reithmayr report, HJ-Bann Allgäu, Oct. 1–31, 1940, SAND, unsign. Best., EAP, 221-b-20/9.

124. Kechele report, Augsburg Stadt, Oct. [1941], and similar such reports, SAND, unsign. Best., EAP 221-b-20/6; Kenkmann, 169.

125. Von Hellfeld, 191; Rempel, 97.

126. For a principal admission of powerlessness vis-à-vis those institutions, see Reichsjugendführung, "Cliquen- und Bandenbildung unter Jugendlichen," Sept. 1942, BA, R22/1177.

127. Anon. to Mulzer, June 15, 1940, SAH, Sozialbehörde I, VT 38.10; Carola Kuhlmann, *Erbkrank oder erziehbar? Jugendhilfe als Vorsorge und Aussonderung in der Fürsorgeerziehung in Westfalen von 1933–1945* (Weinheim, 1989), 200.

128. Reichsjugendführung, "Entwurf: Bekämpfung jugendlicher Cliquen," May 11, 1943; Jugendführer to Führer der Gebiete und Banne, Dec. 10, 1944, BA, R22/1177; Landgerichtspräsident, "Betrifft: Zusammenarbeit in der Jugendrechtspflege," March 9, 1944, ARL, Lü 4.6.1.1 (OLG Oldenburg); Lothar Gruchmann, "Jugendopposition und Justiz im Dritten Reich: Die Probleme bei der Verfolgung der 'Leipziger Meuten' durch die Gerichte," in Wolfgang Benz, ed., *Miscellanea: Festschrift für Helmut Krausnick zum 75. Geburtstag* (Stuttgart, 1980), 122.

129. Axmann to Himmler, Jan. 8, 1942, BA, NS 19/neu 219.

130. Artur Axmann, *"Das kann doch nicht das Ende sein": Hitlers letzter Reichsjugendführer erinnert sich,* 2nd ed. (Koblenz, 1995), 380.

131. Richard F. Wetzell, *Inventing the Criminal: A History of German Criminology, 1880–1945* (Chapel Hill, N.C., 2000), esp. 235.

132. Kershaw, *Nemesis,* 511, 689; Richard J. Evans, *Rituals of Retribution: Capital Punishment in Germany, 1600–1987* (Oxford, 1996), 632, 639–640, 686–720; Dietrich Güstrow, *Tödlicher Alltag: Strafverteidiger im Dritten Reich* (Berlin, 1981).

133. Werner Johe, *Die gleichgeschaltete Justiz: Organisation des Rechtswesens und Politisierung der Rechtsprechung 1933–1945, dargestellt am Beispiel des Oberlandesgerichtsbezirks Hamburg* (Frankfurt am Main, 1967); Walter Wagner, *Der Volksgerichtshof im nationalsozialistischen Staat* (Stuttgart, 1974); Robert Gellately, *Backing Hitler: Consent and Coercion in Nazi Germany* (Oxford, 2002), 47–48.

134. Albrecht Wagner, *Die Umgestaltung der Gerichtsverfassung und des Verfahrens- und Richterrechts im nationalsozialistischen Staat* (Stuttgart, 1968); Robert Wistrich, *Who's Who in Nazi Germany* (New York, 1982), 115–117, 315–316; Gellately, *Hitler,* 79.

135. Albrecht Wagner, 348–359; Hans Frank, *Im Angesicht des Galgens: Deutung Hitlers und seiner Zeit auf Grund eigener Erlebnisse und Erkenntnisse* (Munich-Gräfelfing, 1953); Gellately, *Hitler,* 119.

136. Wetzell, 121.

137. Kuhlmann, 201.

138. Oberkommando der Wehrmacht to Reich justice minister, Aug. 3, 1942, BA, R22/1177; Bormann to Reich justice minister, Oct. 26, 1942, BA, R22/1179.

139. Daniel Horn, "Coercion and Compulsion in the Hitler Youth, 1933–1945," *Historian* 41 (1979): 653–654; "In einer Jugendarrest-Anstalt: Die Tendenzen in der Strafrechtspflege für Minderjährige," *Das Reich,* July 13, 1941 (quote).

140. Hische, "Entwicklung der Jugendkriminalität und Neuordnung der Jugendkriminalstatistik," Nov. 1943, BA, R22/1165.

141. Reich justice minister to Oberlandesgerichtspräsidenten et al., Sept. [?], 1942; and to Himmler, Sept. 25, 1942, BA, R22/5018.

142. Amtsgericht München, judgment against Steigenberger et al., March 27, 1941; Neck to Oberstaatsanwalt München, March 31, 1942, ARL, Lü 6.1.5 (München); minutes of youth courts at Amtsgericht München, March 14, 1941, ARL, Lü 6.1.3 (München).

143. Reichsjugendführung, "Cliquen- und Bandenbildung unter Jugendlichen," Sept. 1942, BA, R22/1177; Reich justice minister to Oberlandesgerichtspräsidenten et al., Sept. [?] 1942, BA, R22/5018; Peukert and Winter, 259 (quote).

144. Thierack memo, Oct. 26, 1944, enclosed with Jugendführer to Führer der Gebiete und Banne, Dec. 10, 1944, BA, R22/1177; Arno Klönne, *Jugend im Dritten Reich: Die Hitler-Jugend und ihre Gegner: Dokumente und Analysen* (Düsseldorf, 1982), 253–254; Kenkmann, 202; Jahnke and Buddrus, 239–243; Von Hellfeld, 126, 133, 171.

145. Kenkmann, 130–132, 203; Von Hellfeld, 130–132; Peukert and Winter, 253, 255.

146. Reichsjugendführung, "Cliquen- und Bandenbildung unter Jugendlichen," Sept. 1942, BA, R22/1177.

147. See the reservations expressed in "Vermerk über eine Besprechung am 16. August 1939 über die Behandlung der sogenannten Meuten in Leipzig," BA, R22/25.

148. Minutes of judgment against Hess et al., Oct. 28, 1938, IfZ, Fa 117/6.

149. Minutes of judgment against Pfloksch et al., June 15, 1942, BA, R22/1177; Jahnke and Buddrus, 428–430; Gruchmann, 103–130.

150. Volksgerichtshof Berlin, judgment against Landgraf et al., Sept. 23, 1942, ARL, Parteikanzlei/Mikrofiches; Von Hellfeld and Klönne, 283–285; Jahnke, *Jugend,* 129–131; Prückner and Waldhier, 51.

151. See Gruchmann, 105, 123.

152. Paul Werner, "Die Einweisung in die polizeilichen Jugendschutzlager," *Deutsches Jugendrecht* 4 (1943): 96.

153. Wetzell, 235.

154. See Patrick Wagner, "Das Gesetz über die Behandlung Gemeinschafts-fremder: Die Kriminalpolizei und die 'Vernichtung des Verbrechertums,'" in Wolfgang Ayass et al., *Feinderklärung und Prävention: Kriminalbiologie, Zigeunerforschung und Asozialenpolitik* (Berlin, 1988), 77.

155. Rietzsch quoted in minutes of "Arbeitsgemeinschaft für Jugendstrafrecht in München am 21. u. 23.11.40," BA, R22/1180; Patrick Wagner, 83–84.

156. Bormann to Lammers, Aug. 30, 1941, BA, R43II/520c.

157. "Verordnung über die Vereinfachung und Vereinheitlichung der Jugend-strafvollstreckung vom 6.11.1943 (Reichsjugendgerichtsgesetz)," *Reichs-gesetzblatt I* (1943): 646; Thierack memo, Oct. 26, 1944 (as in n. 144).

158. Entry for Feb. 2, 1940, in *TGI* 4: 30 (quote); Jörg Wolff, *Jugendliche vor Gericht im Dritten Reich: Nationalsozialistische Jugendstrafrechtspolitik und Justizalltag* (Munich, 1992), 114–115.

159. Nebe/Schefe, "Die Handhabung der Pol. VO.," [March 1940], BA, R22/1176a; "Schutz der Jugend," *Mitteilungsblatt des Reichskriminal-polizeiamts* 3 (Apr. 1940): 239–250, (BA, R22/1175); Kriminalrätin Dr. Isa Koch, "Die Durchführung der Polizeiordnung zum Schutze der Jugend," *Die Ärztin* 17 (1941): 65–66.

160. Kater, *Drummers,* 157–158.

161. Ibid., 151; Rühlig and Steen, 122.

162. Kruse memo, [1942], BA, NL/289.

163. Von Hellfeld, 129.

164. Molden, 175–177.

165. Himmler to Axmann, Jan. 26, 1942, and to Heydrich, Jan. 26, 1942, BA, NS19/neu 219 (quote).

166. See Kater, *Drummers,* 111–211.

167. Madlung-Shelton recorded interview; Ursula Nielsen and Herbert Rönn recorded interview, Hamburg, June 20, 1988.

168. Albath, "Wilde Jugendgruppen—Edelweisspiraten," [spring 1943], BA, R22/1177.

169. Von Hellfeld and Klönne, 272.

170. Werner, "Schnellbrief," June 26, 1940, BA, R22/1189; Heinrich Muth, "Das 'Jugendschutzlager' Moringen," *Dachauer Hefte* 5 (Nov. 1989): 251. See also Gellately, *Hitler,* 46.

171. Joachim S. Hohmann, *Robert Ritter und die Erben der Kriminalbiologie:*

"Zigeunerforschung" im Nationalsozialismus und in Westdeutschland im Zeichen des Rassismus (Frankfurt am Main, 1991), 133–135 (quote, 135).

172. Ibid., 135–136; Robert Ritter, *Ein Menschenschlag: Erbärztliche und erbgeschichtliche Untersuchungen über die—durch 10 Geschlechterfolgen erforschten—Nachkommen von "Vagabunden, Jaunern und Räubern"* (Leipzig, 1937).

173. Hohmann, 136–140; Guenter Lewy, *The Nazi Persecution of the Gypsies* (New York, 2000).

174. Robert N. Proctor, *Racial Hygiene: Medicine Under the Nazis* (Cambridge, Mass., 1988); Michael H. Kater, *Doctors Under Hitler* (Chapel Hill, N.C., 1989).

175. Ferdinand von Neureiter, *Kriminalbiologie* (Berlin, 1940), esp. 5, 16 (quotes); Hohmann, 136–137.

176. Heinrich Wilhelm Kranz, *"Die Gemeinschaftsunfähigen" (Ein Beitrag zur wissenschaftlichen und praktischen Lösung des sog. "Asozialenproblems")* (Giessen, [1939]); Robert Ritter, "Erbärztliche Verbrechensverhütung," *Deutsche Medizinische Wochenschrift* (May 22, 1942): 536–539; Kater, *Doctors,* 115–119; Hohmann, 135; Wolff, 183.

177. Friedrich Schaffstein, *Die Erneuerung des Jugendstrafrechts* (Berlin, [1936]), 10.

178. Werner, 95.

179. On the latter concept, see Michael H. Kater, "Aufnordnung und Ausmerze: 'Volksgesundheit' im Nationalsozialismus: Ein biopolitisches Konzept und seine Anwendung," *Frankfurter Rundschau,* July 24, 2001.

180. Paul Werner, "Die Polizei in ihrem Kampf gegen die Gefährdung der Jugend," *Das Junge Deutschland* (1941): 243–244. See Wolfgang Ayass, ed., *"Gemeinschaftsfremde": Quellen zur Verfolgung von "Asozialen," 1933– 1945* (Koblenz, 1998), xix.

181. Hohmann, 146–148. See Robert Ritter, "Primitivität und Kriminalität," *Monatsschrift für Kriminalbiologie und Strafrechtsreform* 31 (1940): 197–210.

182. Werner, "Einweisung," 97–106; Werner to Kümmerlein, Sept. 6, 1944, BA, R22/1191 (quote).

183. "Dienstliche Anordnung," Moringen, Apr. 16, 1941 (second quote); Wolter-Pecksen to Direktor Landeswerkhaus, Aug. 7, 1942 (first quote), facs. in Martin Guse et al., "Das Jugendschutzlager Moringen—Ein Jugendkonzentrationslager," in Hans-Uwe Otto and Heinz Sühnker, eds., *Soziale Arbeit und Faschismus: Volkspflege und Pädagogik im Nationalsozialismus* (Bielefeld, 1986), 333, 339; Kümmerlein/Eichler travel re-

port, [Apr. 1942], BA, R22/1176; Schmidhäuser to Reichler, July 31, 1943, BA, R22/1306; Patrick Wagner, *Volksgemeinschaft ohne Verbrecher: Konzeptionen und Praxis der Kriminalpolizei in der Zeit der Weimarer Republik und des Nationalsozialismus* (Hamburg, 1996), 376; Hannah Vogt et al., *KZ Moringen—Männerlager, Frauenlager, Jugendschutzlager—Eine Dokumentation* (Göttingen, n.d.), 55.

184. Michael Hepp, "Vorhof zur Hölle: Mädchen im 'Jugendschutzlager' Uckermark," in Angelika Ebbinghaus, ed., *Opfer und Täterinnen: Frauenbiographien des Nationalsozialismus* (Nördlingen, 1987), 202–214 (quote, 211).

185. Patrick Wagner, *Volksgemeinschaft*, 377.

186. Werner, "Einweisung," 99–101; Maike Merten and Katja Limbächer, "Geschichte des Jugendschutzlagers Uckermark," in Katja Limbächer et al., eds., *Das Mädchenkonzentrationslager Uckermark* (Münster, 2000), 16–43.

187. Kümmerlein/Eichler travel report, [Apr. 1942], BA, R22/1176 (quote); Heermann to Oberlandesgerichtspräsident Hamm, July 31, 1944, BA, R22/1191; Paul Werner, "Die polizeilichen Jugendschutzlager," *Deutsche Jugendhilfe* 35 (1944): 101–105; Patrick Wagner, *Volksgemeinschaft*, 378–379.

188. Hepp, 200–201; Erwin Rehn, "Gedächtnisbericht über das Sonderlager (Jugendschutzlager) Moringen und über das Aussenlager Volpriehausen," *Mitteilungen der Dokumentationsstelle zur NS-Sozialpolitik* 1/9–10 (Nov./ Dec. 1985): 94.

189. Ursula Nielsen Rönn and Herbert Rönn recorded interview.

5. Hitler's Youth at War

1. BAB, SS personal file Herbert Taege. First two quotes, SS-Oberscharführer Kramer, "Beurteilungsnotiz," Dec. 1, 1943; last quote, SS-Hauptsturmführer, "Beurteilung," June 16, 1944.

2. Herbert Taege, *Über die Zeiten fort: Das Gesicht einer Jugend im Aufgang und Untergang: Wertung—Deutung—Erscheinung* (Lindhorst, 1978).

3. *Spiegel Online,* Oct. 7, 2002; *www.koninklijkhuis.nl/prinsclaus.*

4. See Omer Bartov, *Hitler's Army: Soldiers, Nazis, and War in the Third Reich* (New York, 1991), esp. 104–105, 108–109, 158–161. On the notorious model of Daniel Jonah Goldhagen, salacious generalizations about *all* German civilians as Nazi racists and *all* German soldiers as

master-race killers have been the subject of less than reliable scholarship. See Clarence Lusane, *Hitler's Black Victims: The Historical Experiences of Afro-Germans, European Blacks, Africans, and African-Americans in the Nazi Era* (New York, 2002), 153; and the egregious Fred Kautz, *Gold-Hagen und die "Hürnen Sewfriedte": Die Holocaust-Forschung im Sperrfeuer der Flakhelfer* (Berlin, 1998).

5. See Detlef Bald et al., *Mythos Wehrmacht: Nachkriegsdebatten und Traditionspflege* (Berlin, 2001), and the convincing testimonies in Michael Burleigh, *The Third Reich: A New History* (New York, 2001), 437, 493, 521, 623.

6. *Der Spiegel* (June 2, 2003): 42–46.

7. On December 30, 1944; quoted in Hermann Langer, "Das 'Gesicht der Schule'—Schüleraufsätze, 1939–1944," in Karl Heinz Jahnke et al., *Deutsche Jugend im Zweiten Weltkrieg* (Rostock, 1991), 77.

8. See the sensible remarks on this by Hans Mommsen, "Kriegserfahrungen," in Ulrich Borsdorf and Mathilde Jamin, eds., *Über Leben im Krieg: Kriegserfahrungen in einer Industrieregion, 1939–1945* (Reinbek, 1983), 8–13.

9. Ursula Baumann, *Vom Recht auf den eigenen Tod: Die Geschichte des Suizids vom 19. bis zum 20. Jahrhundert* (Weimar, 2001), 362.

10. Arne W. G. Zoepf, *Wehrmacht zwischen Tradition und Ideologie: Der NS-Führungsoffizier im Zweiten Weltkrieg* (Frankfurt am Main, 1988).

11. Wladyslaw Szpilman, *The Pianist: The Extraordinary Story of One Man's Survival in Warsaw, 1939–45* (Toronto, 2000), 177–181. See also Hosenfeld's diary, Jan. 18, 1942–Aug. 11, 1944, ibid., 193–208; Michael Beckerman, "The 'Pianist' DVD and the Case of the Missing Nocturne," *New York Times* (June 8, 2003).

12. A condemnable example of this can be found in Andreas Hillgruber, *Zweierlei Untergang: Die Zerschlagung des Deutschen Reiches und das Ende des europäischen Judentums* (Berlin, 1986); see esp. 16, 66–67. The early West German political background to this approach is mentioned in Robert G. Moeller, "War Stories: The Search for a Usable Past in the Federal Republic of Germany," *American Historical Review* 101 (1996): 1018–1019. For Moeller's concise analysis of Hillgruber, see p. 1042. See also Elizabeth Heineman, "The Hour of the Woman: Memories of Germany's 'Crisis Years' and West German National Identity," *American Historical Review* 101 (1996): 372, n. 40.

13. In his new novel *Im Krebsgang: Eine Novelle* (Göttingen, 2002). Grass quoted in *Der Spiegel* (Aug. 25, 2003): 143. On Grass's unsettled boyhood, see Hans Peter Brode, *Günter Grass* (Munich, 1979), 10–14; see also Patrick O'Neill, *Günter Grass Revisited* (New York, 1999), 1–13.

14. John M. Coetzee, "Victims," *New York Review of Books* (June 12, 2003): 24. See also Alan Riding, "Still Intrigued by History's Shadow: Günter Grass Worries About the Effects of War, Then as Now," *New York Times* (Apr. 8, 2003).

15. John Updike, "Suppressed Atrocities," *New Yorker* (Apr. 21/28, 2003): 186.

16. Ingrid Hammer and Susanne zur Nieden, eds., *Sehr selten habe ich geweint: Briefe und Tagebücher aus dem Zweiten Weltkrieg von Menschen in Berlin* (Zurich, 1992), 28–29; Joachim Dollwet, "Menschen im Krieg, Bejahung— und Widerstand? Eindrücke und Auszüge aus der Sammlung von Feldpost-briefen im Landeshauptarchiv Koblenz," *Jahrbuch für Westdeutsche Landes-geschichte* 13 (1987): 309; Walter Manoschek, ed., *"Es gibt nur eines für das Judentum: Vernichtung": Das Judenbild in deutschen Soldatenbriefen, 1939–1944* (Hamburg, 1995), 10; Volker Ullrich, "'Wir haben nichts gewusst'—Ein deutsches Trauma," *1999. Zeitschrift für Sozialgeschichte des 20. und 21. Jahrhunderts,* no. 4 (Oct. 1991): 35.

17. Kreutzer to Melcher, Nov. 24, 1939, in Hermann Melcher, *Die Gefolg-schaft: Jugendjahre im Dritten Reich in Heidelberg, 1933–1945* (Berg, 1990), 45–46.

18. See HJ leader Oskar Riegraf's letters to his wife Lotte from the Danish front, May 1940, SAL, PL 509/1/8; Siegbert Stehmann, *Die Bitternis ver-schweigen wir: Feldpostbriefe, 1940–1945,* ed. Gerhard Sprenger (Hanover, 1992), 30.

19. Quote from Helmut N.'s letter of June 12, 1940, in Marlies Tremper, ed., *Briefe des Soldaten Helmut N., 1939–1945* (Berlin, 1988), 63.

20. Fuchs to Mädi, Sept. 1, 1940, in Horst Fuchs Richardson, ed., *Sieg Heil! War Letters of Tank Gunner Karl Fuchs, 1937–1941* (Hamden, Conn., 1987), 77. See also ibid., 68–69, 72–73; Tremper, 61–62, 67; Herbert Johannes Veigel, *Christbäume: Briefe aus dem Krieg* (Berlin, 1991), 34.

21. Quote from Hans Olte in Poland, Apr. 3, 1941, in Klaus Latzel, *Deutsche Soldaten—nationalsozialistischer Krieg? Kriegserlebnis—Kriegserfahrung, 1939–1945* (Paderborn, 1998), 46.

22. FPN 39690 to family, Nov. 17, 1940, in Manoschek, 18. See also ibid., 16–17, 19; Ullrich, 20.

23. See Wolfgang De Bruyn's undated letter (summer 1941) in Günter De Bruyn, *Zwischenbilanz: Eine Jugend in Berlin* (Frankfurt am Main, 1995), 126. Wehrmacht figure according to Bartov, 36.

24. Hellmut to parents, June 22, 1941, in Hammer and Zur Nieden, 126; also Latzel, 89.

25. Veigel, 53, 89; Jürgen Brautmeier, "'Frontbewährung' in Stalingrad:

Feldpostbriefe des Gefreiten Hans Happe aus Delbrück/Westfalen," *Geschichte im Westen* 8 (1993): 170; Omer Bartov, *The Eastern Front, 1941–45: German Troops and the Barbarisation of Warfare* (New York, 1986), 23–24.

26. Hitler quoted in Jay W. Baird, *The Mythical World of Nazi War Propaganda, 1939–1945* (Minneapolis, 1974), 177.

27. Bartov, *Front,* 83–87; Bartov, *Army,* 83; Lothar Gruchmann, *Der Zweite Weltkrieg: Kriegführung und Politik* (Munich, 1967), 127.

28. Anon. letter, June 26, 1941, in Dollwet, 298 (first two quotes); Korri to Darling, Aug. 3, 1941, in Fuchs Richardson, 122 (last quote). The recurring cattle image is also found in Ortwin Buchbender and Reinhold Sterz, eds., *Das andere Gesicht des Krieges: Deutsche Feldpostbriefe, 1939–1945* (Munich, 1982), 85.

29. Udo von Alvensleben, *Lauter Abschiede: Tagebuch vom Kriege,* ed. Harald von Koenigswald (Frankfurt am Main, 1971), 201.

30. Christian Streit, *Keine Kameraden: Die Wehrmacht und die sowjetischen Kriegsgefangenen, 1941–1945* (Stuttgart, 1978); Gerhard L. Weinberg, *A World at Arms: A Global History of World War II* (Cambridge, 1994), 300; Bartov, *Front,* 107–119; Bartov, *Army,* 88–89.

31. Bartov, *Army,* 83.

32. Hans-Ulrich Greffrath in Johannes Steinhoff et al., eds., *Voices from the Third Reich: An Oral History* (New York, 1994), 277 (quote); Brautmeier, 172.

33. Franzl to parents, July 6, 1941, in Manoschek, 33 (quote); Veigel, 60; Hammer and Zur Nieden, 127.

34. Gruchmann, 131; Weinberg, 300; Bartov, *Army,* 84–87.

35. Bartov, *Front,* 99, 119–126; Bartov, *Army,* 65; Iring Fetscher, *Neugier und Furcht: Versuch, mein Leben zu verstehen* (Hamburg, 1995), 92; Ullrich, 21–22, 24; Ernst Klee et al., eds., *"The Good Old Days": The Holocaust as Seen by Its Perpetrators and Bystanders* (New York, 1991), 107–135. On the soldiers' hatred of Jews on the Russian campaign trail, see Ullrich, 23, 36; Manoschek, 32, 40, 62; Dollwet, 299.

36. Veigel, 53; Hammer and Zur Nieden, 127; Latzel, 55.

37. Latzel, 70; Tremper, 133–134.

38. Guido Knopp, *Hitlers Kinder,* 2nd ed. (Munich, 2000), 285.

39. Hans-Joachim Schröder, "'Man kam sich da vor wie ein Stück Dreck': Schikane in der Militärausbildung des Dritten Reichs," in Wolfram Wette, ed., *Der Krieg des kleinen Mannes: Eine Militärgeschichte von unten,* 2nd ed. (Munich, 1995), 189–194.

40. Jürgen Peiffer, *Vergangenheit, gebrochener Spiegel: Erinnerungen* (Tübingen, 2000), 91.

41. Ralf Roland Ringler, *Illusion einer Jugend: Lieder, Fahnen und das bittere Ende: Hitlerjugend in Österreich: Ein Erlebnisbericht* (St. Pölten, 1977), 98.

42. Melcher, 112–113. Similarly, see Leopold A. in Stefanie Reichelt, *"Für mich ist der Krieg aus!": Deserteure und Kriegsdienstverweigerer des Zweiten Weltkrieges in München* (Munich, 1995), 187.

43. Hans Graf von Lehndorff, *Die Briefe des Peter Pfaff, 1943–1944,* 3rd ed. (Munich, 1988), 95; Kurt Abels, *Ein Held war ich nicht: Als Kind und Jugendlicher in Hitlers Krieg* (Cologne, 1998), 117–118.

44. Willy Schumann, *Being Present: Growing Up in Hitler's Germany* (Kent, Ohio, 1991), 142–153.

45. Bartov, *Army,* 14–15.

46. Weinberg, 270–309 (quote, 298); Gruchmann, 128–132.

47. Stehmann to wife, July 23, 1941, in Stehmann, 116. See also Bartov, *Front,* 21–22.

48. Veigel, 96; Wolfgang Wiesen, ed., *Es grüsst Euch alle, Bertold: Von Koblenz nach Stalingrad: Die Feldpostbriefe des Pioniers Bertold Paulus aus Kastel* (Nonnweiler-Otzenhausen, 1991), 63–64; Bartov, *Front,* 24–25.

49. Von Alvensleben, 217; Veigel, 97, 109; Karl Heinz Jahnke, *Hitlers letztes Aufgebot: Deutsche Jugend im sechsten Kriegsjahr, 1944/45* (Essen, 1993), 155; Bartov, *Front,* 22.

50. Nielsen to family, May 28, 1940, in Walter Bähr and Hans Bähr, eds., *Kriegsbriefe gefallener Studenten, 1939–1945* (Tübingen, 1952), 27.

51. Ibid., 300–301; Bartov, *Front,* 26–27.

52. Friedrich Grupe, *Jahrgang 1916: Die Fahne war mehr als der Tod* (Munich, 1989), 161.

53. Kurt Meyer-Grell quoted in Steinhoff et al., 139.

54. Greffrath quoted ibid., 278.

55. Günter Kaufmann, *Das kommende Deutschland: Die Erziehung der Jugend im Reich Adolf Hitlers,* 3rd ed. (Berlin, 1943), 317.

56. Peter Pechel quoted in Steinhoff et al., 133. See also Hammer and Zur Nieden, 23; Buchbender and Sterz, 54; Peiffer, 94.

57. Horst Lange, *Tagebücher aus dem Zweiten Weltkrieg,* ed. Hans Dieter Schäfer (Mainz, 1979), 87. See also Veigel, 159; Von Alvensleben, 254.

58. Hans Joachim Schröder, *Die gestohlenen Jahre: Erzählgeschichten und Geschichtserzählung im Interview: Der Zweite Weltkrieg aus der Sicht ehemaliger Mannschaftssoldaten* (Tübingen, 1992), 678.

59. Bernhard Haupert and Franz Josef Schäfer, *Jugend zwischen Kreuz und

Hakenkreuz: Biographische Rekonstruktion als Alltagsgeschichte des Faschismus (Frankfurt am Main, 1991), 220. See the text of this chapter at n. 211.

60. Hermann to Rosl, Feb. 28, 1942, in Anatoly Golovchansky et al., *"Ich will raus aus diesem Wahnsinn": Deutsche Briefe von der Ostfront, 1941–1945: Aus sowjetischen Archiven* (Wuppertal, 1991), 67–68. See also ibid., 180; Bähr and Bähr, 301; Bartov, *Front,* 90–91.

61. Hess to Herta, July 22, 1943, in Latzel, 337.

62. Fetscher, 184.

63. Melcher, 168. See also Bartov, *Army,* 25.

64. Bähr and Bähr, 66; Weinberg, 264, 273, 279, 284; Alan Clark, *Barbarossa: The Russian-German Conflict, 1941–45* (New York, 1965), 167.

65. Von Alvensleben, 254.

66. Fetscher, 129; Henry Metelmann, *A Hitler Youth: Growing up in Germany in the 1930s* (London, 1997), 234–235; Veigel, 200; Claus B. Schröder, *Wolfgang Borchert: Biografie* (Hamburg, 1985), 175–176. For official Wehrmacht condemnation of such liaisons, see Bartov, *Front,* 126–129.

67. Burleigh, 530–531; Andreas Hillgruber, "Einführung," in Hillgruber, ed., *Von El Alamein bis Stalingrad: Aus dem Kriegstagebuch des Oberkommandos der Wehrmacht* (Munich, 1964), 7–13; Weinberg, 408–410; Ian Kershaw, *Hitler, 1936–1945: Nemesis* (New York, 2000), 530.

68. William L. Langer, ed., *An Encyclopedia of World History* (Boston, 1968), 1143; *Spiegel Online* (Jan. 29, 2003); *Der Spiegel* (Dec. 16, 2002): 68; Gruchmann, 187–194; Weinberg, 410–417, 420–425 (first quote, 422); entry for Sept. 19, 1942, in Thomas Mann, *Tagebücher, 1940–43,* ed. Peter de Mendelssohn (Frankfurt am Main, 1982), 475 (second quote).

69. The national cover-up is expertly dealt with in Baird, 175–190.

70. Kershaw, 547.

71. Brautmeier, 186; Wiesen, 112. See also Walter Görlitz, ed., *Paulus und Stalingrad: Lebensweg des Generalfeldmarschalls Friedrich Paulus* (Frankfurt am Main, 1964), 255–258.

72. Brautmeier, 175, 178–179, 184, 186; Wiesen, 108–109, 113; Golovchansky, 234–235.

73. Rüdiger Overmans, "Das andere Gesicht des Krieges: Leben und Sterben der 6. Armee," in Jürgen Förster, ed., *Stalingrad: Ereignis—Wirkung—Symbol,* 2nd ed. (Munich, 1993), 420–424, 427; Brautmeier, 175, 179, 185; Wiesen, 108–109, 112–113; Diether Cartellieri, *Die deutschen Kriegsgefangenen in der Sowjetunion: Die Lagergesellschaft: Eine Untersuchung der zwischenmenschlichen Beziehungen in den Kriegsgefangenenlagern* (Munich, 1967), 12–13; *Der Spiegel* (Dec. 16, 2002): 66.

74. Overmans, 422, 426; Brautmeier, 175, 179; Cartellieri, 12–13.

75. Quoted in Overmans, 426. See also ibid., 427–428; Wiesen, 108; Cartellieri, 12; *Der Spiegel* (Dec. 16, 2002): 51.

76. On this phenomenon see Ian Kershaw, *The "Hitler Myth": Image and Reality in the Third Reich* (Oxford, 1987).

77. Joseph Goebbels, "Was ist ein Opfer?", Dec. 28, 1941, in Goebbels, *Das eherne Herz: Reden und Aufsätze aus den Jahren 1941/42,* ed. M. A. Schirmeister (Munich, 1943), 150.

78. Peiffer, 92, 94; Hammer and Zur Nieden, 227–228.

79. Erhard Eppler, *Als Wahrheit verordnet wurde: Briefe an meine Enkelin,* 3rd ed. (Frankfurt am Main, 1995), 153–154.

80. Bähr and Bähr, 67; Von Alvensleben, 203; Melcher, 243–244.

81. See Emmrich's memoirs under the pen name Peter Bamm, *Die unsichtbare Flagge: Ein Bericht,* 8th ed. (Munich, 1957), 199–200; also, from the ideologically opposite point of view, Joseph Goebbels, *Der steile Aufstieg: Reden und Aufsätze aus den Jahren 1942/43,* ed. M. A. Schirmeister (Munich, 1943), 27–28.

82. Steinhoff et al., 133; Buchbender and Sterz, 92; Melcher, 255.

83. Entry for March 23, 1944, in Heinz Boberach, ed., *Meldungen aus dem Reich: Die geheimen Lageberichte des Sicherheitsdienstes der SS, 1938–1945* (Herrsching, 1984), vol. 16, 6439–6445 (quote, 6443). See also Kurt Hass, ed., *Jugend unterm Schicksal: Lebensberichte junger Deutscher, 1946–1949* (Hamburg, 1950), 33–35.

84. *TGII,* vol. 12, 224; *TGII,* vol. 13, 518; Fetscher, 188; Helmut Altner, *Totentanz Berlin: Tagebuchblätter eines Achzehnjährigen* (Offenbach, 1947), 194–195, 204–205; Fred Borth, *Nicht zu jung zum Sterben: Die "Hitler-Jugend" im Kampf um Wien 1945* (Vienna, 1988), 150–152.

85. Ringler, 112.

86. J. S. quoted in Buchbender and Sterz, 40–41.

87. Hammer and Zur Nieden, 230, 243, 250–251; Hartmut von Hentig, *Aufgeräumte Erfahrung: Texte zur eigenen Person* (Munich, 1983), 34; Bähr and Bähr, 134–135. On the Wehrmacht's looting, burning, and destruction, see Bartov, *Front,* 129–136.

88. Entry for Sept. 4, 1941, in Lange, 26 (quote); Ringler, 97.

89. Veigel, 107.

90. Von Hentig, 40. See also Theo Baumeister in Gudrun Norbisrath, ed., *Gestohlene Jugend: Der Zweite Weltkrieg in Erinnerungen* (Essen, 2000), 38–39.

91. Hammer and Zur Nieden, 138; Bertram Otto, *"Wussten wir auch nicht, wohin es geht . . .": Erinnerungen, 1927–1947* (Munich, 2000), 208; Max

von der Grün, *Howl like the Wolves: Growing up in Nazi Germany* (New York, 1980), 253–254; Jahnke et al., *Jugend,* 187–188.

92. Otto, 198–199; De Bruyn, 227.

93. P. G. quoted in Buchbender and Sterz, 123.

94. Baumann, 358.

95. See excerpt from "Militärstrafgesetzbuch," Oct. 10, 1940, in Reichelt, 28; ibid., 29; Bartov, *Army,* 97–100.

96. Reichelt, 29; Norbert Haase, *Deutsche Deserteure* (Berlin, 1987), 23.

97. Reichelt, 27, 106; Jahnke, *Aufgebot,* 73.

98. Gerhard Paul, *Ungehorsame Soldaten: Dissens, Verweigerung und Widerstand deutscher Soldaten (1939–1945)* (St. Ingbert, 1994), 52; Haase, 41. An example of the latter case is in Steinhoff et al., 109.

99. Horst Krüger, *Das zerbrochene Haus: Eine Jugend in Deutschland,* 2nd ed. (Munich, 1967), 206–213.

100. Heinz A. Brenner, *Dagegen: Bericht über den Widerstand von Schülern des Humanistischen Gymnasiums Ulm/Donau gegen die deutsche nationalsozialistische Diktatur* (Leutkirch, [1992]), 39–41. A similar case is related in Reichelt, 190–191.

101. Dieter Knippschild, "'Für mich ist der Krieg aus': Deserteure in der Deutschen Wehrmacht," in Norbert Haase and Gerhard Paul, eds., *Die anderen Soldaten: Wehrkraftzersetzung, Gehorsamsverweigerung und Fahnenflucht im Zweiten Weltkrieg* (Frankfurt am Main, 1995), 133. See also Paul, 64.

102. Hermine Wüllner, ed., *". . . kann nur der Tod die gerechte Sühne sein": Todesurteile deutscher Wehrmachtsgerichte: Eine Dokumentation* (Baden-Baden, 1997), 40–43.

103. Haase, 52 (quote). See also Krüger, 199–201; Bähr and Bähr, 238–241.

104. See Altner, 20–21.

105. Knippschild, 137. See also Elisabeth Abendroth, ed., *Deserteure im Zweiten Weltkrieg: Vaterlandsverräter oder Widerständler* (Oberursel, 1989), 30–31.

106. Ingrid van Bergen, "Mit 13 begegnete ich zum erstenmal dem Tod," *Bild am Sonntag,* Aug. 14, 1977. See also Altner, 86–87; Erhard Lucas-Busemann, *So fielen Königsberg und Breslau: Nachdenken über eine Katastrophe ein halbes Jahrhundert danach* (Berlin, 1994), 59; Doris K. in Lothar Steinbach, *Ein Volk, ein Reich, ein Glaube? Ehemalige Nationalsozialisten und Zeitzeugen berichten über ihr Leben im Dritten Reich* (Berlin, 1983), 104.

107. "Verordnung über das Sonderstrafrecht im Kriege und bei besonderem

Einsatz (Kriegssonderstrafrechtsverordnung)," Aug. 17, 1938, *Reichsgesetzblatt I* (Aug. 26, 1939): 1455.

108. Michael H. Kater, *Doctors Under Hitler* (Chapel Hill, N.C., 1989), 51, 83.

109. Paul, 91.

110. Reichelt, 29.

111. Jahnke, *Aufgebot,* 73.

112. Overmans, 421, 424.

113. Reichelt, 64–65.

114. Ibid., 62–63.

115. Schröder, *Borchert,* 56, 145, 158–164, 185, 232–322; Peter Rühmkorf, *Wolfgang Borchert in Selbstzeugnissen und Bilddokumenten* (Reinbek, 1966).

116. On the Third Reich's gubernatorial structure, see Peter Hüttenberger, "Nationalsozialistische Polykratie," *Geschichte und Gesellschaft* 2 (1976): 417–442; Reinhard Bollmus, *Das Amt Rosenberg und seine Gegner: Studien zum Machtkampf im nationalsozialistischen Herrschaftssystem* (Stuttgart, 1970); Hans Mommsen, "Hitlers Stellung im nationalsozialistischen Herrschaftssystem," in Gerhard Hirschfeld and Lothar Kettenacker, eds., *Der "Führerstaat": Mythos und Realität: Studien zur Struktur und Politik des Dritten Reiches* (Stuttgart, 1981), 43–72.

117. See the text of Chapter 3 at n. 74.

118. Wolfgang Benz, "Vom Freiwilligen Arbeitsdienst zur Arbeitsdienstpflicht," *Vierteljahrshefte für Zeitgeschichte* 16 (1968): 317–346; Michael H. Kater, *Studentenschaft und Rechtsradikalismus in Deutschland, 1918–1933: Eine sozialgeschichtliche Studie zur Bildungskrise in der Weimarer Republik* (Hamburg, 1975), 115, 167–172; Konstantin Hierl, "Die Leistung des Freiwilligen Arbeitsdienstes (Kongressrede)," in *Der Kongress zu Nürnberg vom 5. bis 10. September 1934: Offizieller Bericht über den Verlauf des Reichsparteitages mit sämtlichen Reden* (Munich, 1934), 180–186; Manfred Seifert, *Kulturarbeit im Reichsarbeitsdienst: Theorie und Praxis nationalsozialistischer Kulturpflege im Kontext historisch-politischer, organisatorischer und ideologischer Einflüsse* (Münster, 1996), 27–89; Kurt Stamm, ed., *Der Reichsarbeitsdienst: Reichsarbeitsdienstgesetz mit ergänzenden Bestimmungen und Erläuterungen,* 3rd ed. (Berlin, 1940), 287; Schumann, 136.

119. Stamm, 1.

120. Hermann Kretzschmann, "Der Reichsarbeitsdienst der männlichen Jugend," in Rudolf Benze and Gustav Gräfer, eds., *Erziehungsmächte und Erziehungshoheit im Grossdeutschen Reich als gestaltende Kräfte im Leben*

des Deutschen (Leipzig, 1940), 124; Ringler, 94; Martin Cranz, *Ich, ein Deutscher* (Dülmen, 1987), 176–177; Eppler, 128; Schumann, 139.

121. Hellmut Petersen, *Die Erziehung der deutschen Jungmannschaft im Reichsarbeitsdienst* (Berlin, 1938), 11, 102.

122. The functionality of the spade cult is justified in Petersen, 70–72.

123. Ibid., 80–91; [Martin] Eisenbeck, ed., *Mit Spaten und Waffe in Feindesland: Reichsarbeitsdienst und seine Bautruppen im Feldzug in Polen 1939* (Leipzig, 1939); Grupe, 67–69; De Bruyn, 178–179; Cranz, 176–177, 181, 186; Eppler, 126–138; Schumann, 136–139. On the ineffectiveness of RAD, see Seifert, 100.

124. Artur Axmann, *"Das kann doch nicht das Ende sein": Hitlers letzter Reichsjugendführer erinnert sich,* 2nd ed. (Koblenz, 1995), 282–288. See also Karl Heinz Jahnke and Michael Buddrus, eds., *Deutsche Jugend, 1933–1945: Eine Dokumentation* (Hamburg, 1989), 328–329, 333–334.

125. *Hitler-Jugend, 1933–1943: Die Chronik eines Jahrzehnts* (Berlin, [1943]), 60; Axmann, 283; Jahnke and Buddrus, 365–366; Christoph Schubert-Weller, *Hitlerjugend: Vom "Jungsturm Adolf Hitler" zur Staatsjugend des Dritten Reiches* (Weinheim, 1993), 202–203; Robert Wistrich, *Who's Who in Nazi Germany* (New York, 1982), 7.

126. Axmann, 285; Reich education minister to Unterrichtsverwaltungen et al., Dec. 20, 1944; Brunswick minister of finance to state bureaucracy, Feb. 13, 1945, NSAW, 12 A, Neu, 13h/19597.

127. *Hitler-Jugend . . . Chronik,* 60; Jahnke and Buddrus, 354; Hans Holzträger, *Die Wehrertüchtigungslager der Hitler-Jugend, 1942–1945: Ein Dokumentarbericht* (Ippesheim, 1991), 17–21.

128. Gerhard Rempel, *Hitler's Children: The Hitler Youth and the SS* (Chapel Hill, N.C., 1989), 186.

129. As Gauleiter, Schirach had proceeded to rule Vienna as a personal fiefdom and, with his particular interest in an autonomous cultural policy, was, next to Hitler, raising the ire of Goebbels. See Oliver Rathkolb, *Führertreu und gottbegnadet: Künstlereliten im Dritten Reich* (Vienna, 1991).

130. Dieter Wellershoff in Marcel Reich-Ranicki, ed., *Meine Schulzeit im Dritten Reich: Erinnerungen deutscher Schriftsteller* (Munich, 1984), 149; Axmann, 284, 286–287; Siegfried Lenz, *Beziehungen: Ansichten und Bekenntnisse zur Literatur* (Hamburg, 1970), 24; Knopp, 25–56.

131. *Der Spiegel* (Jan. 6, 2003): 45; Michael H. Kater, *Different Drummers: Jazz in the Culture of Nazi Germany* (New York, 1992), 112.

132. Burleigh, 744.

133. Weinberg, 418–419; Heinz Bude, *Deutsche Karrieren: Lebenskonstruktionen sozialer Aufsteiger aus der Flakhelfer-Generation* (Frankfurt am Main, 1987), 23; Ludwig Schätz, *Schüler-Soldaten: Die Geschichte der Luftwaffenhelfer im Zweiten Weltkrieg* (Frankfurt am Main, 1972), 22; Ludger Tewes, *Jugend im Krieg: Von Luftwaffenhelfern und Soldaten, 1939–1945* (Essen, 1989), 40.

134. *Der Spiegel* (Jan. 6, 2003): 45.

135. Tewes, 38–39, 42; Rolf Schörken, "'Schülersoldaten'—Prägung einer Generation," in Rolf-Dieter Müller and Hans-Erich Volkmann, eds., *Die Wehrmacht: Mythos und Realität* (Munich, 1999), 457; Hans Josef Horchem, *Kinder im Krieg: Kindheit und Jugend im Dritten Reich* (Hamburg, 2000), 142.

136. Jahnke and Buddruss, 359–361; Horchem, 142; Hans-Dietrich Nicolaisen, *Die Flakhelfer: Luftwaffenhelfer und Marinehelfer im Zweiten Weltkrieg* (Berlin, 1981), 11; Schörken, 456; Jahnke, *Aufgebot,* 137. On industrial apprentices, see Schätz, 73; Axmann, 332, 349–350; Jahnke, *Aufgebot,* 63; Schörken, 459.

137. Friedhelm Golücke, *Schweinfurt und der strategische Luftkrieg 1943: Der Angriff der US Air Force vom 14. Oktober 1943 gegen die Schweinfurter Kugellagerindustrie* (Paderborn, 1980), esp. 55–57; Thomas Childers, *Wings of Morning: The Story of the Last American Bomber Shot Down over Germany in World War II* (Reading, Mass., 1995); Georg W. Feuchter, *Der Luftkrieg,* 3rd ed. (Frankfurt am Main, 1964), 174–267.

138. Friedrich Juchter, *Formeln, Fahnen, Flakgeschütze: Eine deutsche Jugend zwischen Schule und Kriegsdienst (1934–1947),* 2nd ed. (Oldenburg, 1999), 154; Schörken, 458.

139. Weinberg, 567–568.

140. Tewes, 40, 63; Schumann, 121; Ernst A. Itschert et al., *"Feuer frei— Kinder!": Eine missbrauchte Generation—Flakhelfer im Einsatz* (Saarbrücken, 1984), 34, 37; Juchter, 164, 166.

141. There are not even approximate estimates for dead or wounded. See Tewes, 43.

142. Schätz, 39; Schörken, 460.

143. Mantz quoted in *Der Spiegel* (Jan. 27, 2003): 63.

144. Schätz, 39; Schörken, 460; Peter Boenisch cited in Knopp, 280.

145. Itschert et al., 42.

146. Horchem, 167.

147. Tewes, 43.

148. Cranz, 165.

149. Nicolaisen, 20. See also ibid., 53.

150. Itschert et. al., 45–46, 186; Nicolaisen, 22–23; Abels, 61–62.

151. Itschert et al., 155.

152. Tewes, 127; Nicolaisen, 39.

153. Nicolaisen, 94; Knopp, 281.

154. Schörken, 458.

155. Itschert et al., 123; Cranz, 149.

156. Itschert et al., 49, 85–86; Martin Greiffenhagen, *Jahrgang 1928: Aus einem unruhigen Leben* (Munich, 1988), 49; Wolfgang Klafki in Klafki, *Verführung, Distanzierung, Ernüchterung: Kindheit und Jugend im National- sozialismus: Autobiographisches aus erziehungswissenschaftlicher Sicht* (Wein- heim, 1988), 141, 161. See the text of Chapter 4 at n. 111.

157. Nicolaisen, 215–216; Itschert et al., 87; Cornelia Rühlig and Jürgen Steen, eds., *Walter: *1926, +1945 an der Ostfront: Leben und Lebensbedin- gungen eines Frankfurter Jungen im III. Reich* (Frankfurt am Main, 1983), 126; Greiffenhagen, 51.

158. Schörken, 466; Tewes, 137; Schumann, 123; De Bruyn, 142.

159. Schumann, 122 (quote). This complaint is echoed in Horchem, 190; Cranz, 150; Eppler, 121; and Abels, 80. For drill details see Itschert et al., 35–36, 123; Juchter, 166; Gunter Otto in Klafki, 127.

160. Eppler, 120–121; Itschert et al., 33–34; Knopp, 279–280.

161. Eppler, 121.

162. Rommel quoted in Schörken, 462. See also Juchter, 164; Horchem, 168; Abels, 80; Itschert et al., 40.

163. Willy Jung, "Junge Luftwaffenhelfer," *Das Reich,* Feb. 21, 1943 (quote); *Das Junge Deutschland* (1943): 87; Nicolaisen, 168.

164. Nicolaisen, 11.

165. Schätz, 57.

166. Rolf Schörken, *Luftwaffenhelfer und Drittes Reich: Die Entstehung eines po- litischen Bewusstseins,* 2nd ed. (Stuttgart, 1985), 118; Schörken, "Schüler- soldaten," 466; Abels, 80; Greiffenhagen, 51; Itschert et al., 48–49, 86.

167. "Reichsbefehl 32/44 K," Sept. 21, 1944, in Nicolaisen, 164–167.

168. Schätz, 56.

169. Wolfgang Klafki in Klafki, 141; Gunter Otto ibid., 126; De Bruyn, 141; Cranz, 173; Schätz, 56; Heinz Boberach, *Jugend unter Hitler* (Düsseldorf, 1982), 127.

170. Eppler, 124; Itschert et al., 35, 126; De Bruyn, 144; Cranz, 156–157; Tewes, 46.

171. "Luftwaffenhelferzeugnis," July 13, 1944, in Hans Scherer, *Ich war Oberschüler und Luftwaffenhelfer, 1927–1948,* vol. 2 (Staffelstein, 1996),

21; Schörken, "Schülersoldaten," 457; Wolfgang Klafki in Klafki, 141; Itschert et al., 133; De Bruyn, 141.

172. Schörken, "Schülersoldaten," 457.

173. Ibid.; Itschert et al., 133.

174. On this concern and the regime's attempt to alleviate it, see entry for July 22, 1943, in Boberach, *Meldungen,* vol. 14, 5521; General Zenetti, "An die Eltern der Luftwaffenhelfer (HJ)," Apr. 11, 1944, in Itschert et al., n.p.; Tewes, 42; Juchter, 156.

175. Wolfgang Klafki in Klafki, 140–141; Tewes, 44; Itschert et al., 37; Schumann, 127; Greiffenhagen, 48.

176. Itschert et al., 36–37; Greiffenhagen, 48.

177. Juchter, 215; Tewes, 86; Greiffenhagen, 52; De Bruyn, 150–151. On the Russian *Hiwis,* see Bartov, *Front,* 138–139.

178. Wolfgang Klafki in Klafki, 161; Schörken, "Schülersoldaten," 465, 467.

179. For an example, see Hildegard Knef, *The Gift Horse: Report on a Life* (London, 1971), 43.

180. Kater, *Drummers,* 195; Hans-Martin Stimpel in Klafki, 116; De Bruyn, 174; Itschert et al., 43; Tewes, 337; Schörken, "Luftwaffenhelfer," 227; Cranz, 156–157, 173.

181. Heinz Höhne, *Der Orden unter dem Totenkopf: Die Geschichte der SS* (Gütersloh, 1967), 414–421.

182. Ibid., 413–414; Bernd Wegner, *Hitlers Politische Soldaten: Die Waffen-SS, 1933–1945: Studien zu Leitbild, Struktur und Funktion einer nationalsozialistischen Elite* (Paderborn, 1982), 217–242; Toni Sch. in *Jugend im nationalsozialistischen Frankfurt: Ausstellungsdokumentation, Zeitzeugenerinnerungen, Publikum* (Frankfurt am Main, 1987), 324–325; Eva Sternheim-Peters, *Die Zeit der grossen Täuschungen: Eine Jugend im Nationalsozialismus* (Bielefeld, 1992), 331; Rempel, esp. 206, 214.

183. See the text of Chapter 2 at n. 255; the text of Chapter 4 at n. 120.

184. George H. Stein, *The Waffen-SS: Hitler's Elite Guard at War, 1939–1945* (Ithaca, N.Y., 1966), 34–35.

185. Franz-Werner Kersting, *Militär und Jugend im NS-Staat: Rüstungs- und Schulpolitik der Wehrmacht* (Wiesbaden, 1989), 92–98, 412–421.

186. Matthias von Hellfeld and Arno Klönne, *Die betrogene Generation: Jugend in Deutschland unter dem Faschismus* (Cologne, 1985), 257, 259–262; Jahnke and Buddrus, 316.

187. Theo Loch in Steinhoff et al., 493; Maili Hochhuth, *Schulzeit auf dem Lande, 1933–1945: Gespräche und Untersuchungen über die Jahre 1933–1945* (Kassel, 1985), 216; Jahnke and Buddrus, 307; Sternheim-Peters, 330.

188. Fetscher, 46; Franz Schönhuber, *Ich war dabei,* 3rd ed. (Munich, 1981), 59–61; Wolfgang Klafki in Klafki, 165; Knopp, 322–323; Eppler, 118; Peter Petersen in Steinhoff et al., 9; Jörg Andrees in Winfried Maass, *Die Fünfzigjährigen: Portrait eine verratenen Generation* (Hamburg, 1980), 38–39; Rempel, 215.

189. Höhne, 428.

190. See Juchter, 264–265.

191. Toni Sch. in *Jugend . . . Frankfurt,* 324; Eppler, 114 (quote).

192. Excerpt report of Navy command, June 17, 1941, in Jahnke and Buddrus, 338 (first quote); Bingger to Ohneberg, Apr. 30, 1942, BA, NS28/25 (second quote).

193. On the former, see Gahrmann to Kaltenbrunner, [summer/fall 1942], BA, Schumacher/474.

194. Höhne, 436–437; Stein, 170–171. Later among ethnic Germans anywhere beyond the Reich's borders. See South Tyrolian Paul Tasser's testimony in Steinhoff et al., 108–109.

195. Eppler, 114–115. See also Alfons Heck, *A Child of Hitler: Germany in the Days when God Wore a Swastika* (Frederick, Colo., 1985), 42.

196. Wolfgang Klafki in Klafki, 165–166; Hans-Martin Stimpel ibid., 117; De Bruyn, 142; Schörken, *Luftwaffenhelfer,* 148–149; Schörken, "Schülersoldaten," 470; entry for March 18–22, 1945, in Nicolaisen, 212; Greiffenhagen, 52.

197. Jüttner to Himmler, Nov. 12, 1942, BA, Schumacher/474; entry for Aug. 1, 1943, in Klaus Granzow, *Tagebuch eines Hitlerjungen, 1943–1945* (Bremen, 1965), 32; Holzträger, 31; Knopp, 285; Rempel, 188–191. On the peremptory skull examination, see Melcher, 228.

198. Stein, 204–205.

199. Martin Broszat et al., eds., *Bayern in der NS-Zeit: Soziale Lage und politisches Verhalten der Bevölkerung im Spiegel vertraulicher Berichte* (Munich, 1977), 165–166; Cranz, 190–191; Knopp, 286.

200. Himmler to Bormann, May 14, 1943, in Jahnke and Buddrus, 368–369.

201. Schlünder to Stinglwagner, Jan. 22, 1944; Brandl to HJ-Banne et al., Feb. 9, 1944; Miller to Führer and K-Führer, Jan. 5, 1945; Flade to Höhere SS- und Polizeiführer, Feb. 11, 1945, BA, Schumacher/239; Broszat et al., 683; Jahnke and Buddrus, 362; Knopp, 286; Rempel, 213.

202. Monthly report of Regierungspäsident Regensburg, Feb. 10, 1944, BA, Schumacher/483 (quote); Axmann to Stinglwagner, Apr. 14, 1944, BA, Schumacher/239; Broszat et al., 179.

203. Hubert Meyer, *Kriegsgeschichte der 12. SS-Panzerdivision "Hitlerjugend"* (Osnabrück, 1982), vol. 1, 24.

204. Ibid., 18.
205. Ibid., 11–16; Himmler in Jahnke and Buddrus, 363–364; Stein, 207–208.
206. Axmann, 337.
207. Schlünder to Stinglwagner, Jan. 22, 1944; Brandl to HJ-Banne et al., Feb. 9, 1944, BA, Schumacher/239.
208. Stein, 206; Meyer, 18–44.
209. Stein, 219; Schubert-Weller, 211; Meyer, 17.
210. Klaus E. in Steinbach, 144.
211. Jahnke, *Aufgebot,* 58.
212. Knopp, 292.
213. Jahnke and Buddrus, 386–387; Axmann, 341–342; Chester Wilmot, *The Struggle for Europe* (London, 1952), 296–297, 413–414; Jack L. Granatstein, *The Generals: The Canadian Army's Senior Commanders in the Second World War* (Toronto, 1993), 169.
214. Höhne, 435; Stein, 277–278. SS-General Kurt Meyer's sentence was later commuted, and he was released in September 1954.
215. Axmann, 337–339.
216. Gruchmann, 292–294; Stein, 225–226, 229.
217. Weinberg, 780–781; Golücke, 393–394; James Dugan and Carroll Stewart, *Ploesti: The Great Ground-Air Battle of 1 August 1943* (London, 1963), esp. 262–277.
218. Weinberg, 810–815; Gruchmann, 422–425.
219. Gruchmann, 432, 434; Weinberg, 817.
220. Weinberg, 799, 822; Gruchmann, 434. Gruchmann and Weinberg differ on the exact date when Vienna was taken.
221. There were over 200,000 of those, mostly Reich Germans. See Gruchmann, 413–414, 417, 419, 448 (second quote); Günter Böddeker, *Die Flüchtlinge: Die Vertreibung der Deutschen im Osten* (Munich, 1981), 197–210; Claus Larass, *Der Zug der Kinder: KLV—Die Evakuierung 5 Millionen deutscher Kinder im 2. Weltkrieg* (Munich, 1983), 245–246; Margarete Schell, *Ein Tagebuch aus Prag, 1945–46* (Bonn, 1957), 9–33; Kershaw, *Hitler,* 764 (first quote); *Der Spiegel* (Jan. 6, 2003): 41, 48.
222. Weinberg, 816–817, 822–825; Gruchmann, 415, 430–431, 441.
223. Albert Speer, *Erinnerungen,* 8th ed. (Berlin, 1970), 274–336; Richard J. Overy, *War and Economy in the Third Reich* (Oxford, 1994), 362–375.
224. Gruchmann, 412.
225. Ibid.; Willy A. Boelcke, ed., *Wollt Ihr den totalen Krieg? Die geheimen Goebbels-Konferenzen, 1939–1943* (Munich, 1969), 24 (quote).
226. Gruchmann, 412.

227. Ibid., 412–413.
228. Jahnke, *Aufgebot,* 89, 96, 106; Hans Wienicke, ed., *"Schon damals fingen viele an zu schweigen . . .": Quellensammlung zur Geschichte Charlottenburgs von 1933–1945* (Berlin-Charlottenburg, 1986), 208–209.
229. Weinberg, 786.
230. See the example of HJ-Volkssturm in Vienna, Jan. 1945, in Ringler, 141; also Holzträger, 98.
231. Jahnke, *Aufgebot,* 123, 135–136, 142–143.
232. Ibid., 151.
233. Entry for March 11, 1945, in *TGII,* vol. 15, 473.
234. Jahnke and Buddrus, 406–408.
235. Ringler, 149.
236. See Von Hellfeld and Klönne, 244–245; Holzträger, 95; Veigel, 281.
237. Entry for Sept. 30, 1944, in *TGII,* vol. 13, 584.
238. Arno Rose, *Werwolf, 1944–1945: Eine Dokumentation* (Stuttgart, 1980), 116; Holzträger, 98–102.
239. Christian Scharnefksy, *Die Gruppe Neupert: Vier Gräber auf dem Einbecker Friedhof* (Oldenburg, 1995), 45–47 (quote, 47).
240. Joe Volmar, *I Learned to fly for Hitler* (Dundee, Mich., 1999), 181–185 (quote, 185). See also Von Lehndorff, 43–44.
241. Otto Lasch, *So fiel Königsberg* (Stuttgart, 1976), 121–122; Silke Spieler, *Vertreibung und Vertreibungsverbrechen, 1945–1948: Bericht des Bundesarchivs vom 28. Mai 1974: Archivalien und ausgewählte Erlebnisberichte* (Bonn, 1989), 166, 212; Jahnke and Buddrus, 404; Lucas-Busemann, 54.
242. Lasch, 125–126.
243. For the Hitler Youths' last stand in and around Vienna, see Ringler, esp. 142–144, 194–205; Borth, esp. 13, 51, 67, 98–99, 106, 133–134, 142, 166–169, 208–209, 277.
244. Rolf Noll in Maass, 18–21; Rose, 114–115; Nicolaisen, 180–181.
245. Hans Holzträger, *Kampfeinsatz der Hitler-Jugend im Chaos der letzten Kriegsmonate* (Dinklage, 1995), 40.
246. Knopp, 324–326; Lucas-Busemann, 68; Nicolaisen, 80–81; Boberach, *Jugend,* 136.
247. Hermann Melcher, *Die Gezeichneten: Das Erleben eines 16jährigen Kriegsfreiwilligen der Waffen-SS beim Endkampf um Prag und in sowjetischer Kriegsgefangenschaft, 1945–1950* (Leoni, 1985), 13 (quote); Böddeker, 206–207.
248. The original report from *Niederdeutscher Beobachter,* March 20, 1945, is reprinted in Jahnke, *Aufgebot,* 155–157.
249. Holzträger, *Kampfeinsatz,* 41.

250. Traudl Junge, *Bis zur letzten Stunde: Hitlers Sekretärin erzählt ihr Leben* (Munich, 2003), 189.

251. Altner, 160–161, 169; Jahnke, *Aufgebot,* 168–169; Rose, 115; Lothar Loewe in Steinhoff et al., 469–471; Melita Maschmann, *Fazit: Kein Rechtfertigungsversuch,* 5th ed. (Stuttgart, 1964), 159.

252. Maschmann, 159; Kurt Schilde, "Artur Axmann auf der Spur: Aktivitäten des letzten Reichsjugendführers nach 1945," in Jahnke et al., *Jugend,* 102–103.

253. Knopp, 222; Altner, 123–124; Axmann, 423.

254. Axmann, 417–442; Holzträger, *Kampfeinsatz,* 54–70; Knopp, 358–359.

255. Axmann, 449–467; Schilde, 100.

256. Charles Whiting, *Hitler's Werewolves: The Story of the Nazi Resistance Movement, 1944–1945* (New York, 1972).

257. Rose, 116.

258. Borth, 102–103.

259. Ibid., 251–252.

260. Cited in Knopp, 299.

261. Boberach, *Jugend,* 138–140. See also Klaus Messmer in Steinhoff et al., 492–493, and Perry Biddiscombe, *Werwolf! The History of the National Socialist Guerilla Movement, 1944–1946* (Toronto, 1998), 59–86. Several of Biddiscombe's assertions regarding HJ Werewolves appear dubious because his documentation is either incomplete or not compelling.

262. Rose, 13–21.

263. Borth, 215–224.

264. Dieter Meichsner, *Versucht's noch mal mit uns* (Hamburg, 1948), 9–112. See also General Vassily Tschuikov's account in Peter Gosztony, ed., *Der Kampf um Berlin 1945 in Augenzeugenberichten* (Düsseldorf, 1970), 251–252.

265. Knopp, 223.

266. De Bruyn, 302–303.

267. *Partei-Statistik* (Munich, [1935]), 10; Ute Frevert, *Women in German History: From Bourgeois Emancipation to Sexual Liberation* (Oxford, 1989), 258; Wolfgang Benz, "Einleitung," in Benz and Angelika Schardt, eds., *Kriegsgefangenschaft: Berichte über das Leben in Gefangenenlagern der Alliierten* (Munich, 1991), 7; Cartellieri, 12; Stefan Karner, "Deutsche Kriegsgefangene und Internierte in der Sowjetunion, 1941–1956," in Müller and Volkmann, 1012.

268. Moeller, 1011; Dennis L. Bark and David R. Gress, *A History of West Germany* (Oxford, 1989), vol. 1, 358–365.

269. Burleigh, 513; Karner, 1012, 1015, 1020; Cartellieri, 38; Heinz Pust in Benz and Schardt, 31, 33, 35.

270. Karner, 1013, 1016, 1020, 1024; Maass, 23–25, 125–126; Bude, 92, 124, 126; Hans R. Queiser, *"Du gehörst dem Führer!"*: *Vom Hitlerjungen zum Kriegsberichter: Ein autobiographischer Bericht* (Cologne, 1993), 211, 217–218, 231; Melcher, *Gezeichneten*, 92, 124–128, 137, 200, 210–211, 247–249, 407; Cartellieri, 16, 25, 50–52, 352–353; Overmans, 431, 446; Hans Heinz Pollack, *Verschleppt und verschollen: Geschichte einer Deportation aus Ostpreussen* (Frankfurt am Main, 1990), 62–70; Heinz Pust in Benz and Schardt, 22–28; Schönhuber, 172–173; Spieler, 33; Jürgen L. in Hass, 150–151.

271. Helmut Wolff, *Die deutschen Kriegsgefangenen in britischer Hand: Ein Überblick* (Munich, 1974), 39; Kurt Glaser in Benz and Schardt, 146–147, 156, 178–180.

272. Hans Jonitz in Benz and Schardt, 85–88.

273. Ibid., 102–104; Johann Möller in Norbisrath, 22.

274. Martin Koch in Norbisrath, 102–103; Cranz, 255–267; Juchter, 272; Paul Carell and Günter Böddeker, *Die Gefangenen: Leben und Überleben deutscher Soldaten hinter Stacheldraht* (Frankfurt am Main, 1980), 147–159. James Bacque, in *Other Losses: An Investigation into the Mass Deaths of German Prisoners at the Hands of the Americans and French after World War II* (Toronto, 1989), has many of the sites and details of the treatment right, but the overall number of captives and resultant deaths is hugely exaggerated, and he misjudges the Americans' intent of killing as many Germans as possible. For definitive rebuttals of his badly documented views, see Günter Bischof and Stephen E. Ambrose, eds., *Eisenhower and the German POWs: Facts against Falsehood* (Baton Rouge, 1992); Rüdiger Overmans, "'Ein untergeodneter Eintrag im Leidensbuch der jüngeren Geschichte'? Die Rheinwiesenlager 1945," in Hans-Erich Volkmann, ed., *Ende des Dritten Reiches—Ende des Zweiten Weltkriegs: Eine perspektivische Rückschau* (Munich, 1995), 259–291.

275. Dan P. Silverman, *Hitler's Economy: Nazi Work Creation Programs, 1933–1936* (Cambridge, Mass., 1998), 203–207, 217; Dörte Winkler, *Frauenarbeit im "Dritten Reich"* (Hamburg, 1977); Jill Stephenson, *Women in Nazi Society* (London, 1975); Kater, *Doctors*, 89–110.

276. See the examples in Maschmann; Renate Finckh, *Mit uns zieht die neue Zeit* (Baden-Baden, 1979); Margarete Hannsmann, *Der helle Tag bricht an: Ein Kind wird Nazi* (Munich, 1984).

277. This figure according to Franz Seidler, *Frauen zu den Waffen? Marketende-rinnen—Helferinnen—Soldatinnen* (Bonn, 1978), 74. See also ibid., 62–72, 77; Seidler, *Blitzmädchen: Die Geschichte der Helferinnen der deutschen Wehrmacht im Zweiten Weltkrieg* (Koblenz, 1979), 11–16; Ursula von Gersdorff, ed., *Frauen im Kriegsdienst, 1914–1945* (Stuttgart, 1969), 61–71, 460–461, 470–473; Jahnke, *Aufgebot,* 119–120; Von Hellfeld and Klönne, 240–241; Elfriede Schade-Bartkowiak, *Sag mir, wo die Blumen sind . . .: Unter der Schwesternhaube: Kriegserinnerungen einer DRK-Schwester im II. Weltkrieg an der Ostfront* (Hamburg, 1989), 7–149.

278. Von Gersdorff, 374, 442; 470; Axmann, 447.

279. Seidler, *Blitzmädchen,* 15–16; Seidler, *Frauen,* 68; Von Gersdorff, 67, 69, 442; Inge Stolten, *Das alltägliche Exil: Leben zwischen Hakenkreuz und Währungsreform* (Berlin, 1982), 117; Knopp, 143; Jahnke, *Aufgebot,* 154; Heinrich Breloer, ed., *Mein Tagebuch, Geschichten vom Überleben, 1939–1947* (Cologne, 1984), 494–495; Von Lehndorff, 24.

280. Karner, 1014–1015; Seidler, *Blitzmädchen,* 28–29; Larass, 245; Carell and Böddeker, 321–325.

281. Seidler, *Blitzmädchen,* 24; Boberach, *Meldungen,* vol. 16, 6485; Golov-chansky, 110; Melcher, *Gefolgschaft,* 220; Pahl in Schröder, *Jahre,* 398.

282. Otto, 228, points directly to this connection.

283. Joachim-Ernst Fromann to Kurt Michaelis, Sept. 28, 1940, quoted in Kater, *Drummers,* 120.

284. For discouragement, see Von Gersdorff, 62; Seidler, *Blitzmädchen,* 18, 24.

285. Golovchansky, 82; Von Alvensleben, 263; Von Lehndorff, 56. In Norway alone, 10,000 children were born to local girls, fathered by Wehrmacht soldiers (*New York Times,* Dec. 18, 2002).

286. See the enthusiastic report by soldier Hans Bergese about willing French girls and even more willing German ones, to his musical mentor Carl Orff, in his letter from France of May 6, 1941, CM; Peter Paul Pauquet, *Gespräche mit der Jugend einer zerschlagenen Nation* (Nuremberg, 1947), 76–77, 115. See also Elizabeth Heineman, "Sexuality and Nazism: The Doubly Unspeakable?", *Journal of the History of Sexuality* 11 (2002): 28.

287. See the text of Chapter 3 at n. 204.

288. On avoidability see Otto, 186–187; Von Gersdorff, 334.

289. Ruth Windisch in Jutta Rüdiger, ed., *Zur Problematik von Soldatinnen: Der Kampfeinsatz von Flakwaffenhelferinnen im Zweiten Weltkrieg—Berichte und Dokumentationen* (Lindhorst, 1987), 94–97.

290. Seidler, *Frauen,* 65–69; Von Gersdorff, 417–418.

291. Von Gersdorff, 70; Jahnke, *Aufgebot,* 153–154; *Frauen im Wehrdienst: Erinnerungen von Ingeborg Hecht, Ruth Henry, Christa Meves* (Freiburg, 1989), 23–38; Windisch in Rüdiger, 95; Seidler, *Frauen,* 86.

292. Statement of Nov. 30, 1944, quoted in Jahnke, *Aufgebot.* See also Von Gersdorff, 411, 417–418; Seidler, *Blitzmädchen,* 14.

293. The transition is described by Erna Tietz in Alison Owings, *Frauen: German Women Recall the Third Reich* (New Brunswick, N.J., 1993), 269.

294. Gerda Szepansky, ed., *"Blitzmädel," "Heldenmutter," "Kriegerwitwe": Frauenleben im Zweiten Weltkrieg* (Frankfurt am Main, 1986), 240; Lore Vogt, "Bericht über den Einsatz als Flakwaffenhelferin," in Rüdiger, 12–73.

295. Erna Tietz in Owings, 270. *Z.b.V.* was one of many standard Wehrmacht designations.

296. Nicolaisen, 158; Tewes, 43.

297. Lisa quoted in Szepansky, 48.

298. Ibid., 241.

299. As reported in Knopp, 144.

300. Ruth Windisch in Rüdiger, 99–101; Erna Tietz in Owings, 272–273; Seidler, *Blitzmädchen,* 16; *Frauen im Wehrdienst,* 39–41.

301. Through rejection of a proposed *Wehrdienstgesetz,* which would have conscripted women for the armed forces on a huge scale. See Seidler, *Frauen,* 69.

302. Quoted ibid., 70.

303. Axmann, 428, 435.

304. Jahnke, *Aufgebot,* 151–152; Holzträger, *Kampfeinsatz,* 57; Birthe Kundrus, "Nur die halbe Geschichte: Frauen im Umfeld der Wehrmacht zwischen 1939 und 1945—Ein Forschungsbericht," in Müller and Volkmann, 721; Knopp, 146.

305. Holzträger, *Kampfeinsatz,* 40, 45, 50.

306. Jahnke and Buddrus, 410; Axmann, 430; Heck, 131.

307. Holzträger, *Kampfeinsatz,* 64–65.

308. Hildegard Morgenthal, *"Rotkopf, die Ecke brennt, Feuerwehr kommt angerennt": Leben in der NS-Zeit und zwei Leben danach* (Frankfurt am Main, 2000), 51–76.

309. Doris Schmid-Gewinner quoted in Knopp, 146.

310. Kershaw, *Nemesis,* 738; Lasch, 121–122.

311. See the brilliantly fictionalized account of this drama by Günter Grass.

312. Lasch, 125.

313. Quotes from Gruchmann, 420.

314. Moeller, 1011.

315. Ingrid van Bergen, "Mit 13 begegnete ich zum erstenmal dem Tod," *Bild am Sonntag,* Aug. 14, 1977.

316. Hannelore Sch. in Hass, 69.

317. Ingeborg P. ibid., 80–81.

318. Atina Grossmann, "Eine Frage des Schweigens? Die Vergewaltigung deutscher Frauen durch Besatzungssoldaten," *Sozialwissenschaftliche Informationen* 24 (1995): 109–119. See also Ingrid Schmidt-Harzbach, "Eine Woche im April: Berlin 1945: Vergewaltigung als Massenschicksal," *Feministische Studien* 2 (1984): 52. One (late) example is Hitler's rhetoric of Apr. 13, 1945, published in Gosztony, 163–164.

319. Schmidt-Harzbach, 59.

320. Jill Stephenson, *Women in Nazi Germany* (Harlow, 2001), 175–176.

321. Schmidt-Harzbach, 59; Frevert, 258; John Willoughby, "The Sexual Behavior of American GIs During the Early Years of the Occupation of Germany," *Journal of Military History* 62 (1998): 155–174; Petra Goedde, *GIs and Germans: Culture, Gender, and Foreign Relations, 1945–1949* (New Haven, Conn., 2003), 58, 65, 84–85.

322. Kershaw, *Nemesis,* 738; Freya Klier, *Verschleppt ans Ende der Welt: Schicksale deutscher Frauen in sowjetischen Arbeitslagern* (Berlin, 1996), 32; Lasch, 121.

323. Lucas-Busemann, 102; Lasch, 74.

324. See Ehrenburg's anti-German article in Gosztony, 59–60; Anatol Goldberg, *Ilya Ehrenburg: Writing, Politics and the Art of Survival* (London, 1984), 207–209; Joshua Rubenstein, *Tangled Loyalties: The Life and Times of Ilya Ehrenburg* (New York, 1996), 190 (quote), 220–221.

325. Ilya Ehrenburg, *The War: 1941–1945* (London, 1964), 162–171; Rubenstein, 222–223; Goldberg, 209; Heinrich Grüber, *Erinnerungen aus sieben Jahrzehnten* (Cologne, 1968), 221–222; Spieler, 222; Klier, 71, 80; Schmidt-Harzbach, 54.

326. See a Soviet Major's rationale cited in Gosztony, 58.

327. Spieler, 146–147; Lasch, 74, 124; Von Lehndorff, 40.

328. Quoted for Feb. 2, 1945, in Gosztony, 64.

329. Quoted in Lasch, 115. Also ibid., 126; Von Lehndorff, 66–85.

330. Entry for Apr. 25, 1945, in Granzow, 175–176. For rural Pomerania, see also Käthe von Normann, *Tagebuch aus Pommern, 1945–1946: Aufzeichnungen* (Munich, 1962), 17, 30–31, 56, 74, 82.

331. Spieler, 221–222.

332. Ibid., 165–168, 208–211; Hammer and Zur Nieden, 312–313, 366–368, 396–399.

333. Johannes Kaps, ed., *Die Tragödie Schlesiens, 1945/46* (Munich, 1962), 117–118.

334. Margret Boveri, *Tage des Überlebens: Berlin 1945* (Munich, 1968), 124.

335. Schmidt-Harzbach, 54.

336. Boveri, 94–95.

337. Schmidt-Harzbach, 53.

338. For one of those exceptions, see Boveri, 103.

339. Generally for these scenarios, see the descriptions ibid., and Gosztony.

340. Gosztony, 281.

341. Marie Mulde in Gabriele Rosenthal, ed., *Die Hitlerjugend-Generation: Biographische Thematisierung als Vergangenheitsbewältigung* (Essen, 1986), 146; Elfriede Schuster, ibid., 168.

342. Boveri, 109.

343. Ibid., 84. See also Knef, 101–102.

344. Grüber, 221–223.

345. *Der Spiegel* (Dec. 16, 2002): 56–57.

346. Ehrenburg, 164.

347. For Pomerania, for example, see Von Normann, 31; Klier, 72; for Lower Silesia, see Klier, 79.

348. Cf. Spieler, 53; Karner, "Kriegsgefangene," 1014.

349. Spieler, 196–197, 203–204, 208–210; Irene Burchert in Owings, 146; Klier, 46–47, 59, 67, 79–80, 86–87, 89.

350. Klier, 54, 101.

351. Erna B. ibid., 73–74.

352. Irene Burchert in Owings, 148.

353. Klier, 160, 166; Spieler, 211; Irene Burchert in Owings, 147.

354. Irene Burchert in Owings, 149.

355. See ibid., 149–151; Hildegard N. in Klier, 205; Carell and Böddeker, 325–330.

6. The Responsibility of Youth

1. Wolfgang Borchert, *Draussen vor der Tür: Ein Stück, das kein Theater spielen und kein Publikum sehen will,* in Borchert, *Draussen vor der Tür und ausgewählte Erzählungen* (Reinbek, 1968; originally published 1947), 27.

2. See the text of Chapter 5 at n. 115.

3. Peter Rühmkorf, *Wolfgang Borchert in Selbstzeugnissen und Bilddokumenten* (Reinbek, 1961), 169–171.

4. From a wealth of documented examples, see the one in the diary of Erika S., entry for May 8, 1945, in Heinrich Breloer, ed., *Mein Tagebuch: Geschichten vom Überleben, 1939–1947* (Cologne, 1984), 187; and Johann Raymann in Gudrun Norbisrath, ed., *Gestohlene Jugend: Der Zweite Weltkrieg in Erinnerungen* (Essen, 2000), 60.

5. Hilde Thurnwald, *Gegenwartsprobleme Berliner Familien: Eine soziologische Untersuchung an 498 Familien* (Berlin, 1948), 52–53, 66; *Jugend in Westdeutschland* (Munich, n.d.), 11–12; Annette Kuhn, "Die vergessene Frauenarbeit in der deutschen Nachkriegszeit," in Anna-Elisabeth Freier and Annette Kuhn, eds., *"Das Schicksal Deutschlands liegt in der Hand seiner Frauen": Frauen in der deutschen Nachkriegsgeschichte* (Düsseldorf, 1983), 184–185; Axel Schildt, "Von der Not der Jugend zur Teenager-Kultur: Aufwachsen in den 50er Jahren," in Axel Schildt and Arnold Sywottek, eds., *Modernisierung im Wiederaufbau: Die westdeutsche Gesellschaft der 50er Jahre* (Bonn, 1993), 335–336; Friedhelm Boll, *Auf der Suche nach Demokratie: Britische und deutsche Jugendinitiativen in Niedersachsen nach 1945* (Bonn, 1995), 31–43; *Der Spiegel* (Jan. 27, 2003): 63.

6. Clemens Vollnhals, "Einleitung," in Vollnhals, ed., *Entnazifizierung: Politische Säuberung und Rehabilitierung in den vier Besatzungszonen, 1945–1949* (Munich, 1991), 11.

7. See, for example, Gerhard Fauth, ed., *Ruf an die deutsche Jugend: Ein Bericht* (Munich, 1948), 10, 41.

8. Breloer, 234; Ralf Roland Ringler, *Illusion einer Jugend: Lieder, Fahnen und das bittere Ende: Hitlerjugend in Österreich: Ein Erlebnisbericht* (St. Pölten, 1977), 168; Wolfgang Klafki in Klafki, ed., *Verführung, Distanzierung, Ernüchterung: Kindheit und Jugend im Nationalsozialismus: Autobiographisches aus erziehungswissenschaftlicher Sicht* (Weinheim, 1988), 168; Herbert Johannes Veigel, *Christbäume: Briefe aus dem Krieg* (Berlin, 1991), 276–277, 334; Edgar Gielsdorf, *Vom Christkind eine Landsknechtstrommel* (Cologne, 1994), 198–199.

9. Arnold P. in Kurt Hass, ed., *Jugend unterm Schicksal: Lebensberichte junger Deutscher, 1946–1949* (Hamburg, 1950), 22 (first quote); Erna Stahl, ed., *Jugend im Schatten von gestern: Aufsätze Jugendlicher zur Zeit* (Hamburg, 1948), 80 (second quote).

10. Knut Pipping et al., *Gespräche mit der deutschen Jugend: Ein Beitrag zum Autoritätsproblem* (Helsingfors, 1954), 326, 329–330; Manfred Rommel, "Die überflüssige Generation—Übersteigerte Hoffnungen," in Claus Richter, ed., *Die überflüssige Generation: Jugend zwischen Apathie und Aggression* (Königstein, 1979), 88; Günter De Bruyn, *Zwischenbilanz: Eine*

Jugend in Berlin (Frankfurt am Main, 1995), 307; Anna J. Merritt and Richard L. Merritt, eds., *Public Opinion in Occupied Germany: The OMGUS Surveys* (Urbana, Ill., 1970), 209; *Jugend zwischen 15 und 24: Eine Untersuchung zur Situation der deutschen Jugend im Bundesgebiet* (Bielefeld, 1954), 307.

11. Roland Gröschel, "Jugendarbeit und Jugendpolitik in Berlin zwischen Krieg, Frieden und Systemkonkurrenz, 1944–1949/50: Forschungsstand—Forschungslücken—Forschungsfragen," in Ulrich Herrmann, ed., *Jugendpolitik in der Nachkriegszeit: Zeitzeugen—Forschungsberichte—Dokumente* (Weinheim, 1993), 53; F. Roy Willis, *The French in Germany: 1945–1949* (Stanford, 1962), 147–161.

12. Karl Heinz Jahnke and Michael Buddrus, eds., *Deutsche Jugend, 1933–1945: Eine Dokumentation* (Hamburg, 1989), 445–446.

13. Heinz Pust in Wolfgang Benz and Angelika Schardt, eds., *Kriegsgefangenschaft: Berichte über das Leben in Gefangenenlagern der Alliierten* (Munich, 1991), 43; Gröschel, 53; Rüdiger Kriemann, "Zur sozialen und politischen Situation von Jugendlichen in Mecklenburg im Sommer 1945," in Karl Heinz Jahnke et al., *Deutsche Jugend im Zweiten Weltkrieg* (Rostock, 1991), 108. On rape especially of young women by Red Army personnel as a constant problem in Soviet-occupied Germany, 1945–1948, see Norman M. Naimark, *The Russians in Germany: A History of the Soviet Zone of Occupation, 1945–1949* (Cambridge, Mass., 1995), 83–90.

14. Mann's BBC address of Oct. 24, 1942, in Jahnke and Buddrus, 446–447.

15. Helmut Schmidt in Schmidt et al., *Kindheit und Jugend unter Hitler,* 2nd ed. (Berlin, 1992), 234 (quote); Helmut Wolff, *Die deutschen Kriegsgefangenen in britischer Hand: Ein Überblick* (Munich, 1974), 46–47; Rolf Schörken, *Jugend 1945: Politisches Denken und Lebensgeschichte* (Opladen, 1990), 83, 119–123; Jürgen Reulecke, "Geboren um 1920: Die Altersgenossen von Hans Scholl und Willi Graf: Zur Diskussion um die junge Generation nach dem Zweiten Weltkrieg," in Michael Kissener and Bernhard Schäfers, eds., *"Weitertragen": Studien zur "Weissen Rose": Festschrift für Anneliese Knoop-Graf zum 80. Geburtstag* (Constance, 2001), 72–73.

16. Willy Schumann, *Being Present: Growing Up in Hitler's Germany* (Kent, Ohio, 1991), 175 (quote); Hans-Günter Zmarzlik, *Wieviel Zukunft hat unsere Vergangenheit? Aufsätze und Überlegungen eines Historikers vom Jahrgang 1922* (Munich, 1970), 25; Gröschel, 52; Schörken, 149–150.

17. Manfred Strack, "Amerikanische Kulturbeziehungen zu (West-)Deutschland, 1945–1955," *Zeitschrift für Kulturaustausch* 37 (1987): 286; Axel Schildt, *Moderne Zeiten: Freizeit, Massenmedien und "Zeitgeist" in der*

Bundesrepublik der 50er Jahre (Hamburg, 1995), 403; Richard Pells, *Not Like Us: How Europeans Have Loved, Hated, and Transformed American Culture Since World War II* (New York, 1997), 52–57.

18. Kurt Lewin, "The Special Case of Germany," *Public Opinion Quarterly* 7 (1943): 555–566, esp. 555, 560–561, 564.

19. Donald McGranahan and Morris Janowitz, "A Comparison of Social Attitudes among American and German Youth," *Journal of Abnormal and Social Pathology* 41 (1946): 3–14, esp. 3, 5.

20. Henry J. Kellermann, *The Present Status of German Youth,* U.S. Department of State, Publication 2583, European Series 11 (Washington, D.C., 1946), 1, 17.

21. Hermann Jung, *Die deutschen Kriegsgefangenen in amerikanischer Hand* (Munich, 1972), 218–238; Hans Jonitz in Benz and Schardt, 112; Glaser in Benz and Schardt, 202–203, 208–209; Klaus Tischler in Gabriele Rosenthal, ed., *Die Hitlerjugend-Generation: Biographische Thematisierung als Vergangenheitsbewältigung* (Essen, 1986), 273–276; Schörken, 29–30; Martin Cranz, *Ich, Ein Deutscher* (Dülmen, 1987), 264–265.

22. *Life,* Overseas Edition for the Armed Forces (Oct. 15, 1945): 21.

23. Kellermann, 5, 11; Saul K. Padover, *Experiment in Germany: The Story of an American Intelligence Officer* (New York, 1946), 72–77; Kurt Piehl, *Schieber, Tramps, Normalverbraucher: Unterwegs im Nachkriegsdeutschland* (Frankfurt am Main, 1989), 16–17. For an early criticism of the U.S. attitude, see Howard Becker, *Vom Barette schwankt die Feder: Die Geschichte der deutschen Jugendbewegung* (Wiesbaden, 1949), 223–224, 227. On the negative German attitude well into the 1970s, see Alfons Kenkmann, *Wilde Jugend: Lebenswelt grossstädtischer Jugendlicher zwischen Weltwirtschaftskrise, Nationalsozialismus und Währungsreform* (Essen, 1996), 212; Elke Nyssen and Sigrid Metz-Göckel, " 'Ja, die waren ganz einfach tüchtig'— Was Frauen aus der Geschichte lernen können," in Freier and Kuhn, 338. On Schaffstein before and after 1945, see the text of Chapter 4 at n. 177, and Rolf Seeliger, *Braune Universität: Deutsche Hochschullehrer gestern und heute* (Munich, 1965), vol. 2, 60–62. It is indicative of the myopia with which the subject of youth in the Third Reich has been and still is treated that, following Schaffstein's interpretation, one of its early chroniclers, Arno Klönne, had no use for *Edelweisspiraten, Meuten,* and Swings as late as 1993. See his "Zur Rekonstruktion von 'Jugendöffentlichkeit' in Deutschland nach dem Ende des NS-Regimes—Hinweise und Fragen," in Ingo Koch, ed., *Deutsche Jugend zwischen Krieg und Frieden, 1944–1946* (Rostock, 1993), 25–26. Similarly: Although Perry Biddiscombe, on the basis

of solely British and U.S. sources, concedes that the *Edelweiss* label was hijacked after 1945 by HJ veterans bent on neo-Nazi, anti-Allied sabotage, he generally echoes, based on the same limited sources, contemporary Western Allied suspicions against surviving *Edelweiss* groups so as to validate *post hoc* their collective condemnation as mere criminals. See his "'The Enemy of Our Enemy': A View of the *Edelweiss Piraten* [*sic*] from the British and American Archives," *Journal of Contemporary History* 30 (1995): 37–62.

24. J. G. Siebert, *The Remaking of German Youth* (London, [1945]), 68.

25. Kellermann, 4.

26. Doris K. in Lothar Steinbach, *Ein Volk, ein Reich, ein Glaube? Ehemalige Nationalsozialisten und Zeitzeugen berichten über ihr Leben im Dritten Reich* (Berlin, 1983), 105–106; Friedrich Grupe, *Jahrgang 1916: Die Fahne war mehr als der Tod* (Munich, 1989), 358–359; Rosenthal, 149; Bodo Brücher, "Jugendarbeit im Spannungsfeld zwischen Überlieferung und Besatzungspolitik: Am Beispiel der 'Falken' nach 1945," in Herrmann, 30–31; Karl-Ernst Bungenstab, *Umerziehung zur Demokratie? Re-education-Politik im Bildungswesen der US-Zone, 1945–1949* (Düsseldorf, 1970), 125–127.

27. "Zeittafel," in Vollnhals, 352.

28. Clemens Vollnhals, "Entnazifizierung: Politische Säuberung unter alliierter Herrschaft," in Hans-Erich Volkmann, ed., *Ende des Dritten Reiches— Ende des Zweiten Weltkriegs: Eine perspektivische Rückschau* (Munich, 1995), 382.

29. On the political objectives, see Schildt, *Zeiten,* 401–402; Strack, 288; Petra Goedde, *GIs and Germans: Culture, Gender, and Foreign Relations, 1945–49* (New Haven, Conn., 2003).

30. Anna J. Merritt and Richard L. Merritt, eds., *Public Opinion in Semi-sovereign Germany: The HICOG Surveys, 1949–1955* (Urbana, Ill., 1980), 39–40; Strack, 290, 297–298; Pells, 50.

31. Maria Höhn, *GIs and Fräuleins: The German-American Encounter in 1950s West Germany* (Chapel Hill, N.C., 2002), 61–62.

32. Ralph Willett, *The Americanization of Germany, 1945–1949* (London, 1989), 91–92; R. Stephen Craig, "American Forces Network in the Cold War: Military Broadcasting in Postwar Germany," *Journal of Broadcasting and Electronic Media* 32 (1988): 309–318.

33. See the articles in *Funk Illustrierte,* no. 17 (1949), and Oliver Hassenkamp, *Der Sieg nach dem Krieg: Die gute schlechte Zeit* (Munich, [1983]), 31–32; Wilfried Breyvogel et al., "'Der Krieg gibt jedem noch ungeahnte Möglichkeiten der Bewährung': Essener Gymnasiasten zwischen 1930 und

1945," in Wilfried Breyvogel and Heinz-Hermann Krüger, eds., *Land der Hoffnung—Land der Krise: Jugendkulturen im Ruhrgebiet, 1900–1987* (Berlin, 1987), 201; Horst H. Lange, *Jazz in Deutschland: Die deutsche Jazz-Chronik, 1900–1960* (Berlin, 1966), 156.

34. Craig, 309.
35. Fritz Eberhard, *Der Rundfunkhörer und sein Programm: Ein Beitrag zur empirischen Sozialforschung* (Berlin, 1962), 157; Willett, 97; Axel Schildt, "Hegemon der häuslichen Freiheit: Rundfunk in den 50er Jahren," in Schildt and Sywottek, 473–474.
36. McGranahan and Janowitz, 9; Heinz Kluth, "Das Verhältnis der arbeitslosen Jugendlichen zum Staat und zur Politik," in *Arbeitslosigkeit und Berufsnot der Jugend* (Cologne, 1952), vol. 2, 191; Breloer, 417; Schörken, 29; Wilhelm Jurzek, "Von der Hitlerjugend zum 'Berliner Gespräch': Meine Erinnerungen als Politologe und Zeitzeuge," in Franz-Werner Kersting, ed., *Jugend vor einer Welt in Trümmern: Erfahrungen und Verhältnisse der Jugend zwischen Hitler- und Nachkriegsdeutschland* (Weinheim, 1998), 160.
37. Rommel as quoted in Winfried Maass, *Die Fünzigjährigen: Porträt einer verratenen Generation* (Hamburg, 1980), 145.
38. Claus Larass, *Der Zug der Kinder: KLV—Die Evakuierung 5 Millionen deutscher Kinder im 2. Weltkrieg* (Munich, 1983), 211; Roswitha Fröhlich, *Ich konnte einfach nichts sagen: Tagebuch einer Kriegsgefangenen* (Reinbek, 1979), 46, 70.
39. Schumann, 173.
40. Kellermann, 15–16; Heinz Westphal, "Junge Menschen 1945—Am Anfang einer neuen Zeit," in Kersting, 287; De Bruyn, 304, 308; Jurzek, 159–160; Cranz, 48.
41. Christian Schneider et al., *Das Erbe der NAPOLA: Versuch einer Generationengeschichte des Nationalsozialismus* (Hamburg, 1996), 140–142.
42. Stephen Spender, *European Witness* (New York, 1946), 32–33.
43. Steven P. Remy, *The Heidelberg Myth: The Nazification and Denazification of a German University* (Cambridge, Mass., 2002), 124, 167; Anson Rabinbach, *In the Shadow of Catastrophe: German Intellectuals between Apocalypse and Enlightenment* (Berkeley, 1997), 133–134.
44. Kellermann, 3, 10.
45. Boll, 199–222.
46. Bungenstab, 154–155.
47. See the text of Chapter 1 at n. 38.
48. Kellermann, 2.

49. McGranahan and Janowitz, 10.

50. *German Youth between Yesterday and Tomorrow: 1 April 1947–30 April 1948* (Berlin, 1948), 1 (quote); Thurnwald, 148, 151.

51. Helmut Schelsky, *Die skeptische Generation: Eine Soziologie der deutschen Jugend* (Düsseldorf, 1963; first printing 1957).

52. Schelsky, esp. 77–82, 109–110, 355 (quote), 356.

53. On Schelsky's Nazi past, see Seeliger, vol. 3, 79–83. On the SS-infiltrated Reichsuniversität Strassburg, see Michael H. Kater, *Das "Ahnenerbe" der SS: Ein Beitrag zur Kulturpolitik des Dritten Reiches,* 3rd ed. (Munich, 2001), 285–286.

54. For a contemporary critique of Schelsky see Boll, esp. 20, 224.

55. Ernst Samhaber, "Die erste Probe," *Die Zeit* (Feb. 21, 1946): 1.

56. Annemarie Krapp, "Was ist Demokratie?", in Fauth, 43–44. See also ibid., 57.

57. Jost Hermand, *Als Pimpf in Polen: Erweiterte Kinderlandverschickung, 1940–1945* (Frankfurt am Main, 1993), 112; Zmarzlik, 26–28; Heinrich Kupffer, *Swingtime: Chronik einer Jugend in Deutschland, 1937–1951* (Berlin, 1987), 98–100.

58. Stahl, 77; Hass, 39; Grupe, 363; De Bruyn, 307. See also Maass, 145; Westphal, 283–284; Heinz Bude, *Deutsche Karrieren: Lebenskonstruktionen sozialer Aufsteiger aus der Flakhelfer-Generation* (Frankfurt am Main, 1987), esp. 45, 53.

59. Hildegard Milberg, "Zwischen gestern und morgen: Hamburgs Jugend nach 1945—Ist das Dritte Reich überwunden?", *Junges Hamburg* 12 (1958): 4.

60. Milberg, 4–5.

61. Schmidt, 189. See also Kluth, 134–136.

62. Merritt and Merritt, *OMGUS Surveys,* 86.

63. Otto Haase, "Die soziale Lage der Jugend," in Adolf Grimme and Otto Haase, *Befreiter Geist: Vorträge der kulturpädagogischen Woche in Hannover vom 25.–27. September 1945* (Hanover, 1946), 31–33; Hartmut von Hentig, *Aufgeräumte Erfahrung: Texte zur eigenen Person* (Munich, 1983), 38; Kluth, 142.

64. Kluth, 133–158. See already Kellermann, 6.

65. *German Youth,* 1, and Table 3. The timing for the reauthorization of political groups varied according to group type and Allied zone. In the British Zone, for instance, a Social Democratic Student club was functioning at Hamburg University as early as 1945 (Schmidt, 236). See also the text above at n. 45. Politically oriented groups were permitted in the U.S. Zone

only in March 1947 (Bungenstab, 128). For a description of the spectrum of new West German youth groups, see *Jugend in Westdeutschland,* 46–53.

66. Theodor Heuss, *Reden an die Jugend,* ed. Hans Bott (Tübingen, 1956), 80.

67. Hitler's political testament of Apr. 29, 1945, as quoted in Percy Ernst Schramm, ed., *Die Niederlage 1945: Aus dem Kriegstagebuch des Ober-kommandos der Wehrmacht* (Munich, 1962), 415.

68. Boll, 133; Kurt Schilde, "Artur Axmann auf der Spur: Aktivitäten des letzten Reichsjugendführers nach 1945," in Jahnke et al., 99–105.

69. Jutta Rüdiger in Gisela Miller-Kipp, ed., *"Auch Du gehörst dem Führer": Die Geschichte des Bundes Deutscher Mädel (BDM) in Quellen und Dokumenten* (Weinheim, 2001), 312–313; Rüdiger, *Die Hitler-Jugend und ihr Selbst-verständnis im Spiegel ihrer Aufgabengebiete* (Lindhorst, 1983); Rüdiger, *Der Bund Deutscher Mädel: Eine Richtigstellung* (Lindhorst, 1984).

70. Baldur von Schirach, *Ich glaubte an Hitler* (Hamburg, 1967), 312–318; Michael Wortmann, *Baldur von Schirach: Hitlers Jugendführer* (Cologne, 1982), 10–11.

71. Von Schirach on May 24, 1946, cited in *Der Prozess gegen die Haupt-kriegsverbrecher vor dem Internationalen Militärgerichtshof Nürnberg, 14. November 1945 – 1. Oktober 1946* (Munich, 1984), vol. 13, 477.

72. Robert Wistrich, *Who's Who in Nazi Germany* (New York, 1982), 273.

73. Borchert, 59.

74. Peter H. Merkl, *The Origins of the West German Republic* (New York, 1963); Elmer Plischke, *Contemporary Government of Germany* (Boston, 1964); Geoffrey K. Roberts, *West German Politics* (London, 1972); Kurt P. Tauber, *Beyond Eagle and Swastika: German Nationalism since 1945,* vol. 1. (Middletown, Conn., 1967).

Acknowledgments

The idea for this book came to me after years of work, earlier in my career, on both German youth and various institutions of the Nazi movement, in particular the Nazi Party. Over several years, research for the book was generously supported by grants from the Social Sciences and Humanities Research Council of Canada, the Alexander von Humboldt-Stiftung (Konrad Adenauer Research Award), a two-year Senior Killam Fellowship of the Canada Council, and York University. Without this financial assistance, the opportunities for gathering basic materials from German, Austrian, and U.S. archives, as well as university release time to write, could never have been provided.

As my plan for the book took shape, I was able to present and discuss it in colloquia arranged by colleagues in North America and Germany. At York University, the Canadian Centre for German and European Studies, where I am based, arranged a meeting with faculty and students through the good offices of its directors, Jeffrey Peck and Mark Webber. At the Historisches Kolleg in Munich, Jürgen Reulecke, Reinhard Spree, Gerhard A. Ritter, Hans Mommsen, and Wolfgang Hardtwig convened colleagues for several hours of presentation and lively discussion. Hans Rudolf Vaget did the same for me at Smith College. Hartmut Lehmann of the Max Planck-Institut für Geschichte in Göttingen discussed with me some of my earlier ideas for this book, as did Jörg Wolff at the Institut für Rechtswissenschaften (Arbeitsgruppe

Jugend und Strafrecht) of the Universität Lüneburg. Before I spoke there, Jörg Wolff had generously made available to me the entire records of his research for his own important work on the regimentation of youth during the Third Reich. I have benefited immensely from the help I received from these colleagues, and I am very grateful to them.

As always, the experienced librarians at York University helped me to obtain less accessible books and sources, some of which dated from the Nazi period and were available only from other Canadian and American libraries, not to mention European ones. Even if sometimes I monopolized the books for longer than I should have, Mary Lehane, Gladys Fung, and Julie Pippo never lost their patience with me. For this they deserve my gratitude.

I would also like to thank Edward Shorter, who hosted me in 1997–1998 as the Jason A. Hannah Visiting Professor of the History of Medicine at the University of Toronto. This position gave me an opportunity to study problems arising from the psychology of adolescence. My insights into the pathologization and criminalization of youth in the Nazi system resulted, not least, from fruitful conversations with Ned, his colleagues at the university, and several visiting scholars.

I owe a special debt to Joyce Seltzer, my editor at Harvard University Press. The combination of intelligence, experience, intuition, and empathy that she brought to her reading of the manuscript was extremely helpful, especially in the final shaping of the book. Errors which remain, however, are entirely my own liability.

Index